CHICAGO PORTRAITS

Chicago Tribune

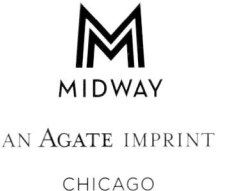

AN AGATE IMPRINT

CHICAGO

Copyright 2014 by the Chicago Tribune.

All rights reserved. No part of this book may be reproduced or transmitted in any form or by any means, electronic or mechanical, including copying, recording, or by any information storage and retrieval system, without express written permission from the publisher.

Printed in China

Chicago Tribune

Tony W. Hunter, CEO & Publisher
Gerould W. Kern, Senior Vice President, Editor
Bill Adee, Executive Vice President/Digital
Joycelyn Winnecke, Vice President, Associate Editor
Jane Hirt, Vice President, Managing Editor
Peter Kendall, Deputy Managing Editor

Library of Congress Cataloging-in-Publication Data

Chicago portraits / Chicago tribune.
　　　pages cm

Includes index.

 Summary: "Portraits of both everyday and well-known Chicagoans compiled from the Chicago Tribune's historical archives"-- Provided by publisher.

 ISBN 978-1-57284-165-9 (hard cover) -- ISBN 1-57284-165-6 (hard cover) -- ISBN 978-1-57284-743-9 (ebook) -- ISBN 1-57284-743-3 (ebook)

1. Celebrities--Illinois--Chicago--Portraits. 2. Portrait photography. I. Chicago tribune.

 TR681.F3C4884 2014

 770.9773'11--dc23
　　　　　　　　2014017730

10 9 8 7 6 5 4 3 2 1

Midway is an imprint of Agate Publishing.
Agate books are available in bulk at discount prices.
For more information visit agatepublishing.com.

Foreword **4**

Introduction **6**

Subject Index **284**

Foreword

You will see many, many talented and famous and gifted and interesting and provocative people on the pages of this captivating book. You will not see the faces of the photographers who took these images, but it can be argued that they are every bit as talented and gifted as their subjects.

The photographers are not famous. They are all but anonymous. Such is the lot of the newspaper photographer, whose only acknowledgment is often relegated to tiny type, a name affixed below or next to his or her photos, easy to miss.

I have known and worked with newspaper photographers for nearly half a century, starting during a time when cameras were bulky and film was, well, film. That amount of time should have allowed me to figure out how they do what they do. I have not. I have not because there is magic in what they do. I know they are seekers of truth, an image that offers more than the physical or superficial.

Most of the photos in this book have involved a subtle dance between photographer and subject. The subjects have agreed to be photographed and so are hoping to look their best, or at least not to look foolish. The photographers are trying to do their jobs and capture something that will grab a reader's eye.

I know this because I have been with some of these people when their photographs were taken, none more involved than that of former Bears quarterback Jim McMahon when photographer Chris Walker and I visited the Northbrook home where McMahon lived with his family in 2002.

I watched and listened as Walker and McMahon talked, as McMahon balked at a few ideas, as Walker suggested more. It worked. That's Jim alright, and have a look at his little dog on page 171, also presumably beguiled by Walker.

There are some photos in this book that are not technically portraits, for the subjects are caught not in pose but in action: poet Gwendolyn Brooks walking down a street; Harold Washington amid a large crowd; former Cicero Mayor Betty Loren-Maltese, smoking a cigarette and autographing a dollar bill.

This is a remarkable gathering, some of the people from long ago: Maurice Chevalier, Louise Brooks, Rudolph Valentino and Richard J. Daley. And try to name another book that features Steve "Mongo" McMichael and Lady Gaga? Former Mayor William Hale "Big Bill" Thompson and Zac Efron? Walter Payton and Woody Allen? Charlie Chaplin and O.J. (a pit bull puppy)?

Some of the photos will introduce you to people you've never met, and you'll be glad to make their acquaintance, to have looked into their eyes.

I know as much about photography as I know about cooking, which is in the neighborhood of nothing. But I do know that these are not the sort of photos an amateur can get from a cellphone or other high-tech gizmo. It takes a professional's eye. Wandering through the following photos, as if through some timeless gallery, I realize that there is beauty in some, mystery in others, and truth and art in them all.

Rick Kogan
SENIOR WRITER, CHICAGO TRIBUNE

Introduction

A portrait is much more than a picture of a person. When it's done well, even a seemingly simple photograph can speak volumes about a person's character. The potential for that has driven photographers — and artists of all kinds — for centuries.

As you will see on the pages of this book, Tribune photographers strive to transform a photograph into something more: a reflection of who that person may be at that exact time and place. A tall order.

They must rely on their wits, people skills and creativity to make the most of the location, the light and the willingness of the subject to buy into their ideas. Sometimes cooperation is not a given.

Often they have only a moment of a person's time in an unforgiving setting. Rarely do they have the luxury of hours, and sometimes they must deal with the mixed blessings of press agents, prop and clothing stylists, hair and makeup people, and other fussers.

The goal, always, is to go beyond the obvious and the expected, to get under the skin of the person and show the essence of his or her character, or, at a minimum, channel the person's personality and mood in the photograph.

With portraiture, photographers have a degree of control over the look of the photograph. How they choose to exercise that tells us something about the photographer as well. They want not only an illuminating and aesthetically pleasing portrait for posterity, but one that satisfies their own estimation of who that person is. Tribune photographers bring a wealth of expertise and talent to the portrait session, and the interchange between photographer and subject, however brief, can be a dance between the aspirations of both.

These portraits, selected from our vast archive of contemporary and vintage pictures by Tribune photographers, span almost a century, from 1922 to 2014. Many are from the Tribune's archive of glass-plate negatives, delicate and luminous records of the Jazz Age and before. Others were recorded with the latest digital technology. In between, they cover almost the entire history of film in photography.

The cameras used span the history of photographic technology as well, from accordion-style view cameras to the iPhone (naturally).

These are Chicago portraits, though the locations and settings they were made in encompass the metropolitan area, and in a couple of instances reach out from the city to where the corn and soybeans grow. Our region is a wonderfully diverse cultural, societal and political ecosystem, and the evidence is seen on the faces in this book. The connective tissue is the conversation a daily newspaper has with its readers in words and, of course, in pictures.

Michael Zajakowski
PICTURE EDITOR, CHICAGO TRIBUNE

CHICAGO PORTRAITS

Brian Bannon

Brian Bannon, then the new head of Chicago Public Library, holds an iPad displaying a digital photo of himself next to books in the special collections room at the Harold Washington Library Center.

ALEX GARCIA, 2012

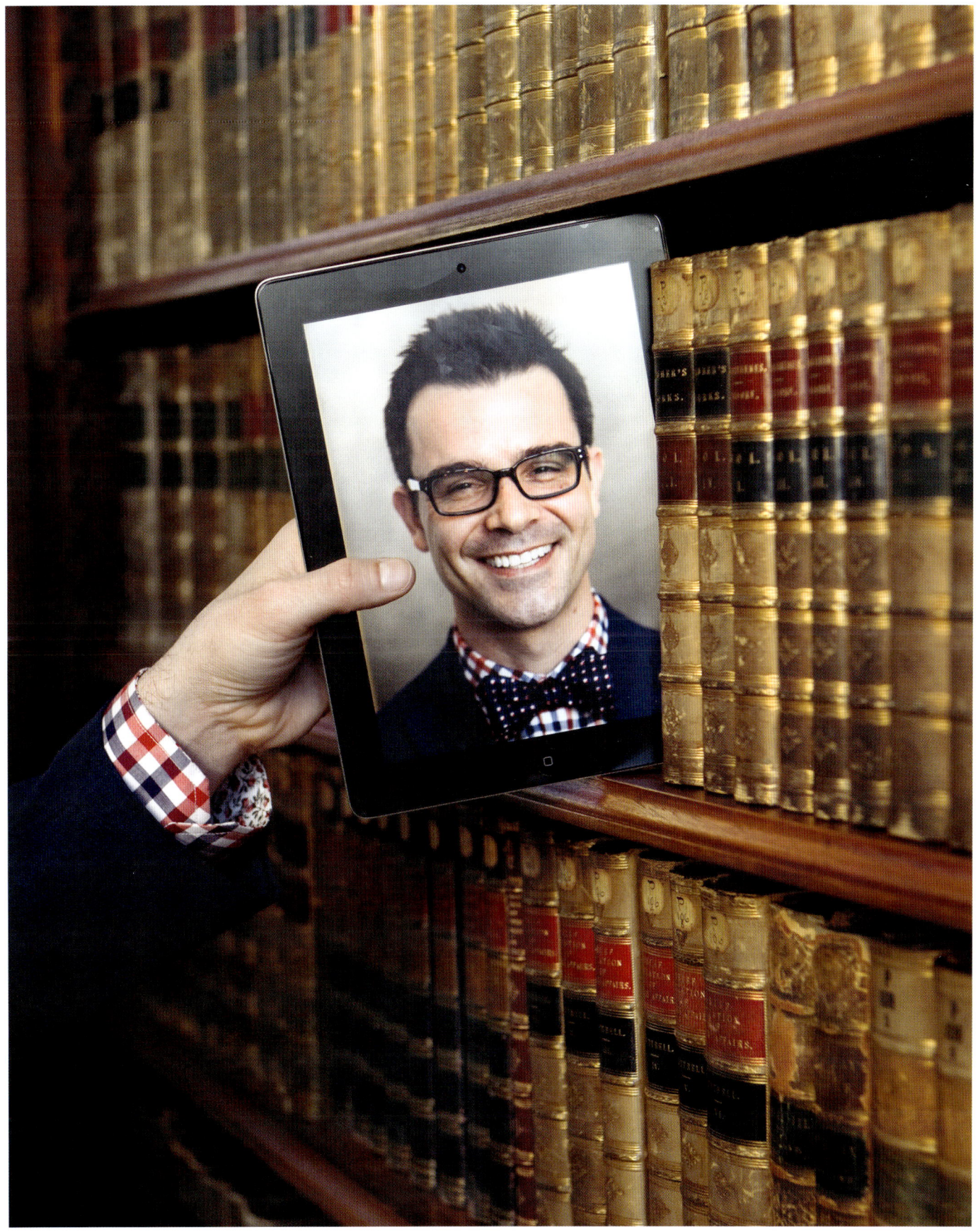

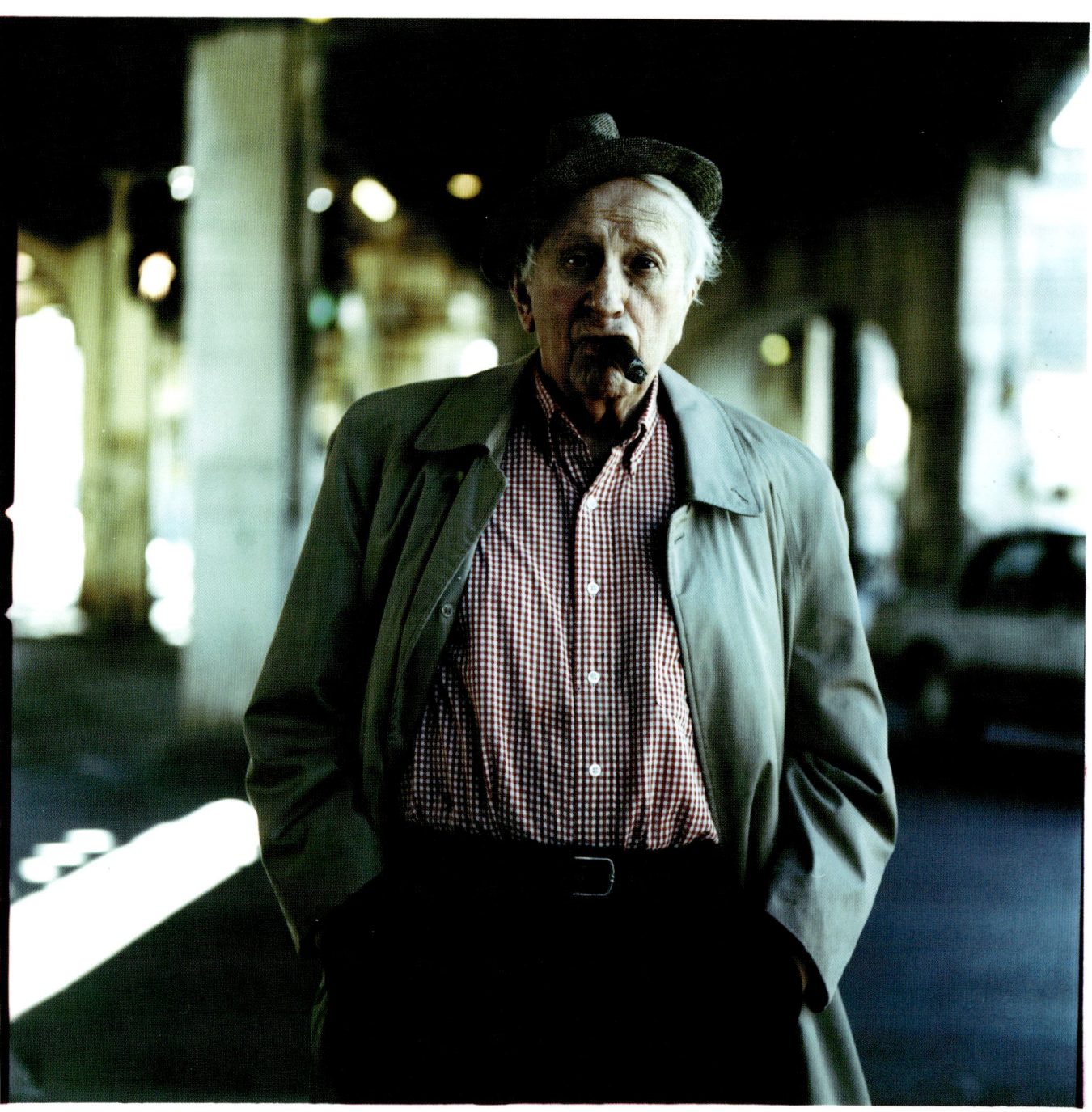

Studs Terkel

Author and activist Louis "Studs" Terkel arrived in the Windy City as a child from New York City. In Chicago he found not only a new name but also a place that perfectly matched his own personality — in its energy, its swagger, its charms, its heart.

CHRIS WALKER, 2001

Frank Bausch

Chicago Bears center Frank Bausch demonstrates life as a football player in the time before face guards. Under the titillating headline "The Private Life of a Football Lineman," the Tribune did a photo spread of a couple of Bears' faces having intimate but anonymous encounters with elbows, knees, cleats and hands. This move, the caption read, "adds zest to the game—for the pushee. Nothing illegal about it. Just a trifle discommoding." It wasn't till the 1950s that it occurred to someone to invent the face mask.

CHICAGO TRIBUNE HISTORICAL PHOTO, 1938

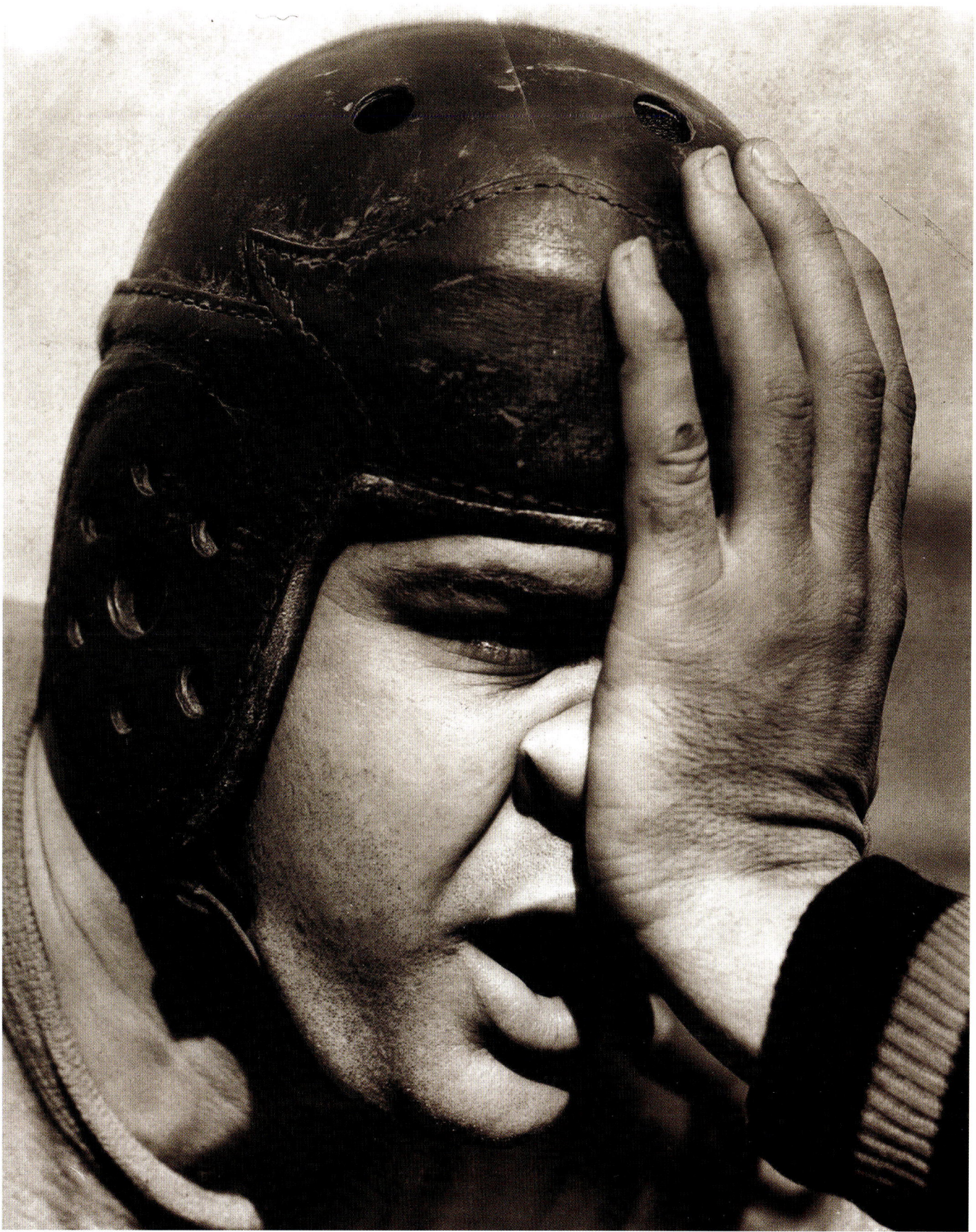

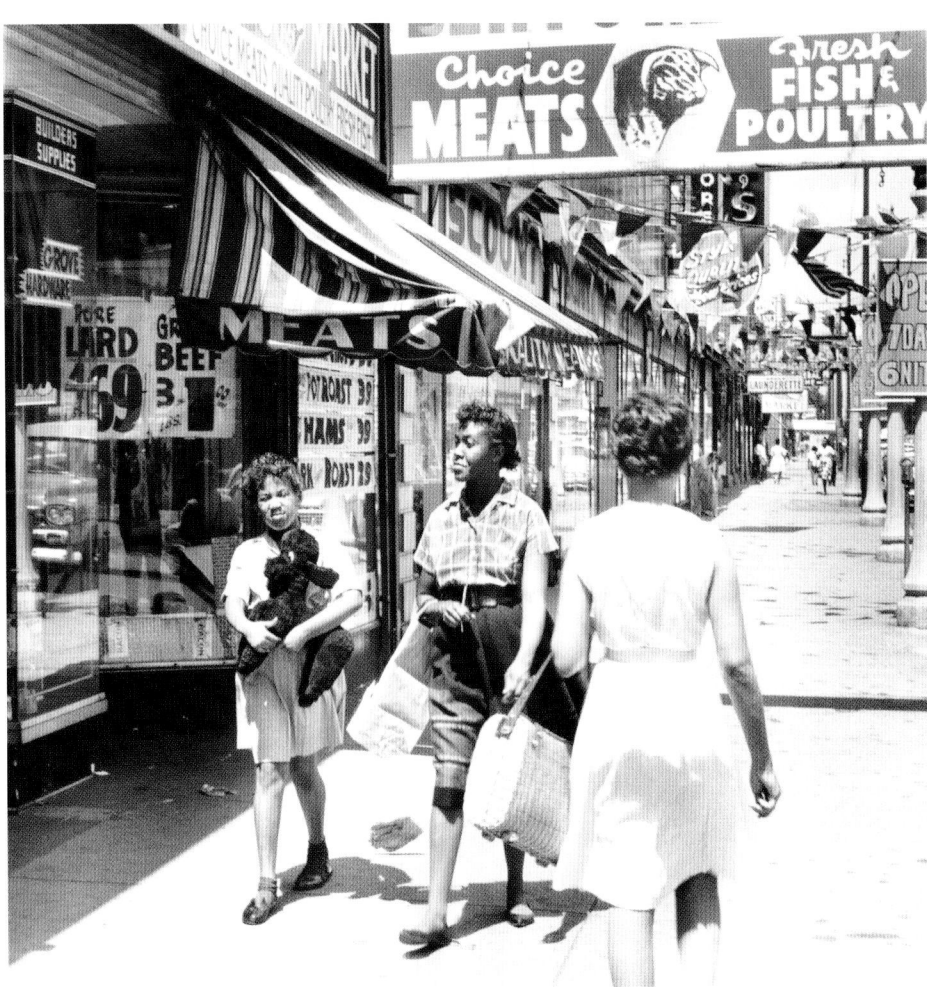

Gwendolyn Brooks

Poet Gwendolyn Brooks, center, lived on the South Side all of her life. She walks unrecognized by passersby in Chicago. She was the first African-American to win a Pulitzer Prize.

CHICAGO TRIBUNE HISTORICAL PHOTO, 1961

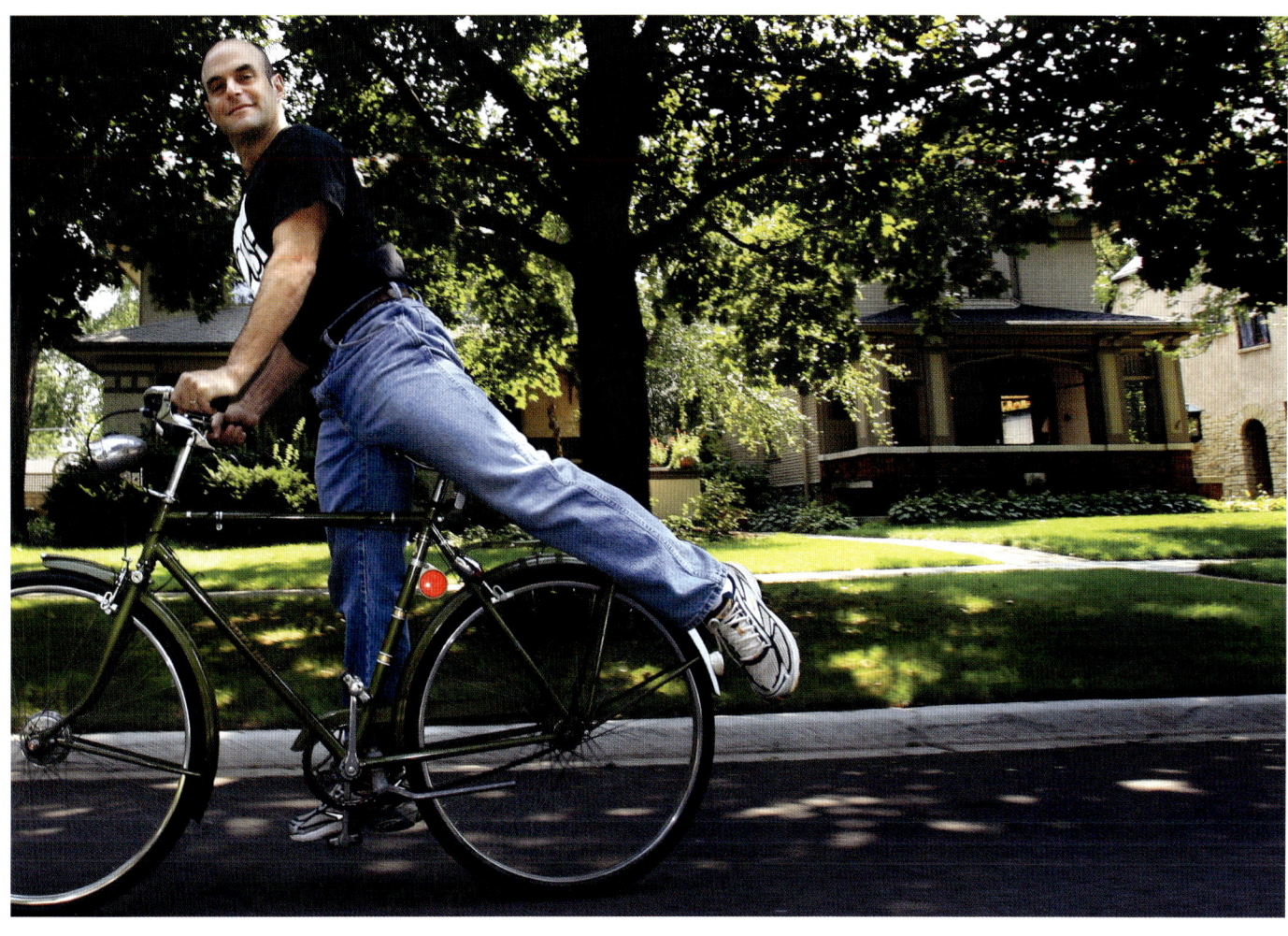

Peter Sagal

Peter Sagal, host of NPR's "Wait Wait … Don't Tell Me!" hops aboard his 1970 Raleigh Superbe three-speed bike in Oak Park. The popular quiz show is performed and recorded at the Chase Auditorium in downtown Chicago.

ALEX GARCIA, 2007

Janice Dickinson

Janice Dickinson, who calls herself the world's first supermodel, dons a lifesaver after taking a dip in the pool — fully clothed — at the InterContinental Hotel in Chicago.

HEATHER STONE, 2002

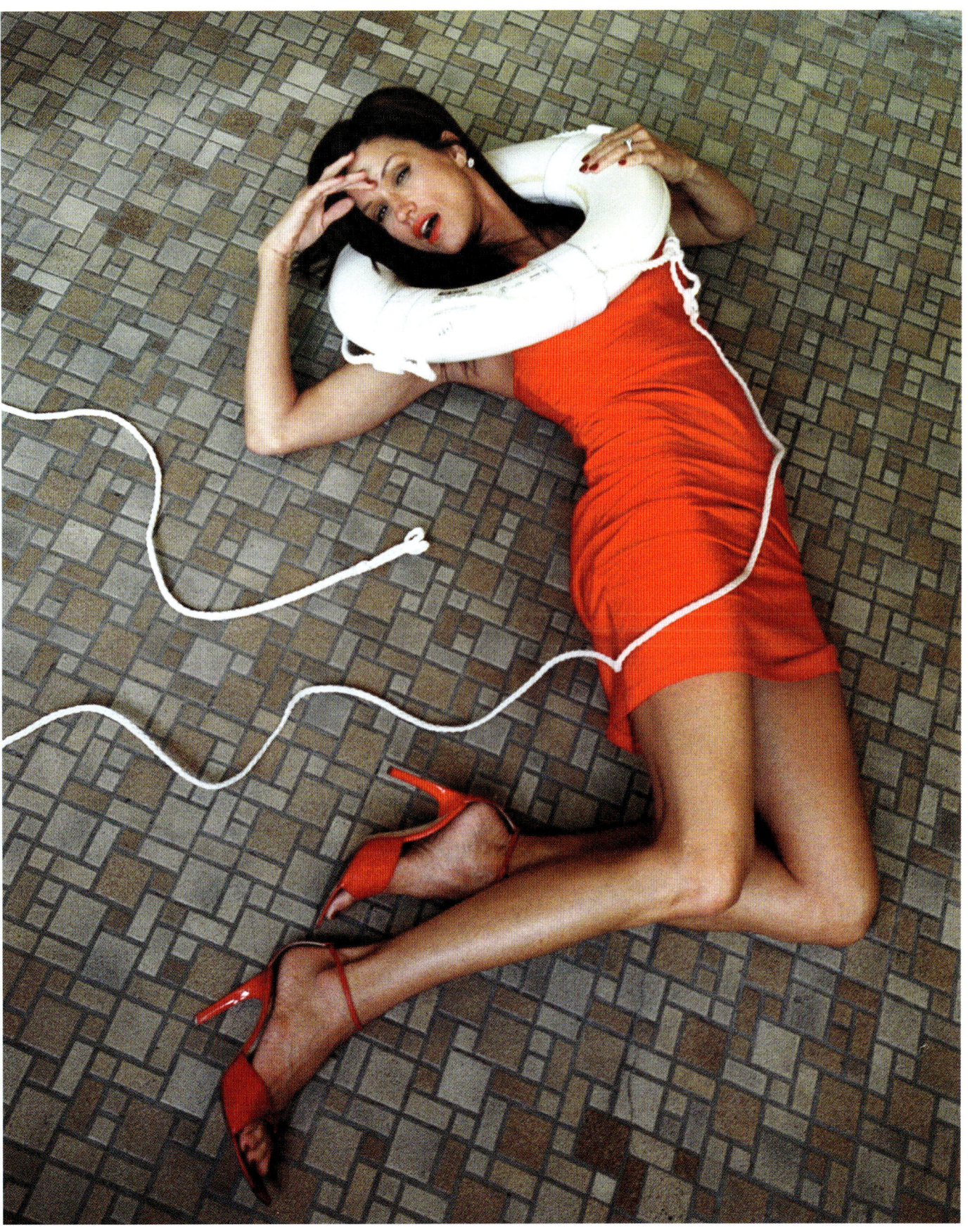

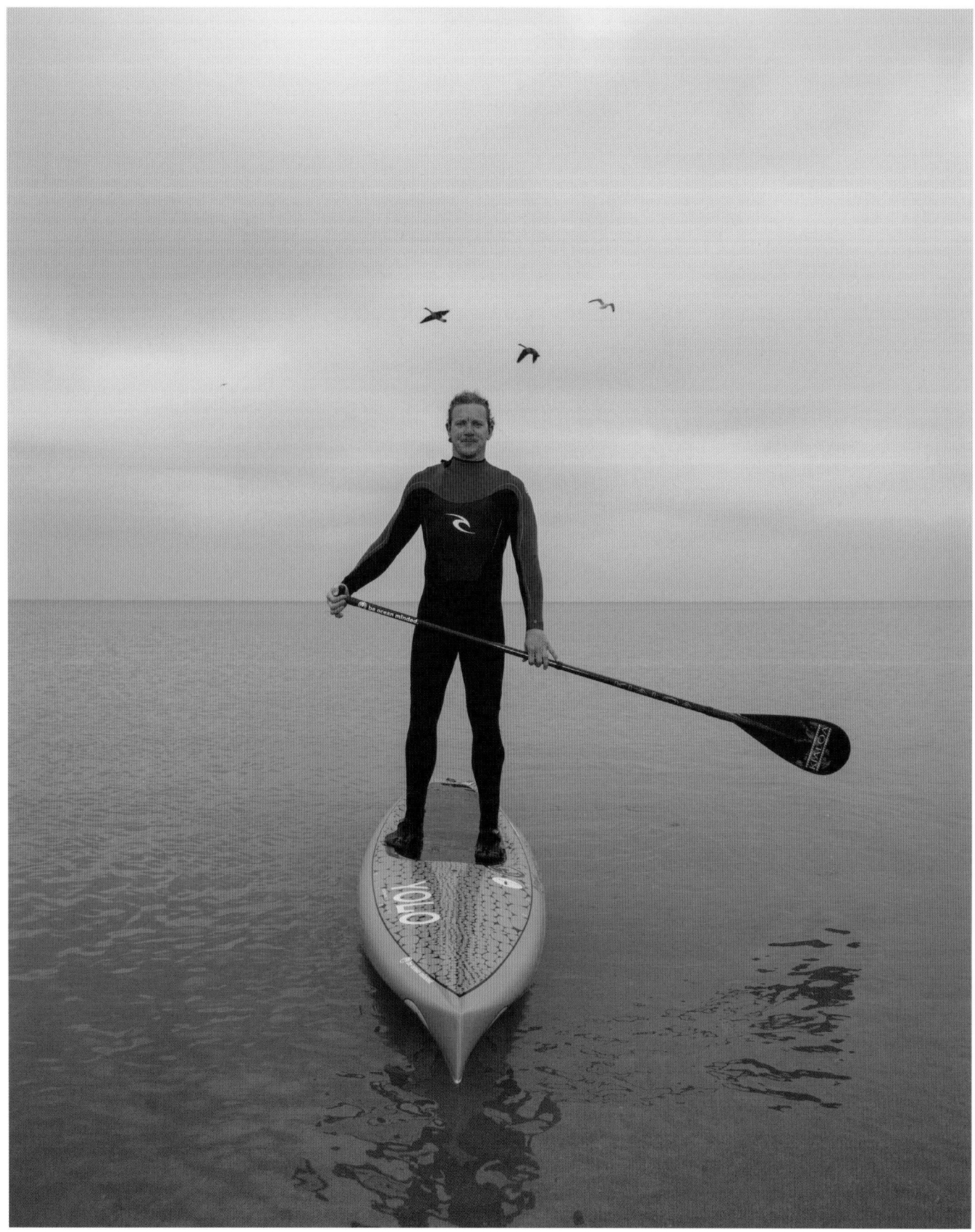

Michael Westenberger

Michael Westenberger, an expert stand-up paddle boarder, balances on Lake Michigan.

ALEX GARCIA, 2013

Pauline Palmer

Pauline Palmer, aka Mrs. Potter Palmer Jr., gives off a distinctive air of high society in this undated photo.

CHICAGO TRIBUNE HISTORICAL PHOTO, 1920s

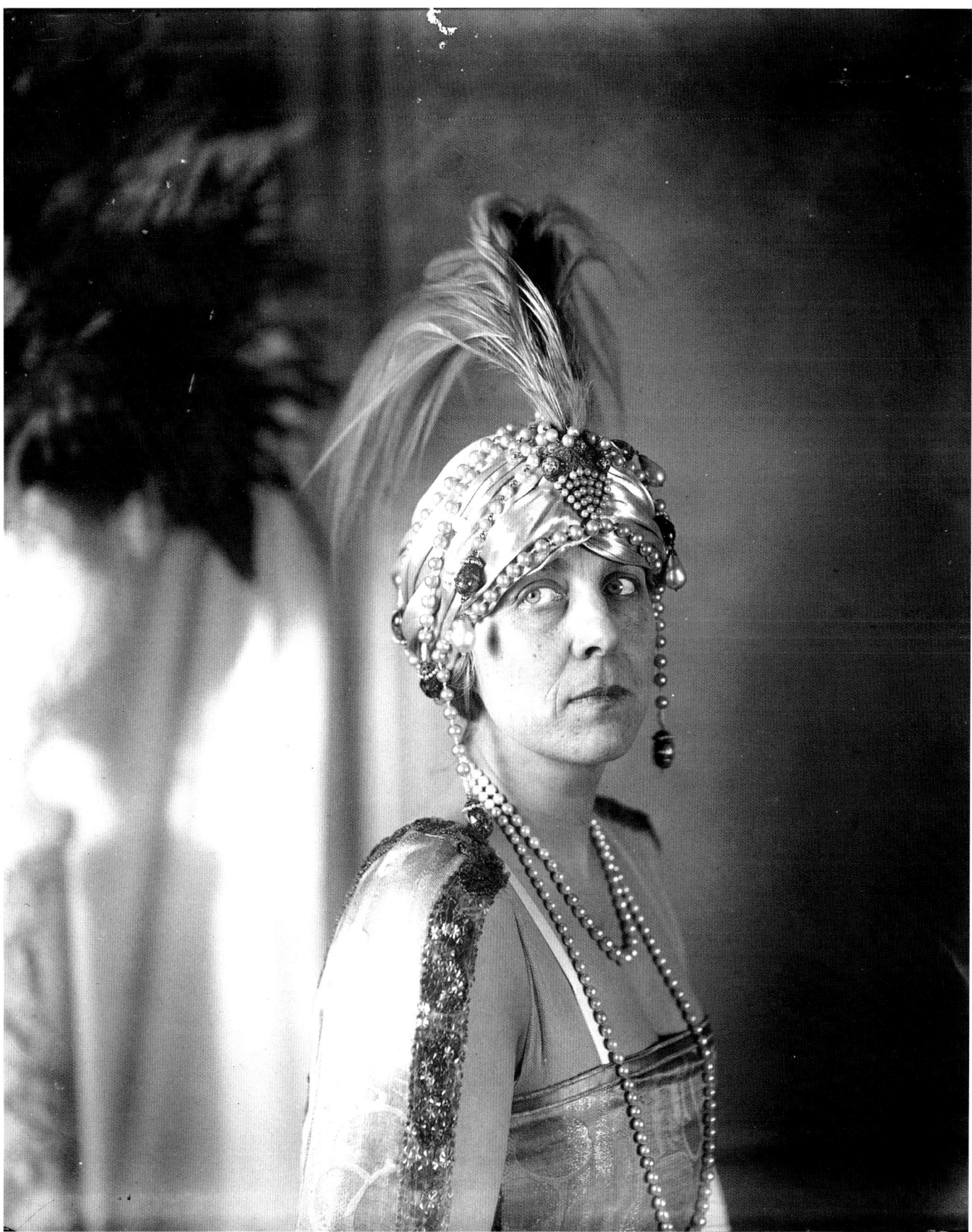

Lady Gaga

Pop superstar Lady Gaga listens to hip-hop artist Kendrick Lamar's set during the Pitchfork Music Festival in Chicago's Union Park.

SCOTT STRAZZANTE, 2012

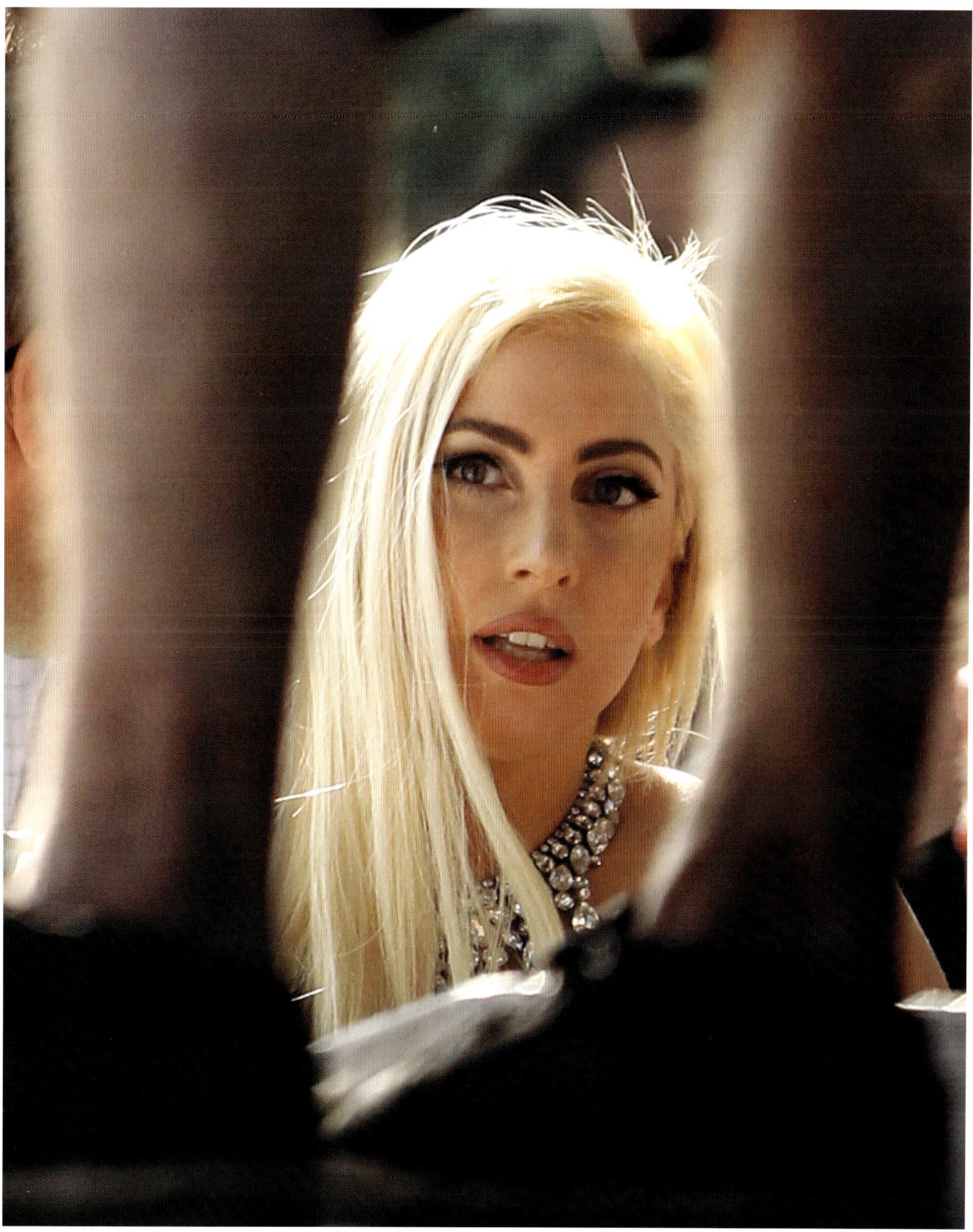

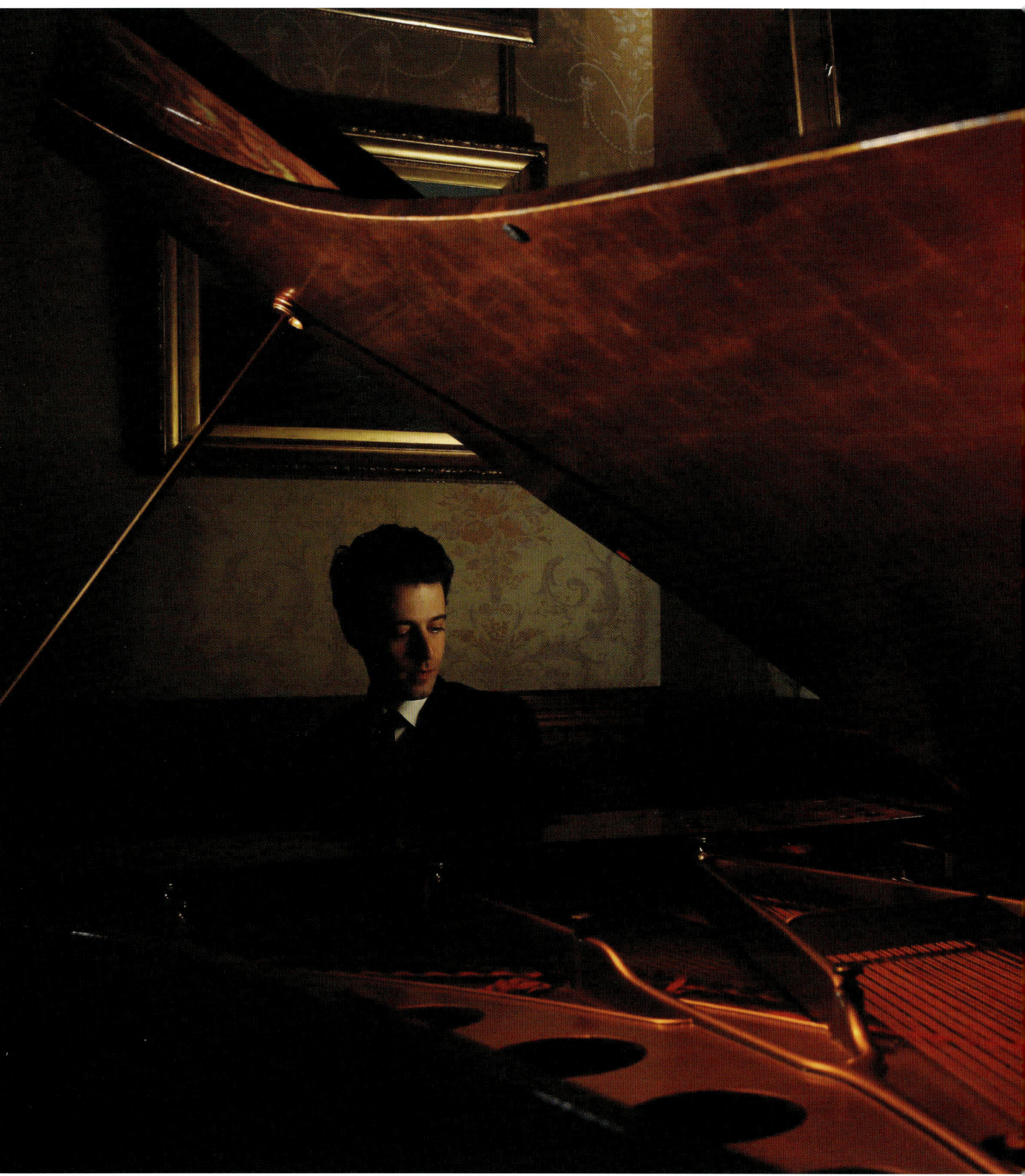

George Lepauw

George Lepauw, a prodigious pianist who maintains close ties to Chicago, sits at a Chickering piano at the Driehaus Museum on the Near North Side.

CHRIS WALKER, 2012

Jose Contreras

Chicago White Sox pitcher Jose Contreras regroups after a rough fourth inning against the Los Angeles Angels at U.S. Cellular Field in Chicago.

PHIL VELASQUEZ, 2005

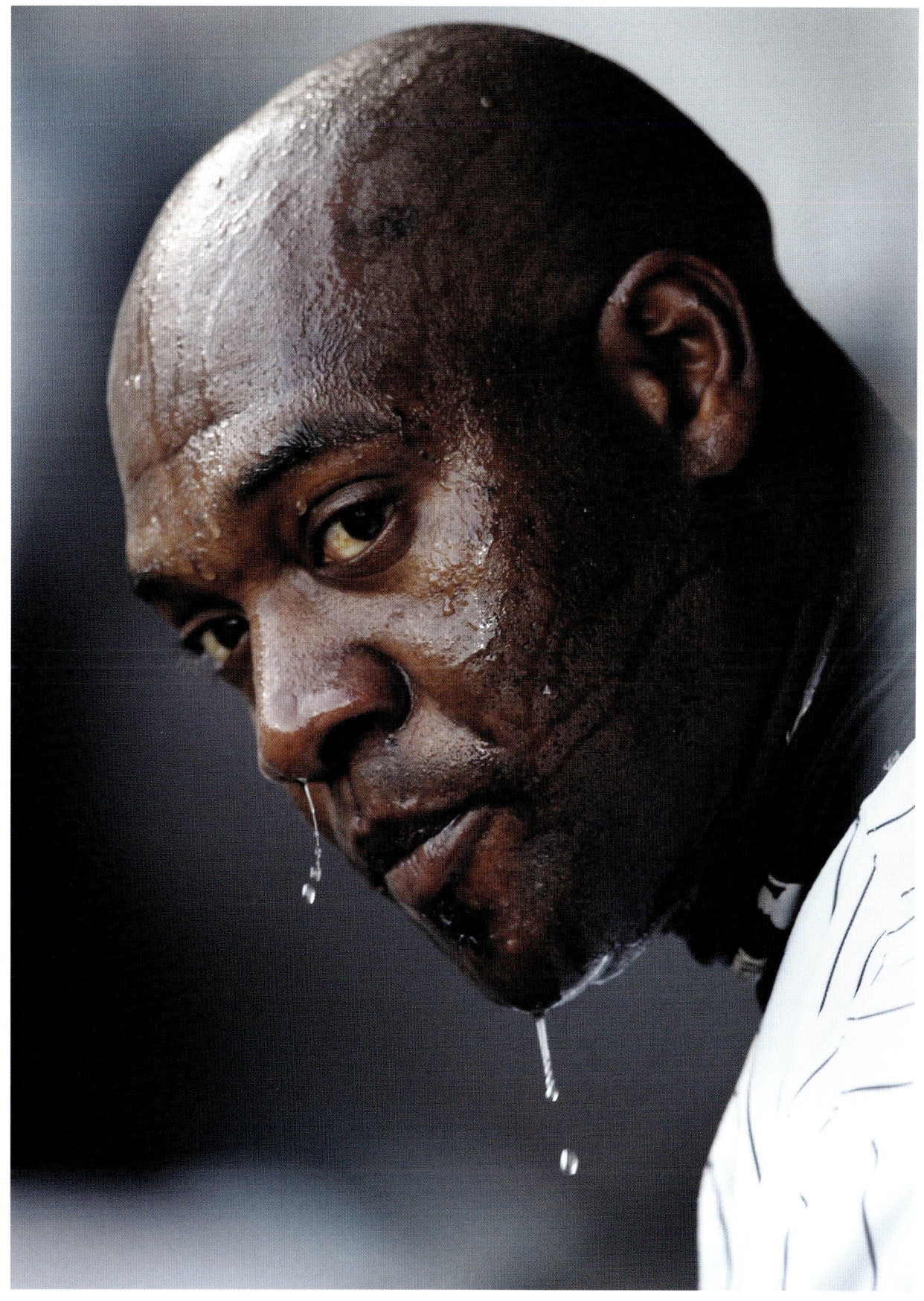

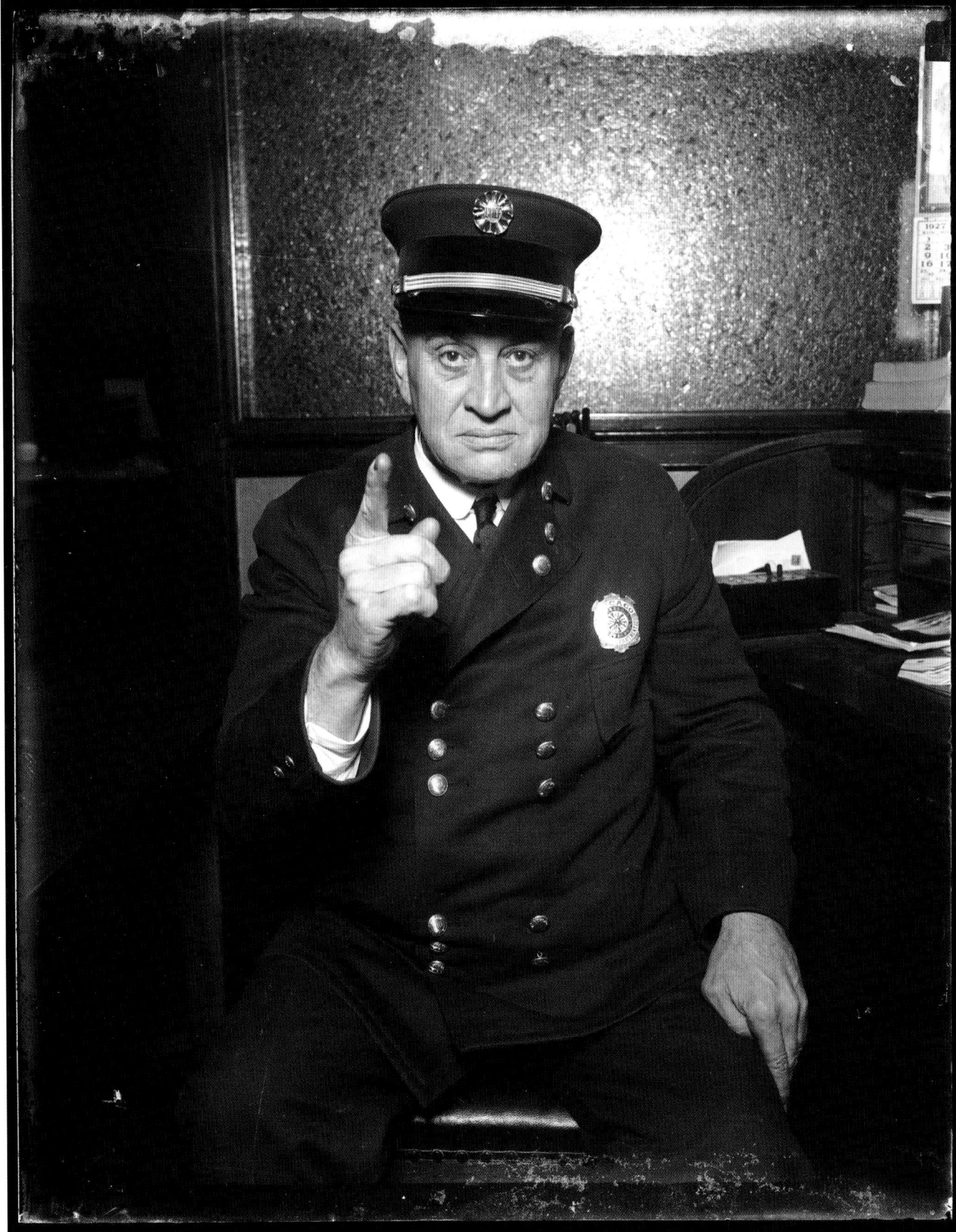

Arthur Seyferlich

Chicago Fire Department Chief Arthur Seyferlich strikes an authoritative pose.

CHICAGO TRIBUNE HISTORICAL PHOTO, 1927

Carrie Secrist

Carrie Secrist's West Loop garden was featured in the May 9, 2010, issue of Chicago Tribune Magazine. Secrist turned a barren, stamp-size plot in front of her town house into a mini-paradise.

BILL HOGAN, 2009

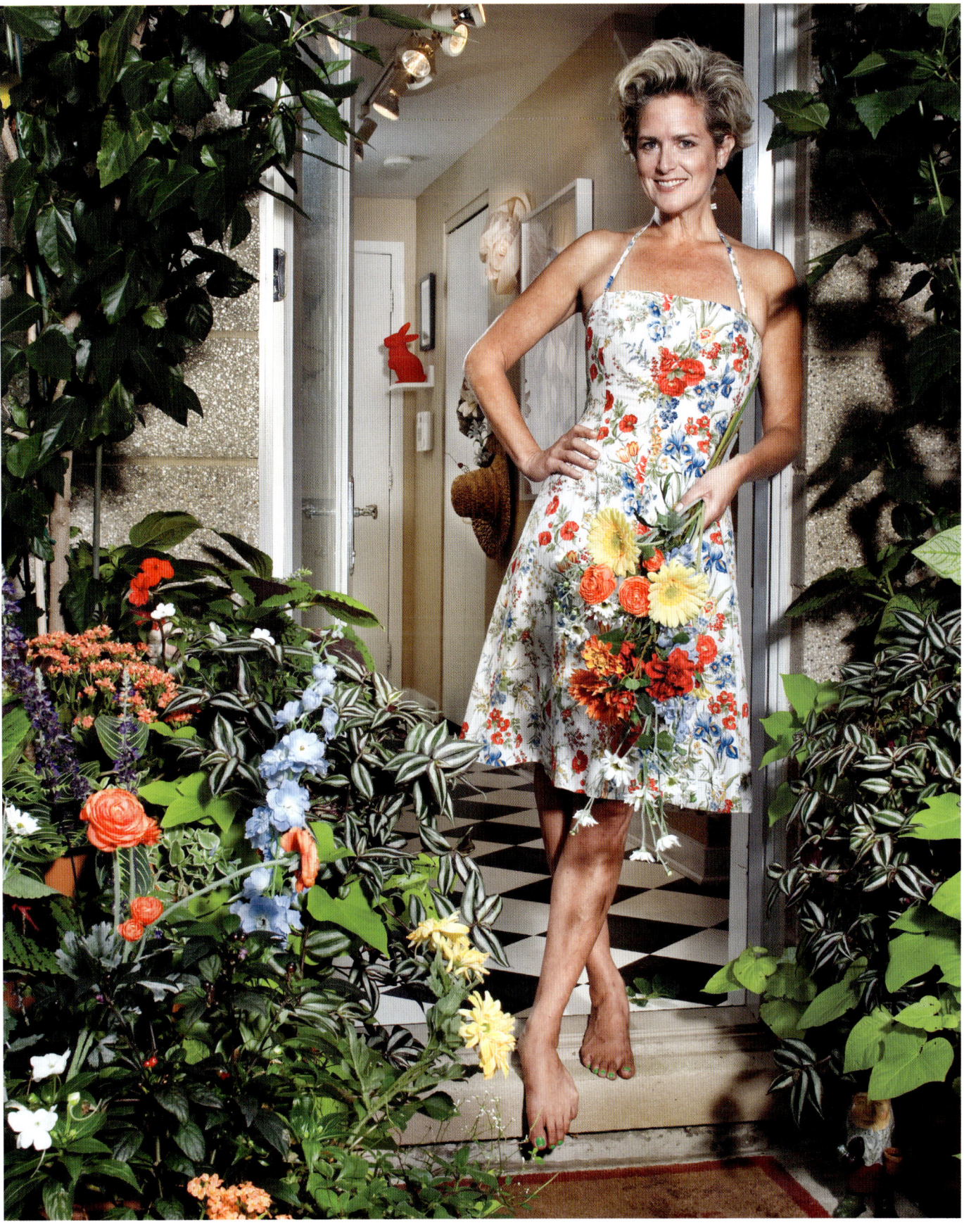

Robert Hanson AND Edward Murphy

Robert Hanson, 8, left, and Edward Murphy, 9, beam after being removed from a ventilation duct at Chicago's Ramova Theater in the Bridgeport neighborhood. Lacking the 15 cents or so for a matinee, they crept up the theater's fire escape to the roof, pried open a skylight and dropped into a ventilation duct. "Destination uncertain, they trudged on," the Tribune reported, until they reached a massive fan. The boys settled into the knee-high dust and watched the show between the blades of the fan, which only had to be switched on by an unknowing employee to slice them up. Eventually rescued by ushers, the boys were sent to the local police station for a lecture, glorification by the local media and, later, likely strong censure from their parents.

CHICAGO TRIBUNE HISTORICAL PHOTO, 1942

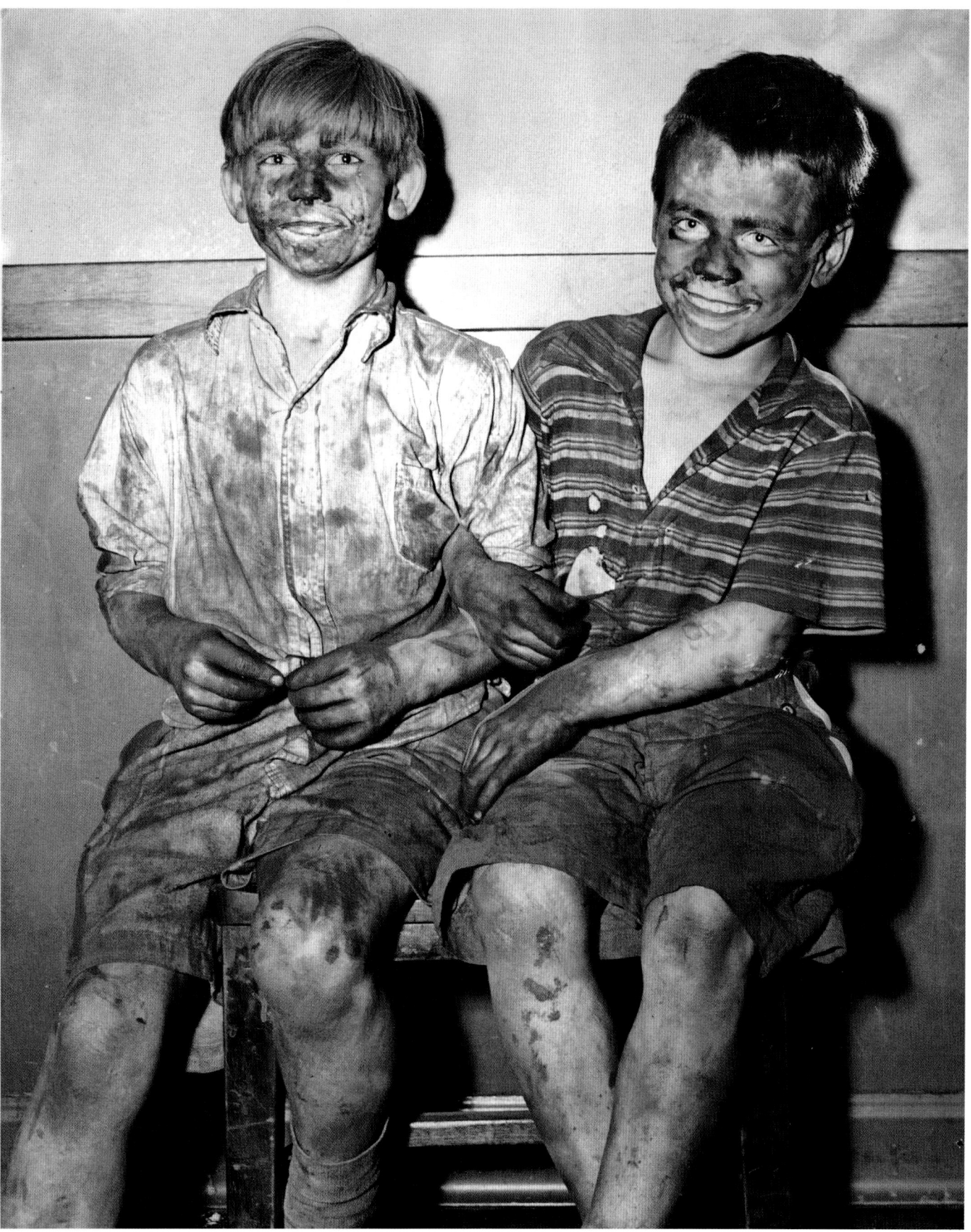

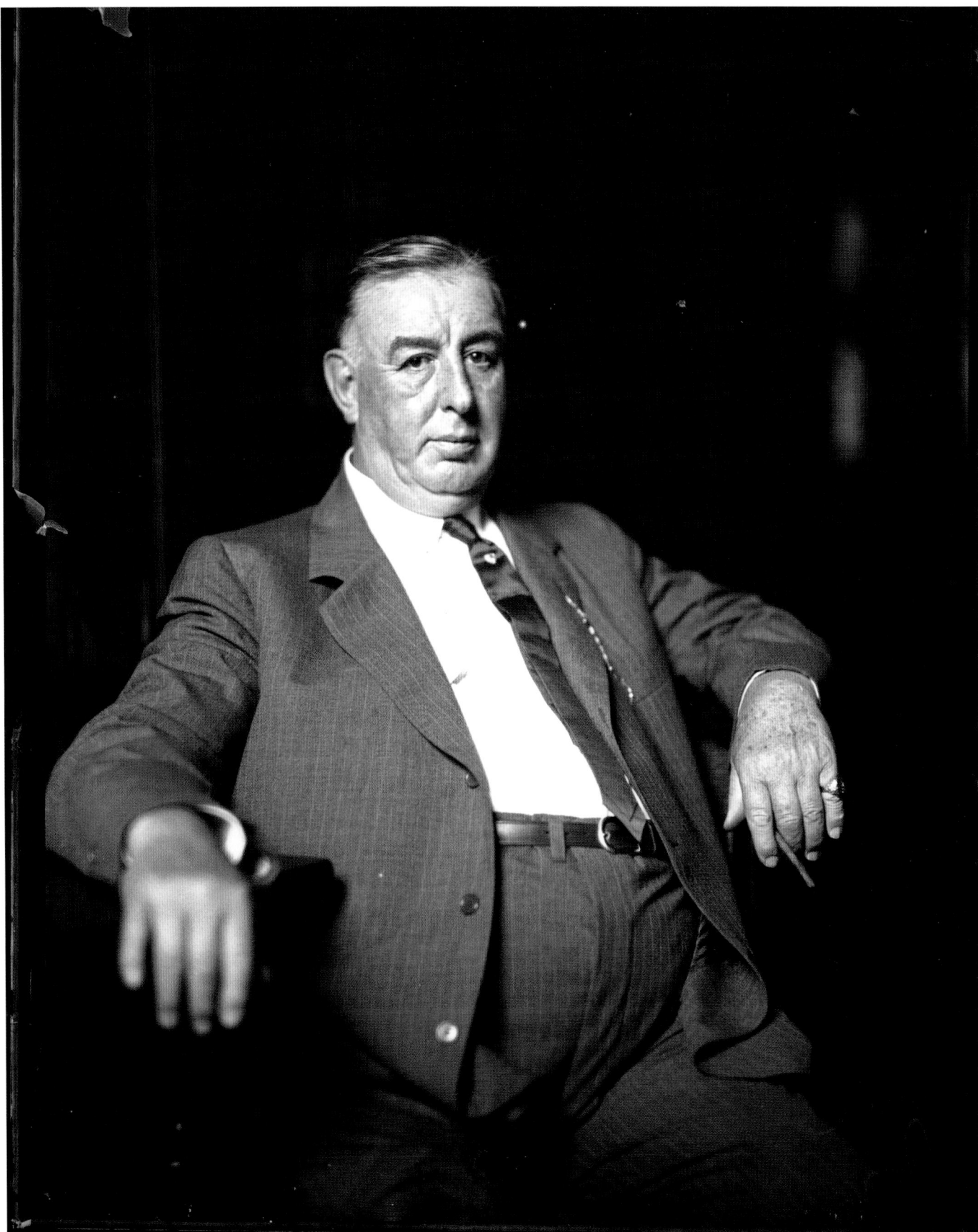

William Hale Thompson

Mayor William Hale Thompson was elected to lead Chicago three times, serving from 1915 to 1923 and again from 1927 to 1931. The city's current mayor, Rahm Emanuel, appears to have a flair for drama, but he will never rival the theatrics of Thompson. During the 1927 election, in which he was abetted by mobster boss Al Capone, Thompson held a debate between himself and two live white rats, which he carried onto a stage to represent his opponents. He also, in no particular order, threatened to punch England's King George V "in the snoot," began an expedition to the South Seas to discover tree-climbing fish and brought horses into the City Council chambers.

CHICAGO TRIBUNE HISTORICAL PHOTO, UNDATED

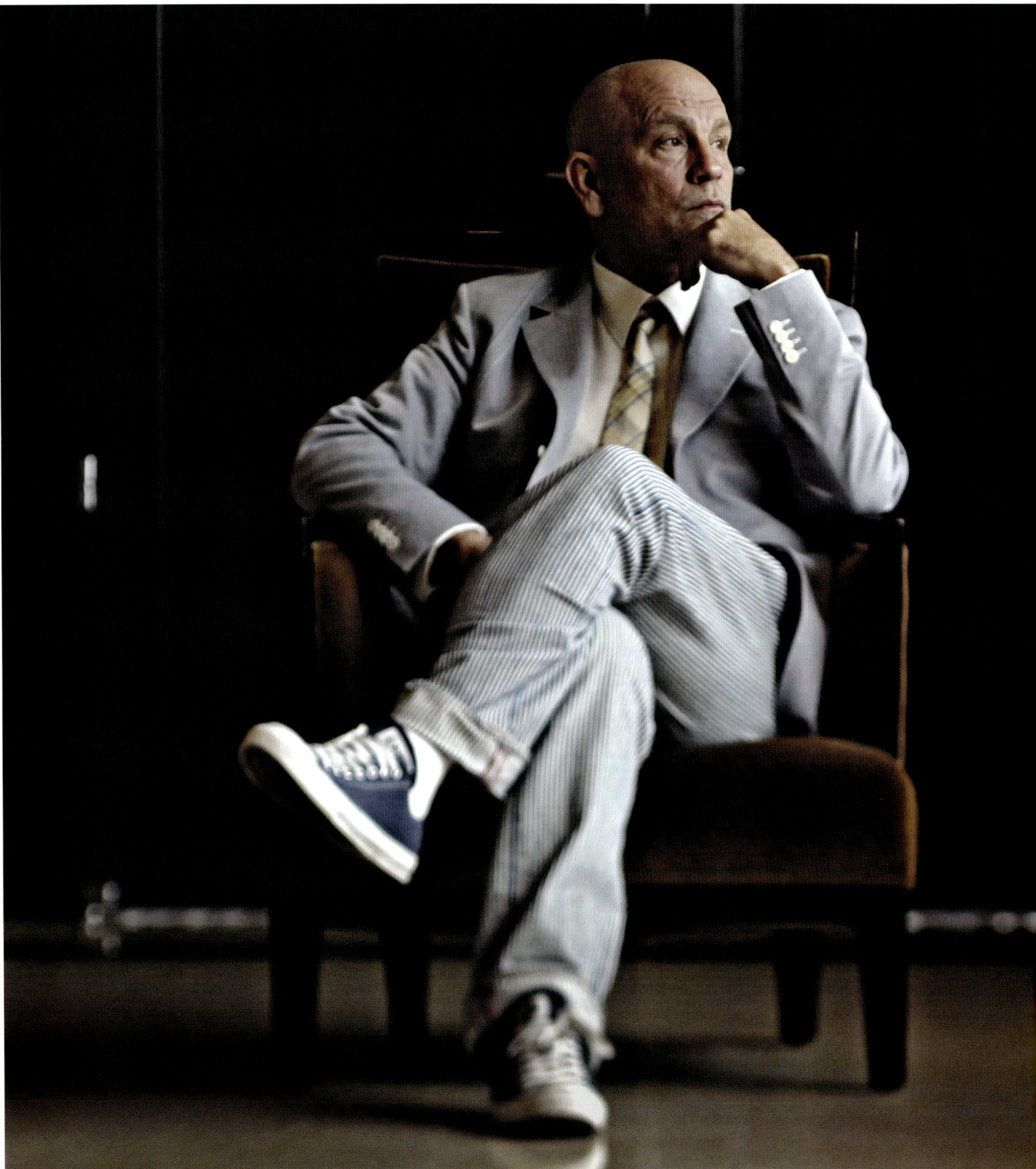

John Malkovich

Actor John Malkovich poses for a portrait at Trump International Hotel while in Chicago to promote his film "Secretariat." Malkovich is a longtime ensemble member with Chicago's Steppenwolf Theatre Co.

BRIAN CASSELLA, 2010

Victoria Jaiani

Ballerina Victoria Jaiani, shown at the Joffrey Ballet studios in Chicago, was named 2010 Chicagoan of the Year in Dance after her artistry soared to new heights.

ALEX GARCIA, 2010

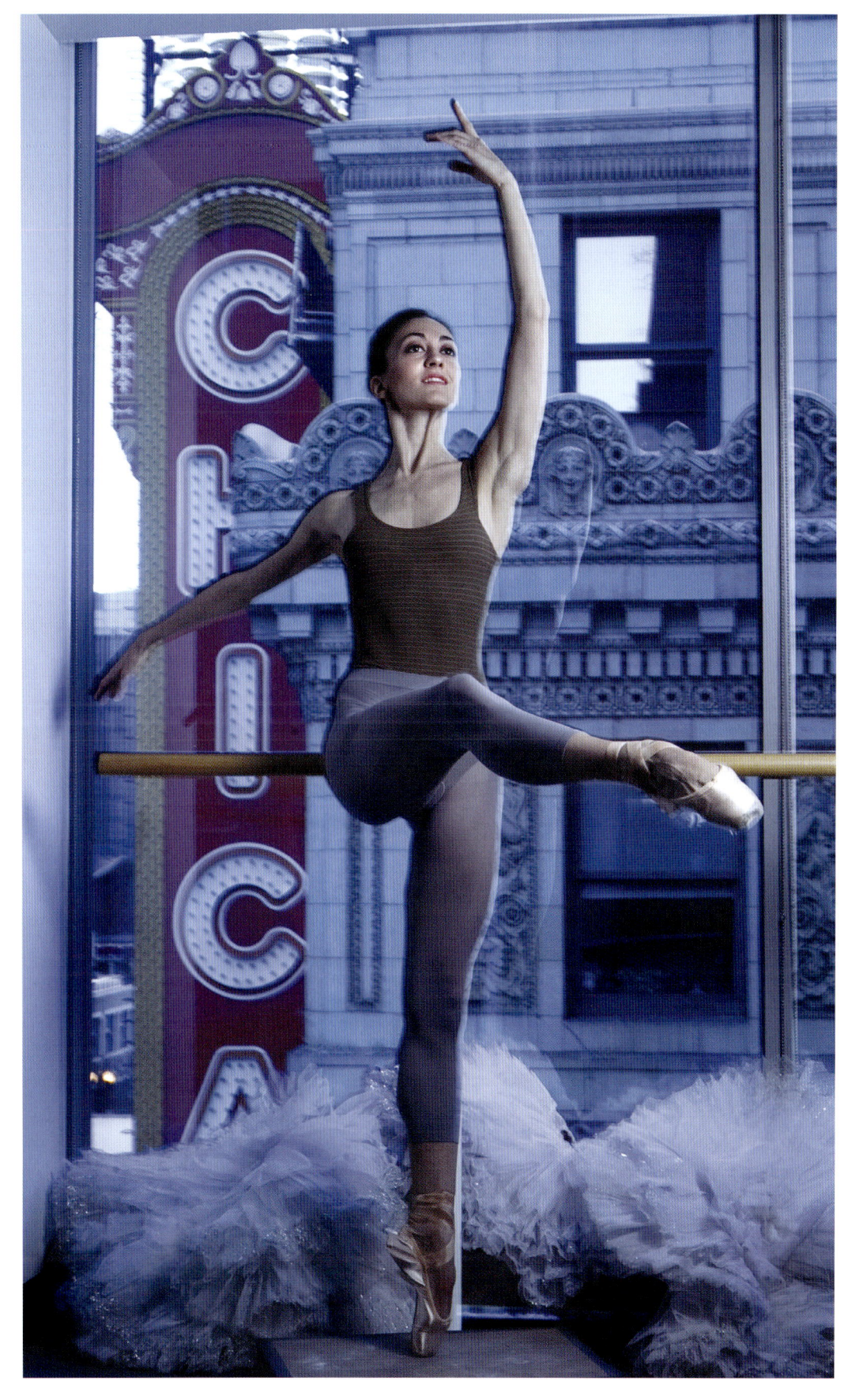

Harold Washington

Harold Washington is surrounded by supporters as he campaigns April 6, 1983, on Chicago's South Side. The former state senator and U.S. representative made history that month by being elected the city's first black mayor.

FRANK HANES, 1983

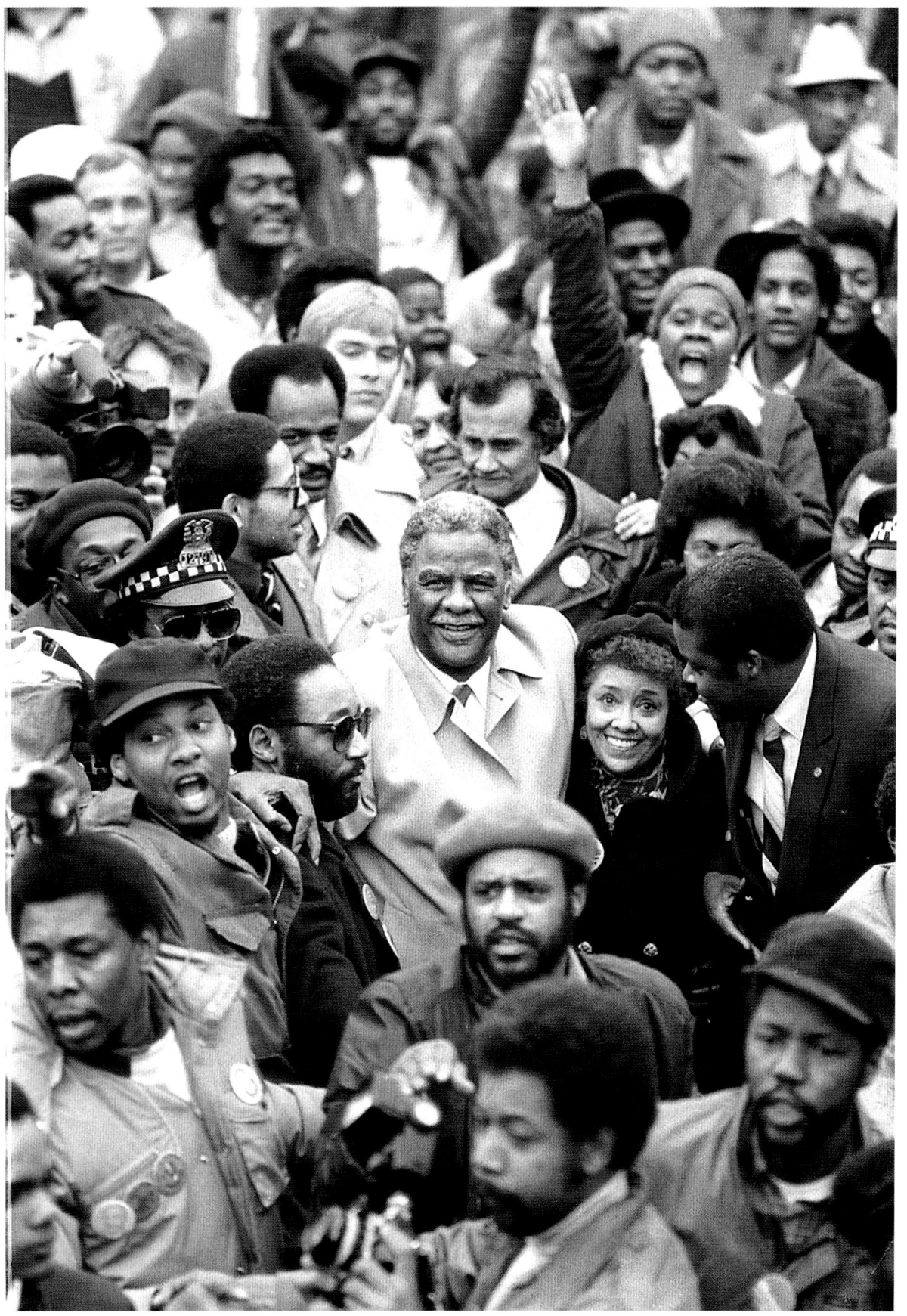

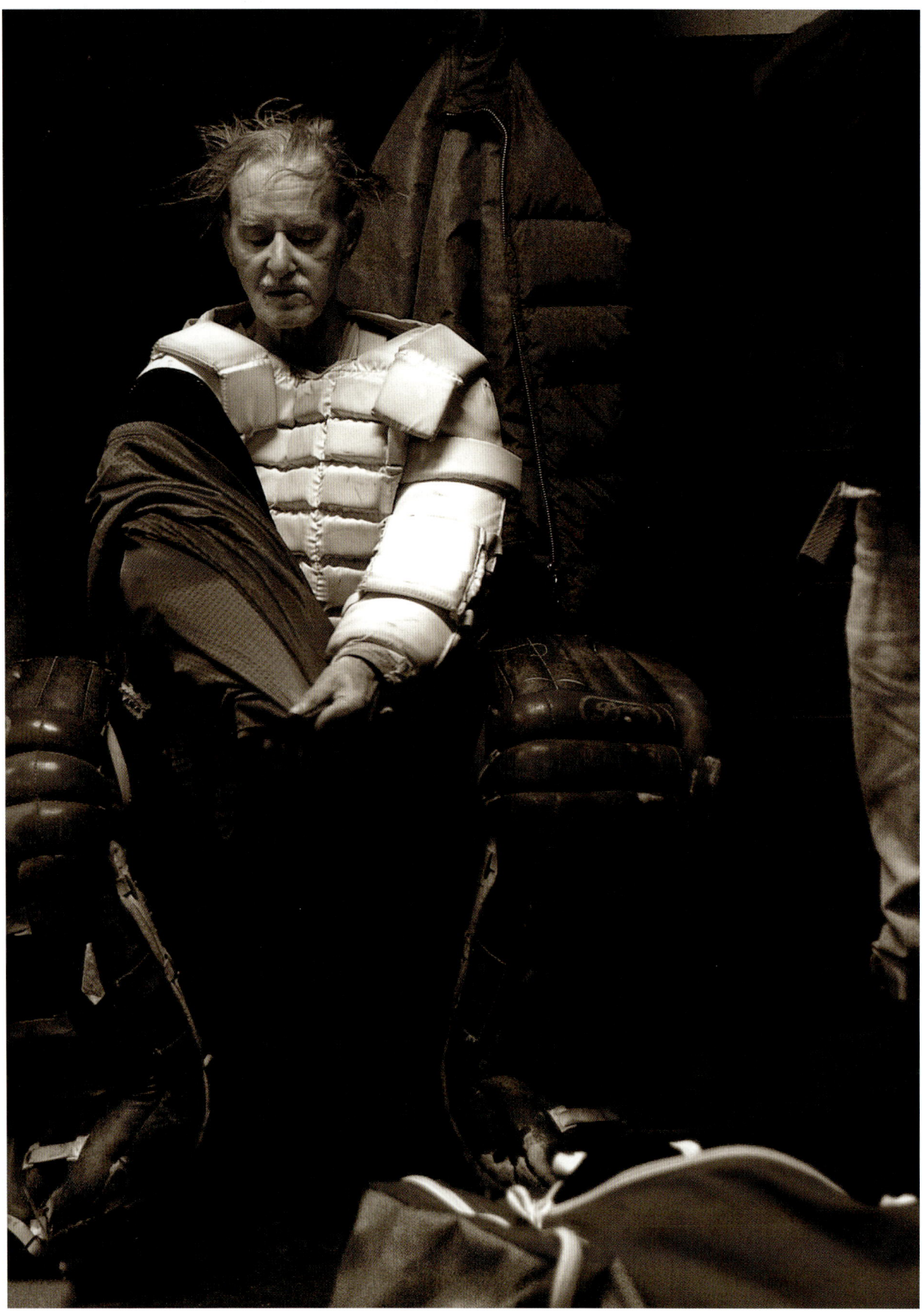

Ron Fedor

Ron Fedor, 72, of Mount Prospect, undresses in a locker room. At the time, the veteran hockey player was serving as a goalie in the 50-and-older pick-up league at Johnny's IceHouse in Chicago.

CHARLES CHERNEY, 2004

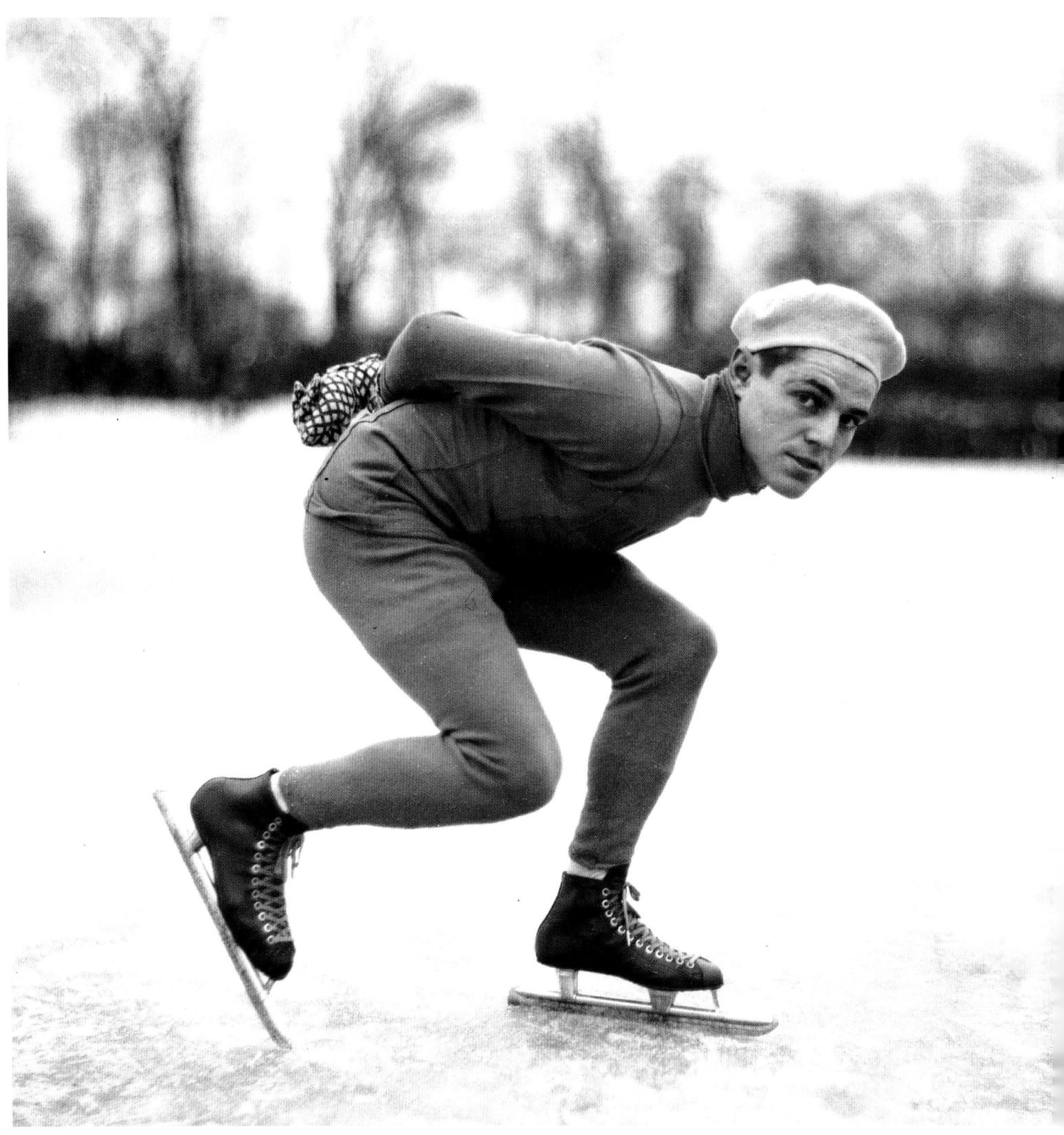

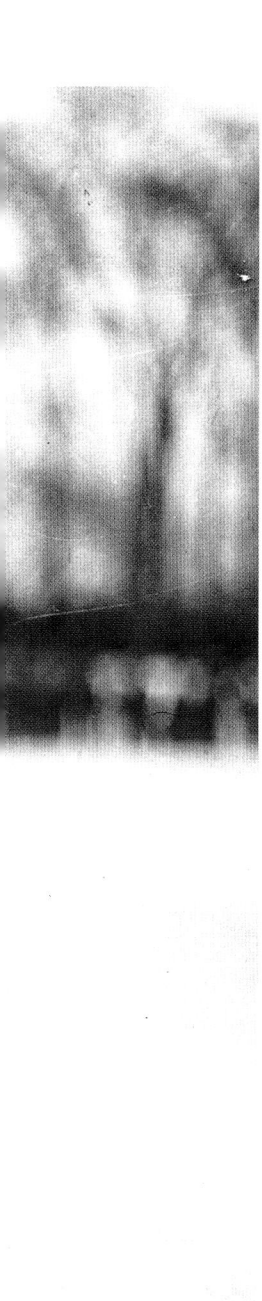

Eddie Schroeder

Olympic speedskater Eddie Schroeder, shown in an undated photo, was a product of Chicago's South Side and a member of the Walton Arrow Athletic Club in Chicago.

CHICAGO TRIBUNE HISTORICAL PHOTO, UNDATED

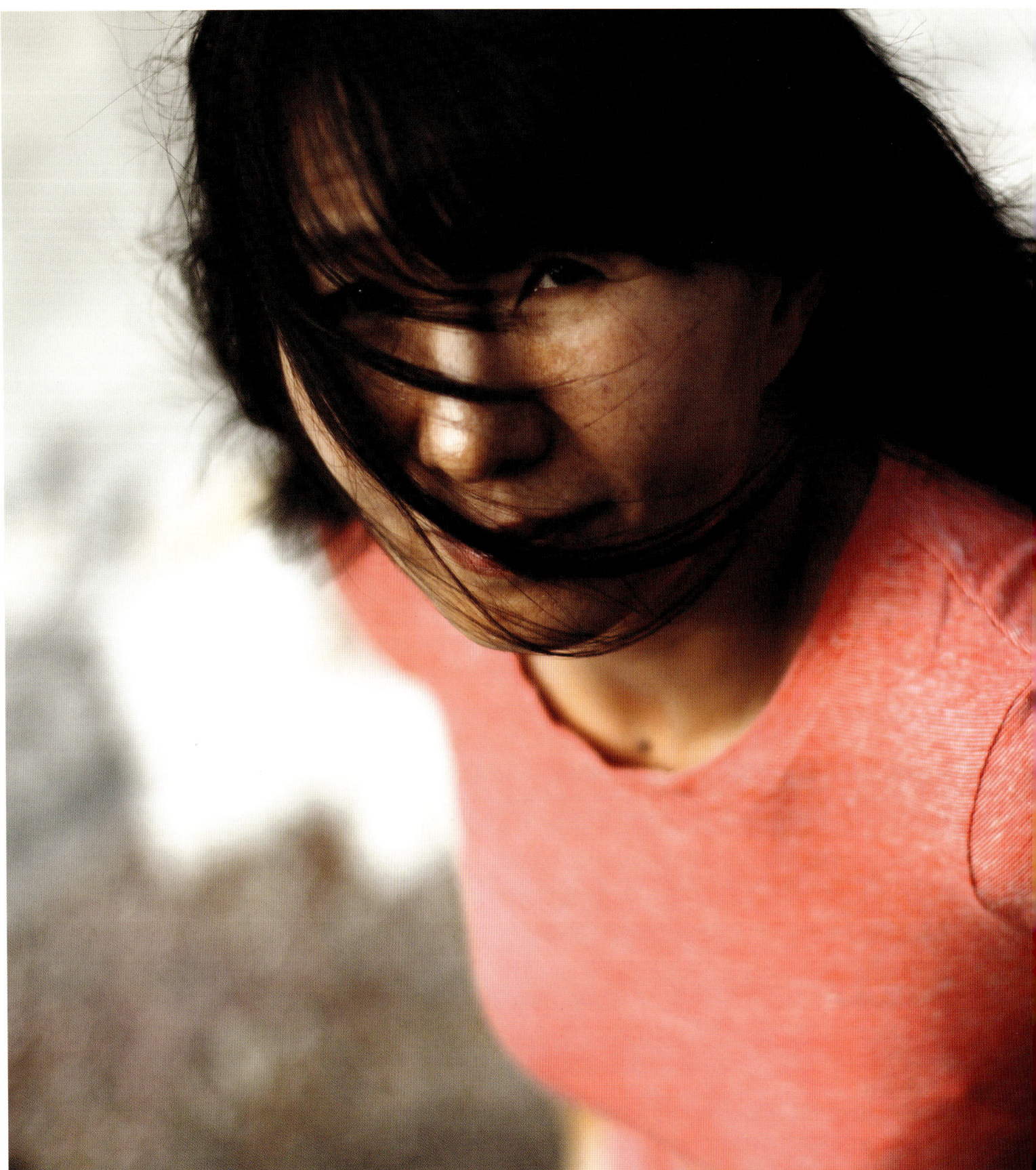

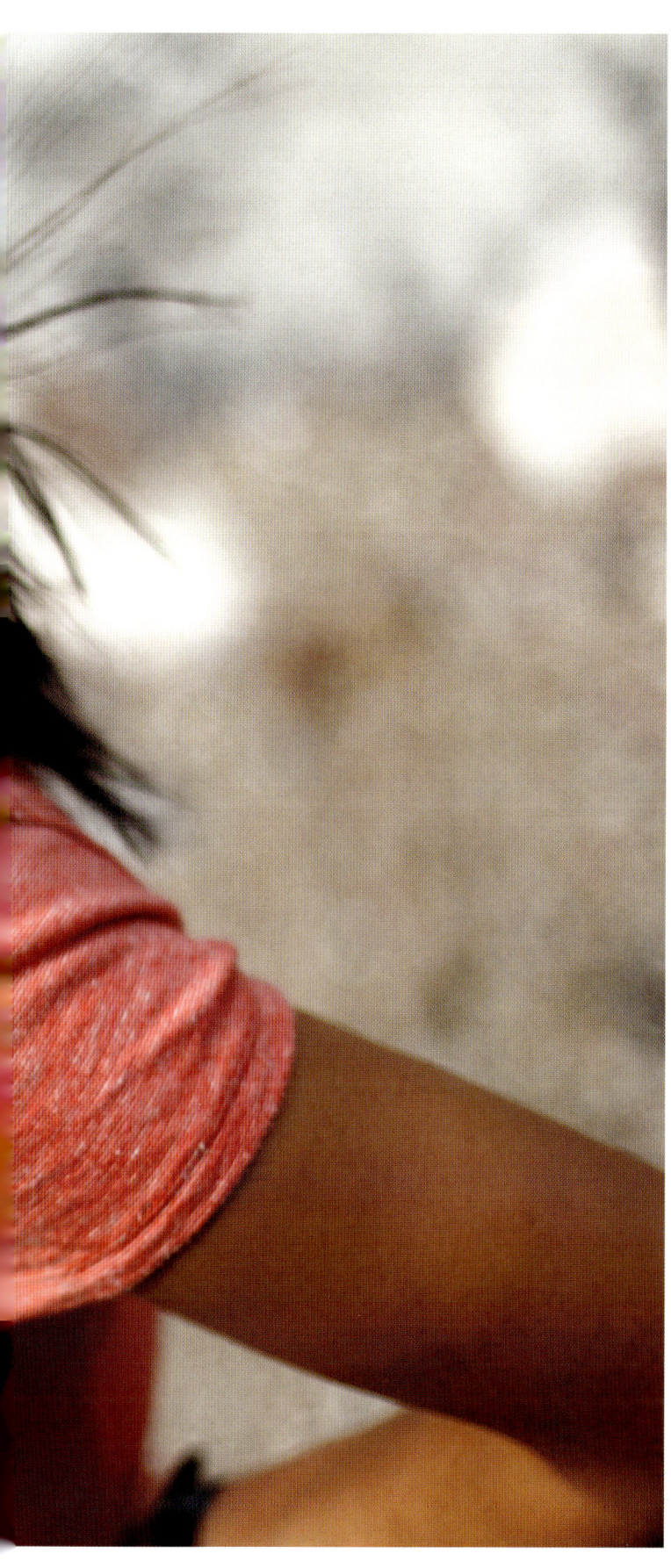

Nami Mun

Author Nami Mun, shown on Chicago's North Side, went from being a homeless teen to an acclaimed author, but, she says, "I didn't do it alone."

CHRIS WALKER, 2012

Rosie Simpson

Rosie Simpson stands at 73rd Street and Lowe Avenue on Chicago's South Side, where more than 40 years prior she participated in a civil rights protest. Simpson dropped out of school at age 15 to work at the stockyards, but the mother of six wanted much more for her children. She helped organize the school boycotts that brought the Rev. Martin Luther King Jr. to Chicago to lead the Chicago Freedom Movement. And so when the telephone rang in her South Side apartment at 5 a.m. on a rainy day in 1963, she was ready to go to jail. Simpson, who was 32 at the time, dialed the next name on the list of mothers willing to join her behind bars. "The bulldozers are here," she said, and with her heart racing, she hung up, quickly got dressed and rushed out the door for the showdown in a vacant lot at 73rd and Lowe.

CHRIS WALKER, 2006

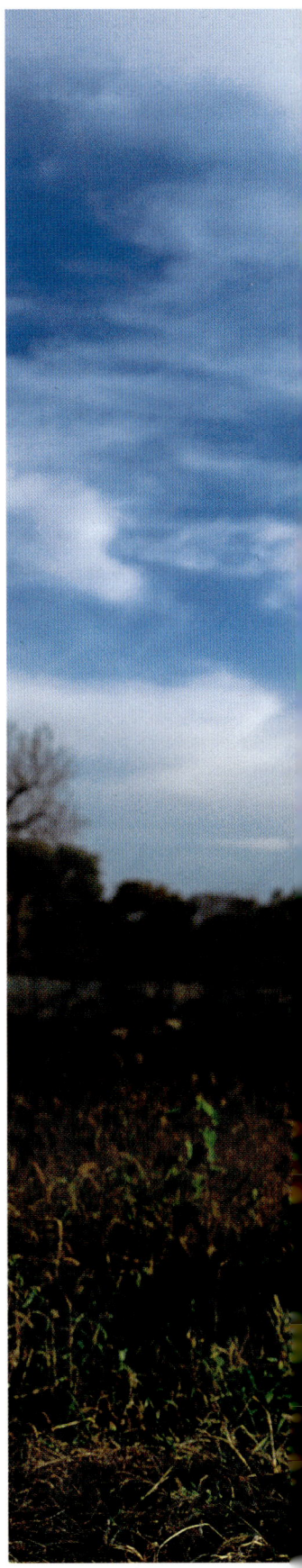

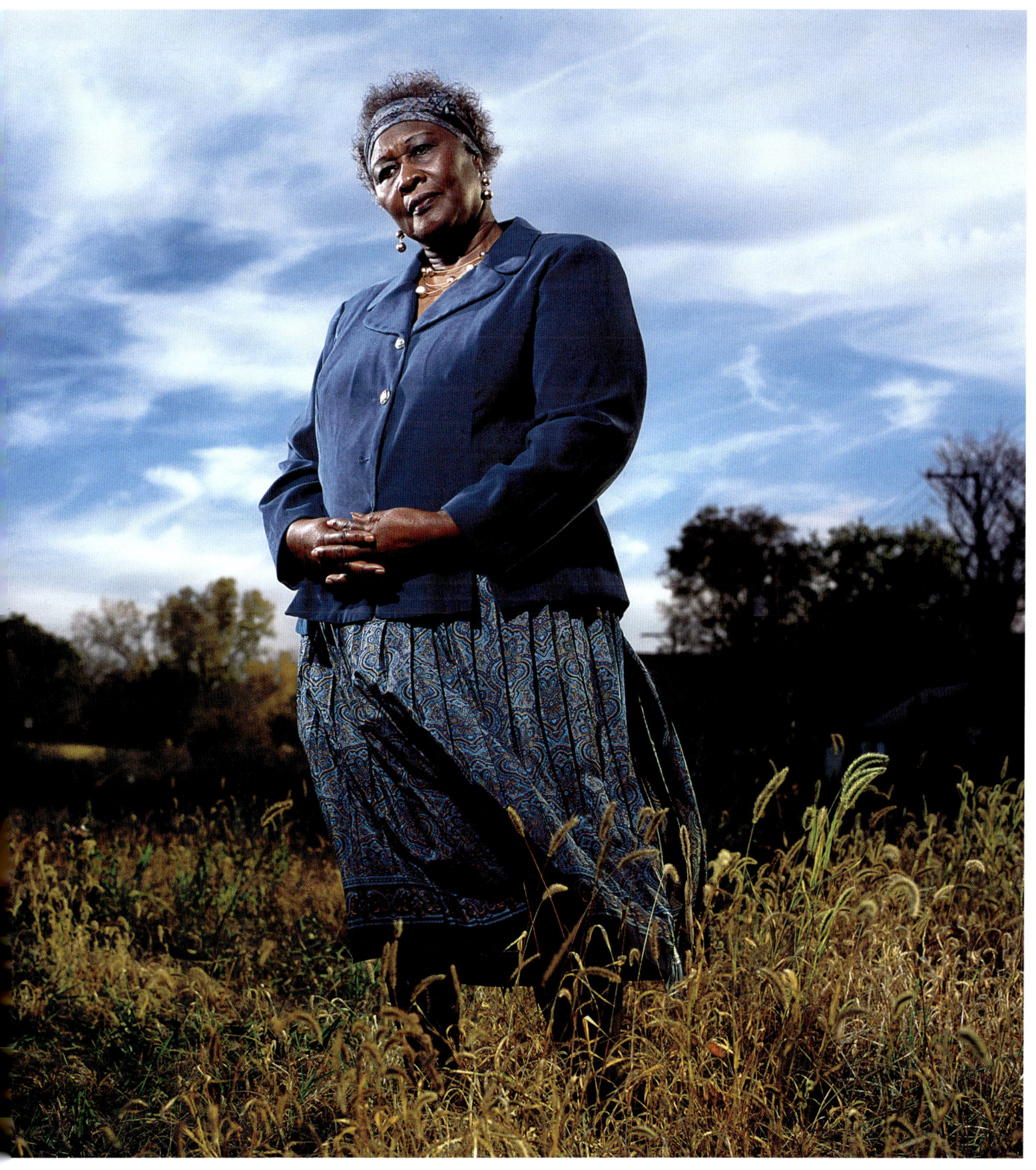

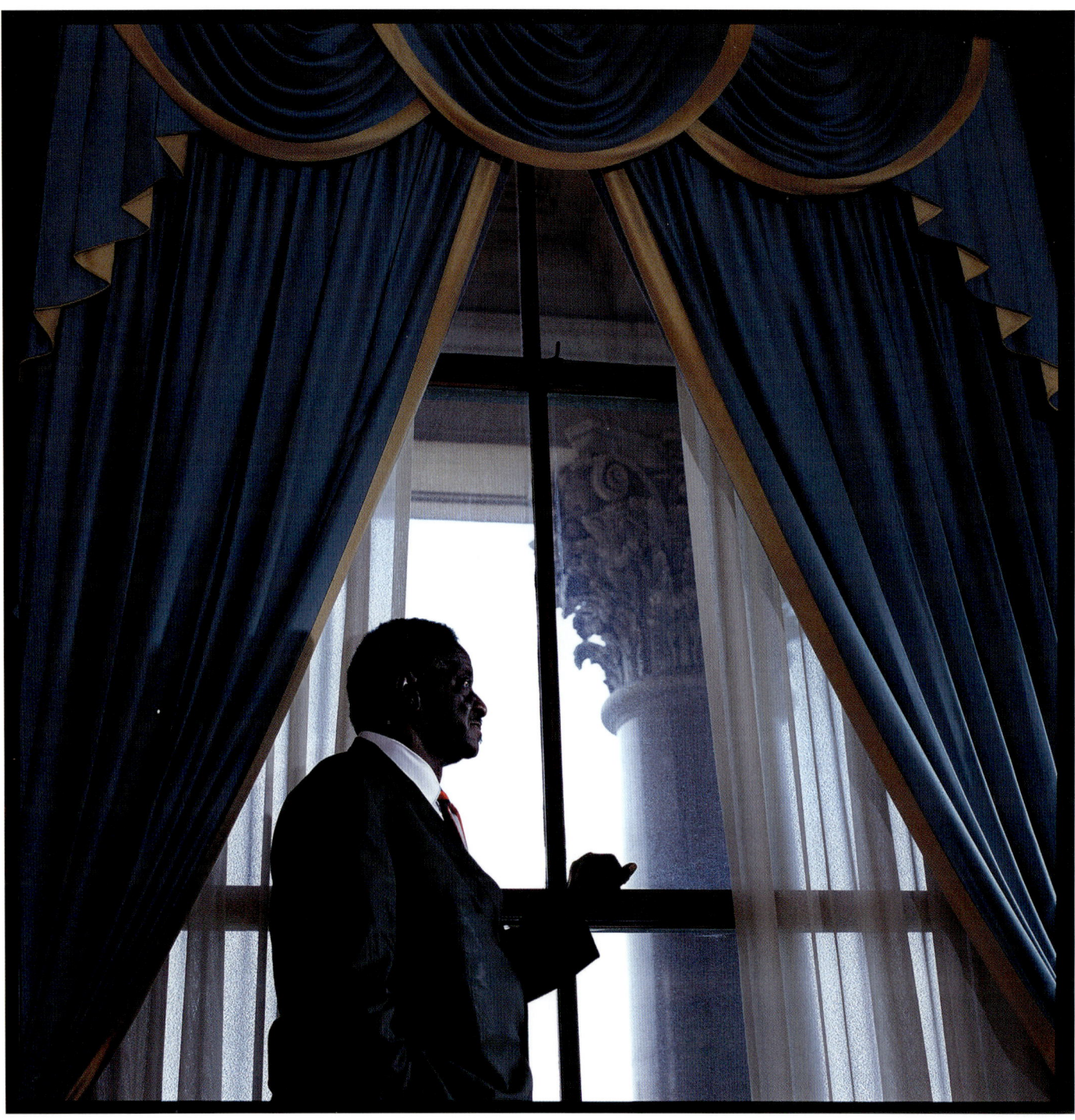

Emil Jones III

Illinois Senate President Emil Jones III peers out a window in the Capitol rotunda in Springfield.

STACEY WESCOTT, 2004

Gerald Arpino

Gerald Arpino surveys a thriving troupe at the Joffery Ballet in Chicago's Loop. The choreographer and dance impresario led the ballet company's move to Chicago from New York in 1995, helping it survive financial ruin.

BILL HOGAN, 2005

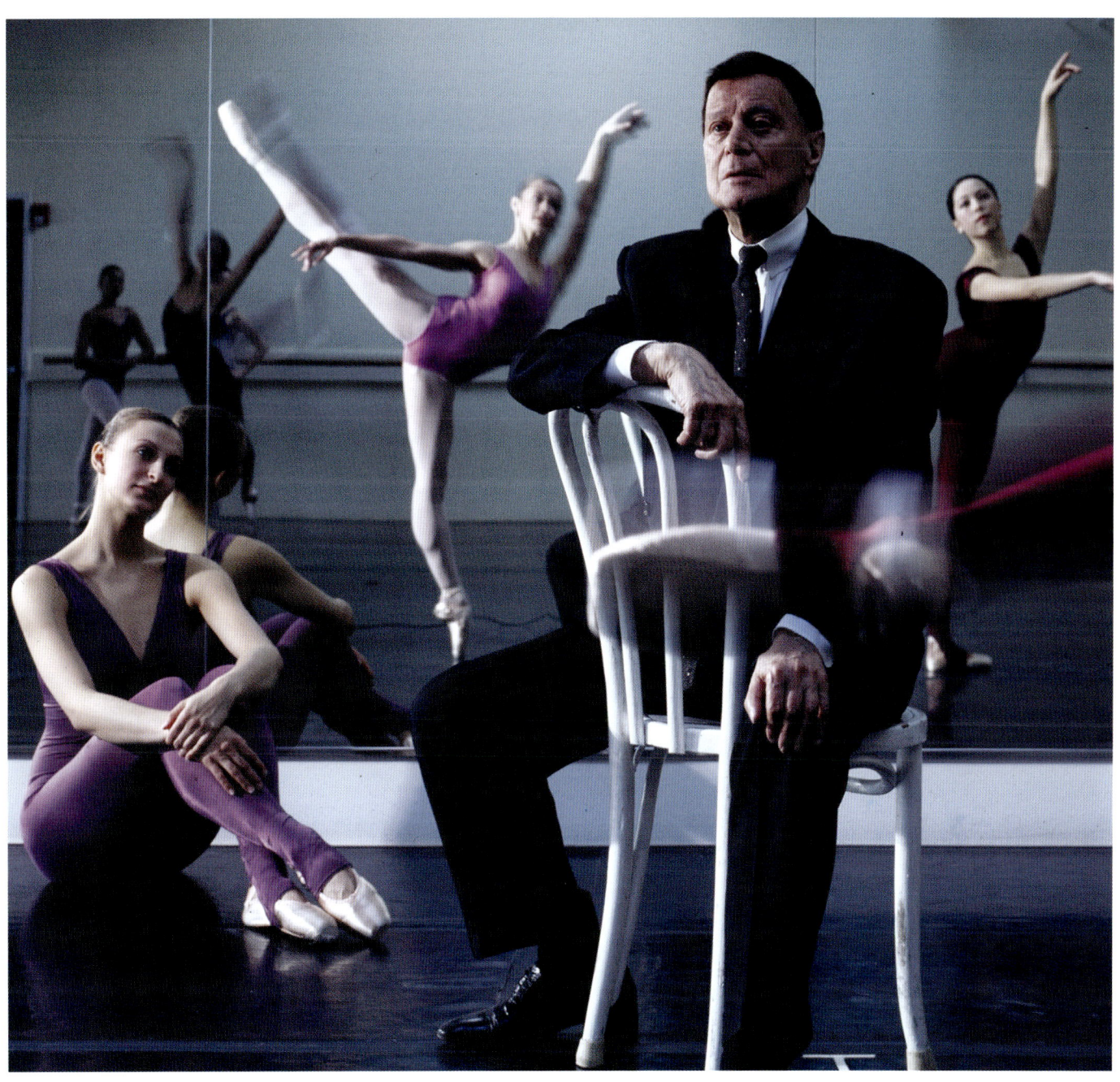

Autumn Eckman

Autumn Eckman, a choreographer with Giordano Dance Chicago, strikes a pose at the American Rhythm Center in Chicago.

ZBIGNIEW BZDAK, 2012

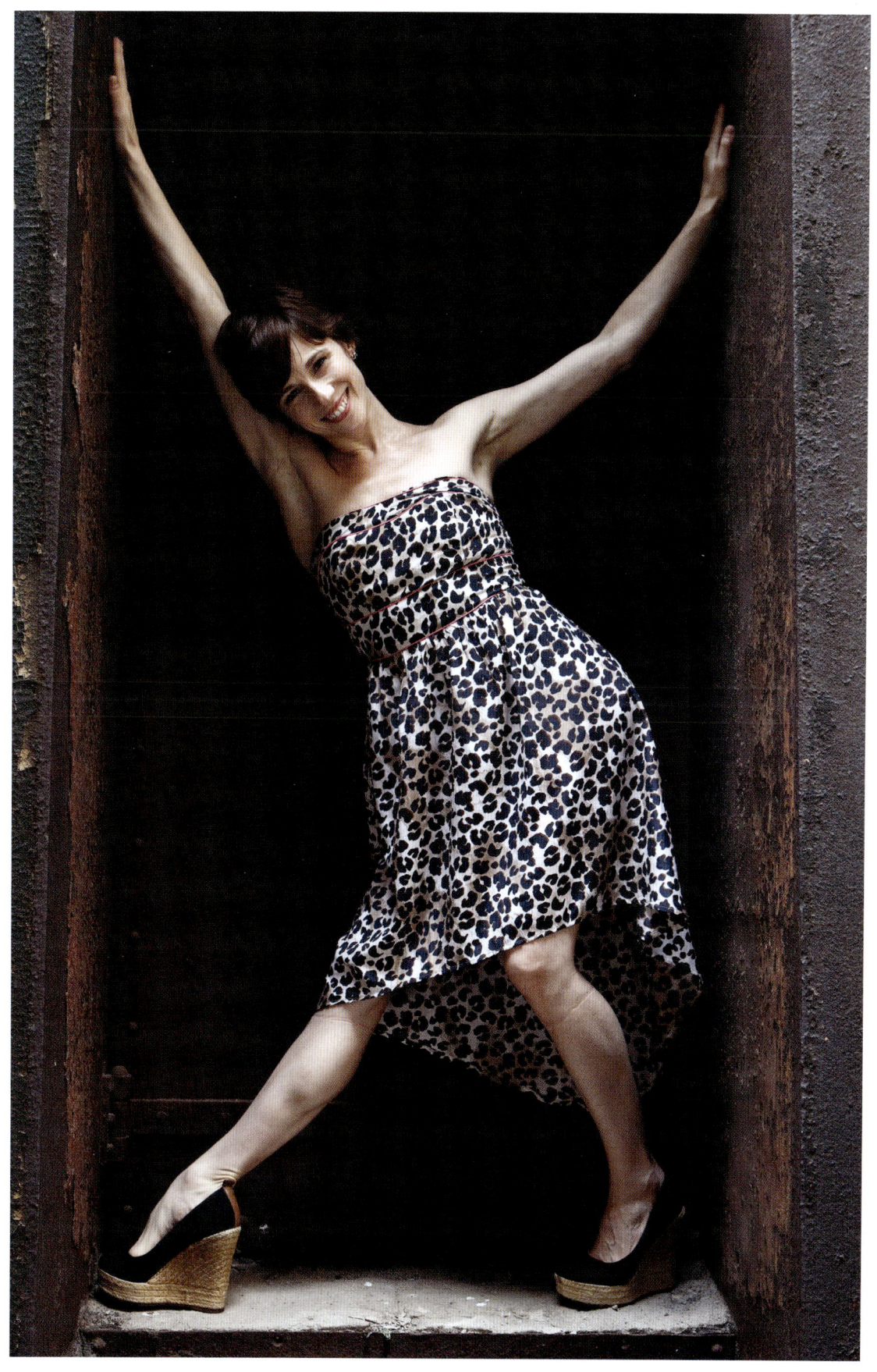

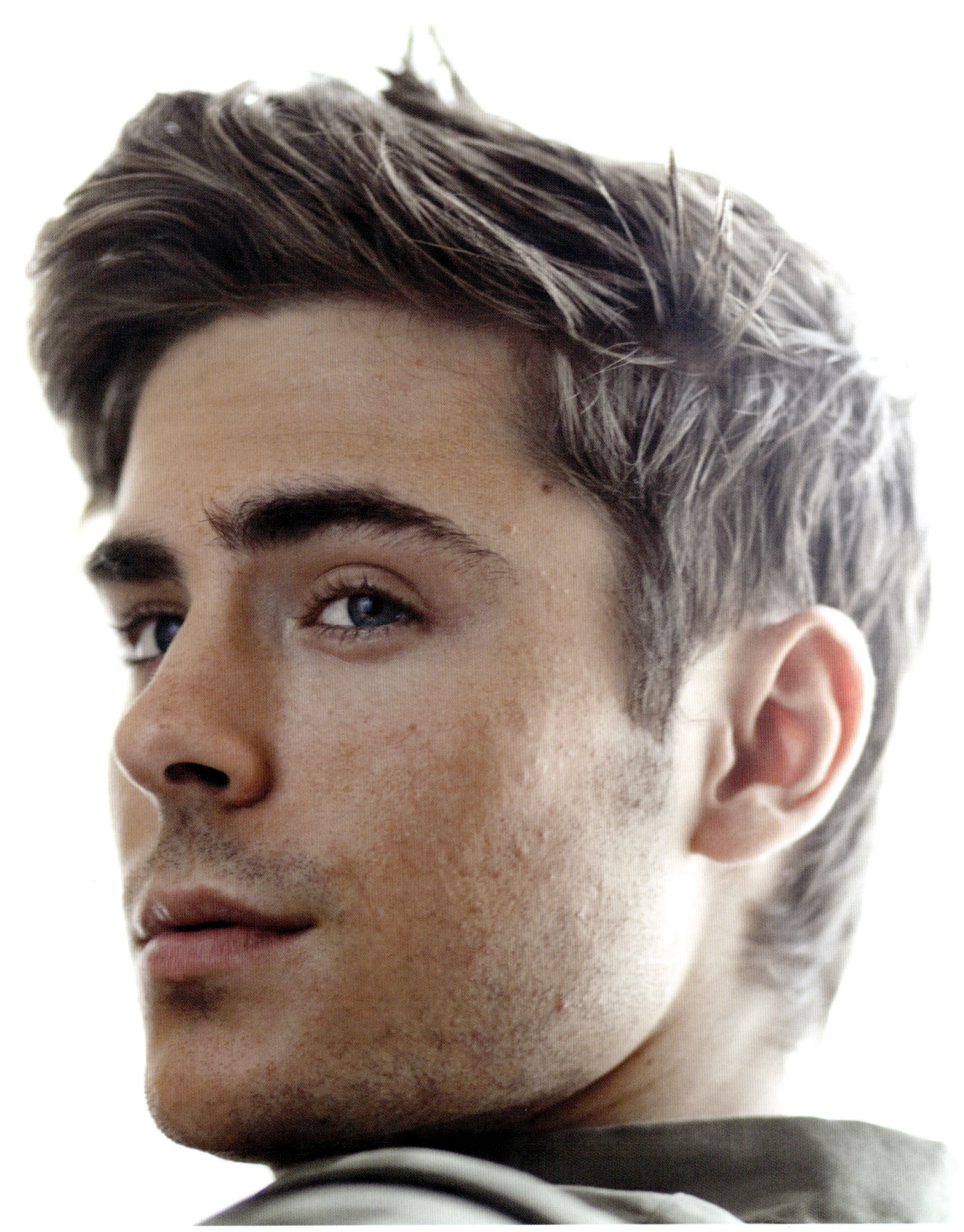

Zac Efron

With only five minutes to capture a portrait of actor Zac Efron, an over-the-shoulder shot does the trick. Efron, who broke out as an actor in Disney films, was at The Peninsula Hotel in Chicago.

ALEX GARCIA, 2010

Tree

Chicago rap artist Tree, at a home studio in the city's Logan Square neighborhood, performed at the Pitchfork Music Festival that summer.

CHRIS SWEDA, 2013

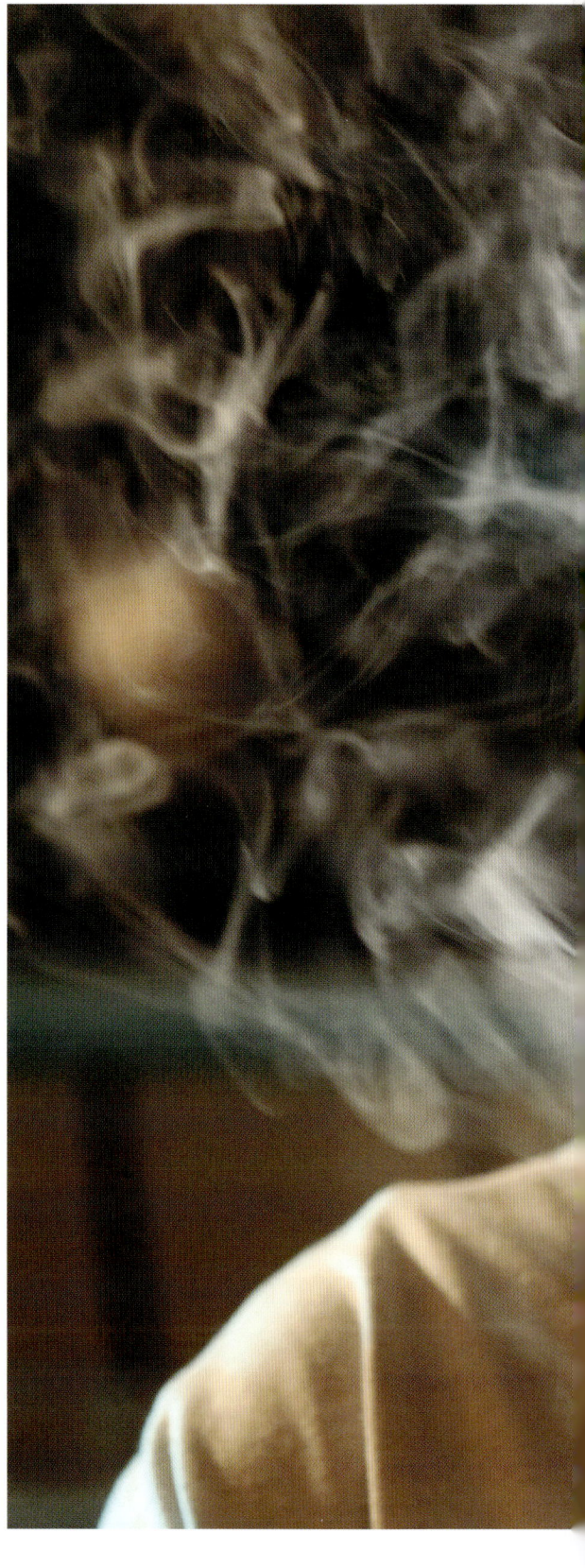

Walter Payton

Chicago Bears player Walter Payton watches from the sidelines. The beloved running back known as "Sweetness" was with the Bears for 13 seasons.

CHARLES CHERNEY, UNDATED

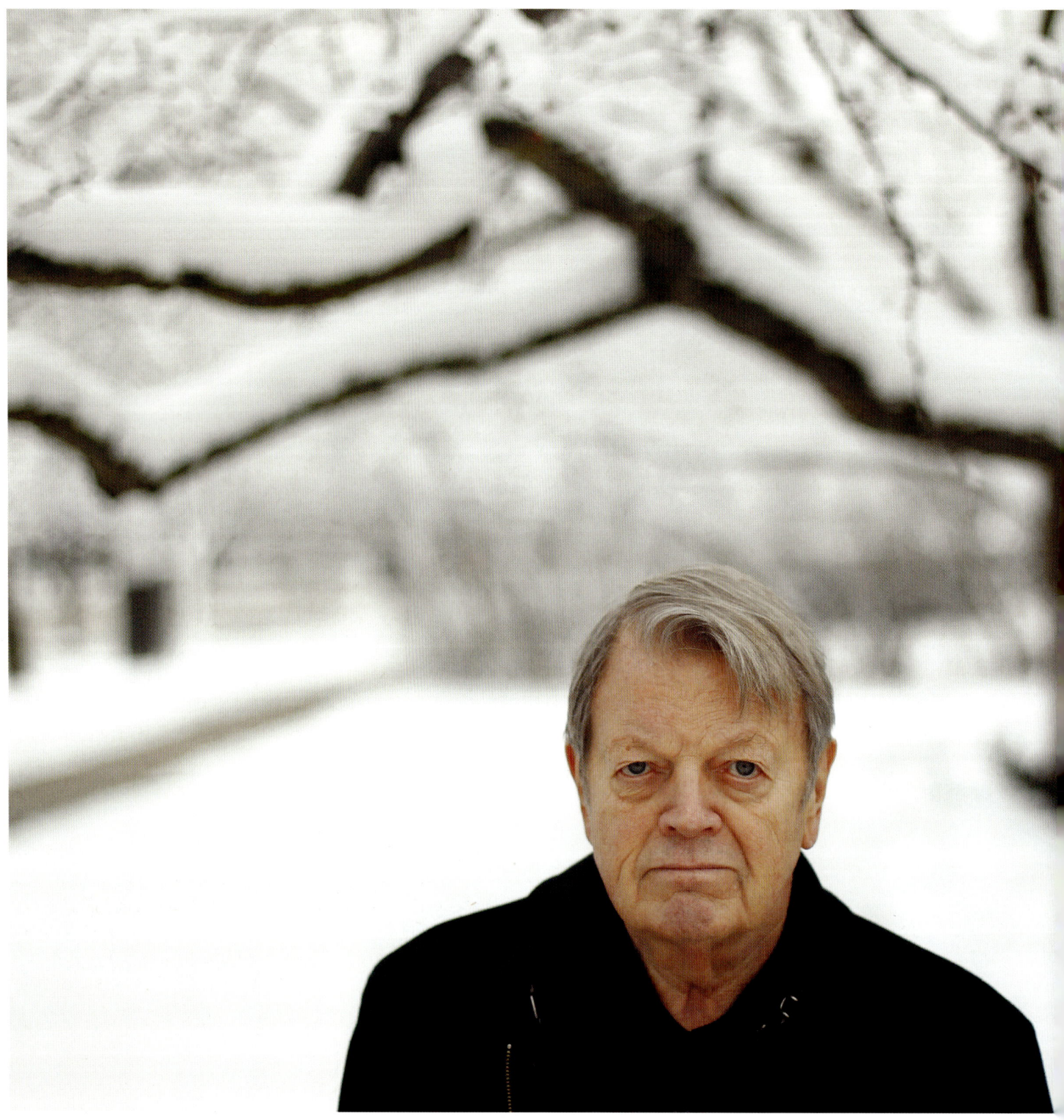

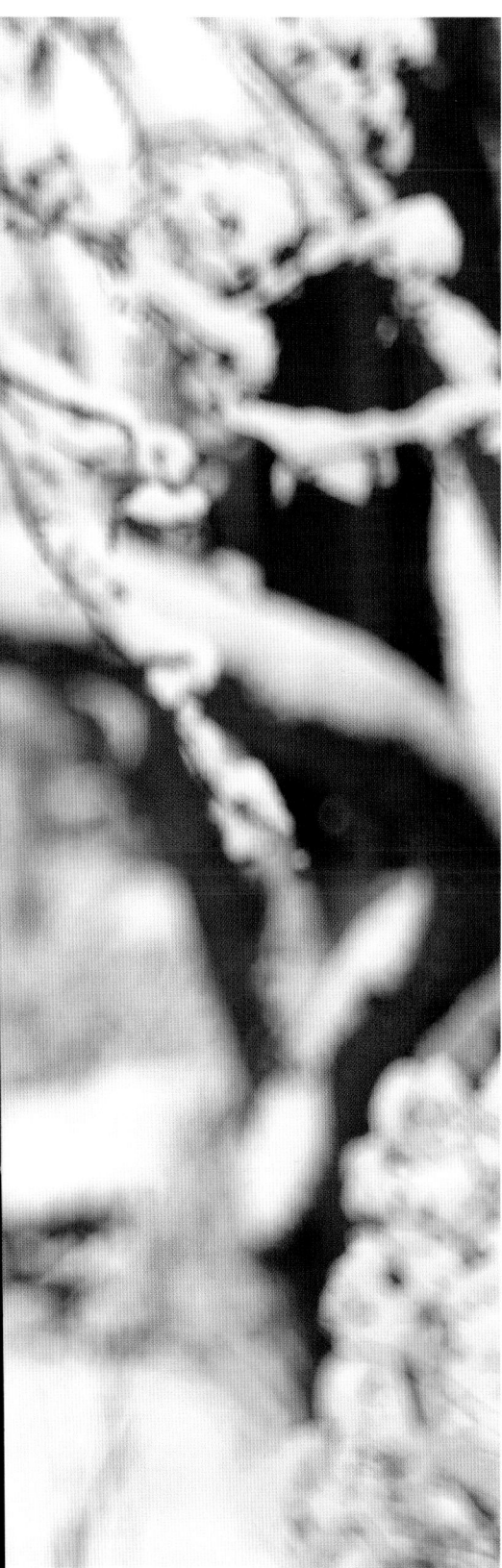

Garry Wills

Author and historian Garry Wills — a political conservative turned liberal, lifelong Roman Catholic and world-class curmudgeon — poses outside Northwestern University's Sheil Catholic Center in Evanston, Ill.

CHRIS WALKER, 2012

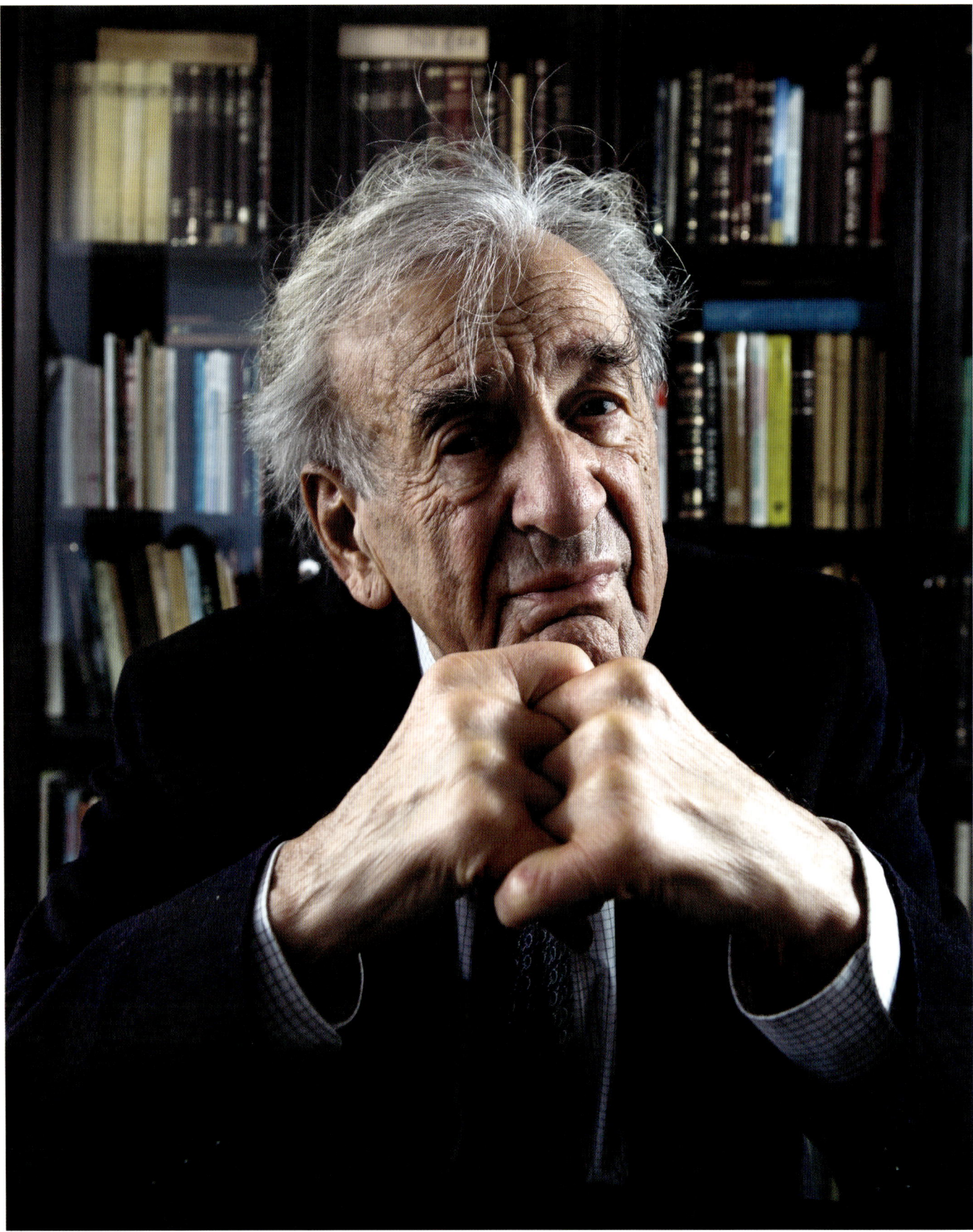

Elie Wiesel

Elie Wiesel reflects in his office in New York City. The prolific author is renowned for his memoir "Night," which describes his experiences in Nazi death camps during the Holocaust. The educator has won many accolades for his life's work, including the Nobel Peace Prize in 1986 and the 2012 Chicago Tribune Literary Award, and has advised numerous U.S. presidents. "Have I changed that much? I'm still looking. I'm still searching. I'm still wondering," Wiesel said in an interview before receiving the Tribune honor.

ZBIGNIEW BZDAK, 2012

Iggy Pop

Fans rush the stage upon invitation as Iggy Pop and the Stooges ratchet up the energy at the Lollapalooza music festival in Chicago's Grant Park. "No fun to be alone," Pop said. The proto-punk band enjoyed its heyday from 1969 to 1973, creating a template for punk, postpunk and just about every permutation of garage rock.

E. JASON WAMBSGANS, 2007

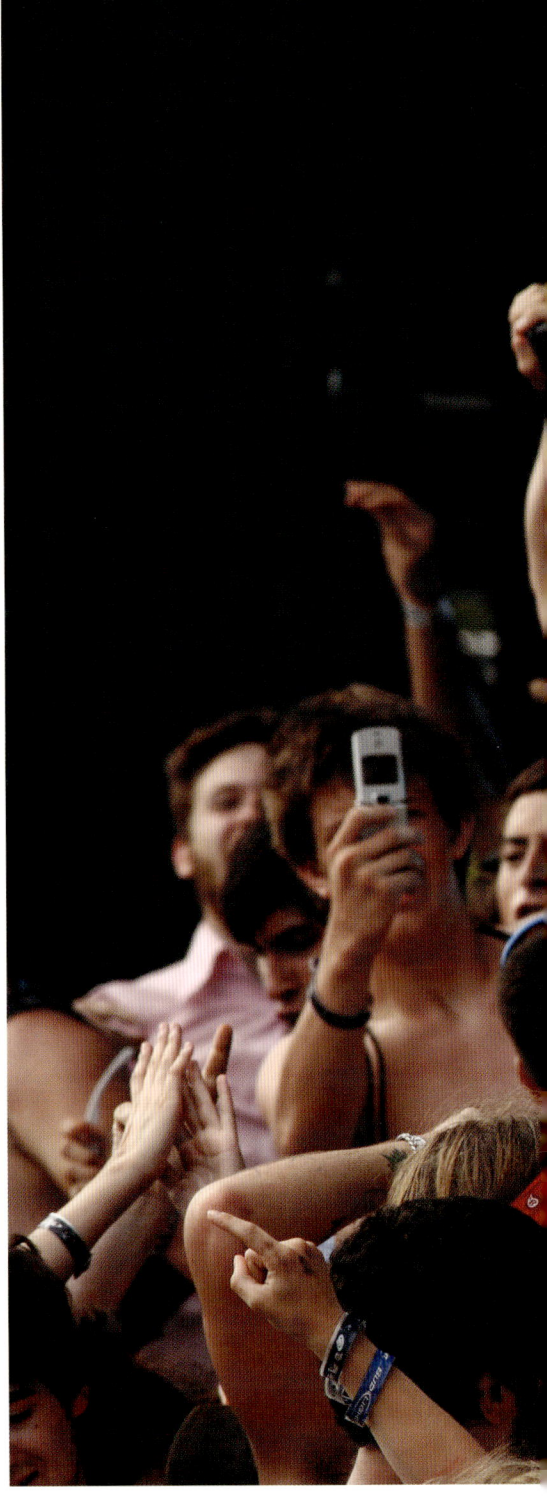

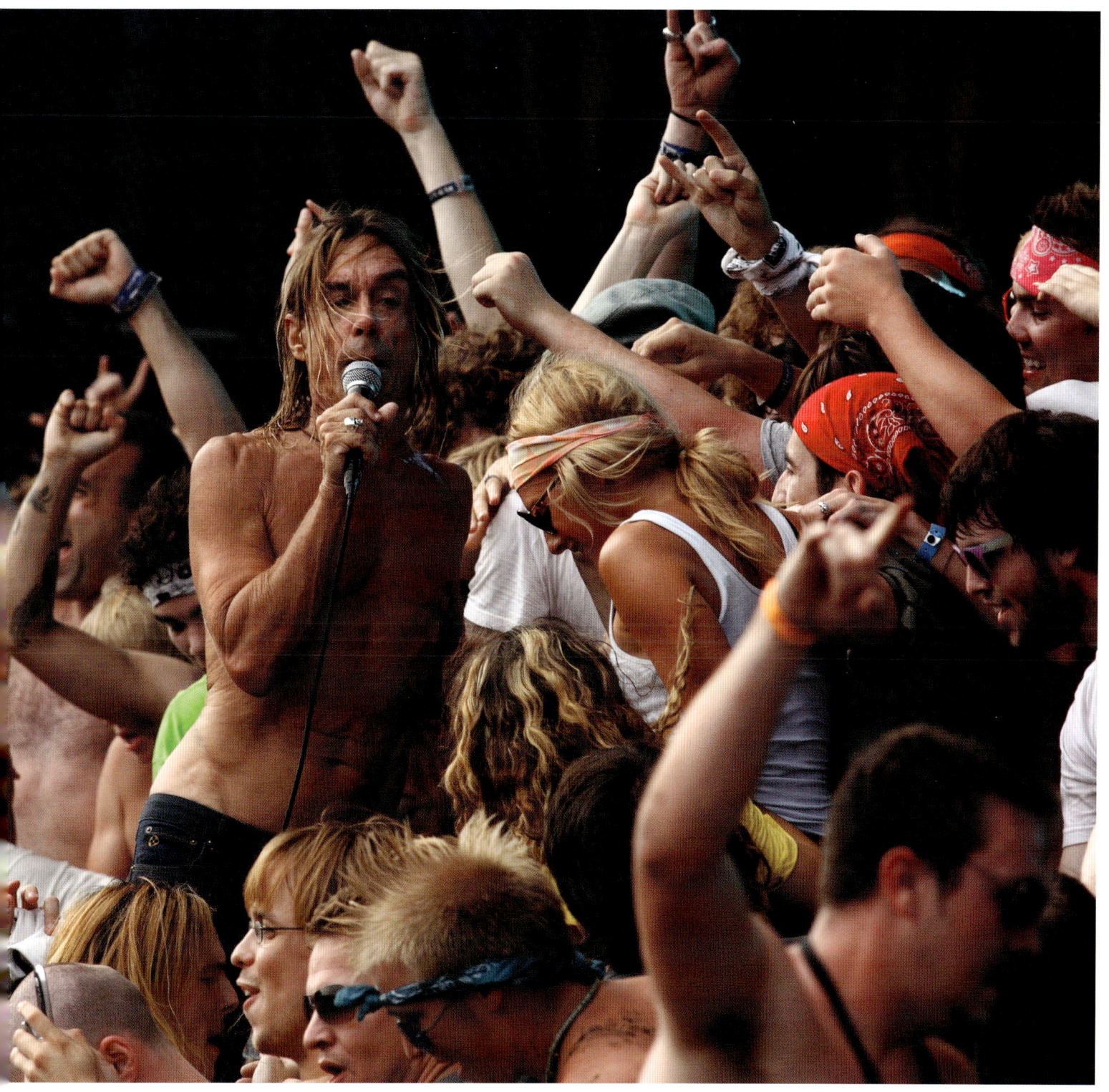

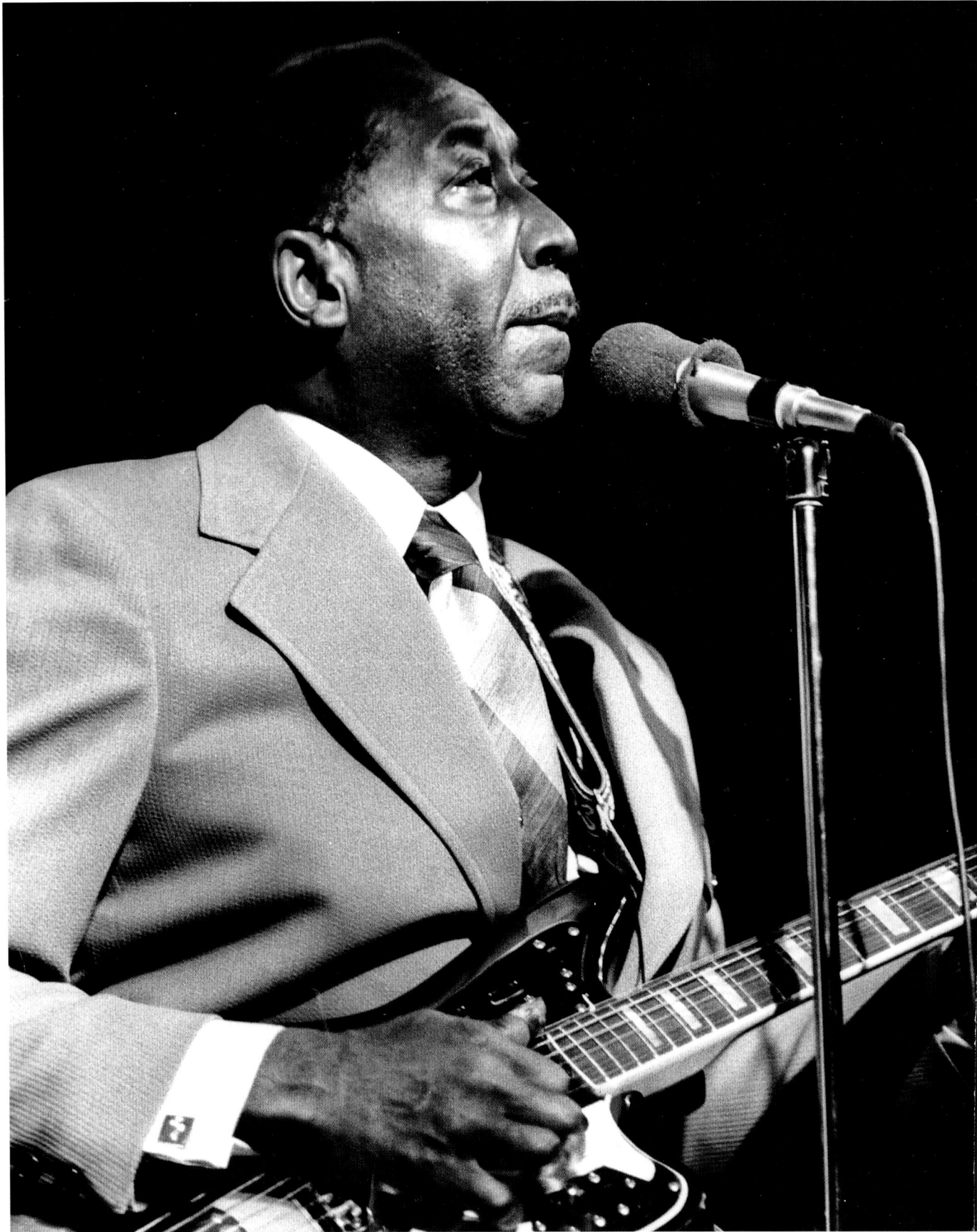

Muddy Waters

Blues icon Muddy Waters earned his musical stripes playing bars on Chicago's South and West sides.

VAL MAZZENGA, 1972

Sara Levine

Evanston author Sara Levine and a feathered friend take in their surroundings at the pet store Thee Fish Bowl in Evanston, Ill. A talking parrot serves as a character in her novel, "Treasure Island!!!"

CHRIS WALKER

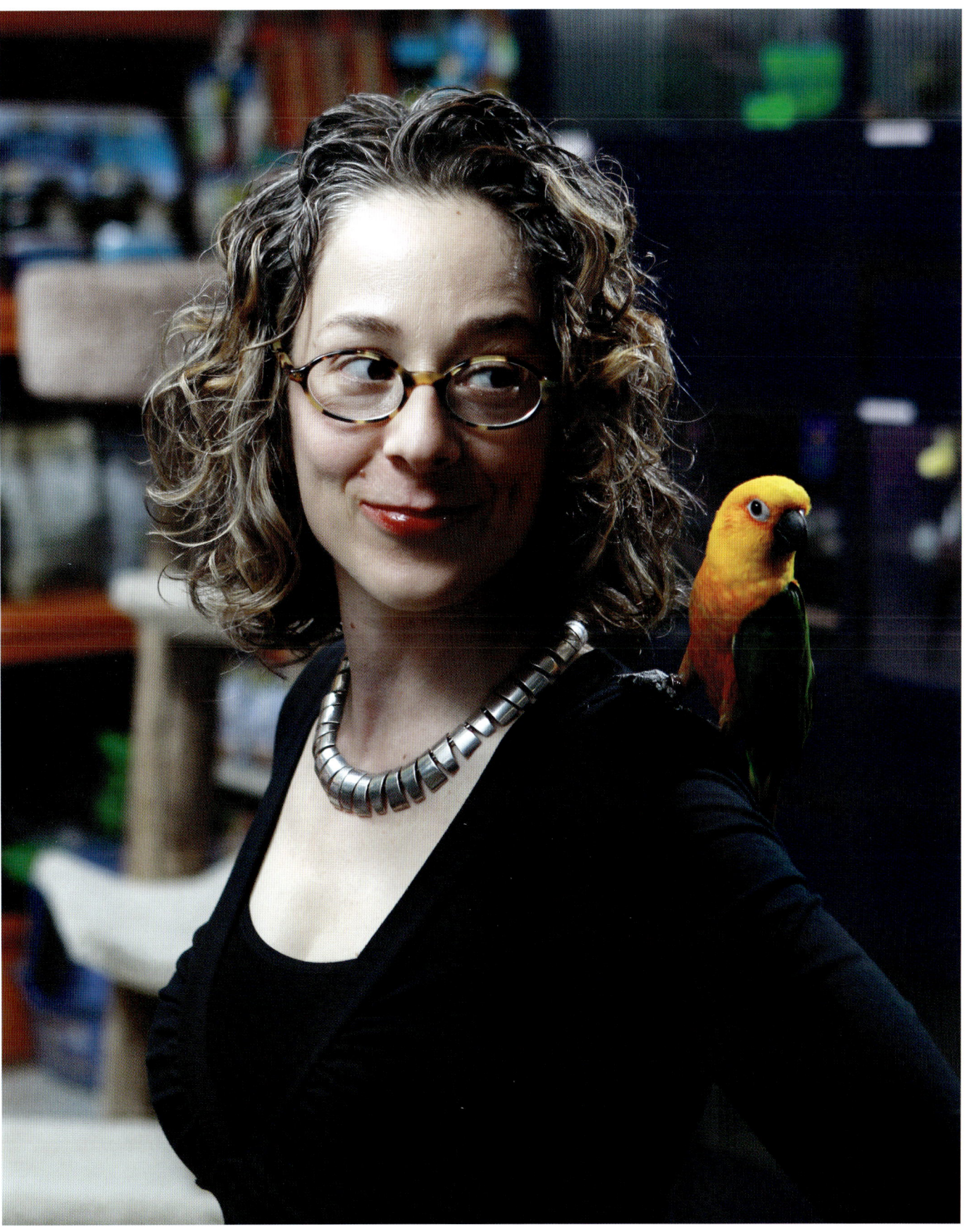

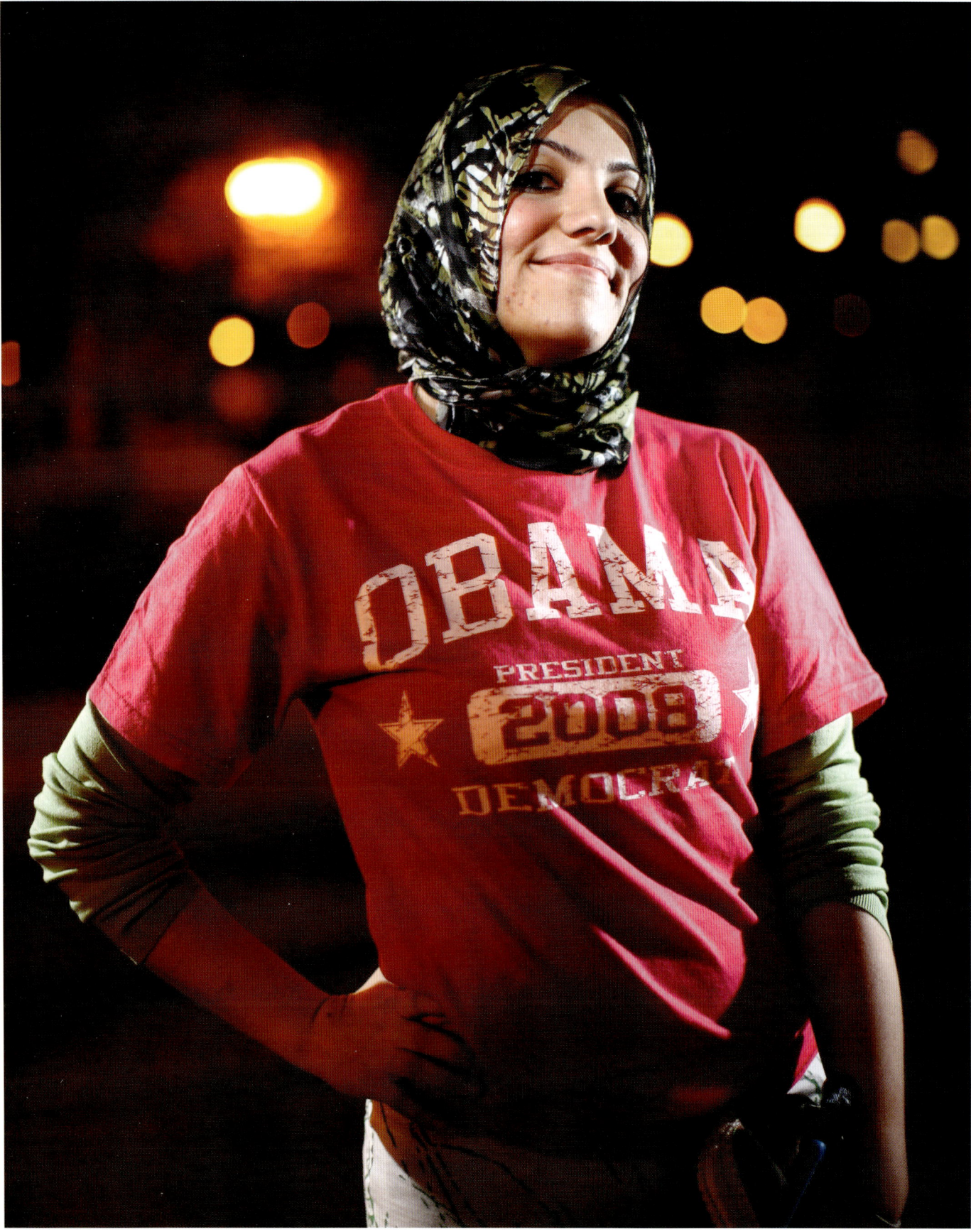

Tahani Hassan

Tahani Hassan, 23, of Orland Park, smiles at Barack Obama's presidential victory rally in Chicago's Grant Park. Hassan, her sister Ahlam and three of their friends took a Metra train into the city to attend the rally and weren't sure how they'd get back if the event went past 11:40 at night. But Hassan, a teacher, wasn't sweating the details. Asked if her group might take a taxi home, she said, "Maybe. To the suburbs? I don't know. It's a little expensive."

E. JASON WAMBSGANS, 2008

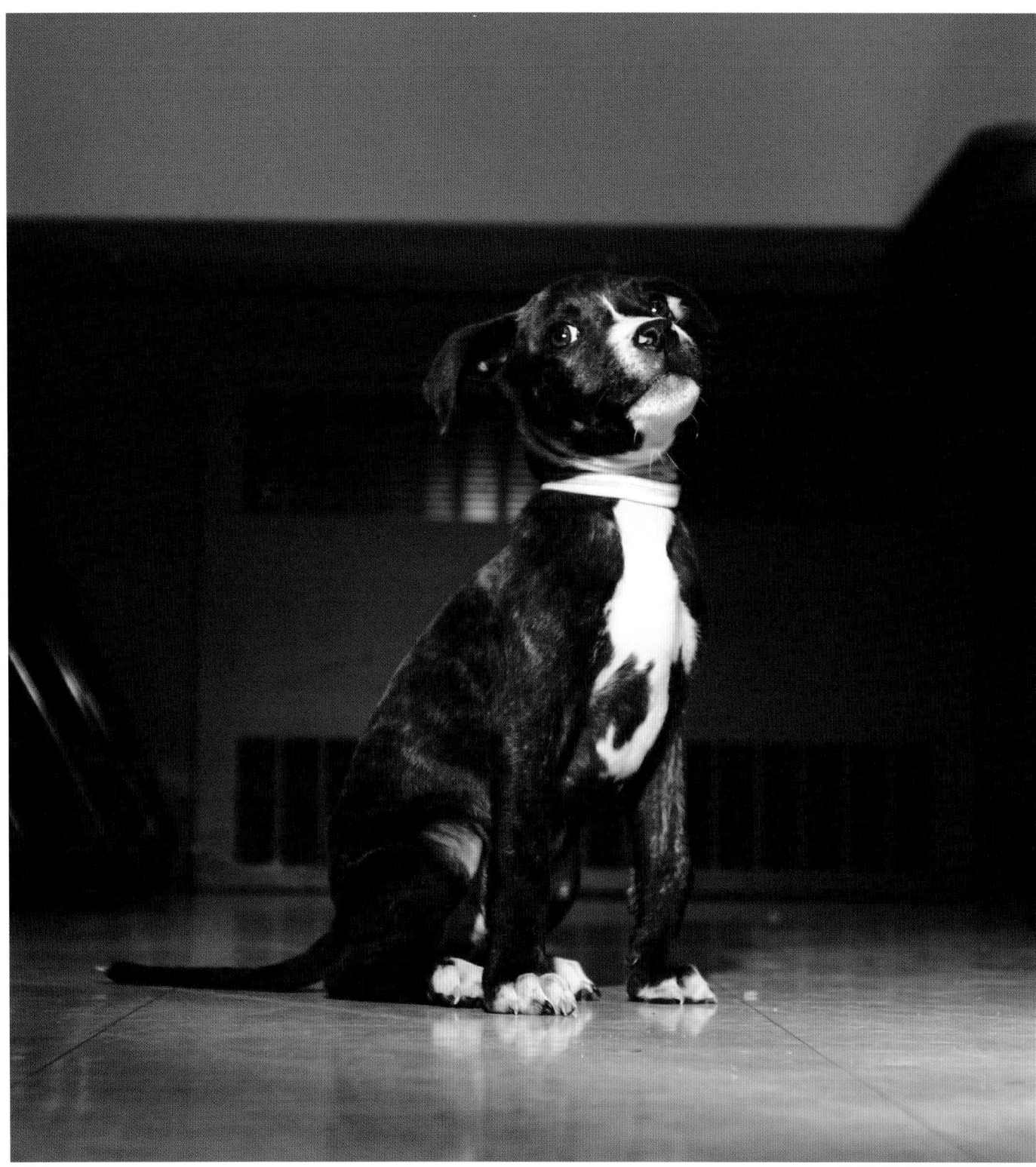

O.J.

O.J., a 2 1/2-month-old pit bull puppy, shows quiet resolve during a training class at the Nash Community Center in Chicago.

BRIAN CASSELLA, 2009

Douglas Fairbanks

Actor Douglas Fairbanks was one of the silver screen's first swashbuckling heroes, and his marriage to actress Mary Pickford created one of Hollywood's first power couples. Fairbanks hosted the first Academy Awards ceremony in 1929.

CHICAGO TRIBUNE HISTORICAL PHOTO, 1933

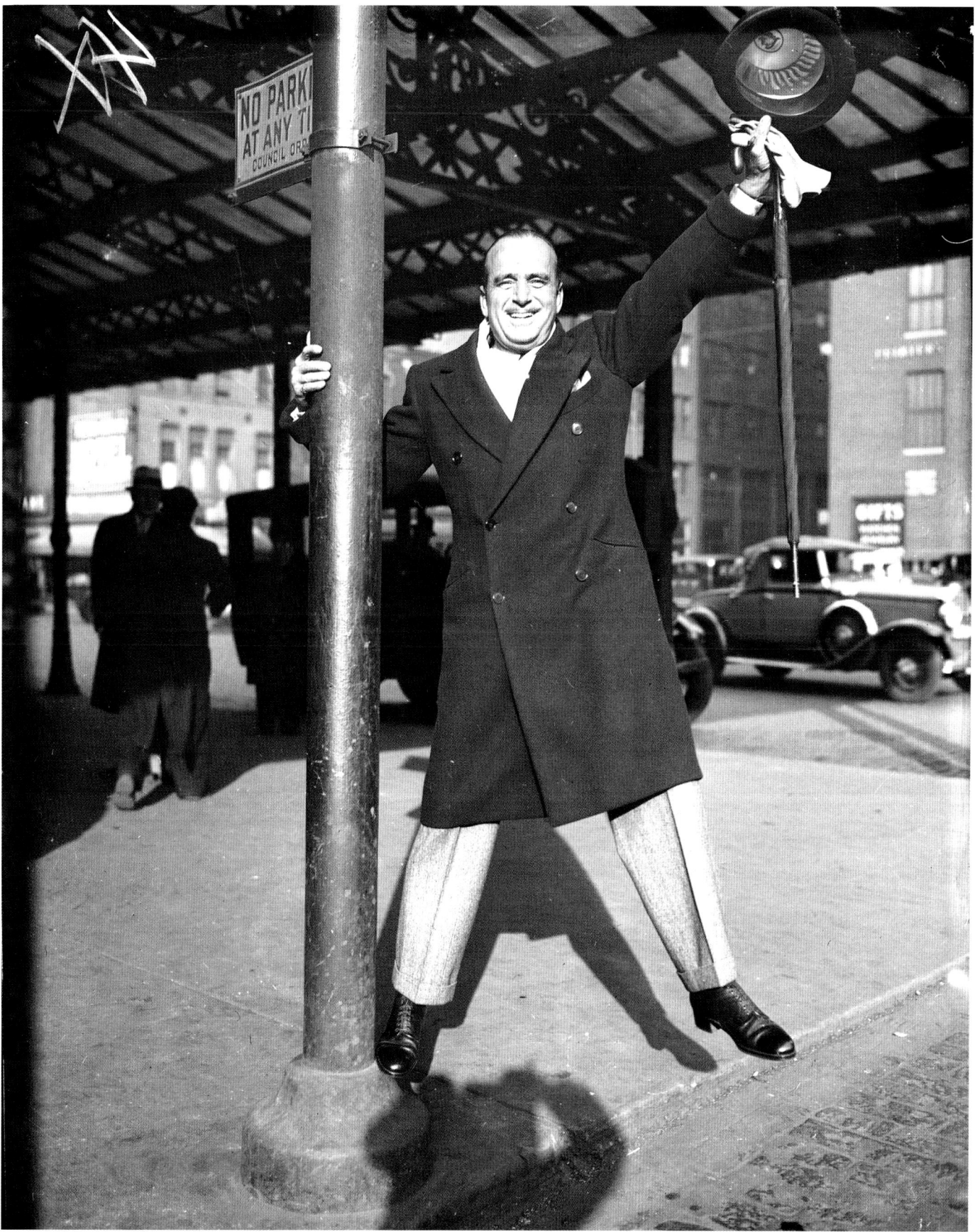

Manuel Lopez

Street artist Manuel Lopez takes a break while painting a mural on Ashland Avenue in Chicago's Back of the Yards neighborhood.

SCOTT STRAZZANTE, 2012

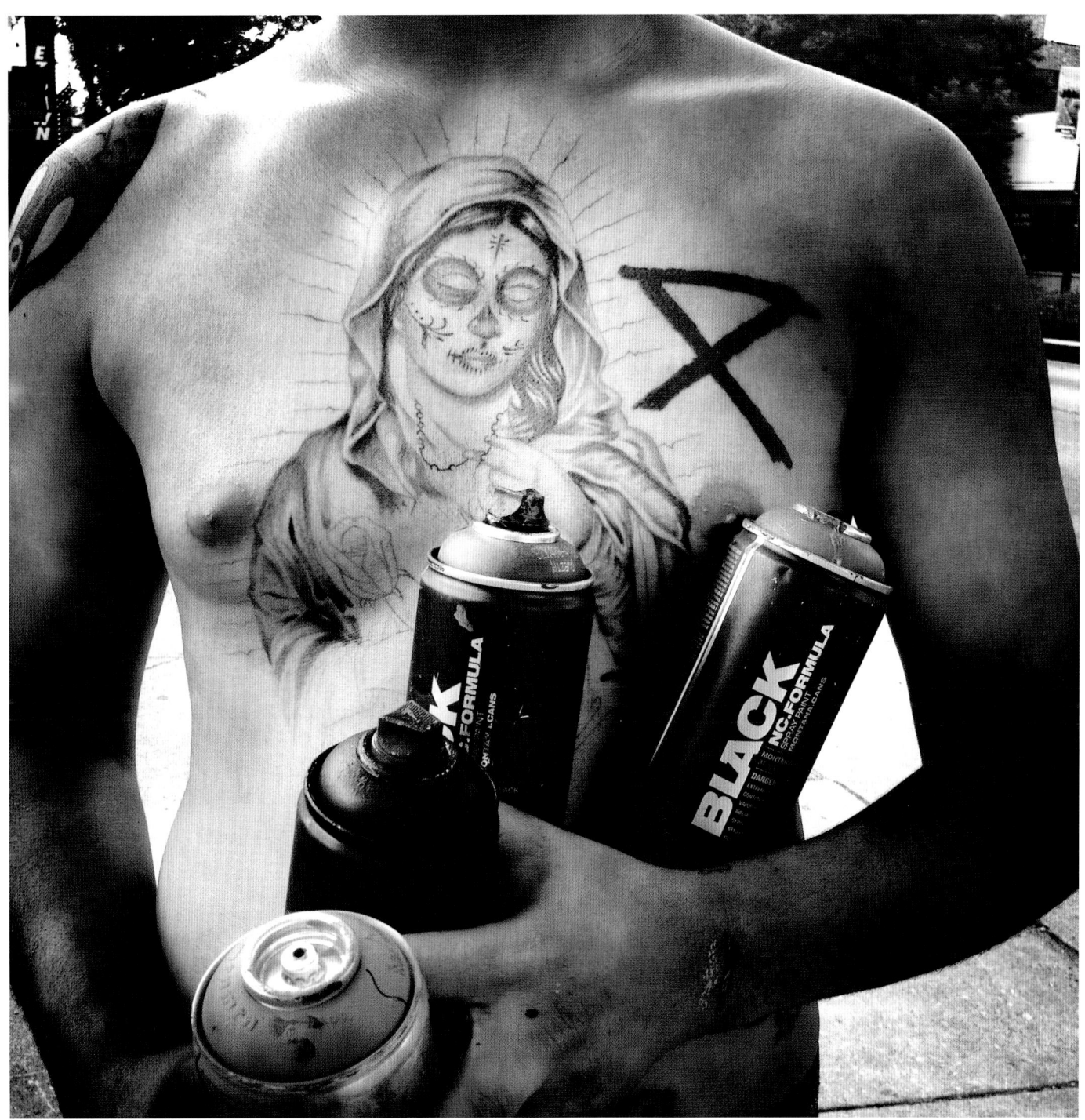

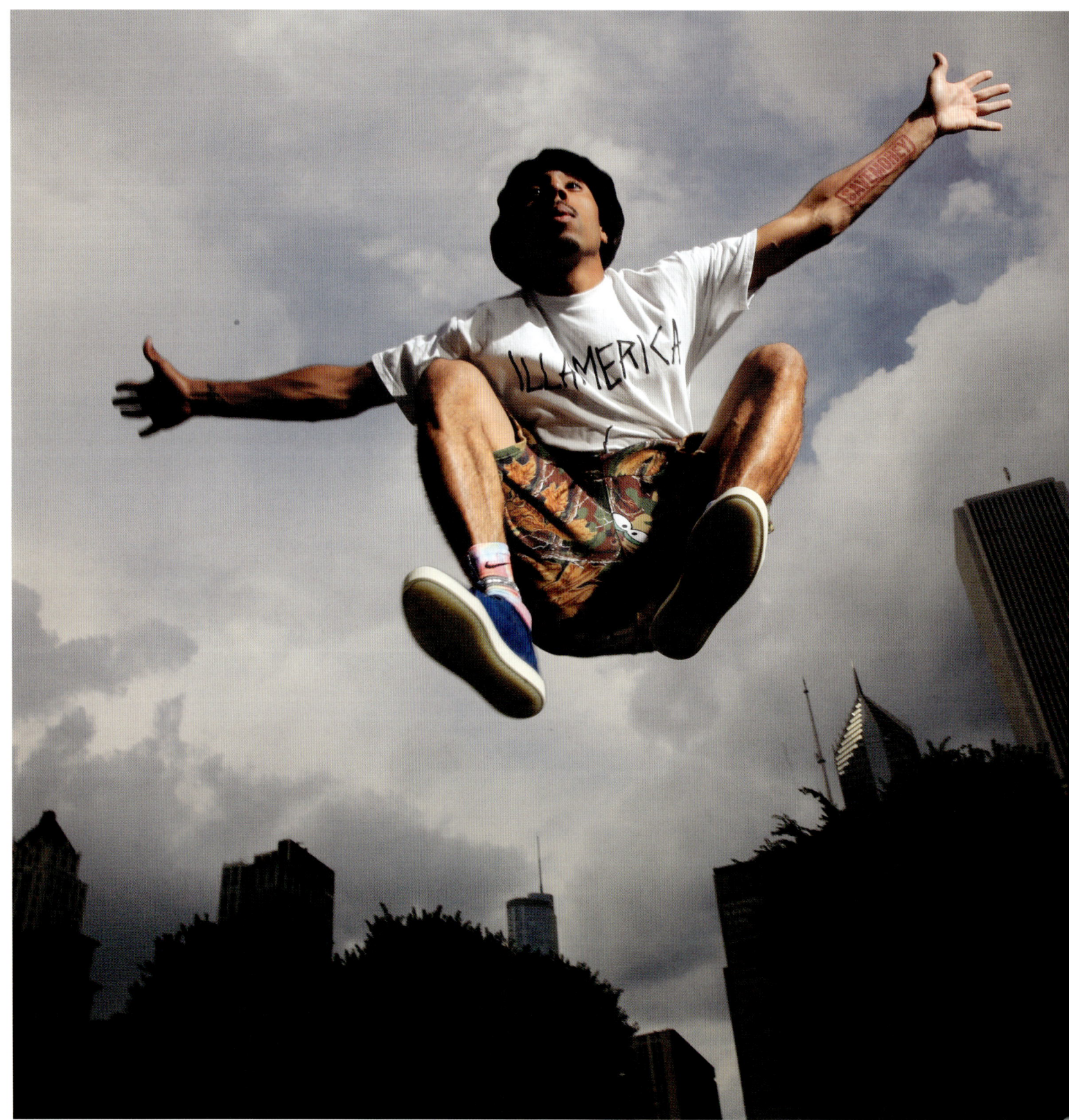

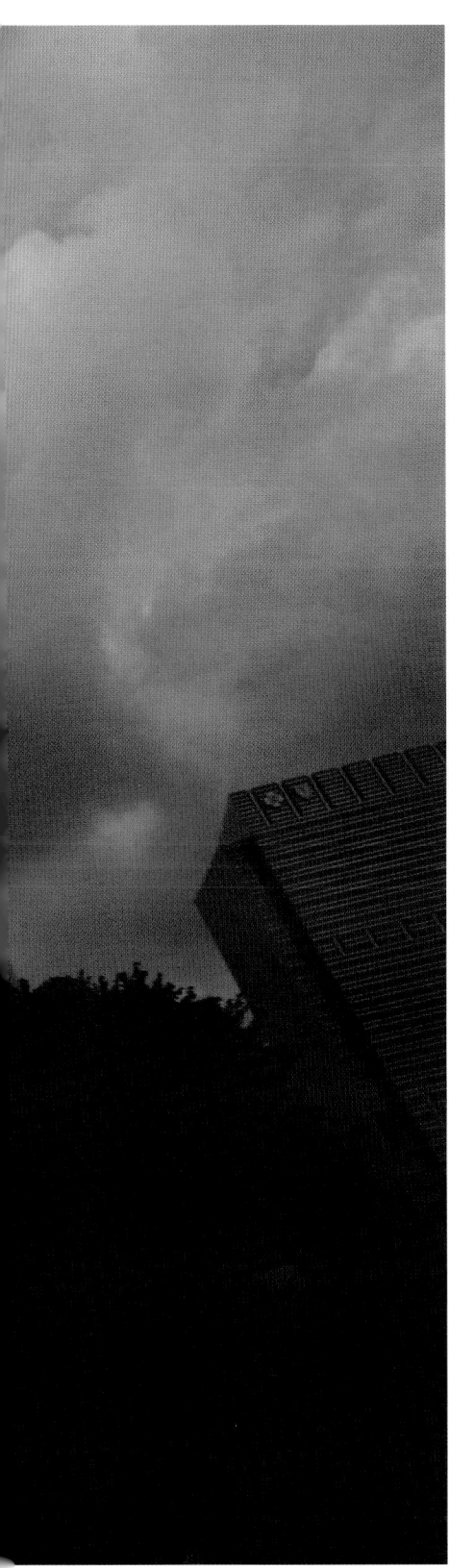

Vic Mensa

Chicago rapper Vic Mensa jumps in the air on Monroe Street east of Michigan Avenue, near where he fell onto railroad tracks in 2010 and was burned by an electrical transformer while trying to sneak into the Lollapalooza music festival. He didn't have to sneak into the event in 2013 — he was one of the performers.

CHRIS WALKER, 2013

Atalee Judy

Atalee Judy throws her body into her work as artistic director with Breakbone Dance Co., a Chicago-based troupe known for its avant-garde physicality.

ZBIGNIEW BZDAK, 2003

Johari Cole-Kweli

Johari Cole-Kweli overlooks her farm atop a tractor in Pembroke, Ill., about 60 miles from Chicago. The self-described "country chick," a former Chicagoan and fashion model, moved to Pembroke with her family to dig in the fields of her dreams. The community is one of the poorest in Illinois.

MICHAEL TERCHA, 2007

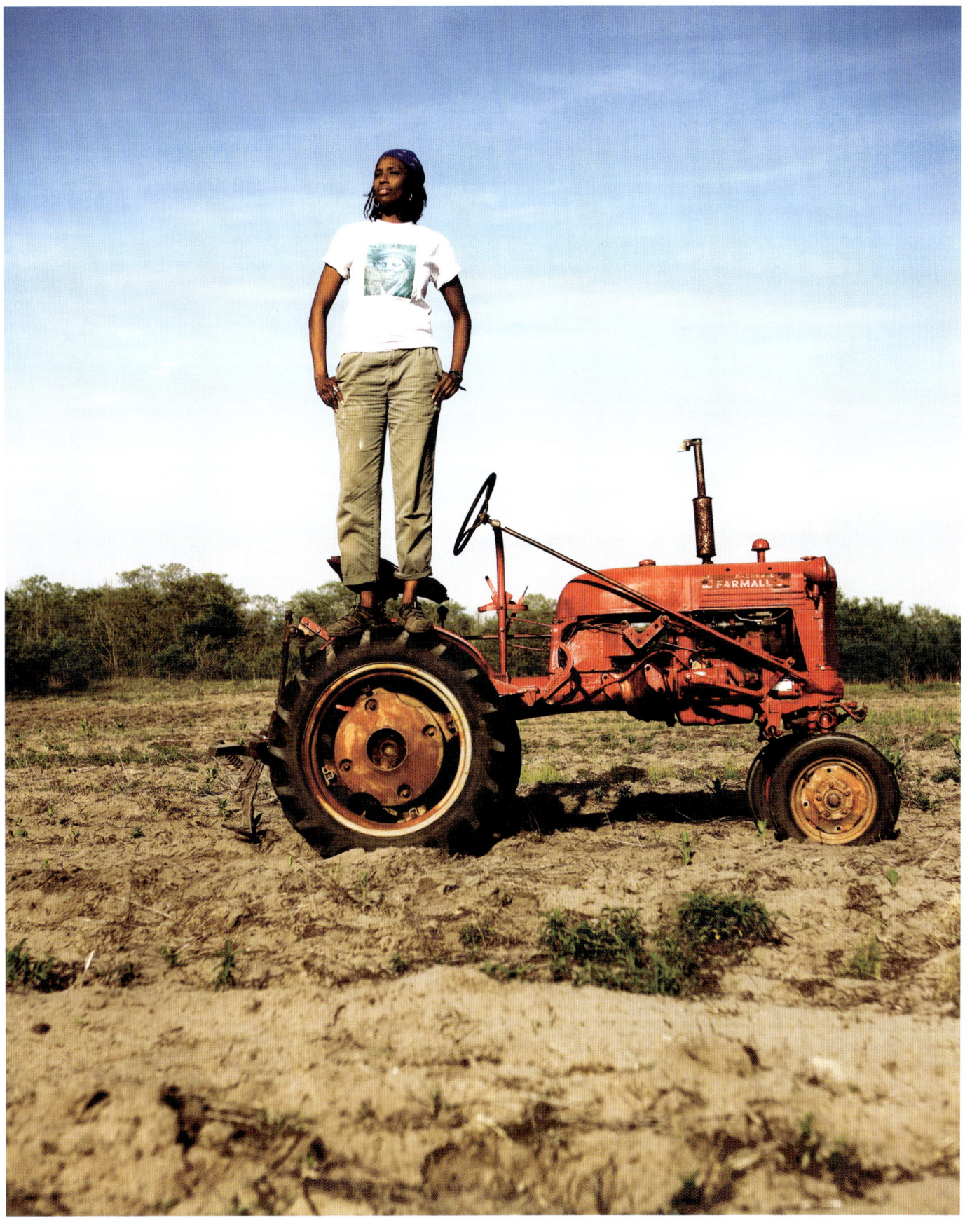

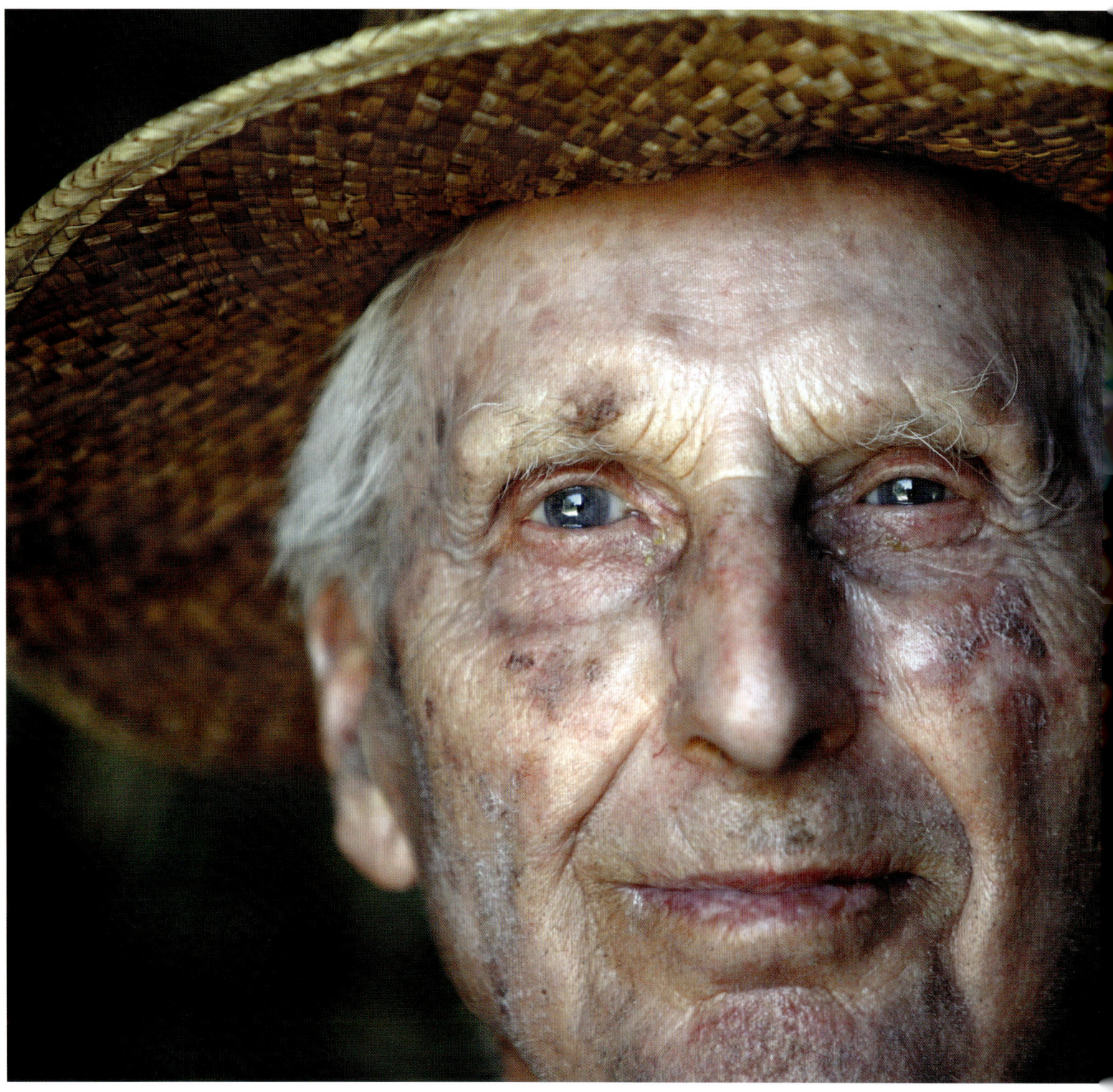

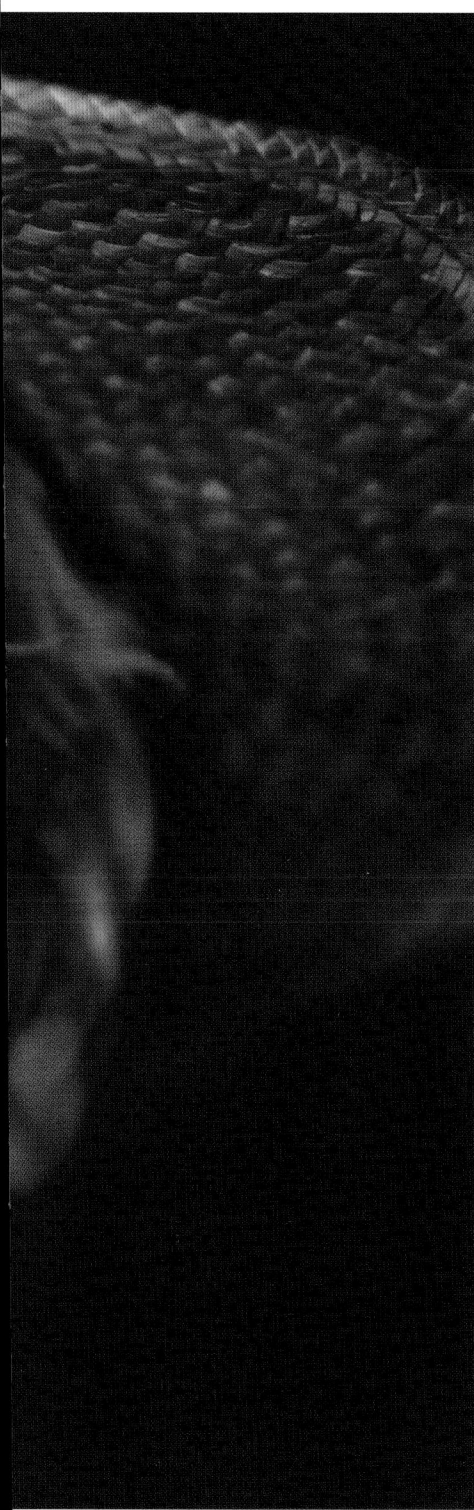

Harold Bergman

Harold Bergman, 93, then one of the oldest farmers in Cook County, Ill., poses in his barn.

LANE CHRISTIANSEN, 2009

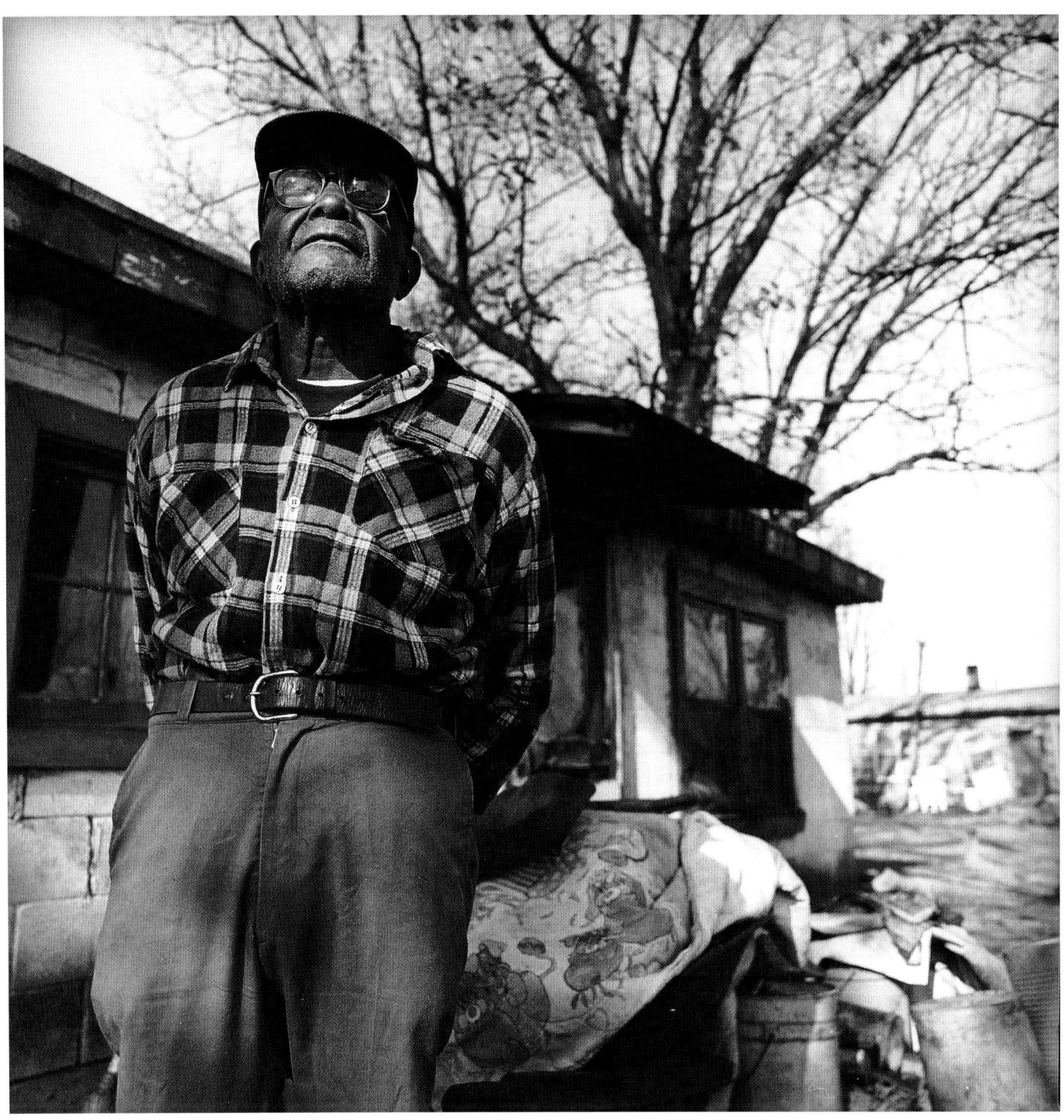

Eugene Thomas

Eugene Thomas, 89, watches as a construction crew works on six modular homes near his house in Hopkins Park, Ill. Thomas and his extended family were set to take possession sometime that March.

TODD PANAGOPOULOS, 1999

Grant Achatz

Chef Grant Achatz works in the kitchen of his Chicago restaurant Alinea in preparation for dinner.

ZBIGNIEW BZDAK, 2011

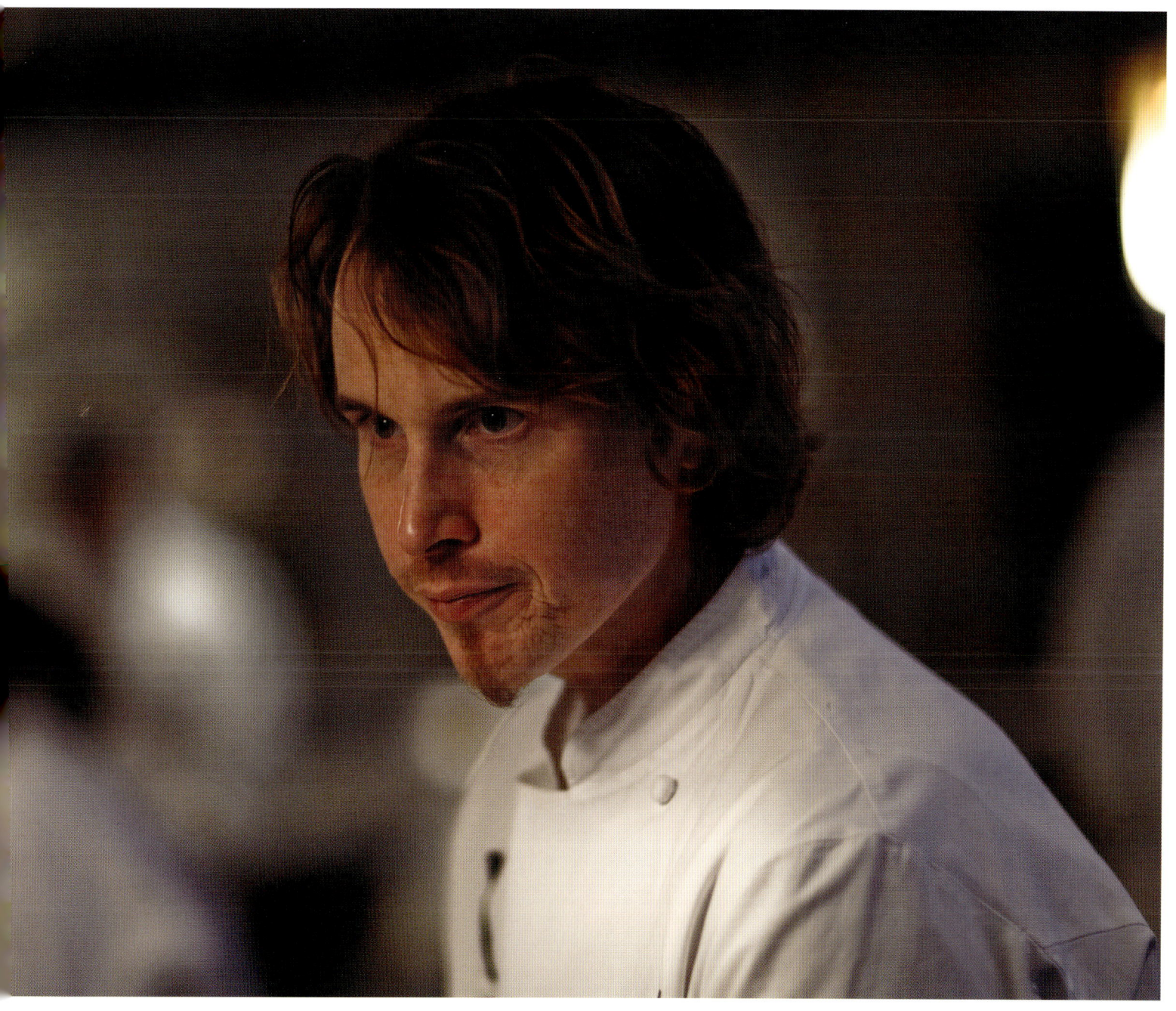

Sho Yano

Medical student Sho Yano in 2004 on the University of Chicago campus in the city's Hyde Park neighborhood. Sho created a stir in 2000 when he entered Loyola University at the age of 9 and graduated summa cum laude just three years later. His admission into the U. of C.'s Pritzker School of Medicine in the fall of 2003 revived the debate among parents and educators about whether someone that young is emotionally prepared for college.

CHRIS WALKER, 2004

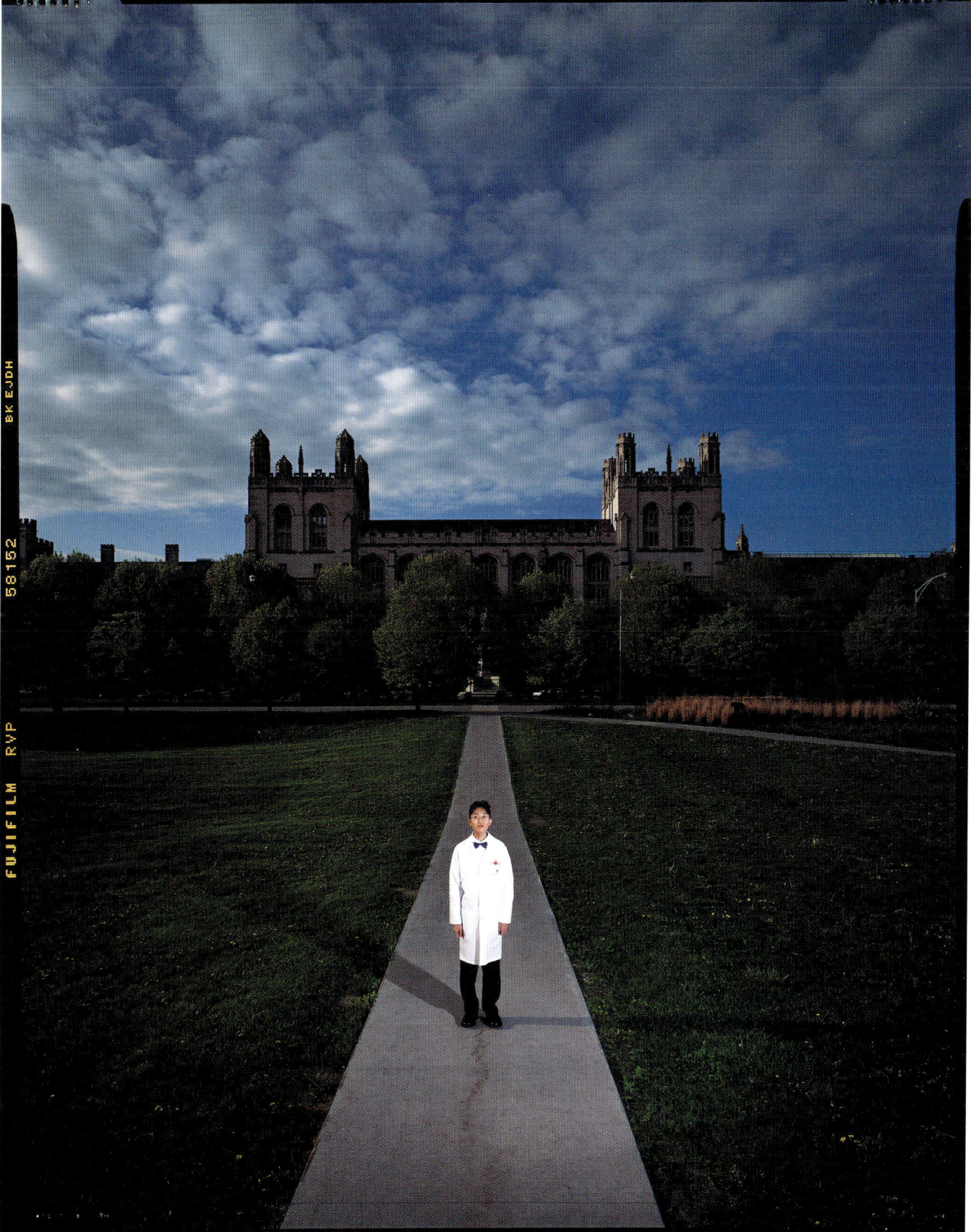

Nick Cave

Chicago artist and educator Nick Cave listens to the sounds of the surf and one of his creations at the 31st Street Beach in Chicago. Cave is the creator of full-body Soundsuits, which are made from layers of metal, plastic, fabric, hair, found objects and other materials that make noise when they rub together.

CHRIS WALKER, 2010

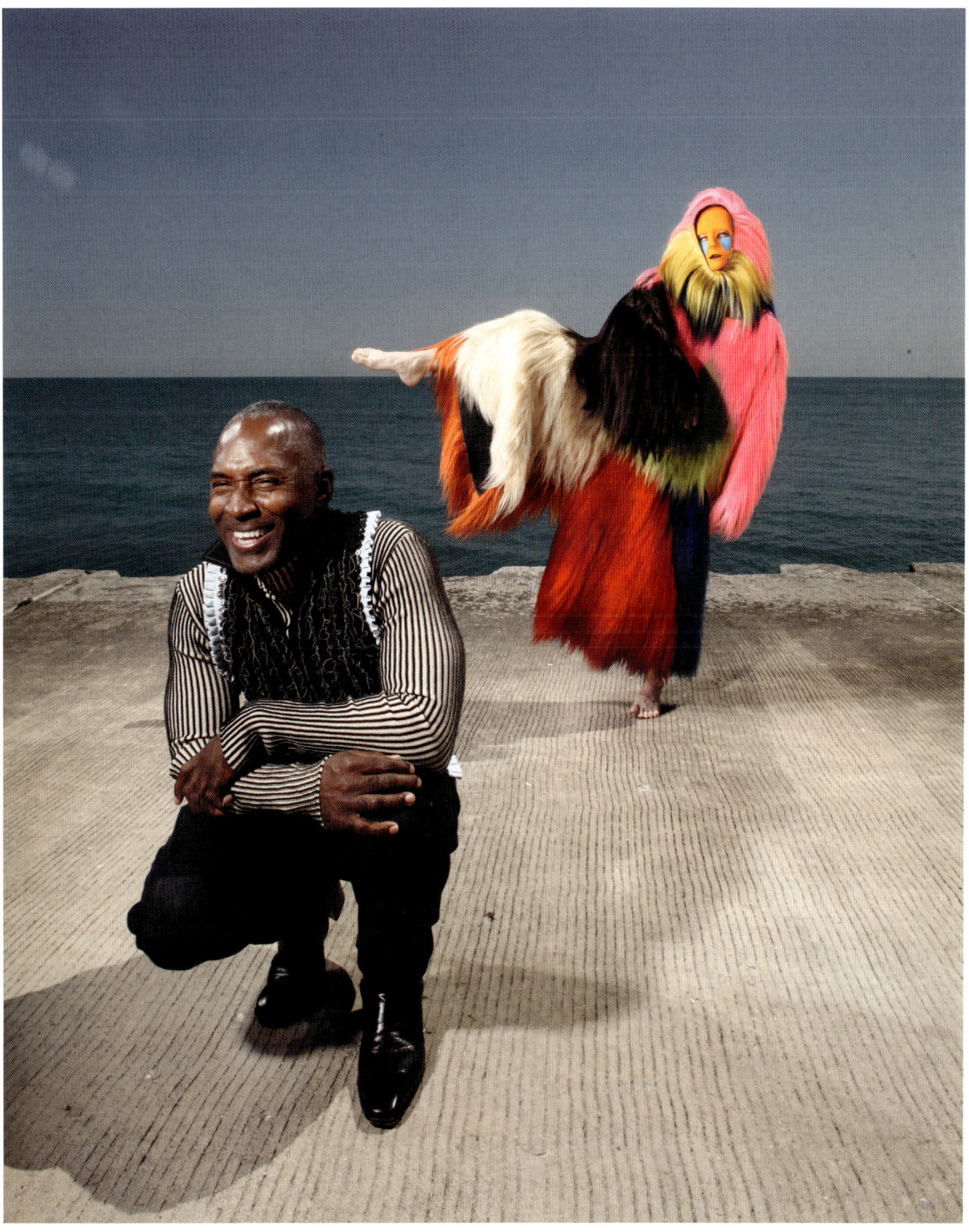

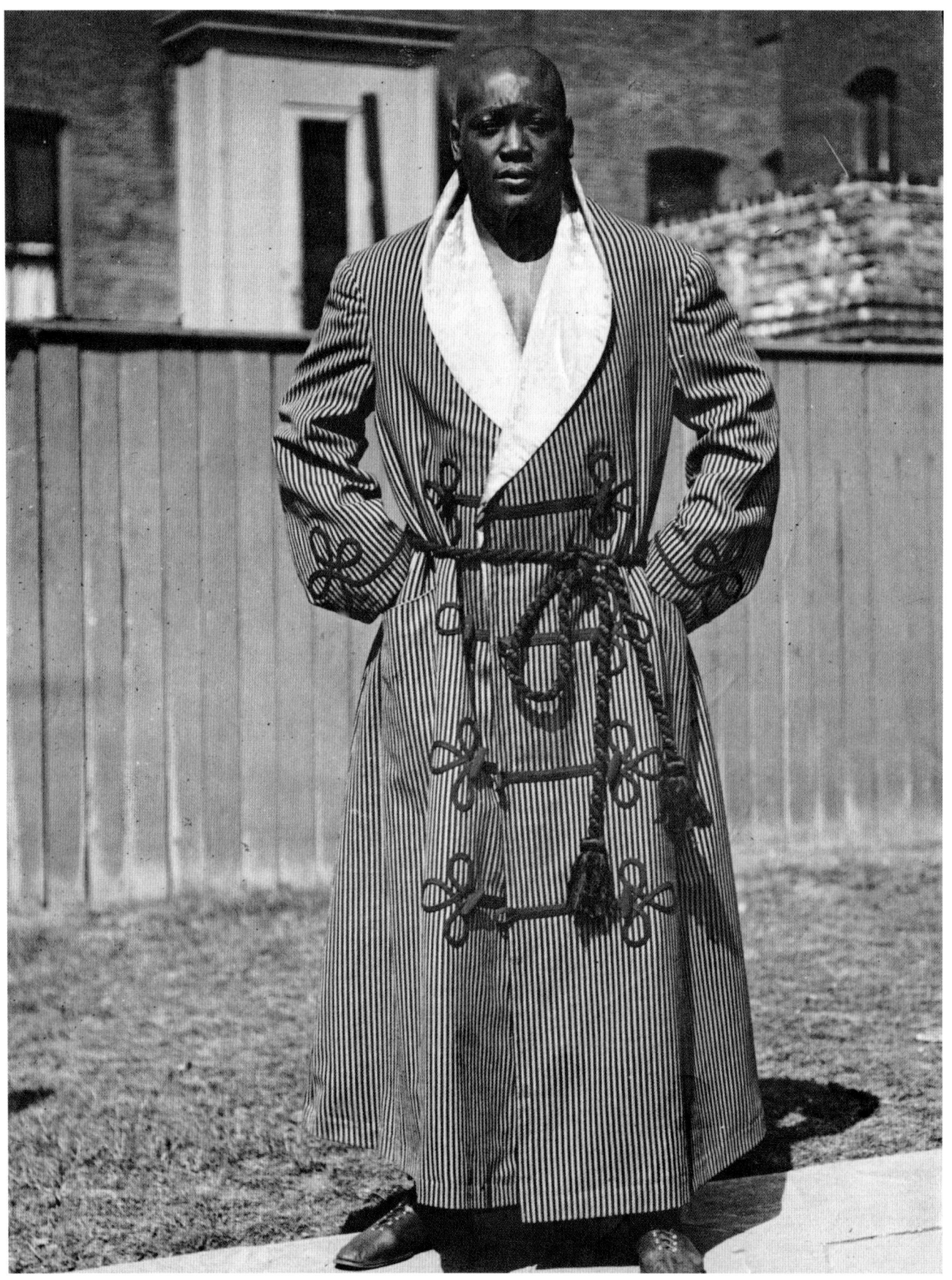

Jack Johnson

Jack Johnson, shown in an undated photo, was the first black world heavyweight boxing champion.

CHICAGO TRIBUNE HISTORICAL PHOTO, UNDATED

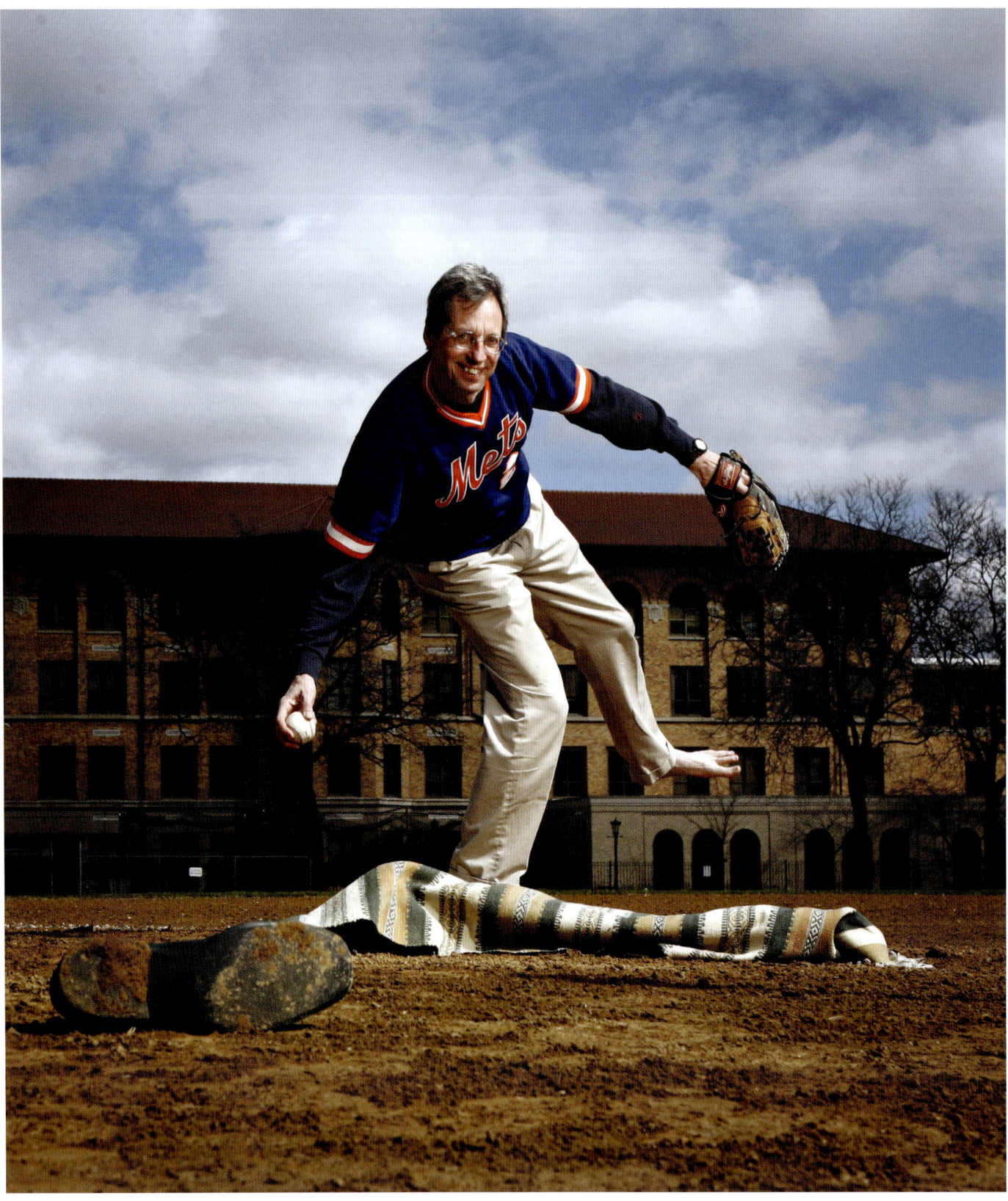

Joe Berton

Joe Berton, who posed as fictional Sidd Finch in a Sports Illustrated hoax for April Fool's Day 1985, re-enacts his famous shot outside Oak Park High School in Oak Park, Ill.

BRIAN CASSELLA, 2011

Ben Huh

Ben Huh, founder of the Cheezburger Network, a website featuring funny video clips and Internet memes, does his "invisible bicycle" impression in Chicago.

CHRIS WALKER, 2010

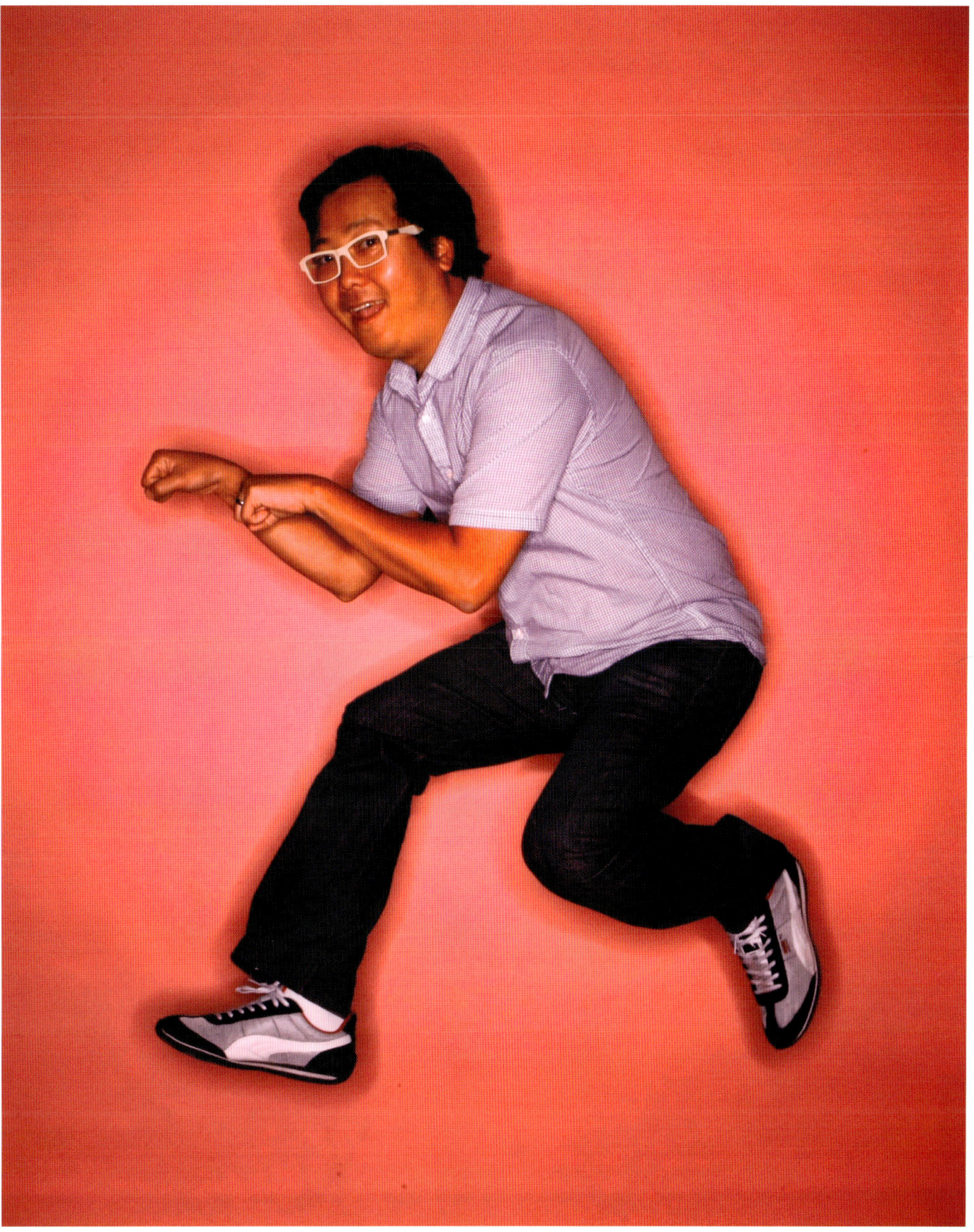

Helen Langos Phillips AND
Irene O'Malley Graham

Great-grandmothers Helen Langos Phillips, left, 90, of Niles, said she takes requests on her ukulele, while Irene O'Malley Graham, 100, of Libertyville, said she loves a good cup of coffee.

HEATHER STONE, 2005

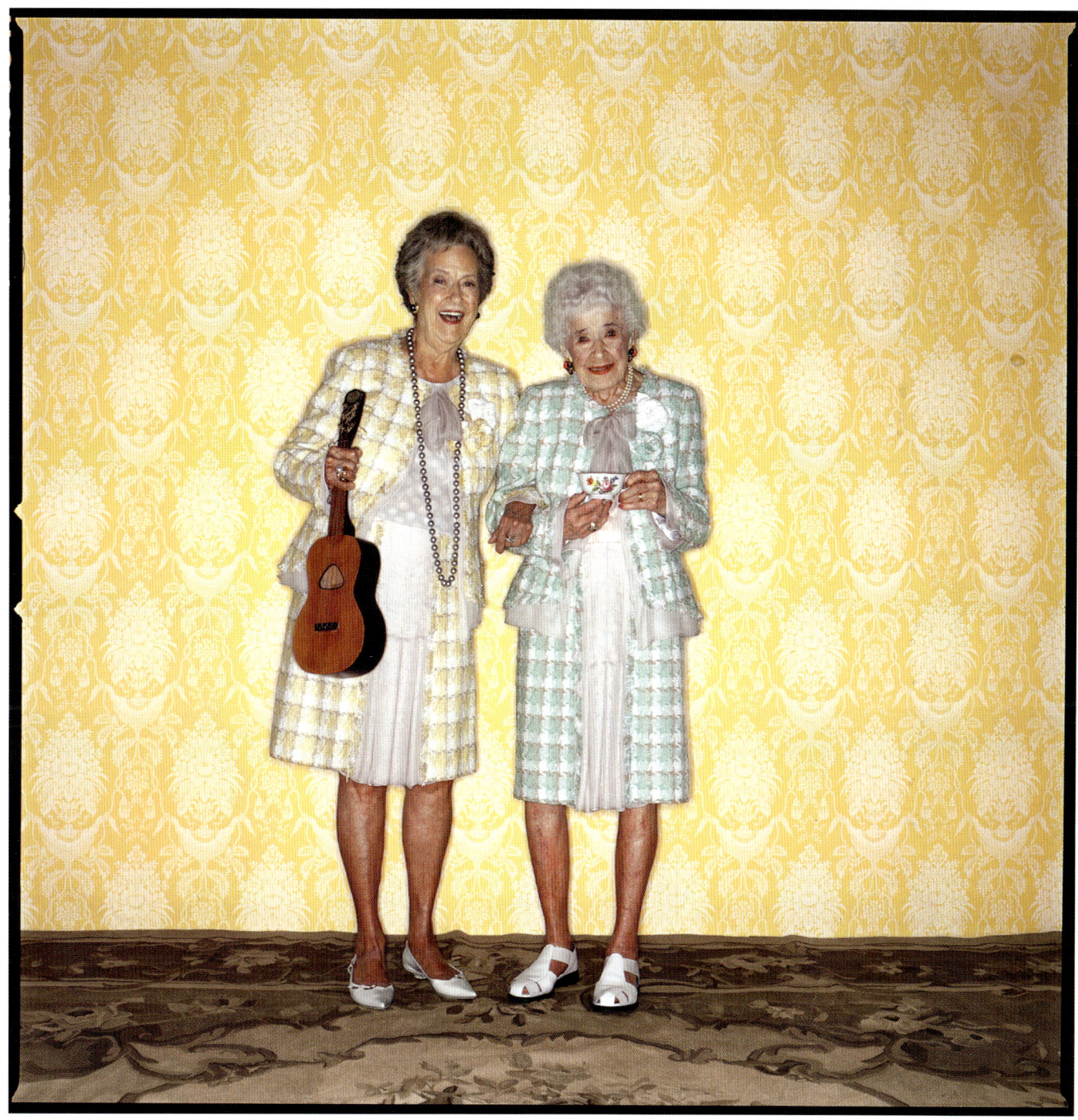

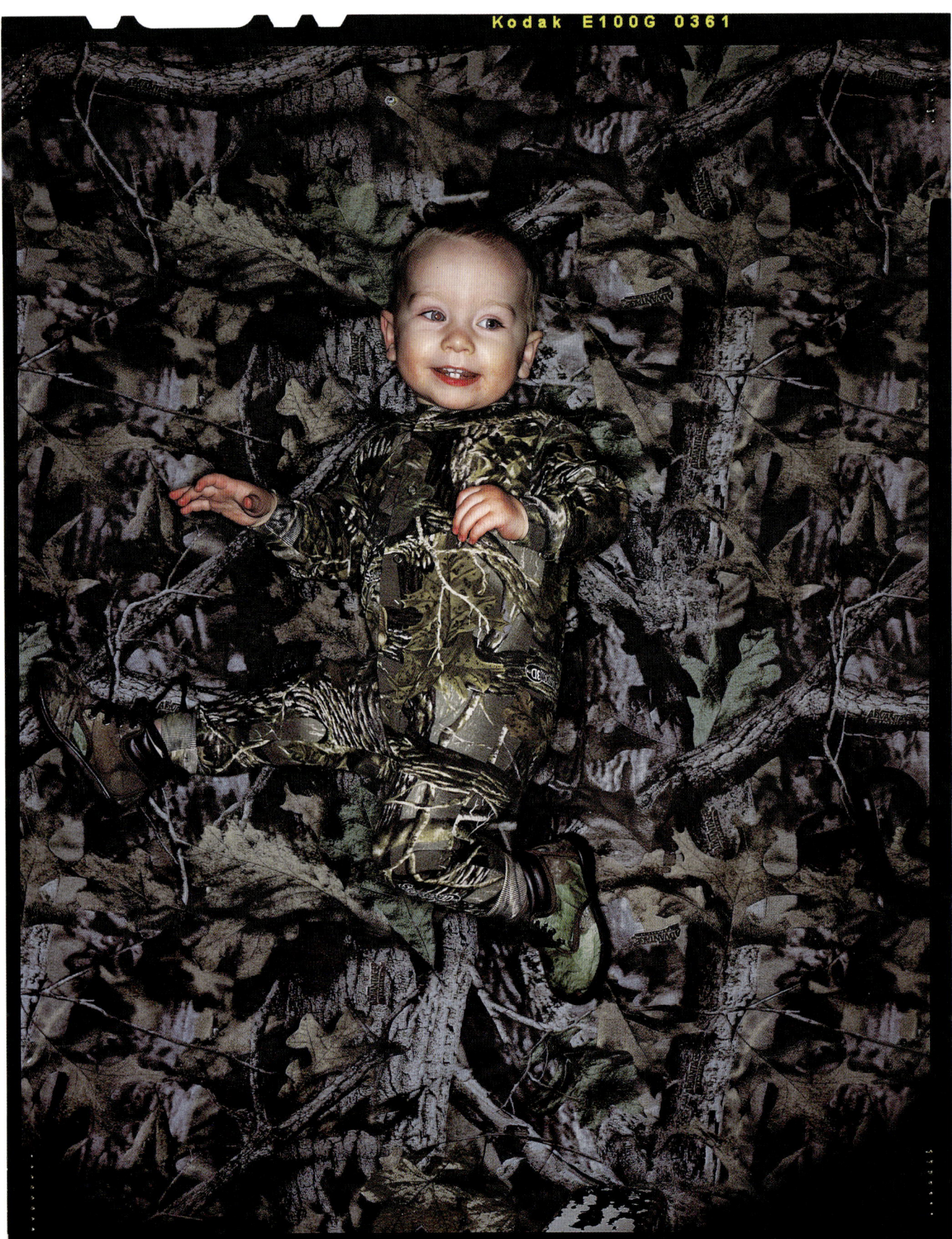

June Stevens

June Stevens, daughter of a Chicago Tribune reporter, demonstrates why outdoor outfitters are adding sections to their stores and catalogs for young children.

BILL HOGAN, 2006

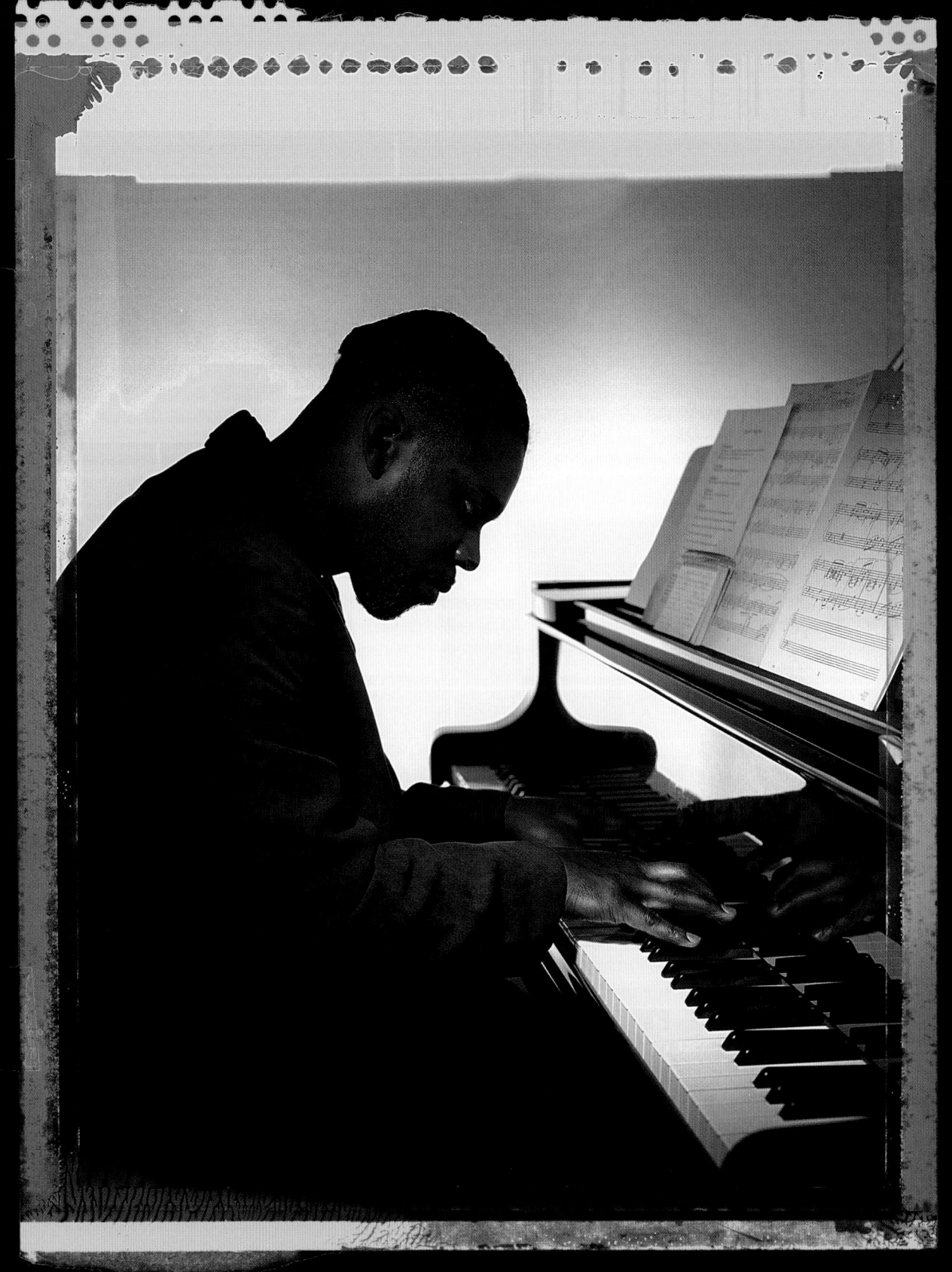

Reginald Robinson

Ragtime piano virtuoso Reginald Robinson has proved through his fiercely original compositions and thoroughly persuasive pianism that the genre Scott Joplin brought to a high point early in the 20th century still has new things to say in the 21st.

CHRIS WALKER, 2005

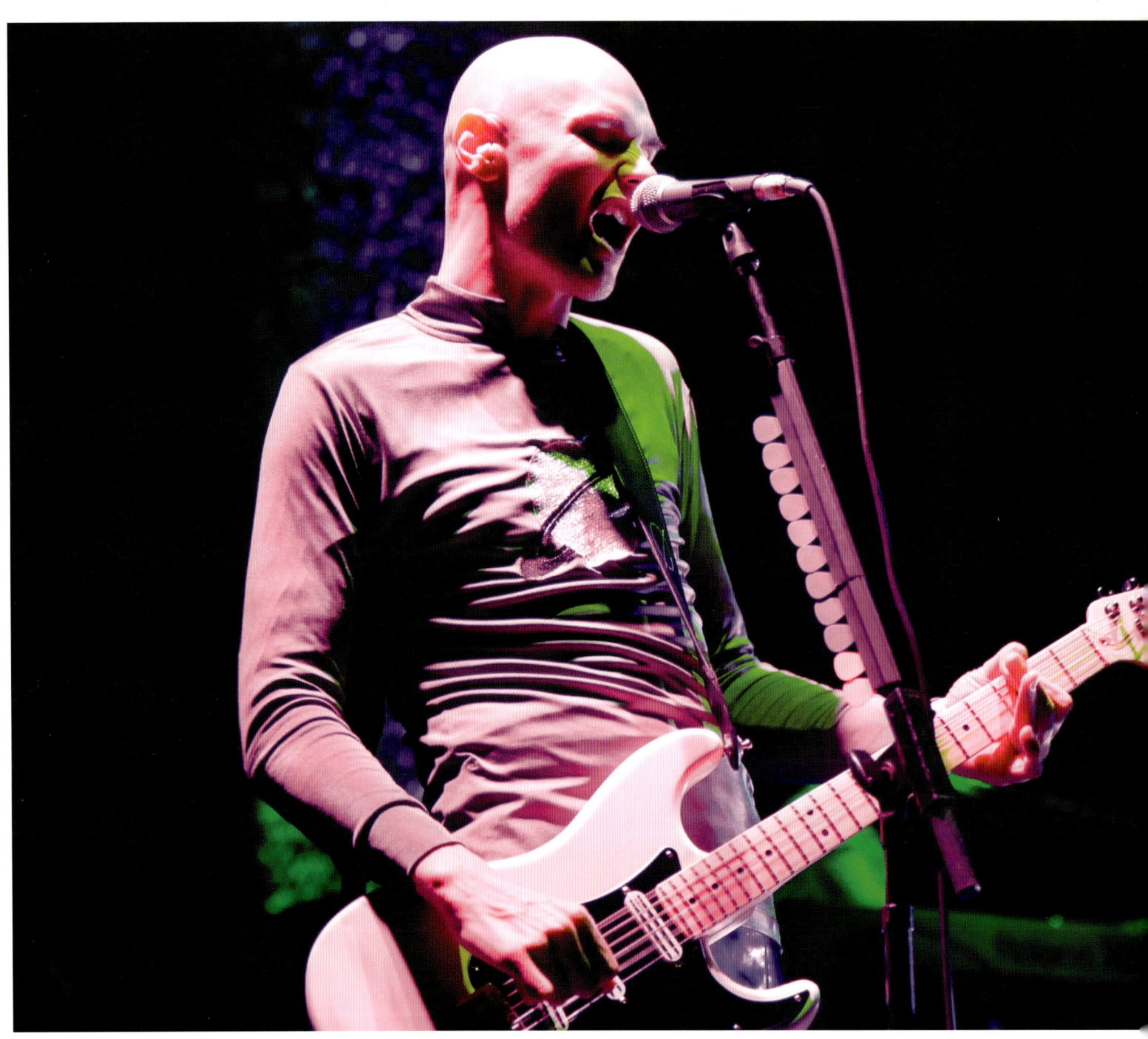

Billy Corgan

Lead singer Billy Corgan and the Smashing Pumpkins perform at The Venue at Horseshoe Casino in Hammond, Ind. The Chicago-area native and the rock band reunited in 2006 after breaking up in 2000. Corgan also owns a tea shop, Madame ZuZu's, in north suburban Highland Park.

CANDICE C. CUSIC, 2008

Liz Phair

Veteran Chicago rocker Liz Phair plays around in a public pool in Chicago's Bucktown neighborhood.

NANCY STONE, 1994

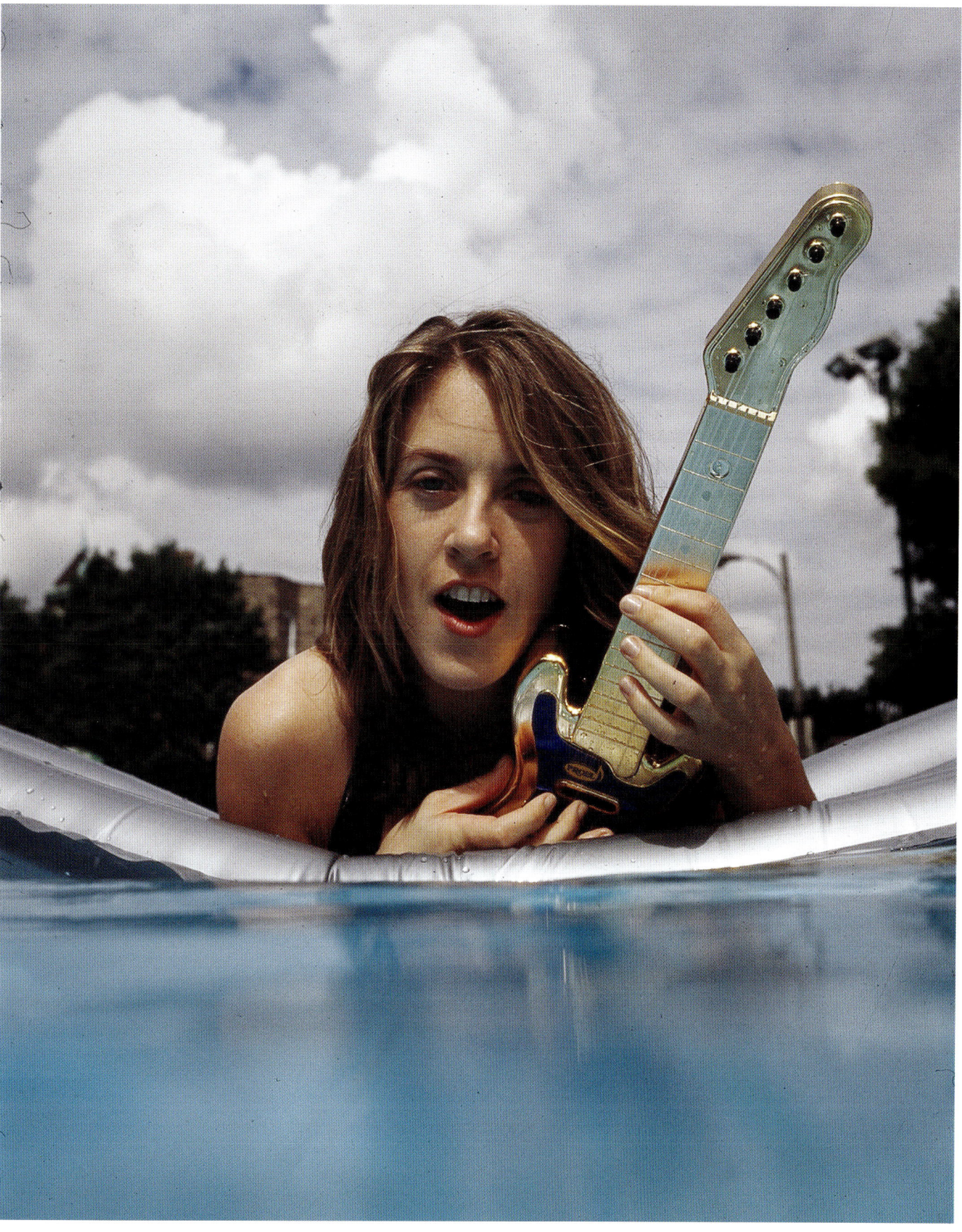

David McCullough

Author David McCullough works in his studio, a small cabin by his house near the coast of Maine. The two-time Pulitzer Prize winner was awarded the Chicago Tribune Literary Prize in 2008.

CHRIS WALKER, 2008

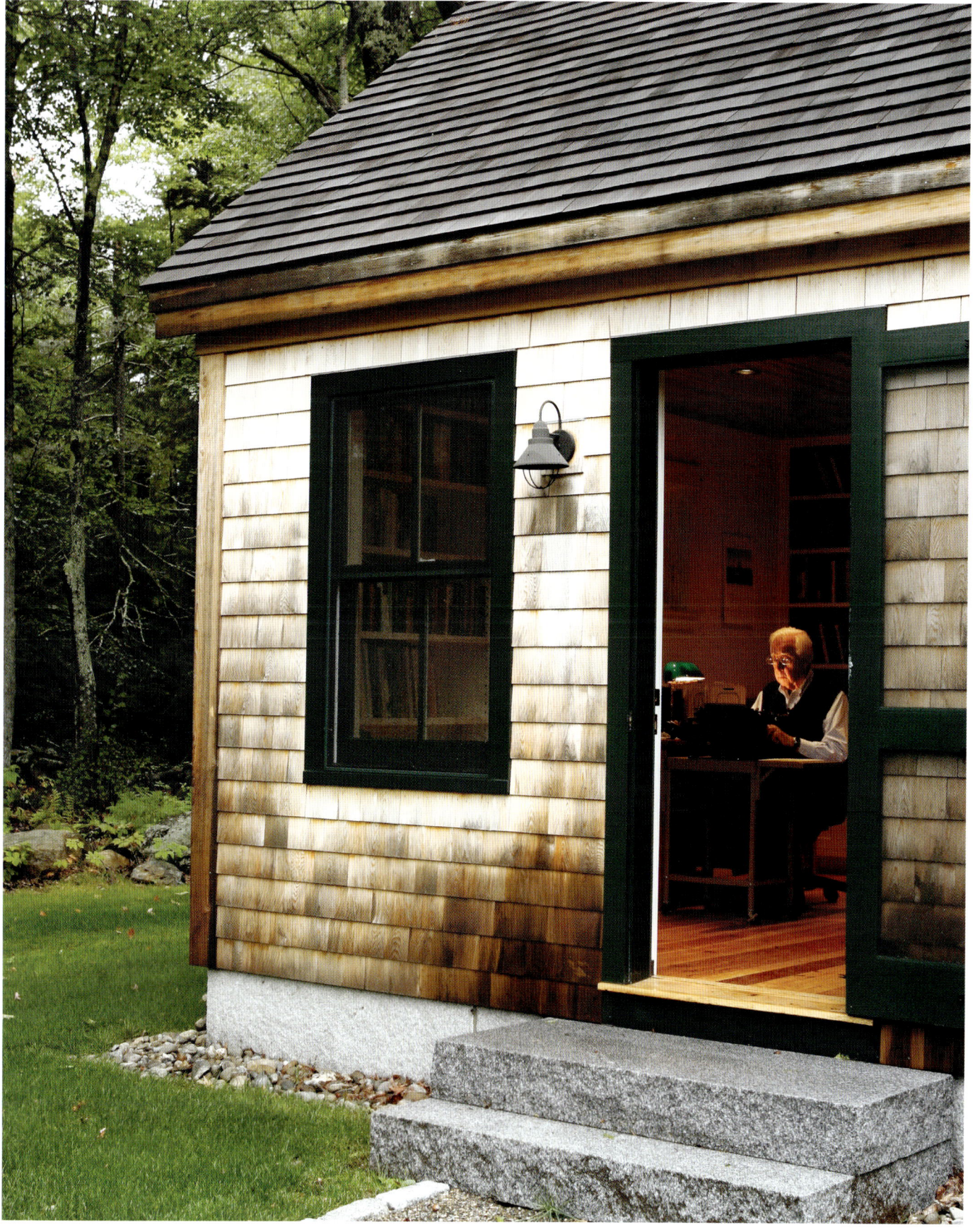

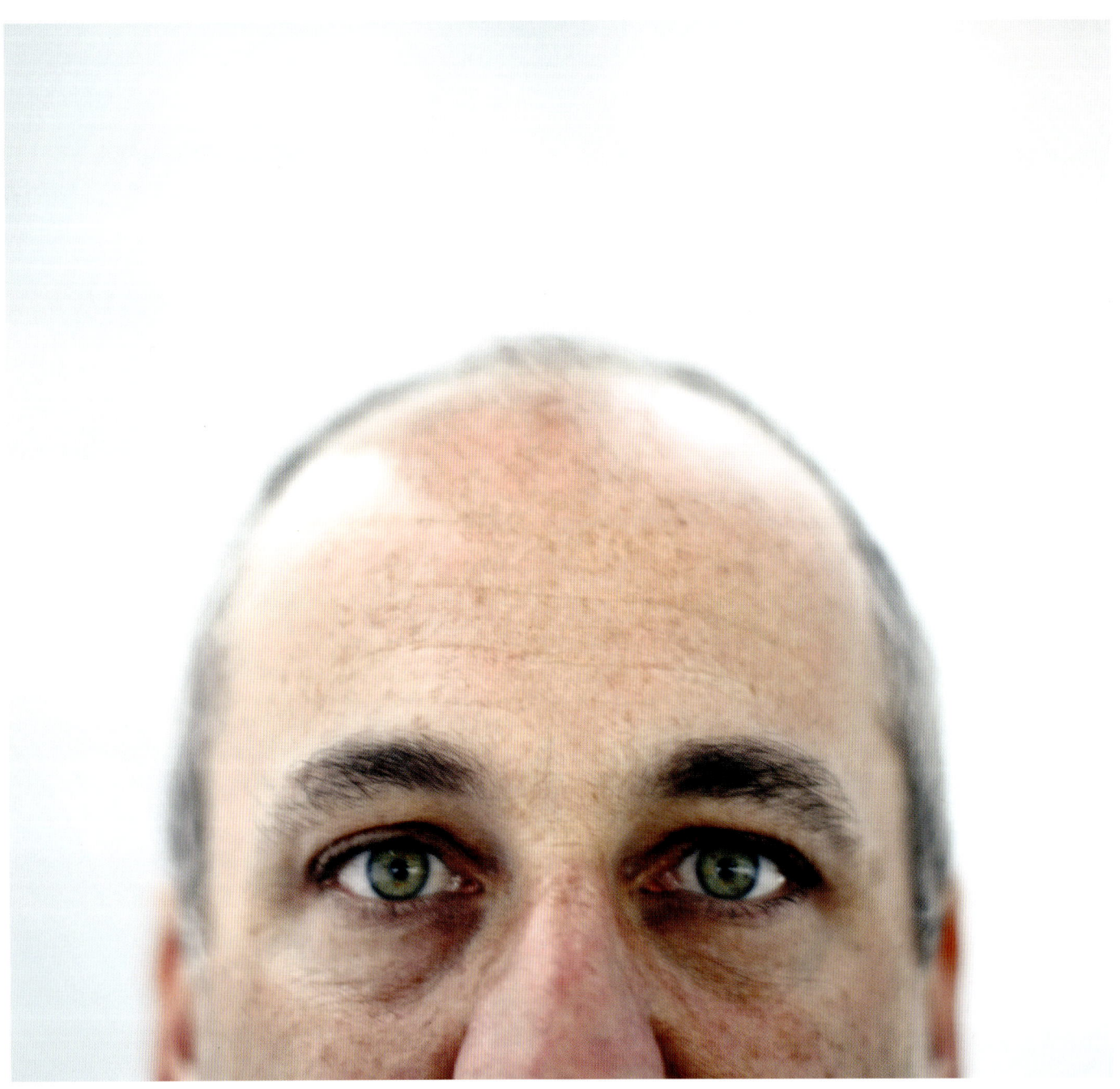

Jim Lasko

Jim Lasko, shown at Chicago's Millennium Park, was named the city's first artist in residence that year. Lasko is the co-founder of Redmoon Theater, which uses the public art of spectacle.

SCOTT STRAZZANTE, 2009

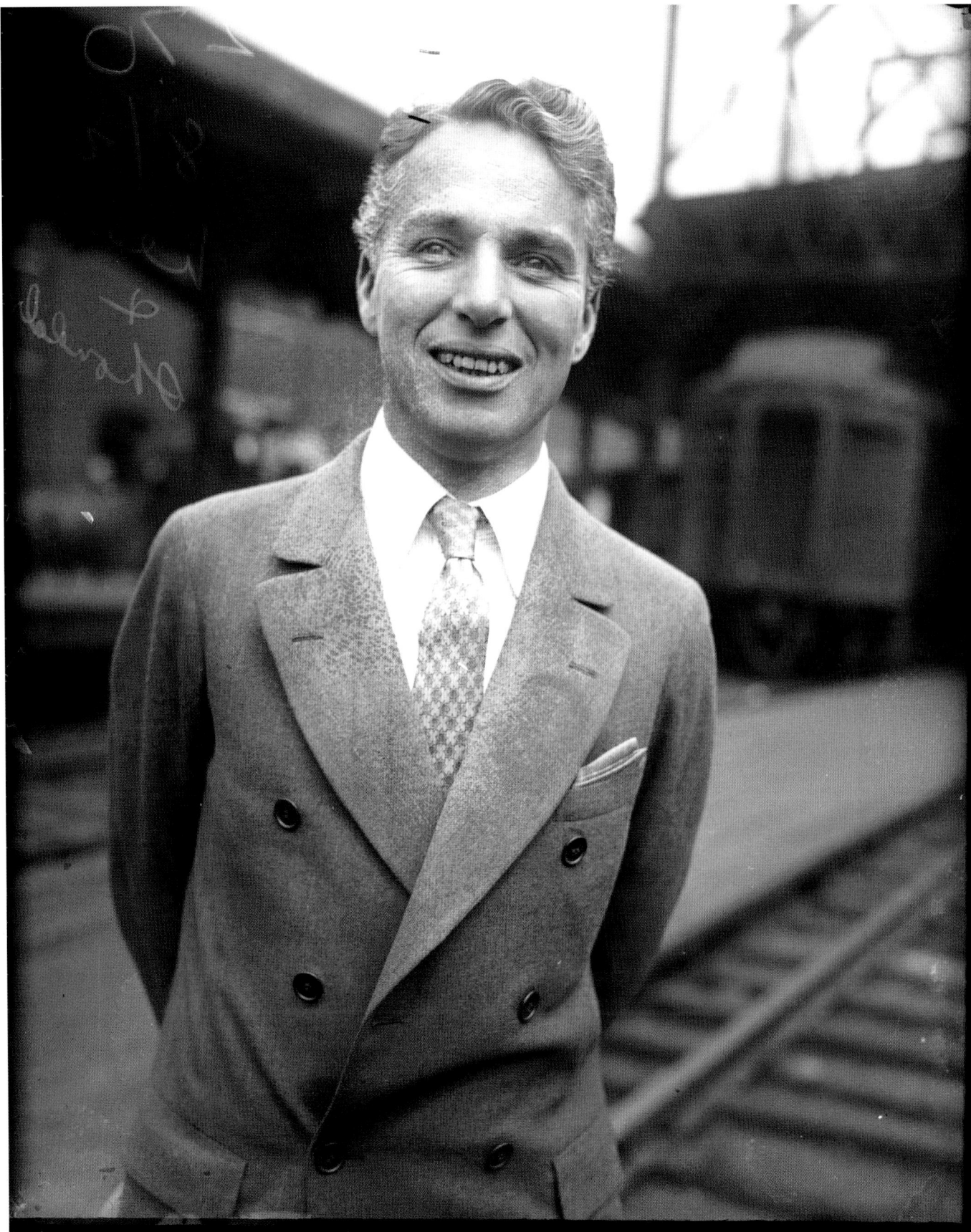

Charlie Chaplin

Silent film actor-director Charlie Chaplin starred in comedies produced by Chicago's Essanay Studios in the early 1900s.

CHICAGO TRIBUNE HISTORICAL PHOTO, UNDATED

Clara Bow

Film actress Clara Bow, striking a pose at a train station, was the original "It" girl, a silent film star and a symbol of the Roaring '20s.

CHICAGO TRIBUNE HISTORICAL PHOTO, 1930

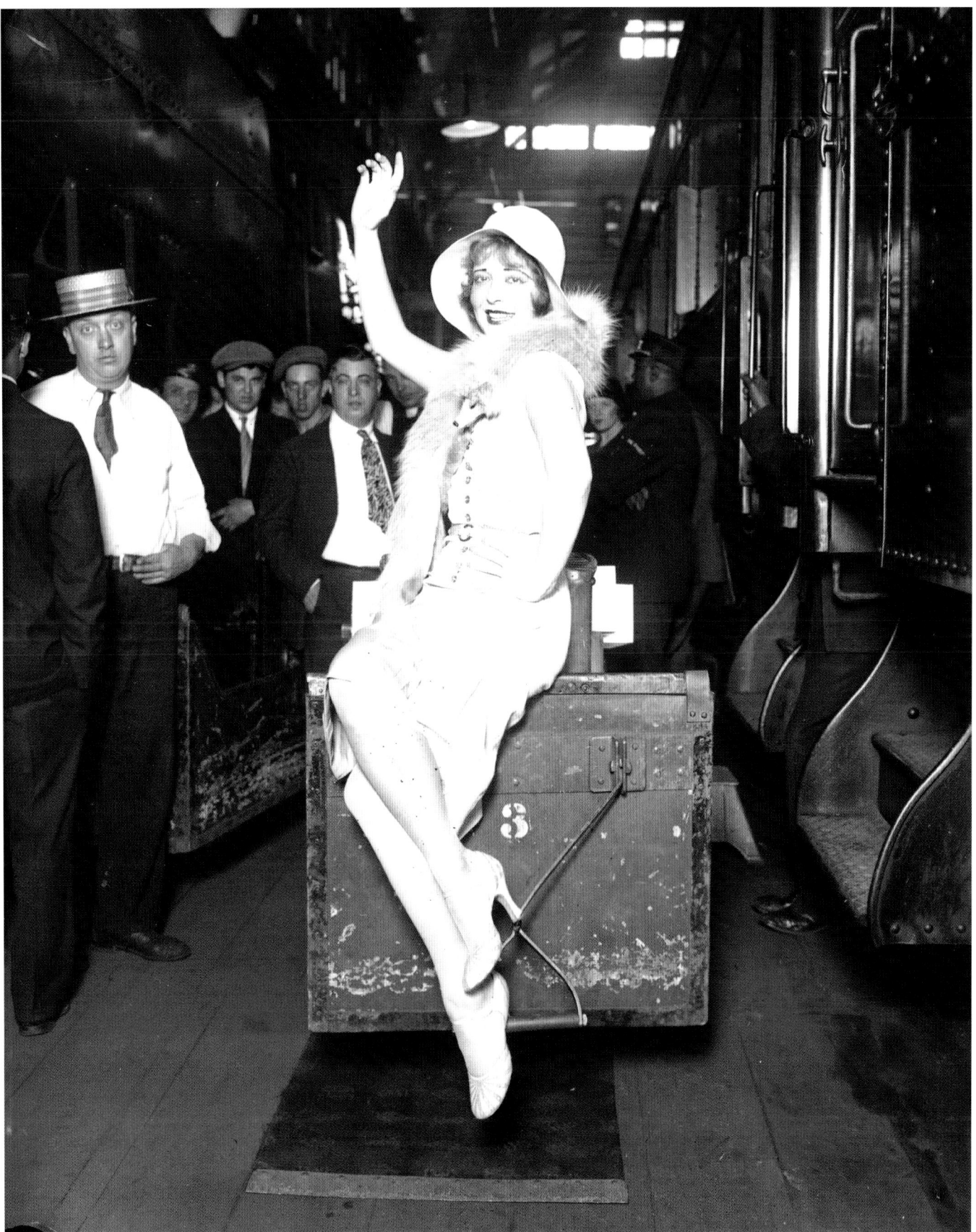

Kim Novak

Chicago-born actress Kim Novak, then known as Marilyn Novak, was a candidate for "Queen of Lake Michigan." She later made waves on film. In arguably her most famous role, she played a duplicitous woman in Alfred Hitchcock's "Vertigo."

CHICAGO TRIBUNE HISTORICAL PHOTO, 1947

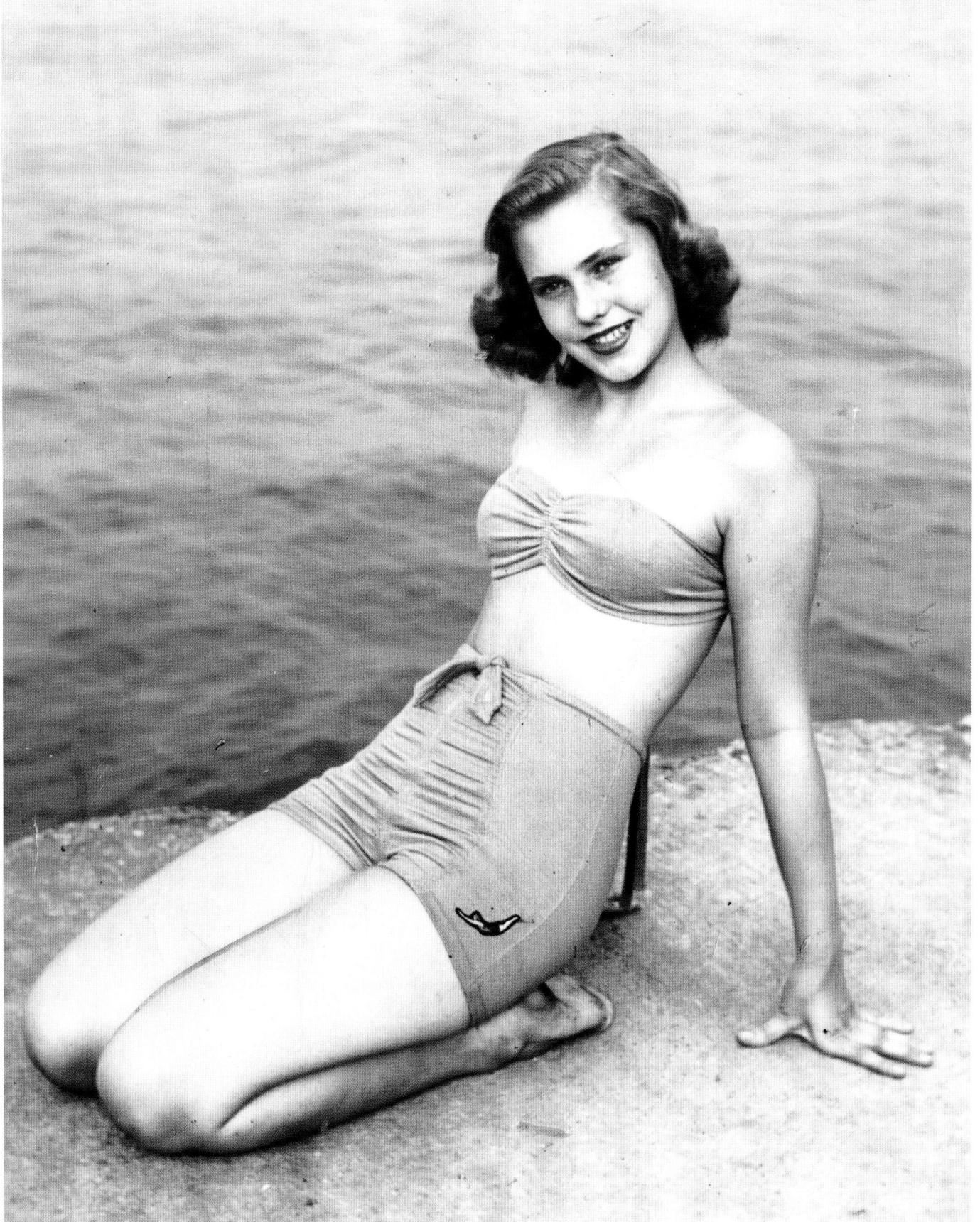

Marilyn Monroe

Long before the Marilyn Monroe statue famously graced Michigan Avenue, the real-life actress and bombshell arrived at Midway Airport to promote her new movie, "Some Like It Hot."

CHICAGO TRIBUNE HISTORICAL PHOTO, 1959

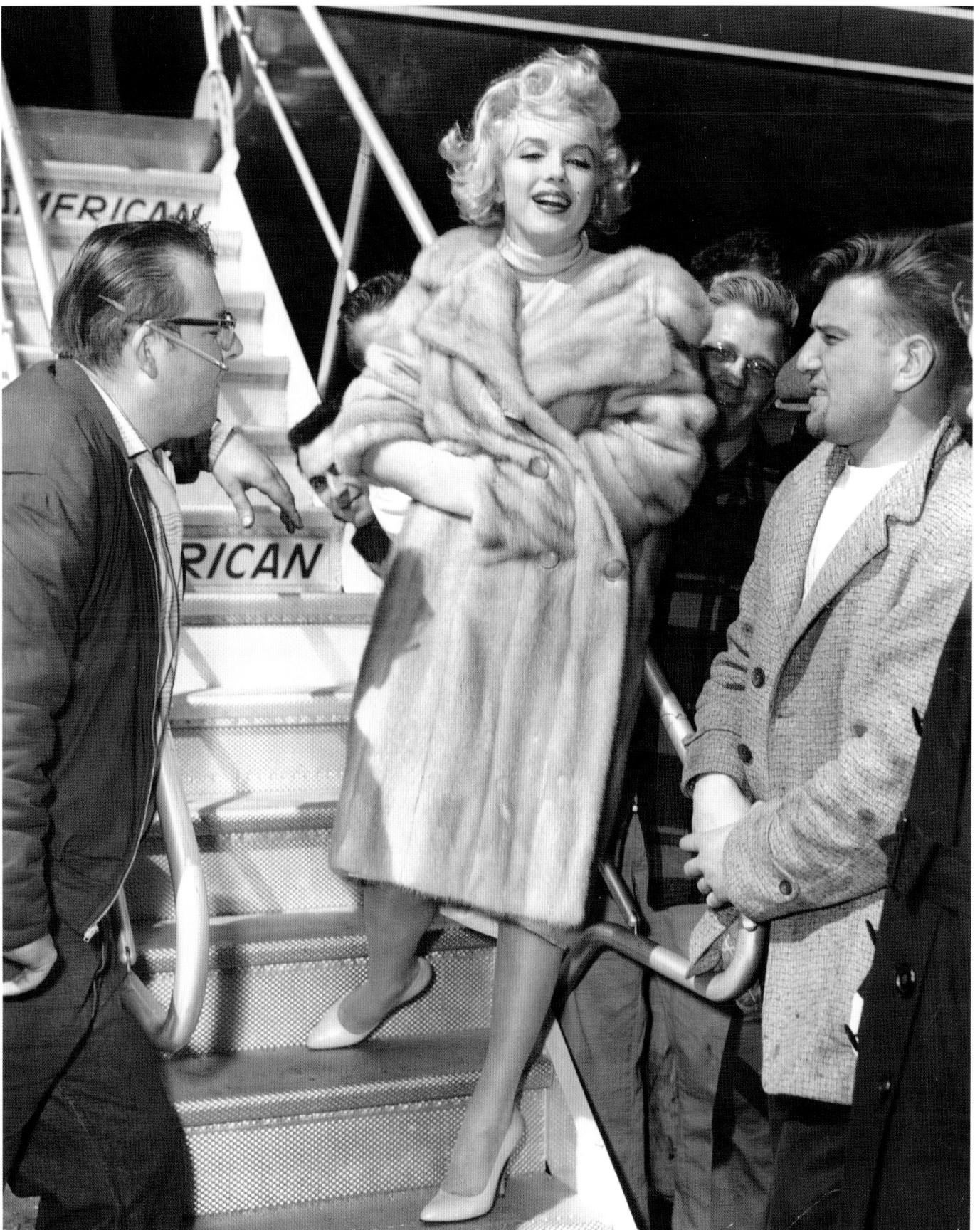

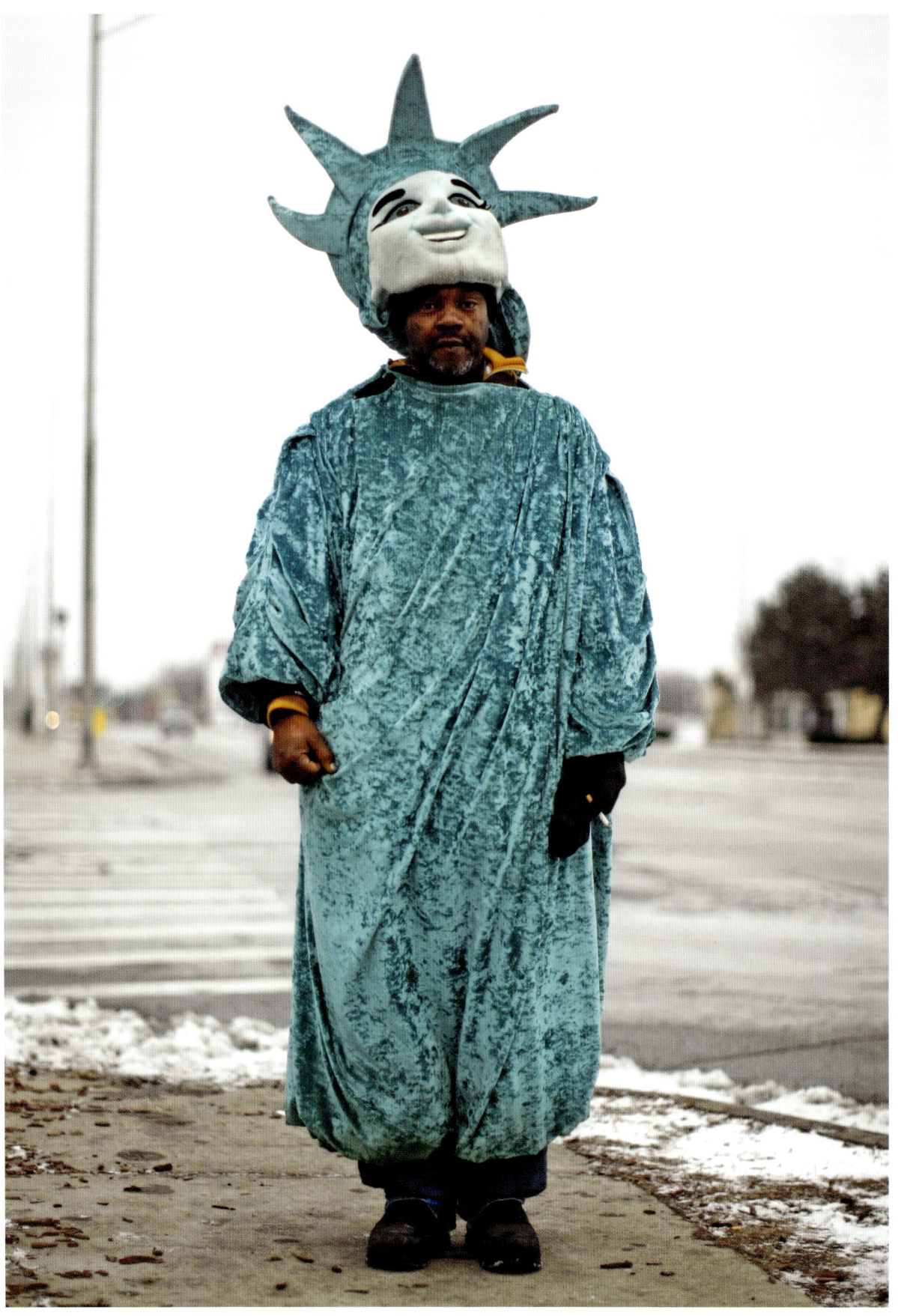

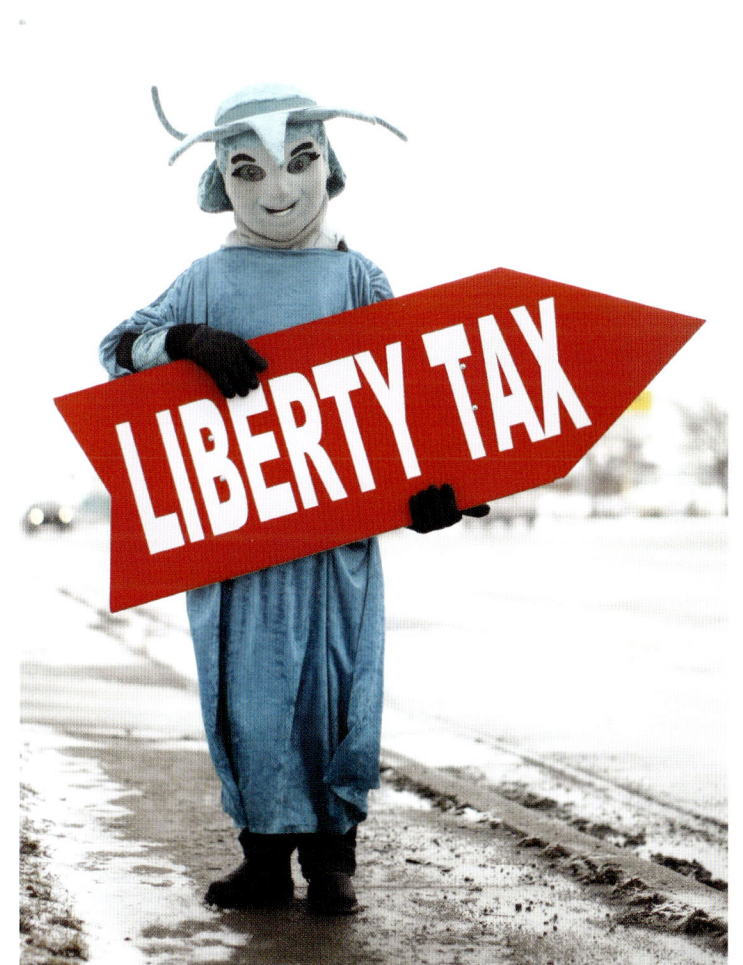
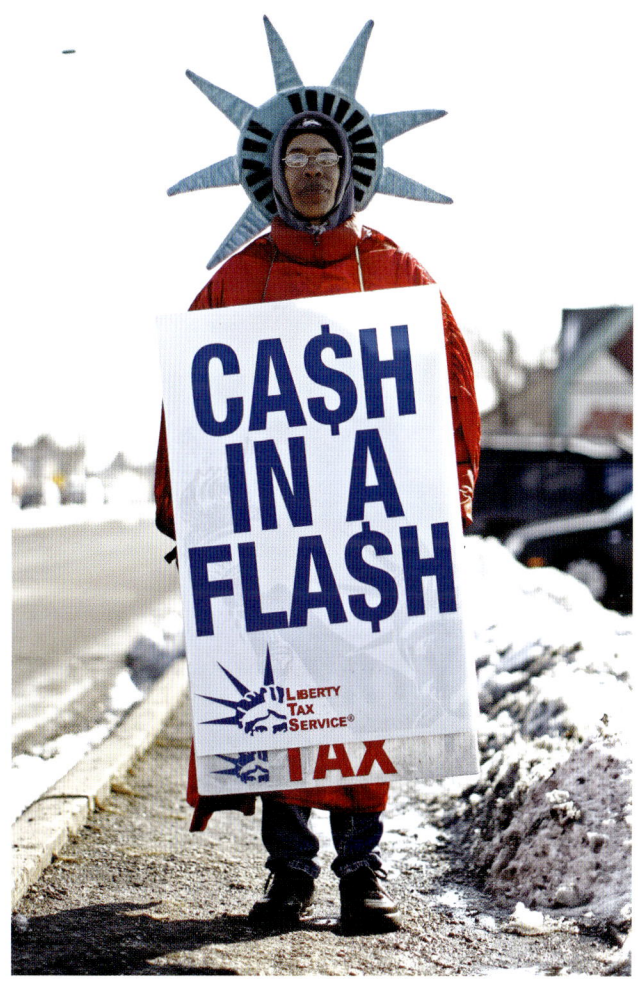

Derek Warlick, Fernando Cruz AND Corina Fowler

Derek Warlick, Fernando Cruz and Corina Fowler are among the hundreds who promote Liberty Tax Service, rain or shine.

SCOTT STRAZZANTE, 2010

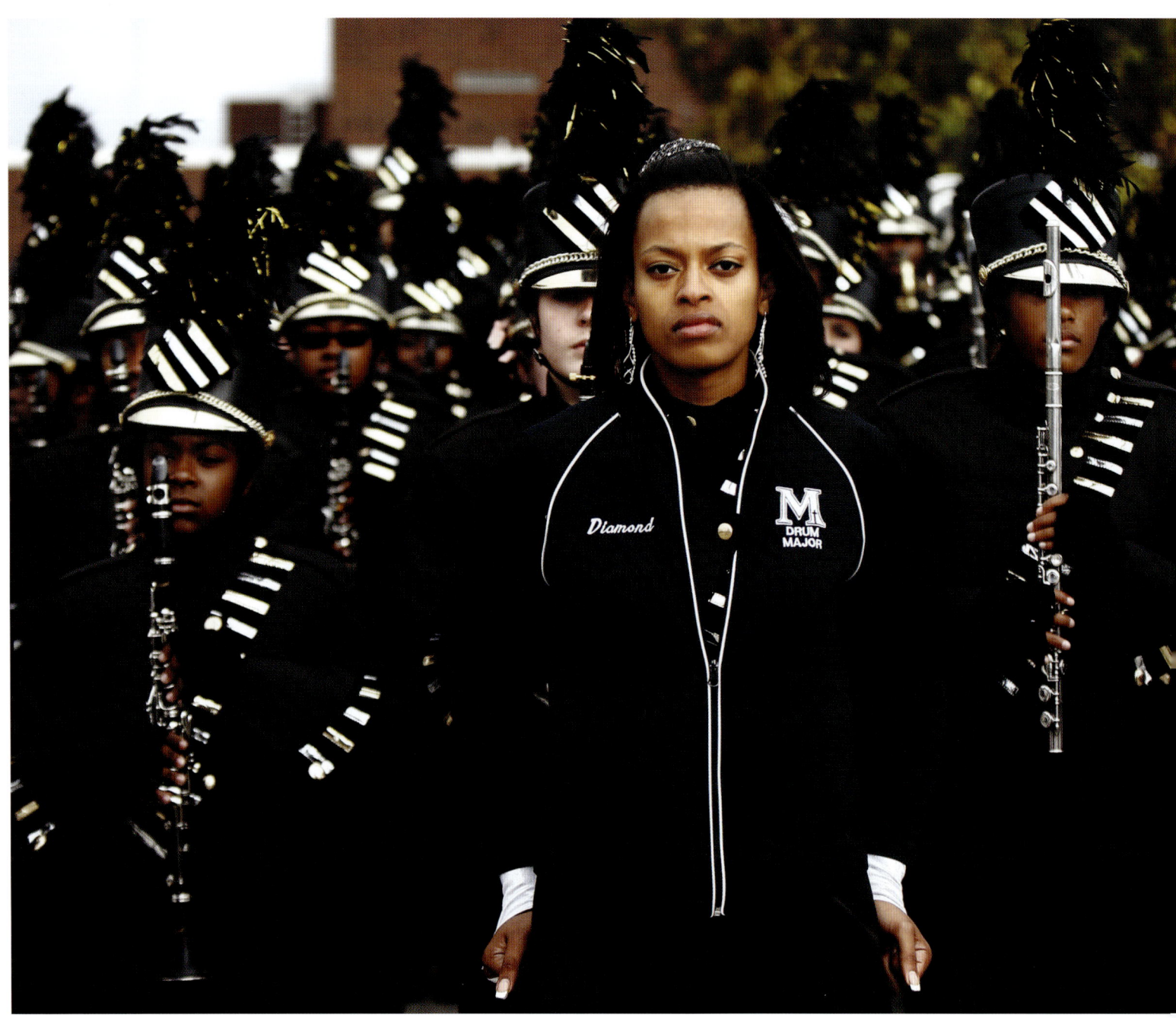

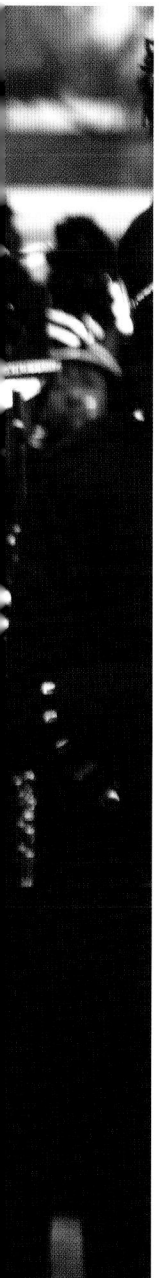

Diamond Murphy

Head drum major Diamond Murphy, center, leads Marian Catholic High School's decorated marching band to the field before preliminaries at a competition for the state title in Normal, Ill. "I'm here (with the band) more than I'm with my family," Murphy said. Marian Catholic is in Chicago Heights.

WILLIAM DESHAZER, 2009

Frank Capra

Frank Capra, director of beloved films such as "It's a Wonderful Life" and "Mr. Smith Goes to Washington," steps up to the camera.

TRIBUNE HISTORICAL PHOTO, 1931

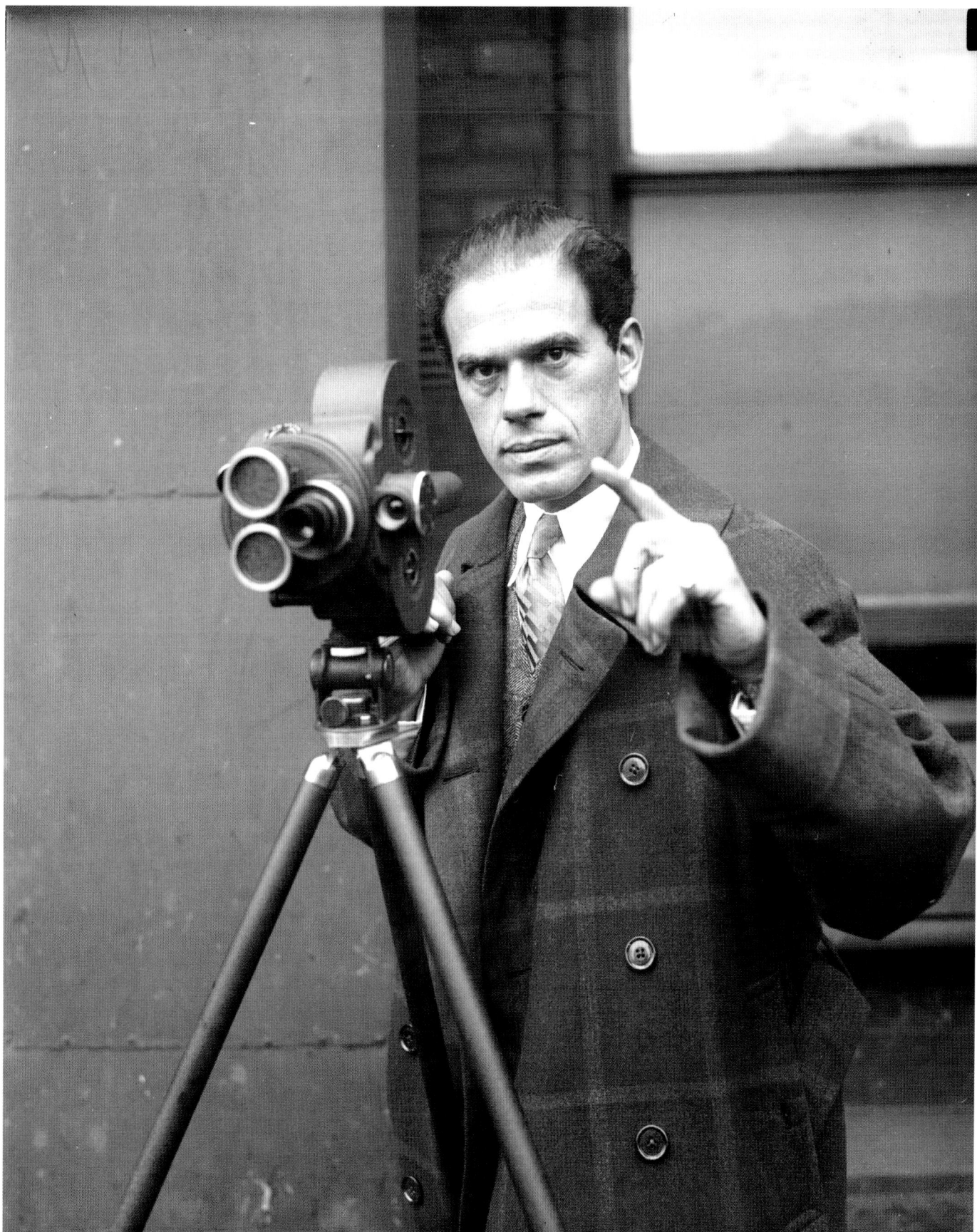

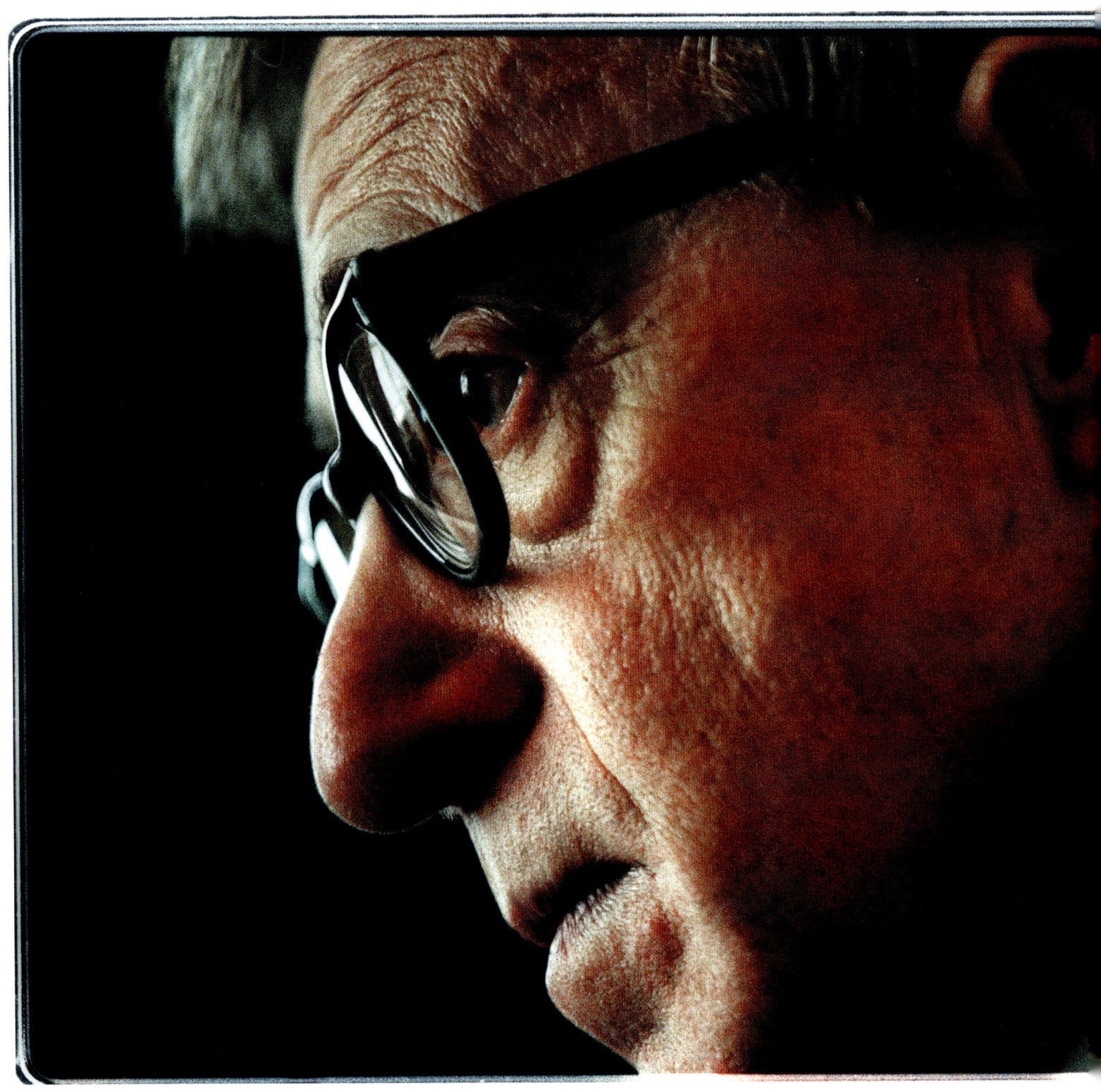

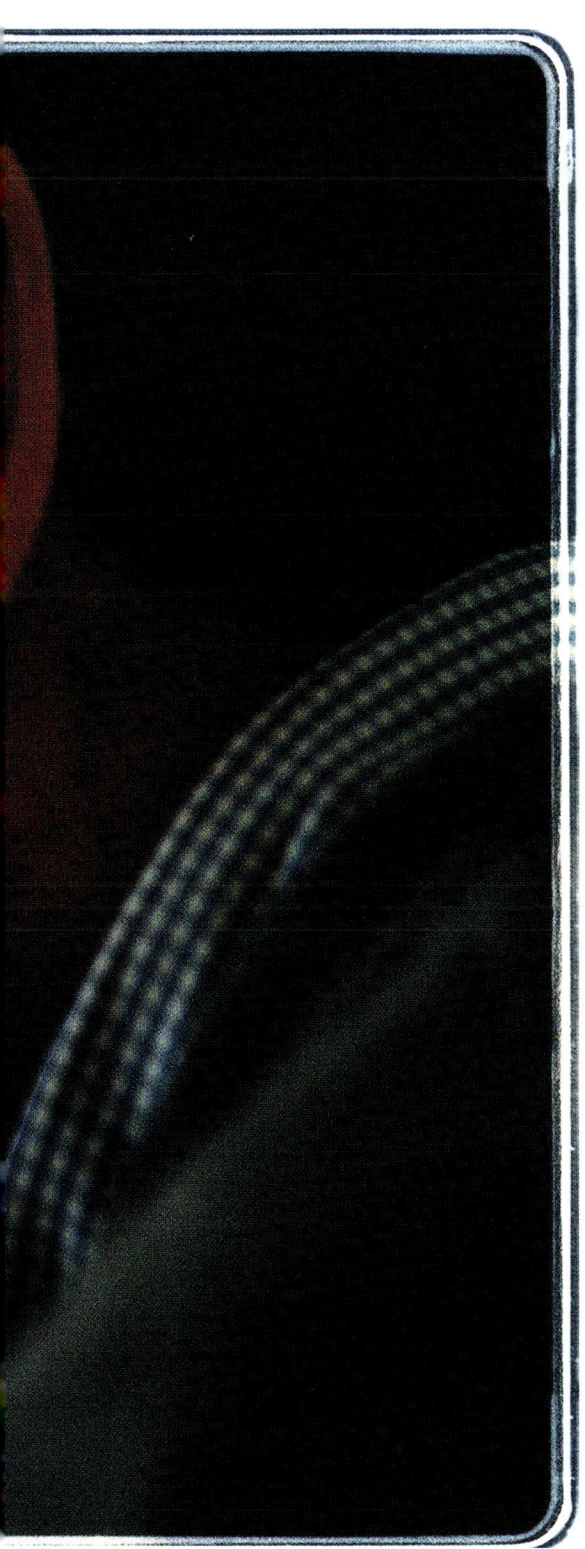

Woody Allen

Director, writer and actor Woody Allen considers a question during a Tribune interview at the Drake Hotel in Chicago. He was in town promoting his film "Small Time Crooks."

ALEX GARCIA, 2000

Christina Hendricks

Actress Christina Hendricks, of AMC's "Mad Men" fame, in Chicago to host a fashion show.

ANTONIO PEREZ, 2013

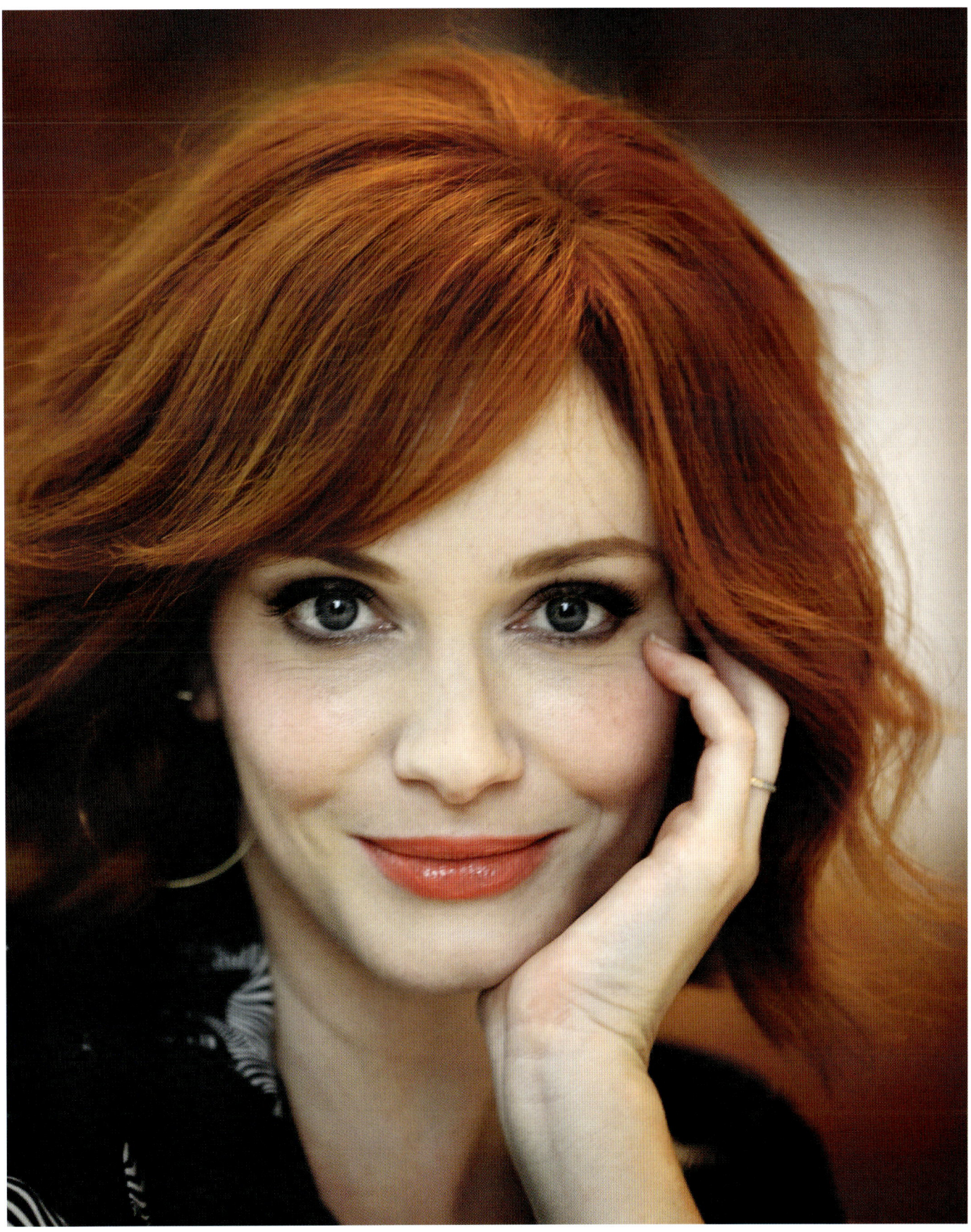

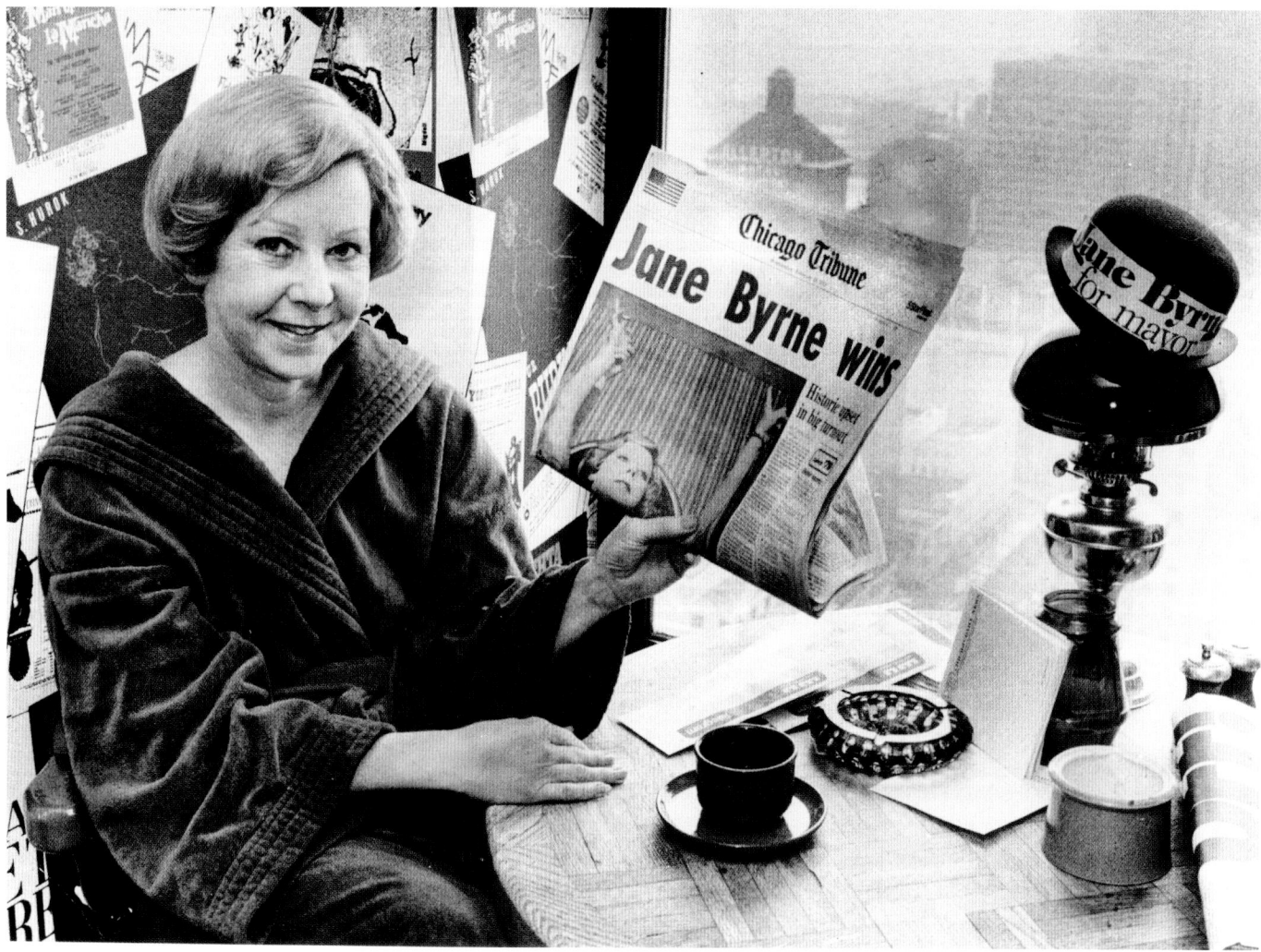

Jane Byrne

Jane Byrne savors her February 1979 victory in the Democratic primary, defeating Chicago Mayor Michael Bilandic. She was elected the city's first female mayor two months later.

CARL HUGARE, 1979

John Belushi

John Belushi appears on the main stage at ChicagoFest as his alter ego Jake Blues from "Saturday Night Live's" famous "Blues Brothers" skit. Belushi appealed that year to Mayor Jane Byrne to allow the filming of the "Blues Brothers" in Chicago, which he told her would include driving a car through the lobby windows at Daley Plaza. She offered her blessing.

WALTER KALE, 1979

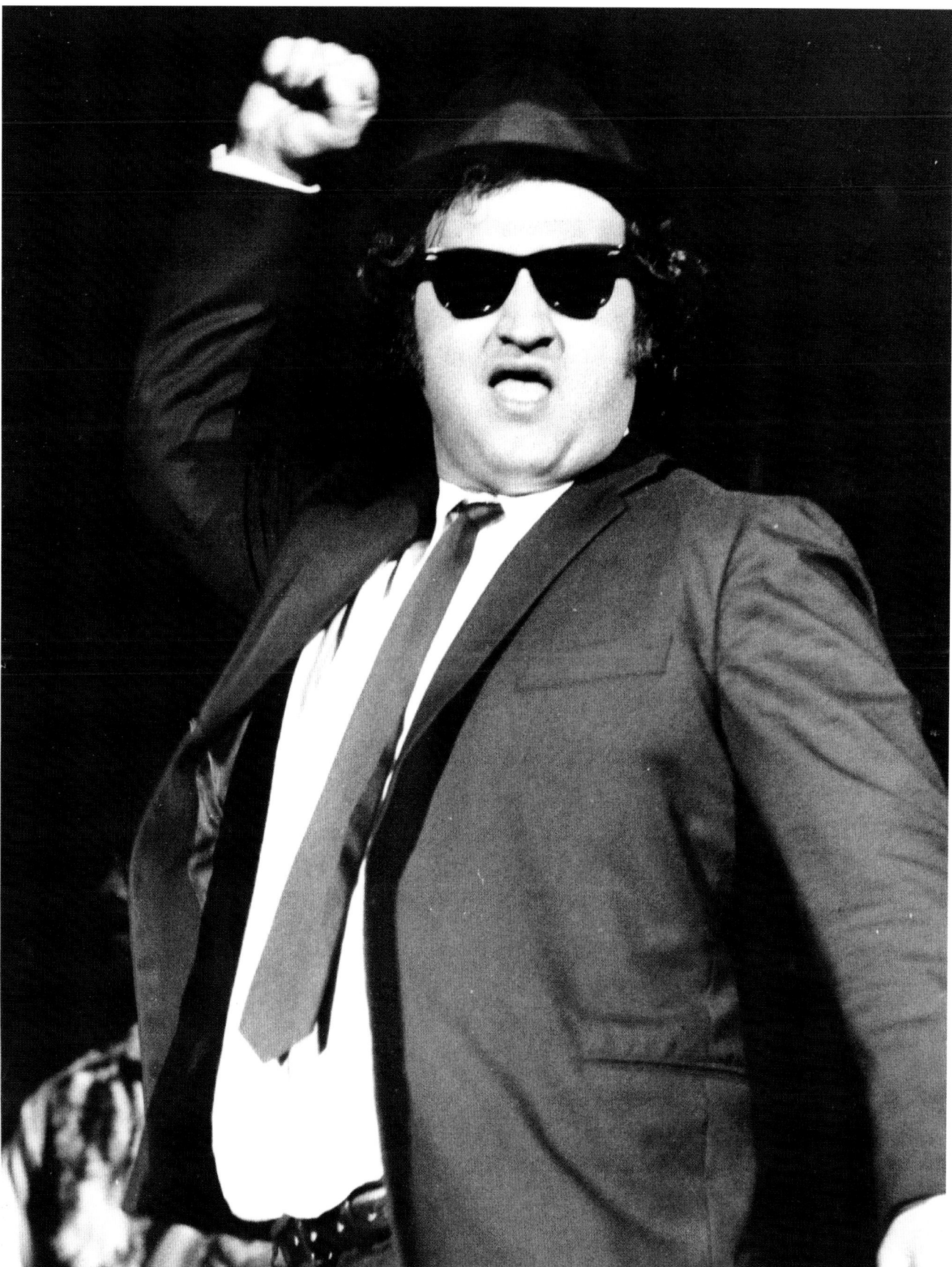

Vince Vaughn

Actor Vince Vaughn hangs out near an "L" platform while in Chicago to film "The Break-Up" with Jennifer Aniston. Vaughn, who grew up in north suburban Lake Forest, has lived in Chicago on and off.

ALEX GARCIA, 2005

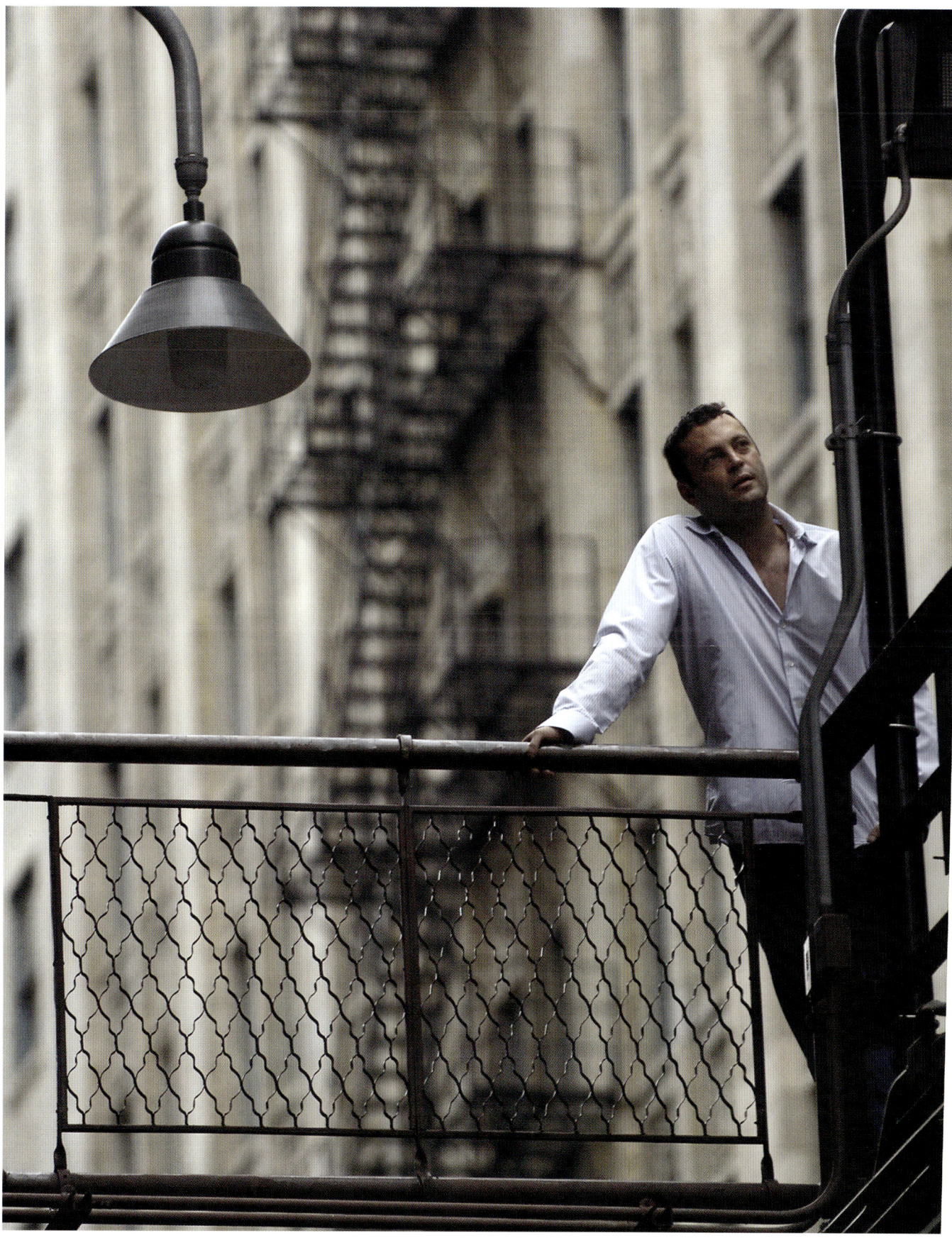

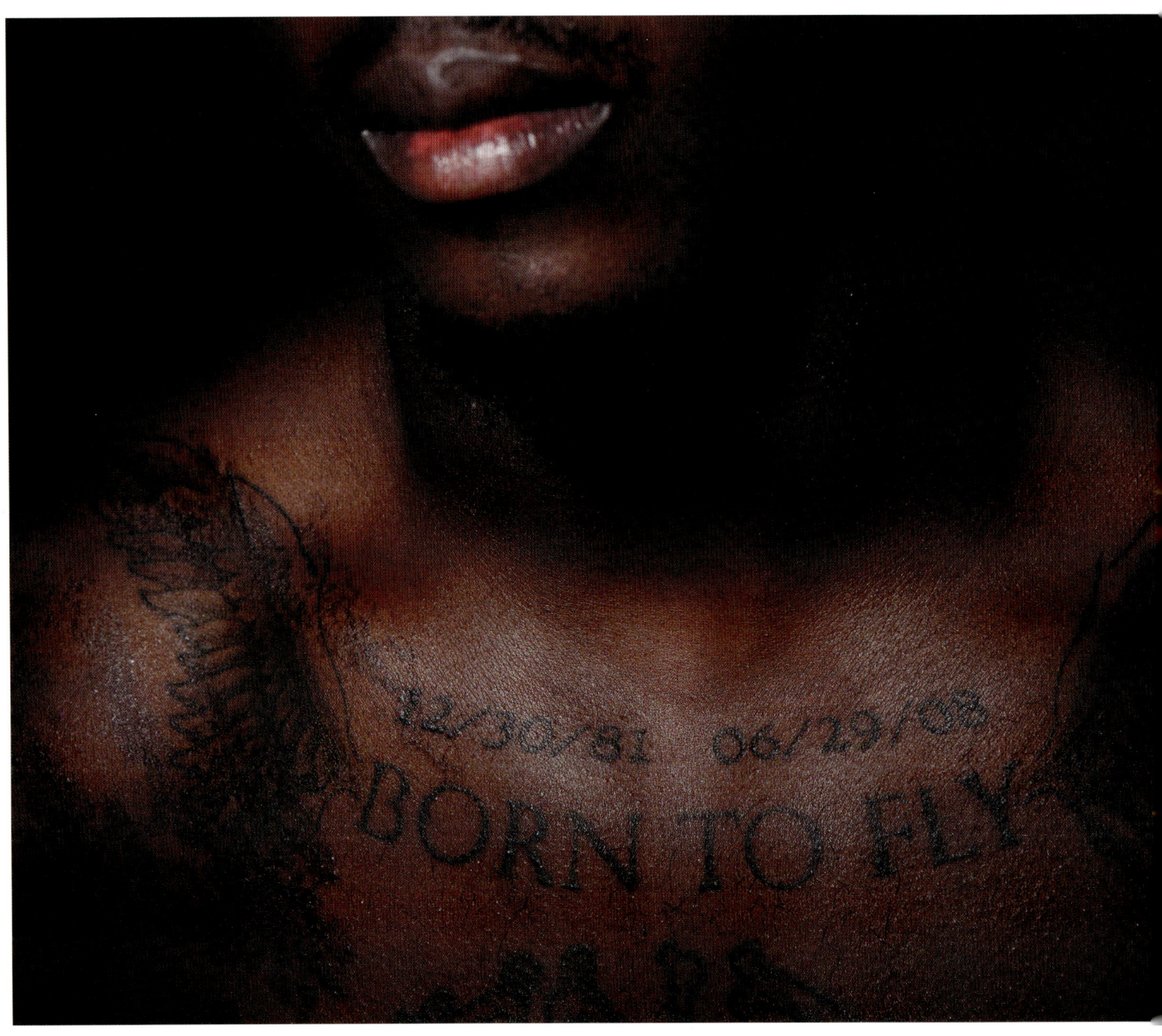

Jarred Fayson

University of Illinois wide receiver Jarred Fayson has the birth and death dates of his brother Arius tattooed between his collarbones. His brother died that June in a motorcycle accident.

E. JASON WAMBSGANS, 2009

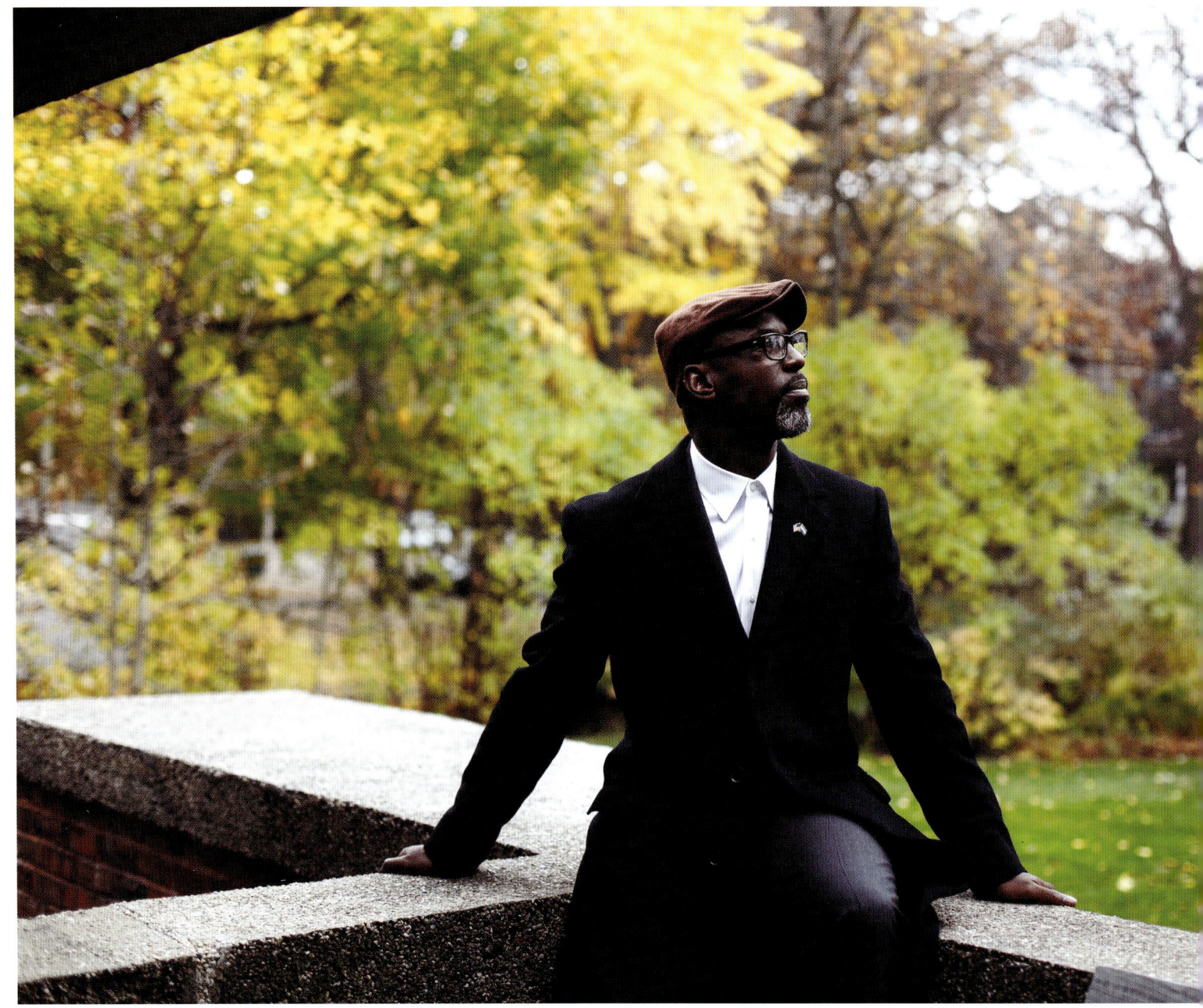

Isaiah Washington

Actor Isaiah Washington, best known for his role on "Grey's Anatomy," sits on the back porch of the Frank Lloyd Wright-designed Peter A. Beachy House in Oak Park, Ill. Washington is a fan of Wright's style.

KERI WIGINTON, 2010

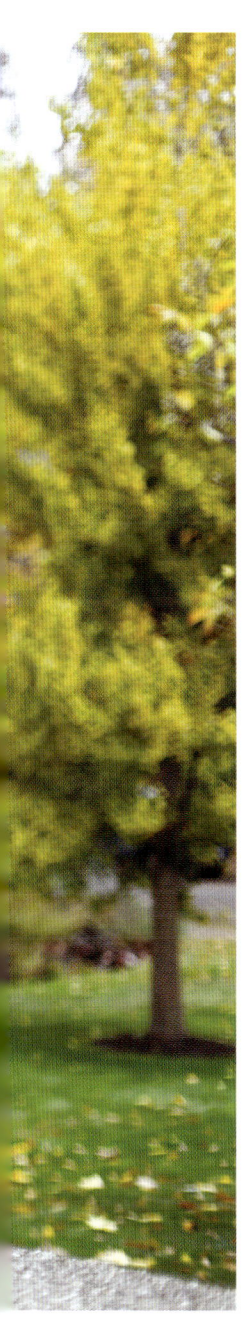

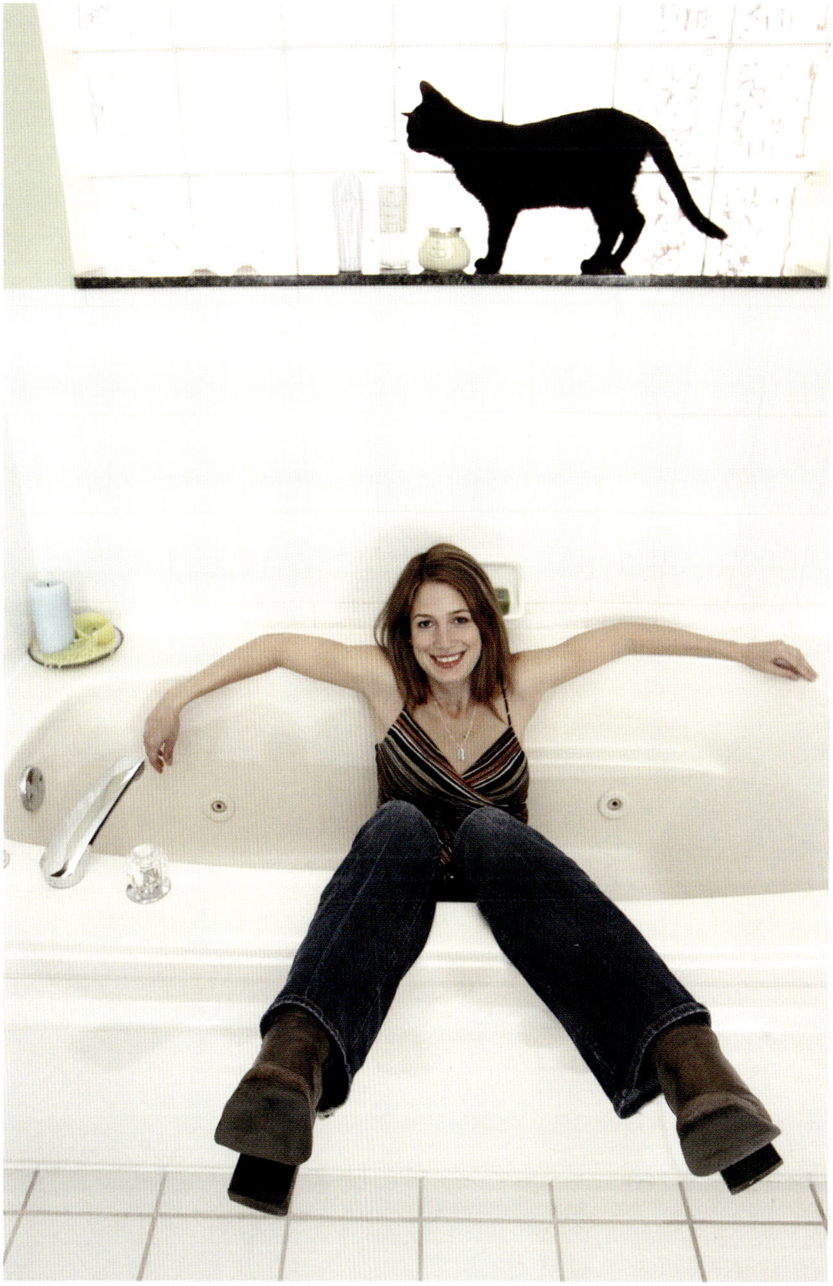

Gillian Flynn

Chicago author Gillian Flynn sometimes does her writing in her bathtub. Her cat Roy is often nearby.

HEATHER STONE, 2006

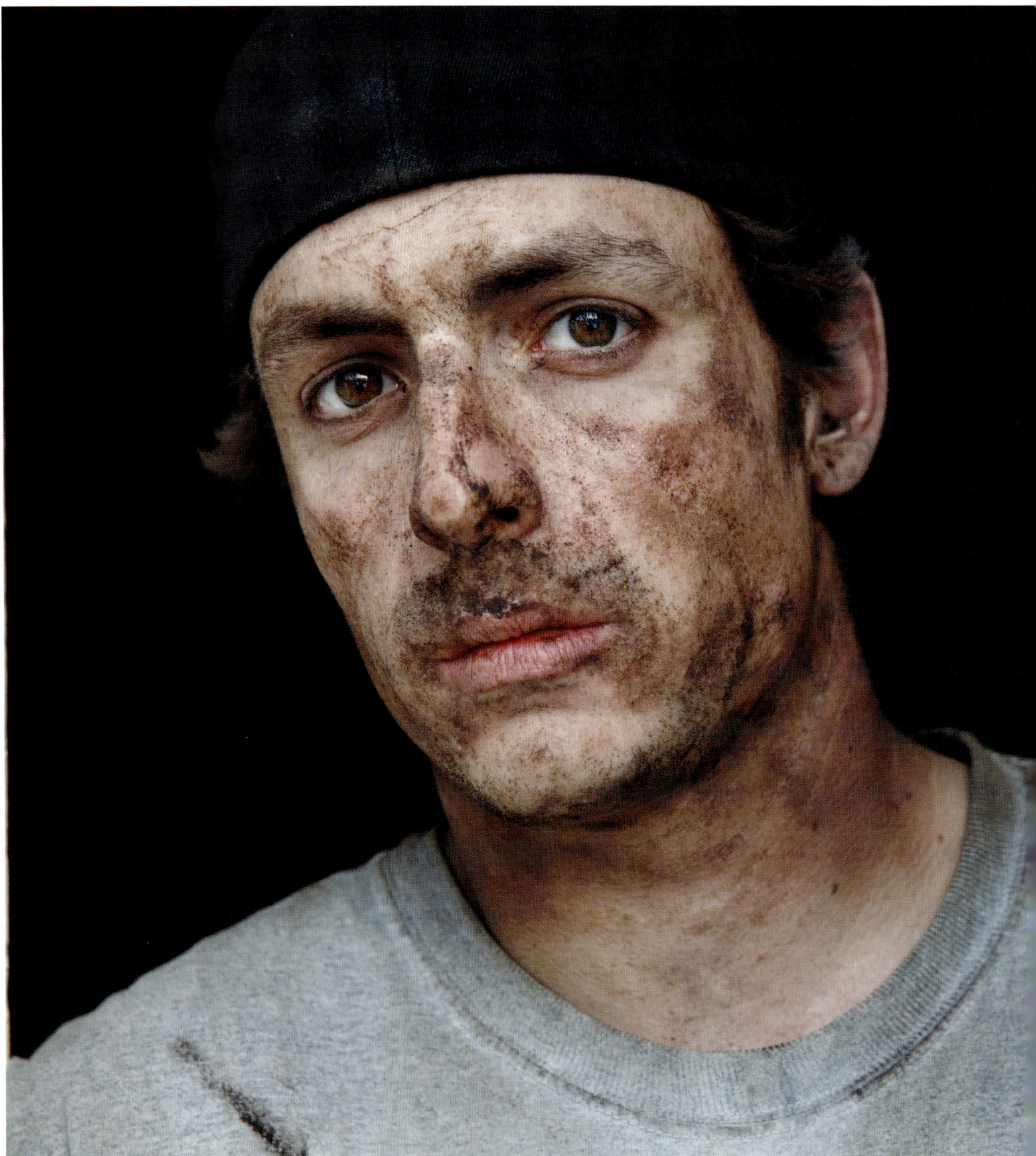

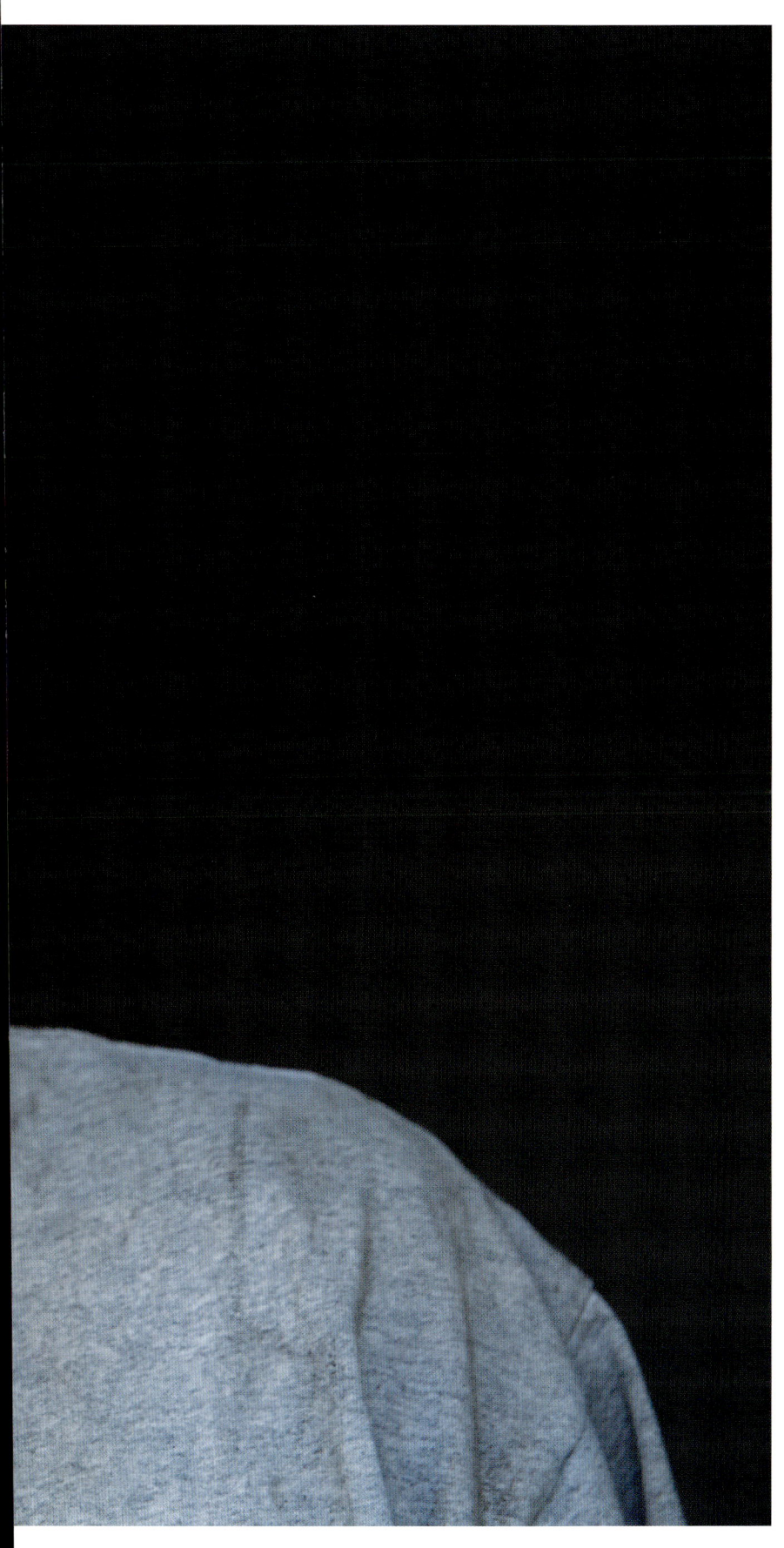

Andy Turco

The rigors of his work show on Andy Turco's face after he returns to his apartment from a 12-hour shift on an oil rig south of Williston, N.D. Turco left the north suburbs of Chicago to go west and take advantage of a modern-day gold rush — fracking, or hydraulic fracturing, which extracts oil from shale thousands of feet deep in the earth. In Williston, fracking has brought with it thousands of jobs, explosive population growth and an array of consequences.

ZBIGNIEW BZDAK, 2013

Jeremy Van Ek

Adventure racer Jeremy Van Ek strikes a familiar pose: resting in the woods. "I had so much fun it shouldn't even be legal," Van Ek, of Glen Ellyn, Ill., said of the Michigan Coast to Coast race he ran that June. He lacked feeling in several toes after spending so much time on his feet. "Most people wonder why in the world would you want to do that. I'm coming at it from the opposite perspective: Why not? It's just so fun." Adventure racers hike and bike during competitions, with added challenges such as whitewater rafting, glacier trekking or camel riding, depending on the locale.

E. JASON WAMBSGANS, 2005

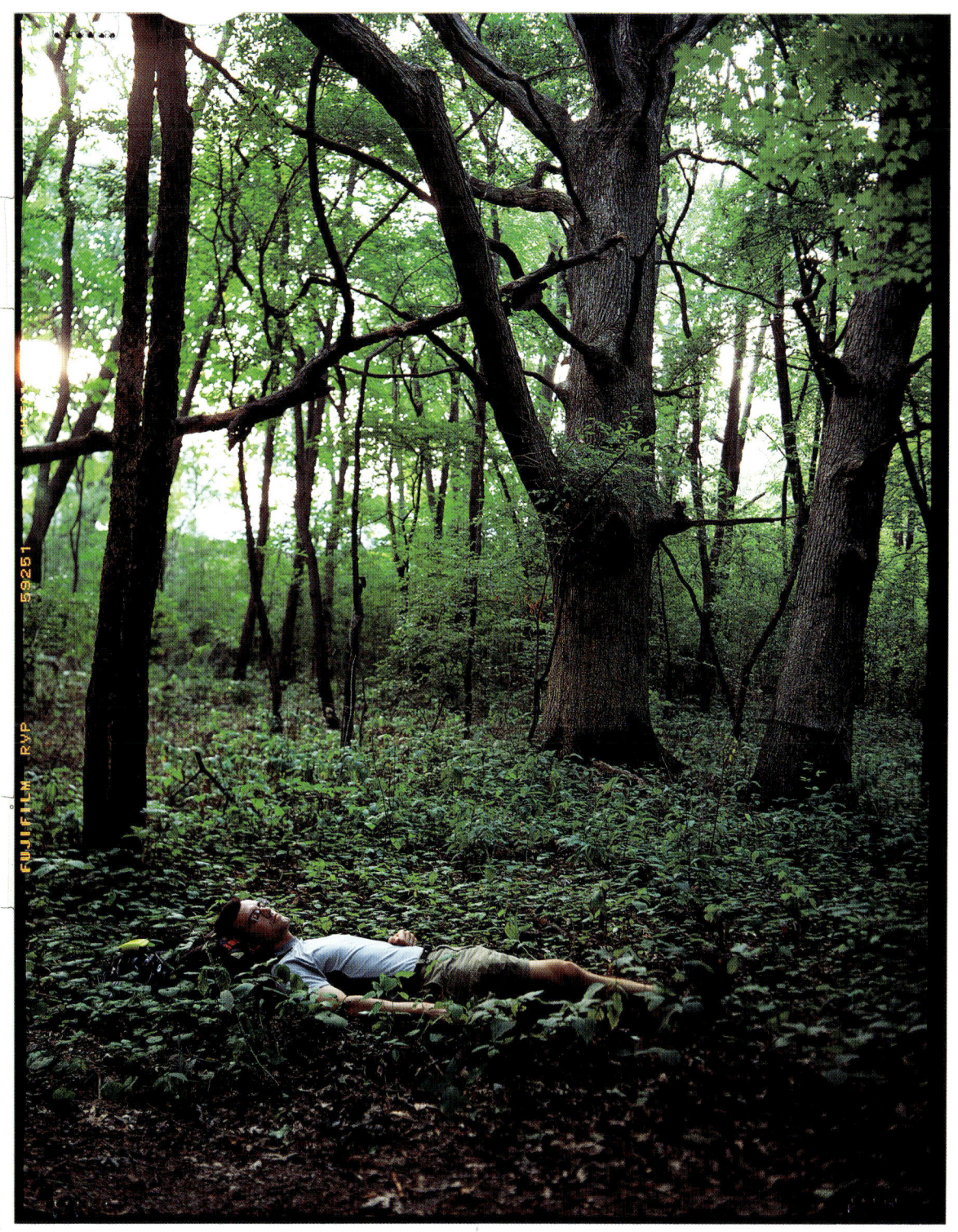

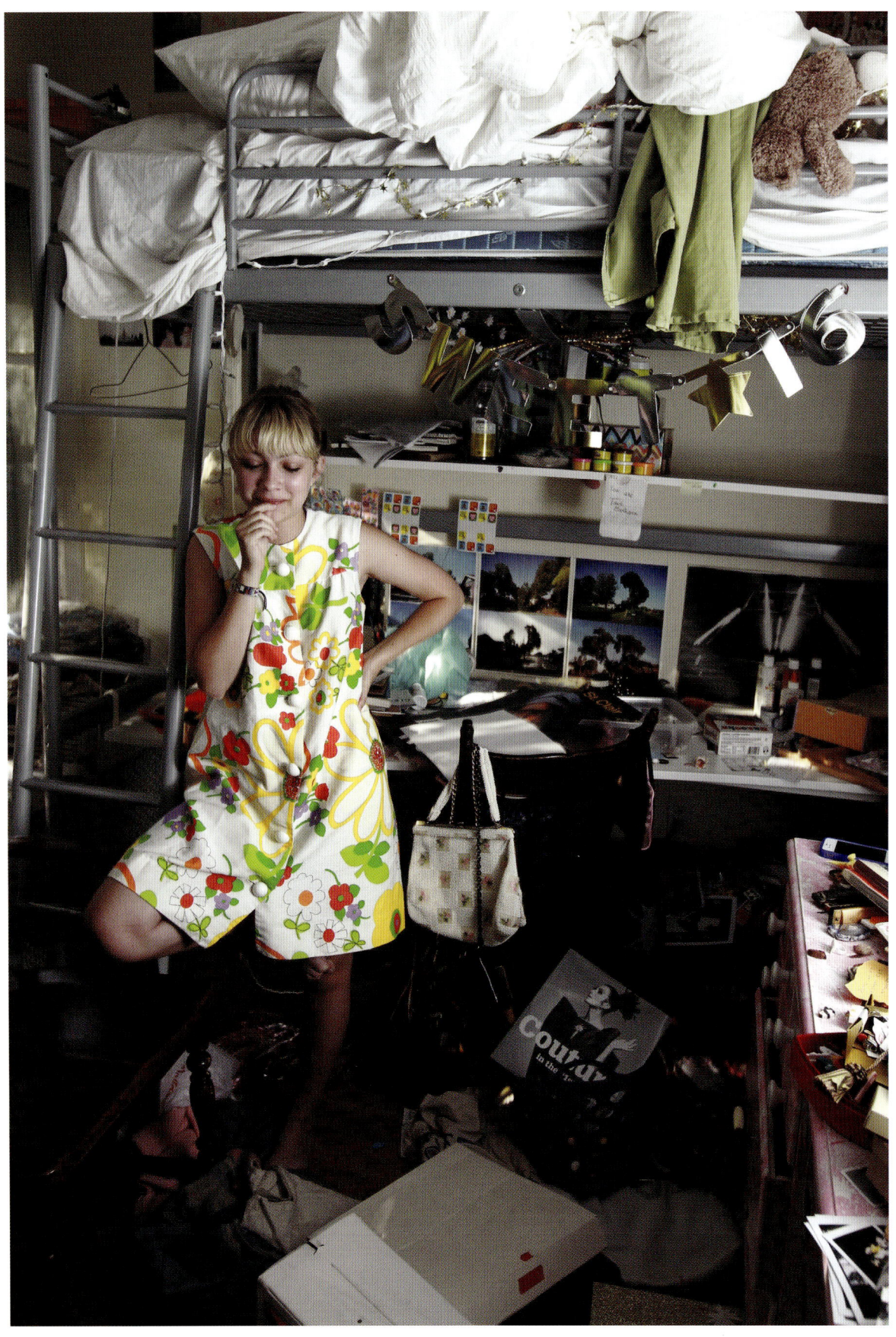

Tavi Gevinson

Young fashion maven Tavi Gevinson, 16, shown in her Oak Park, Ill., bedroom, was profiled by the New Yorker at 14 and feted by the fashion industry at 12.

ANTONIO PEREZ, 2012

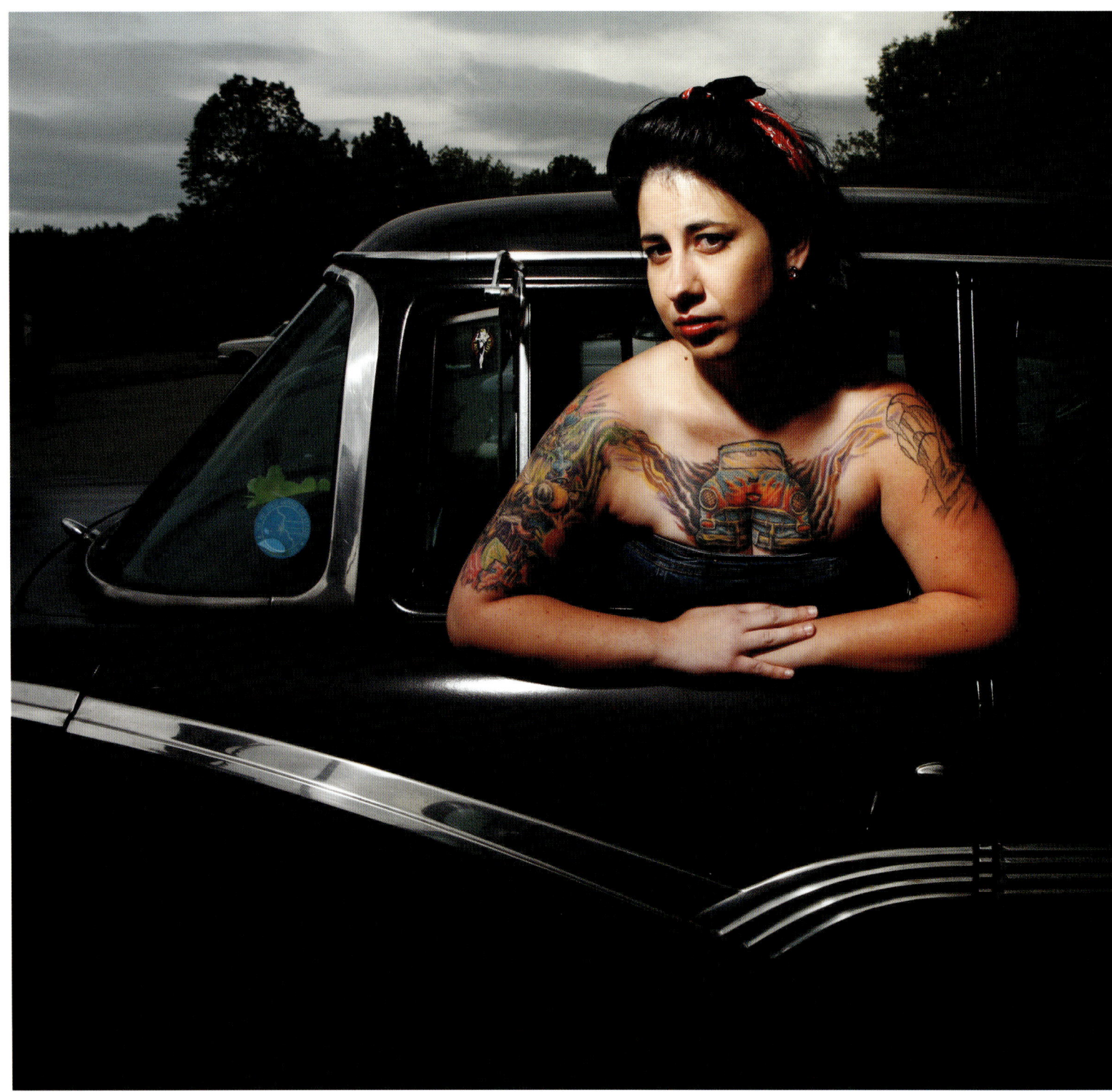

Patricia Kush

Patricia Kush, who owns a 1951 Buick Special, leans out the window of a 1956 Ford at Busse Woods in Schaumburg, Ill. The St. Charles, Ill. woman's favorite "kustom kulture" accessory is her chest tattoo of a 1954 Chevrolet.

E. JASON WAMBSGANS, 2007

Nellie Fox

White Sox second baseman Nellie Fox in classic pinstripes. Fox was considered a catalyst for the "Go-Go" White Sox of the 1950s. A 12-time American League All-Star, he was the league's most valuable player in 1959, when he led the White Sox to their first World Series in 40 years.

CHICAGO TRIBUNE HISTORICAL PHOTO, 1959

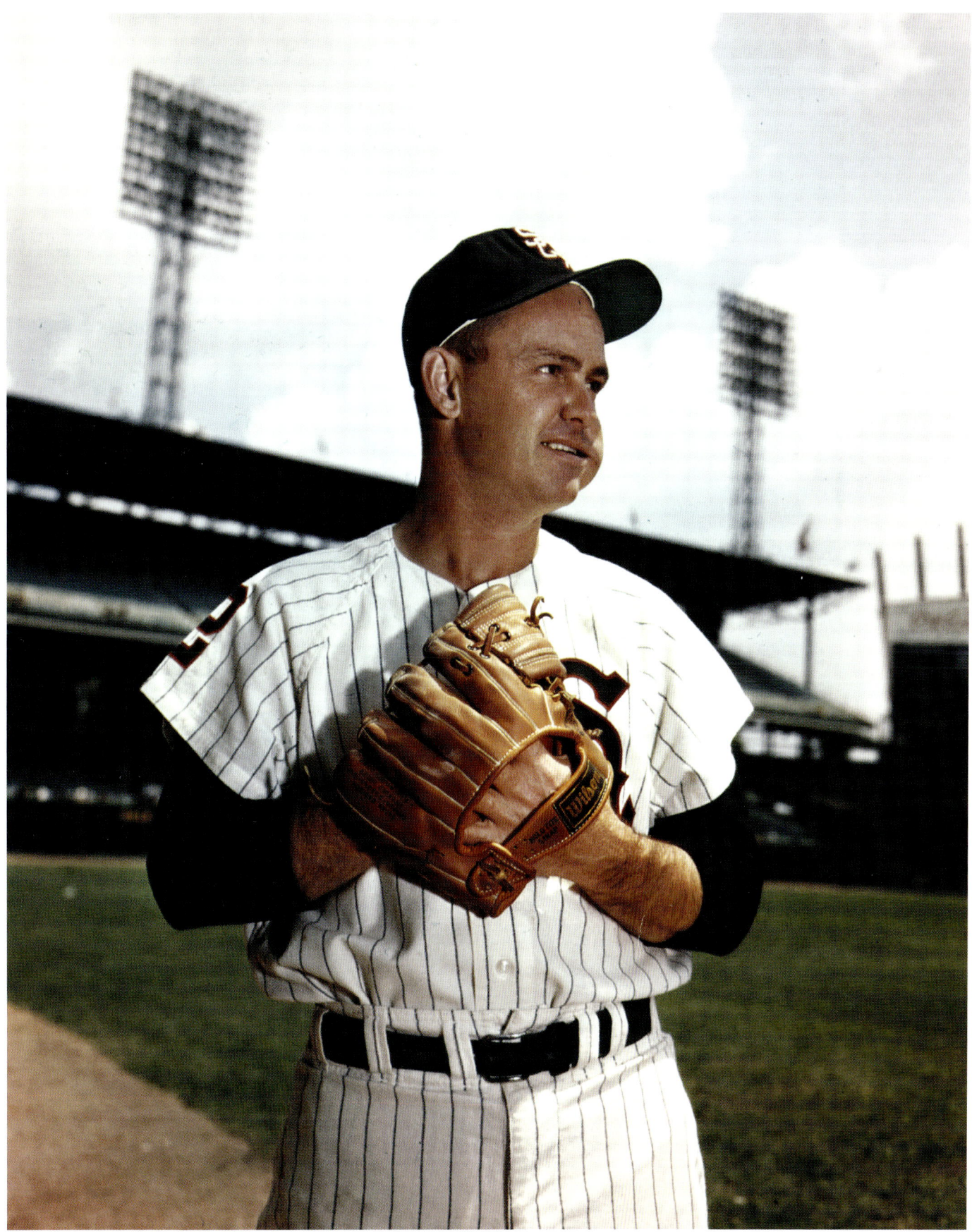

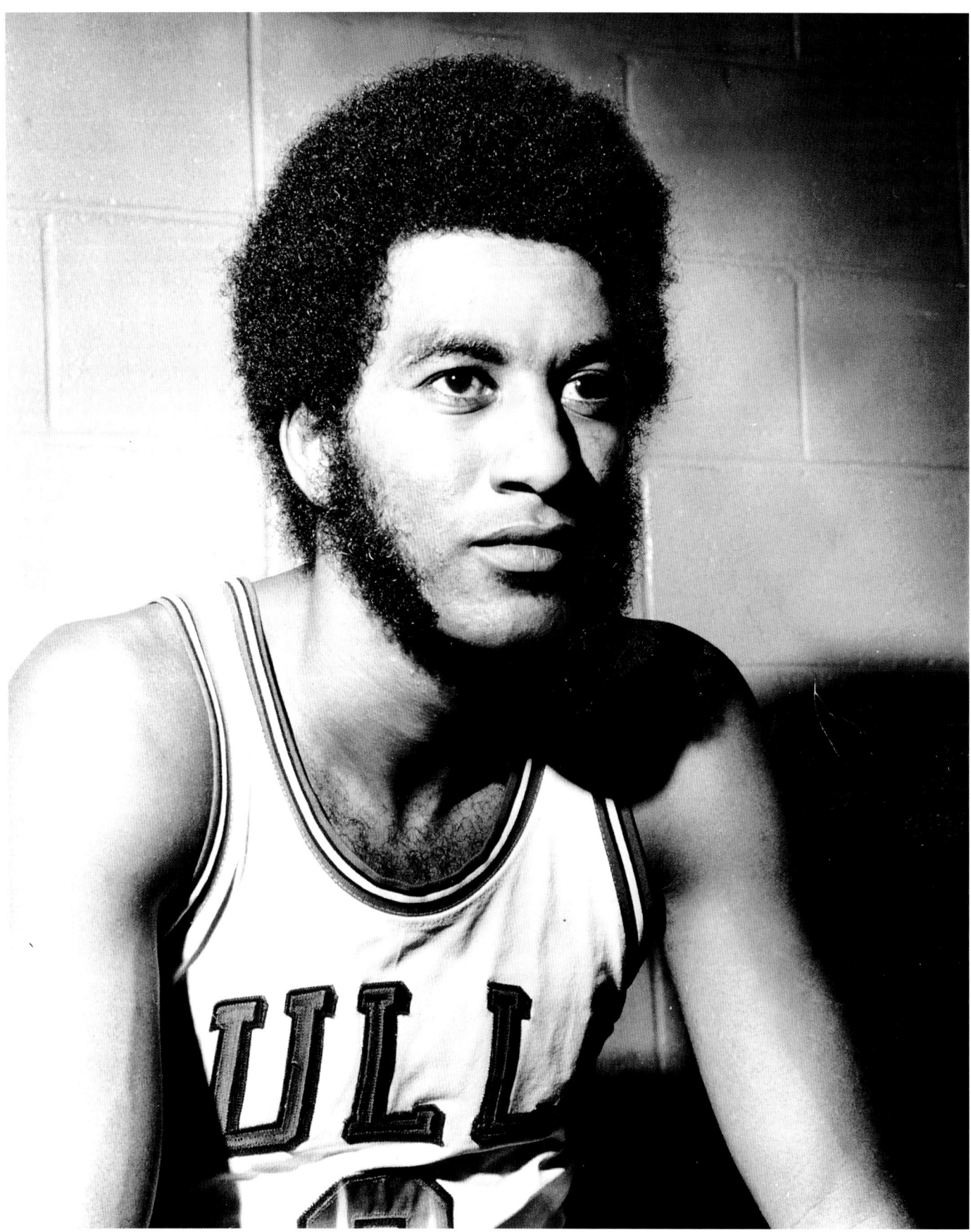

Norm Van Lier

Norm Van Lier, shown at a Chicago Bulls picture day, played for the team throughout the 1970s. The point guard wasn't a superstar, but he was a definite presence on the court.

CHICAGO TRIBUNE HISTORICAL PHOTO, 1972

Jesse Sullivan

Jesse Sullivan stands against a 1953 GMC truck outside his home in Dayton, Tenn. The prosthesis that serves as his left arm is controlled through thought. He was the first person to be outfitted with such a bionic arm at the Rehabilitation Institute of Chicago. He lost his limbs at the shoulders in 2001 after he grabbed a high-tension wire as a lineman for a Tennessee power company.

ZBIGNIEW BZDAK, 2004

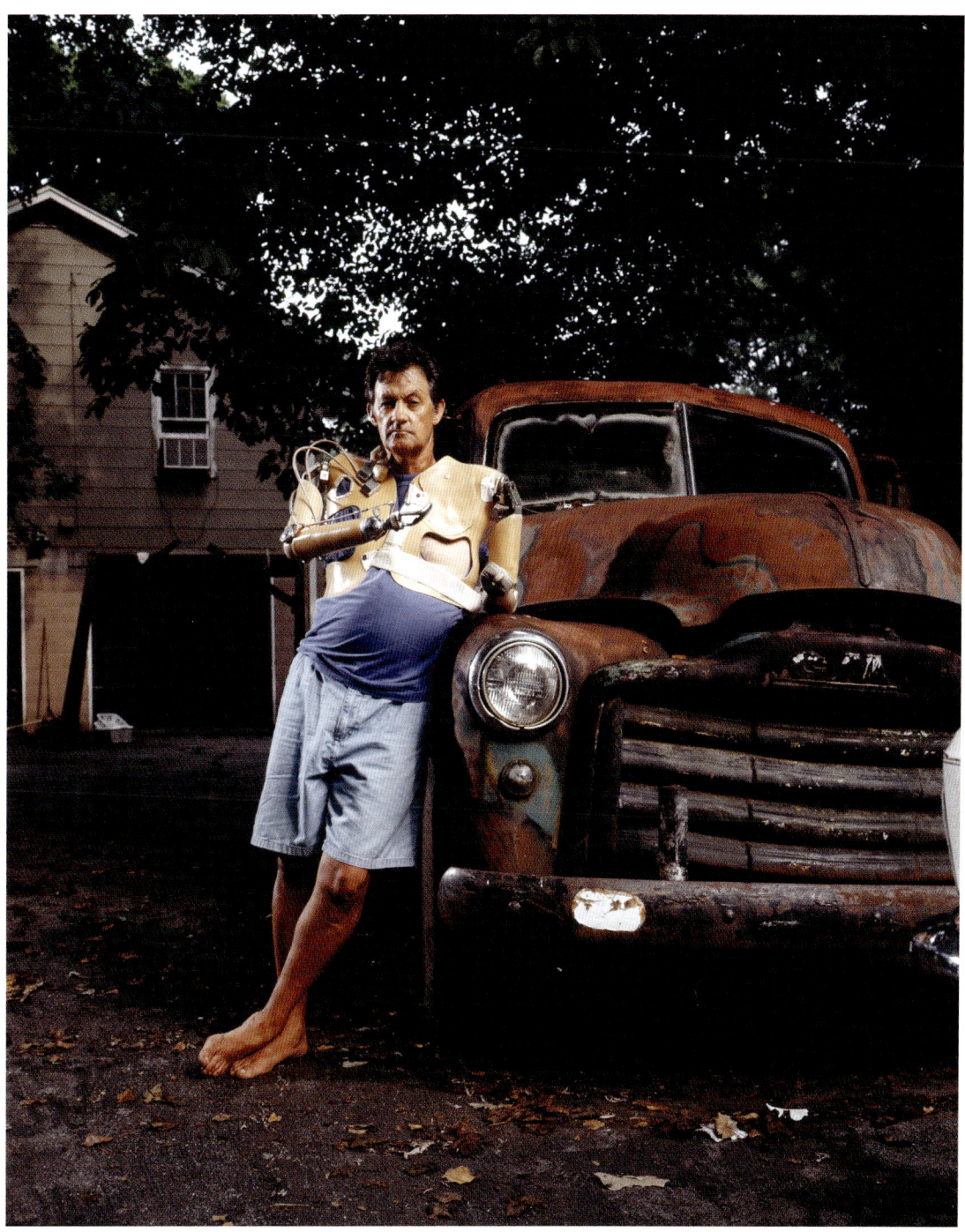

Margaret Marsh

Margaret Marsh, a flapper, in an undated photo. Flappers broke sartorial, sexual and social boundaries in their determination to live on their own terms.

CHICAGO TRIBUNE HISTORICAL PHOTO, 1920s

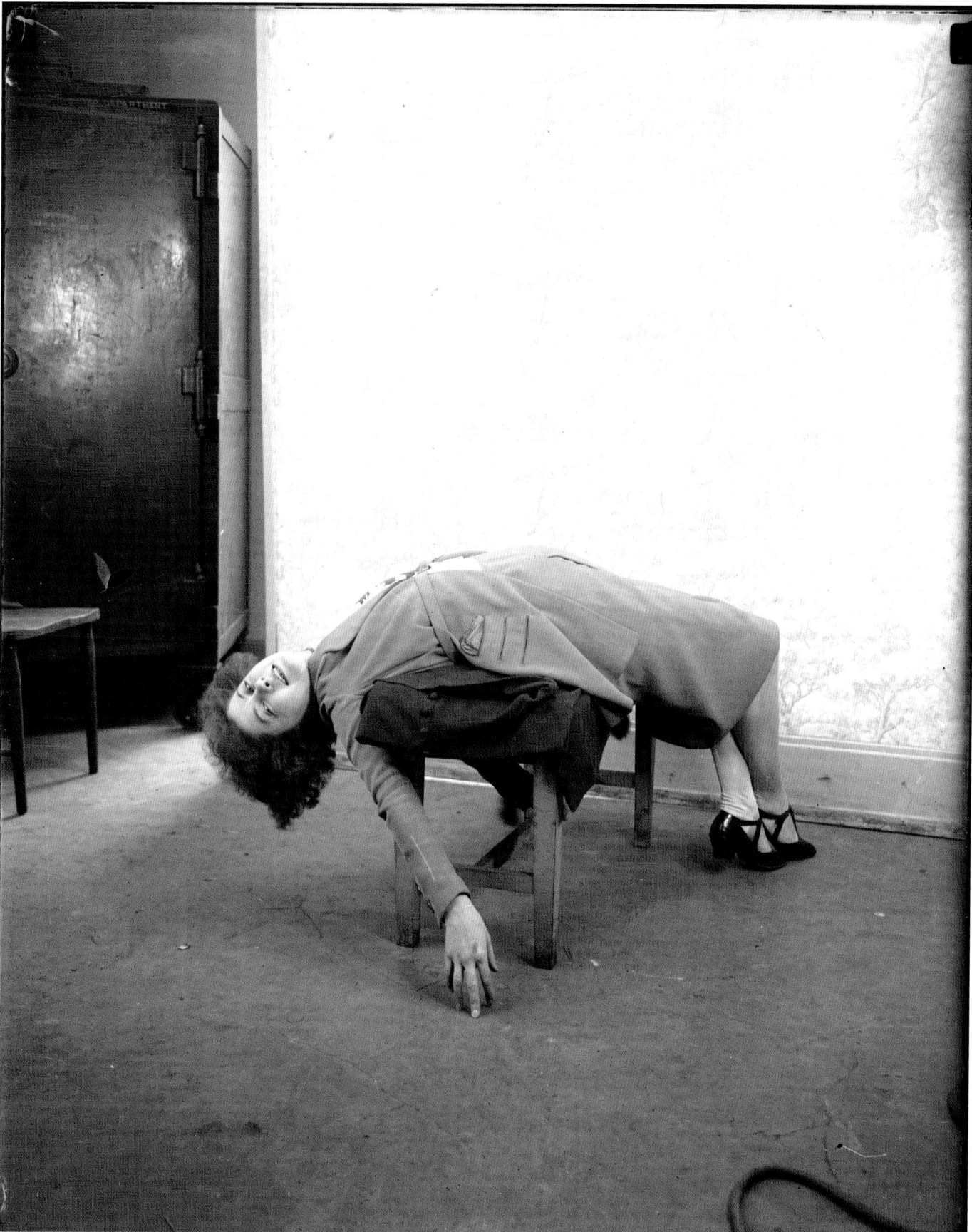

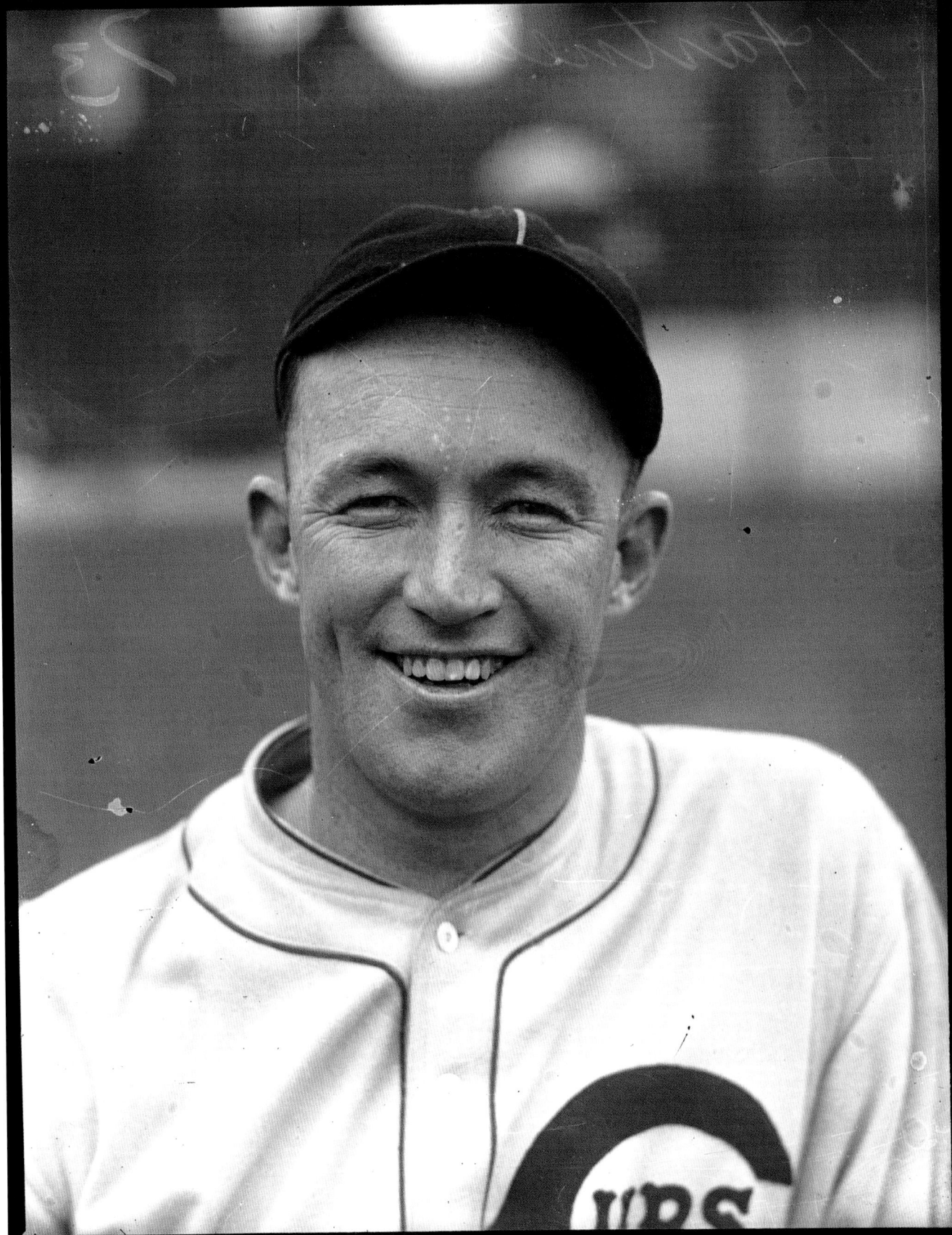

Charles Leo "Gabby" Hartnett

Charles Leo "Gabby" Hartnett played almost his entire major league career as a catcher for the Chicago Cubs. He was inducted into the Baseball Hall of Fame in 1955.

CHICAGO TRIBUNE HISTORICAL PHOTO, 1932

Kurt Perry

Kurt Perry, 26, at home in a Chicago suburb. Perry had to suspend his plans to end his life Feb. 26 because of the legal troubles faced by the Final Exit Network. He had decided to commit suicide because of his severe form of Charcot-Marie-Tooth disease, a neurological disorder. Less than 24 hours before Perry's chosen time, two Final Exit members in Georgia and in Baltimore were arrested, essentially shutting down the volunteer organization. Perry said he didn't want to die without the aid of his guides.

SCOTT STRAZZANTE, 2009

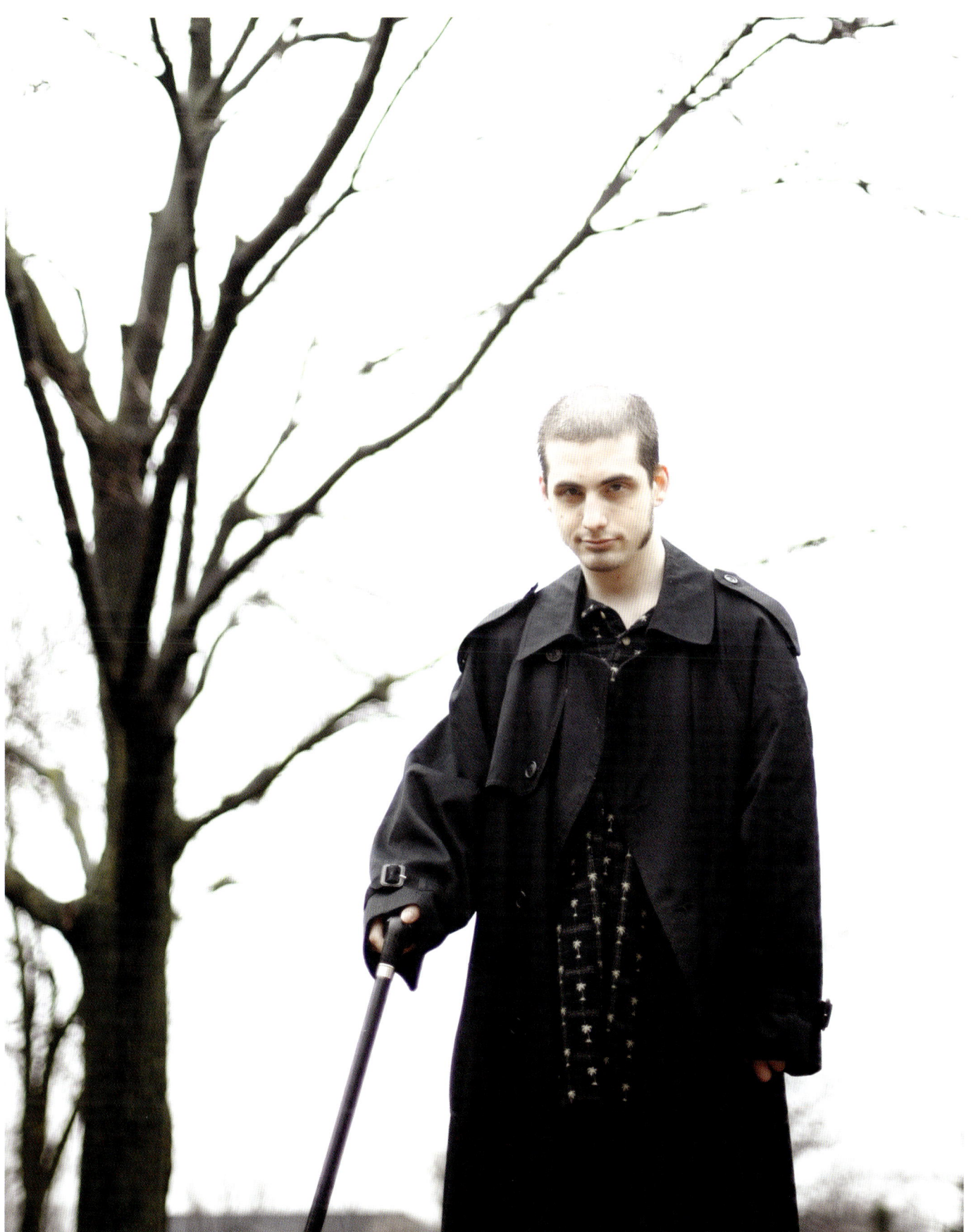

Gary Sinise

Actor-director Gary Sinise stands in front of the Above and Beyond sculpture at the National Veterans Art Museum in Chicago. Dog tags suspended from the ceiling commemorated the more than 58,000 servicemen and women who died in the Vietnam War. Sinise, one of the founders of Chicago's Steppenwolf Theatre Co., was promoting a new documentary he produced, "Brothers at War," directed by a Decatur, Ill., native who embedded with troops in the Middle East to tell his brothers' stories.

E. JASON WAMBSGANS, 2009

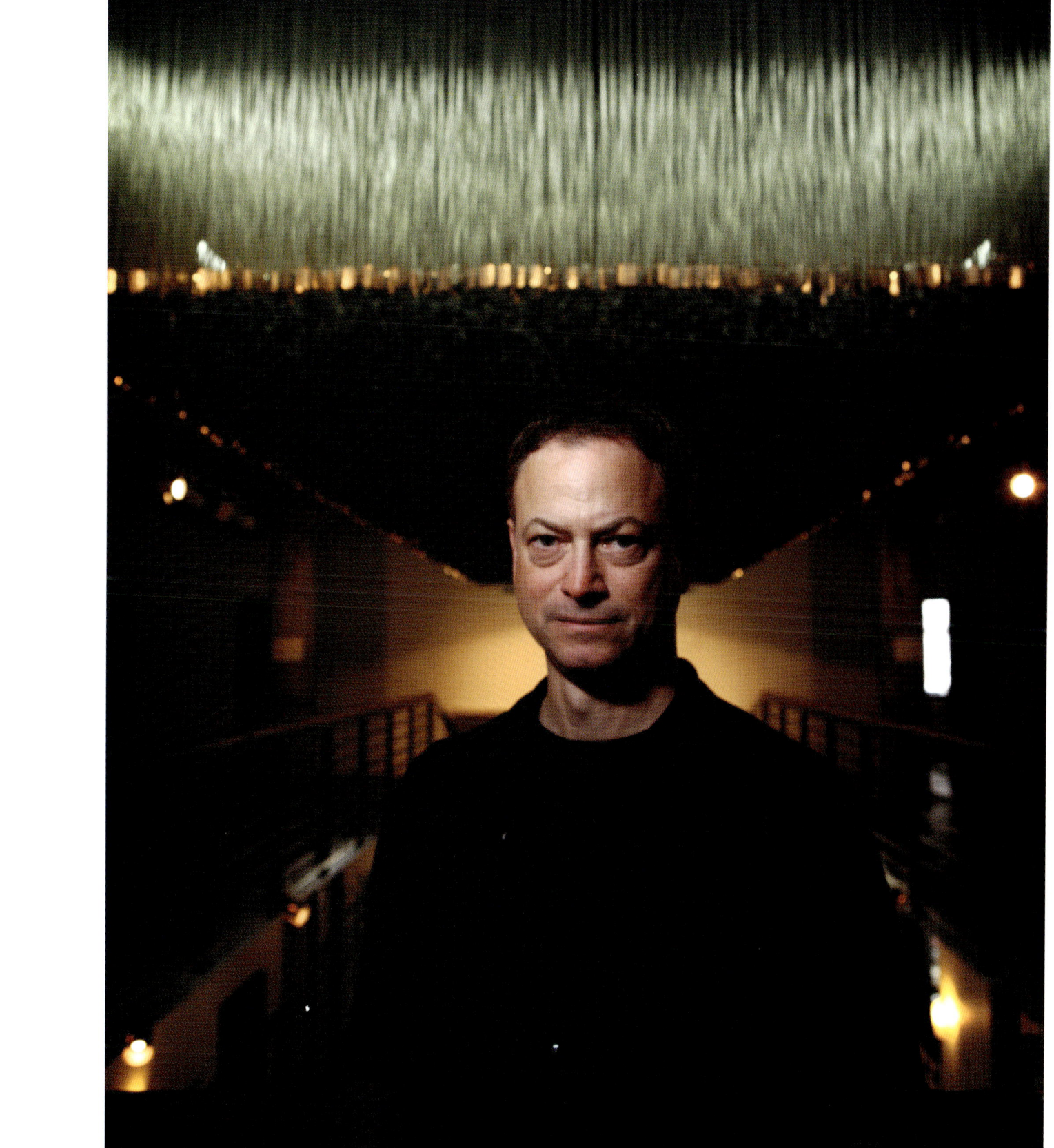

Dick Butkus

Chicago native Dick Butkus, shown in an undated photo, played for the Chicago Bears from 1965 to 1973 and was elected to the Hall of Fame in 1979, his first year of eligibility.

CHICAGO TRIBUNE HISTORICAL PHOTO, UNDATED

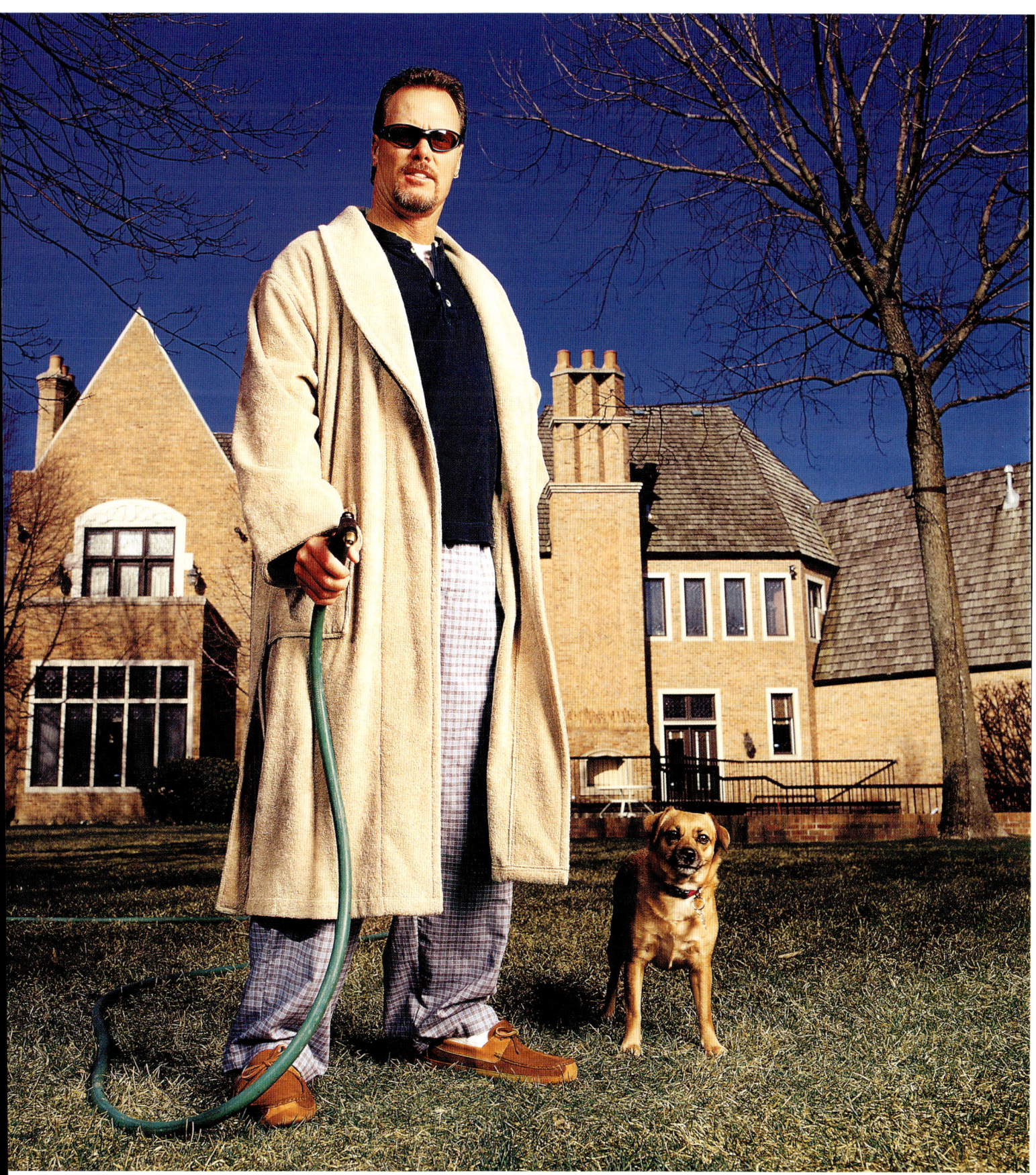

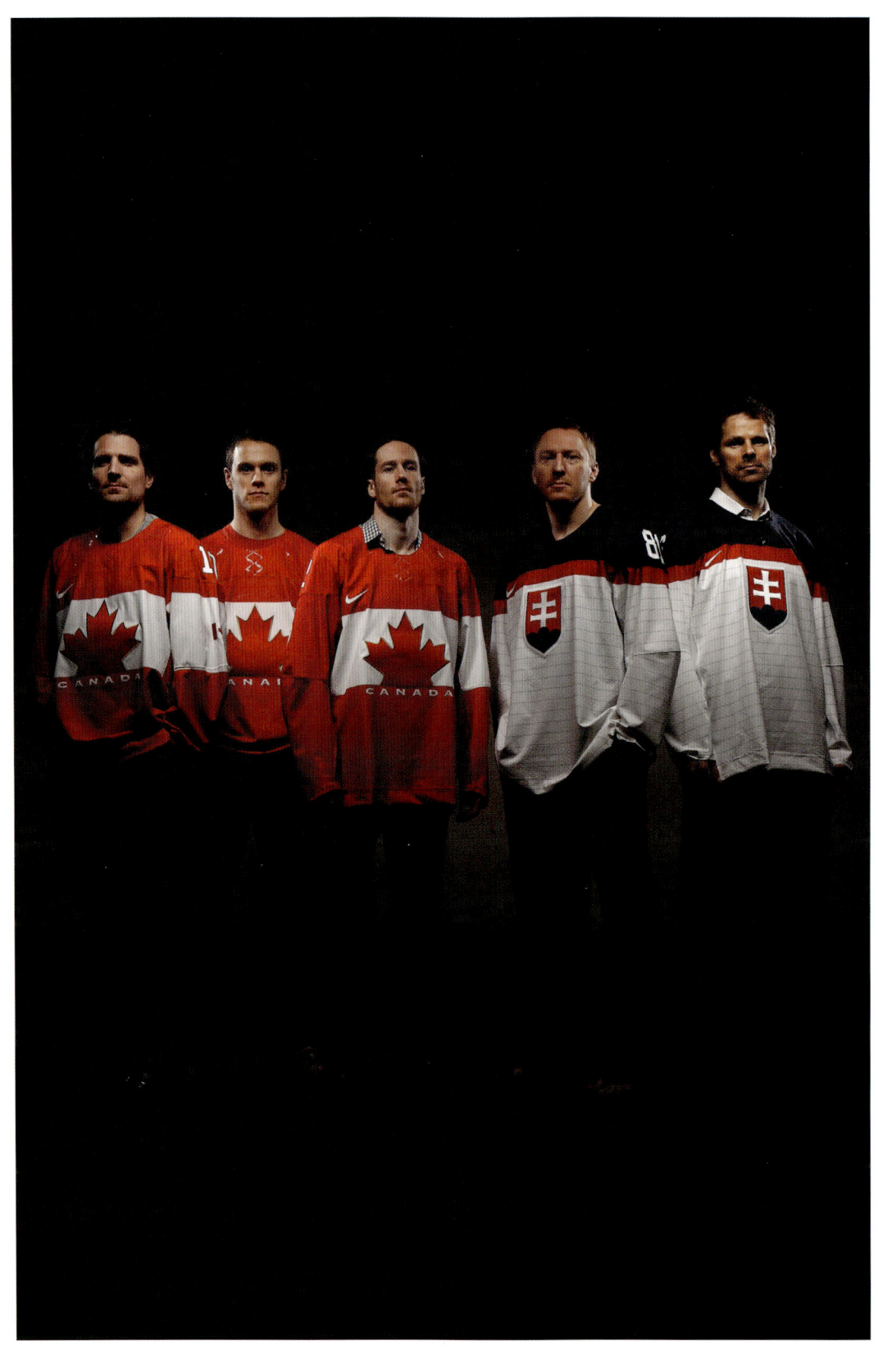

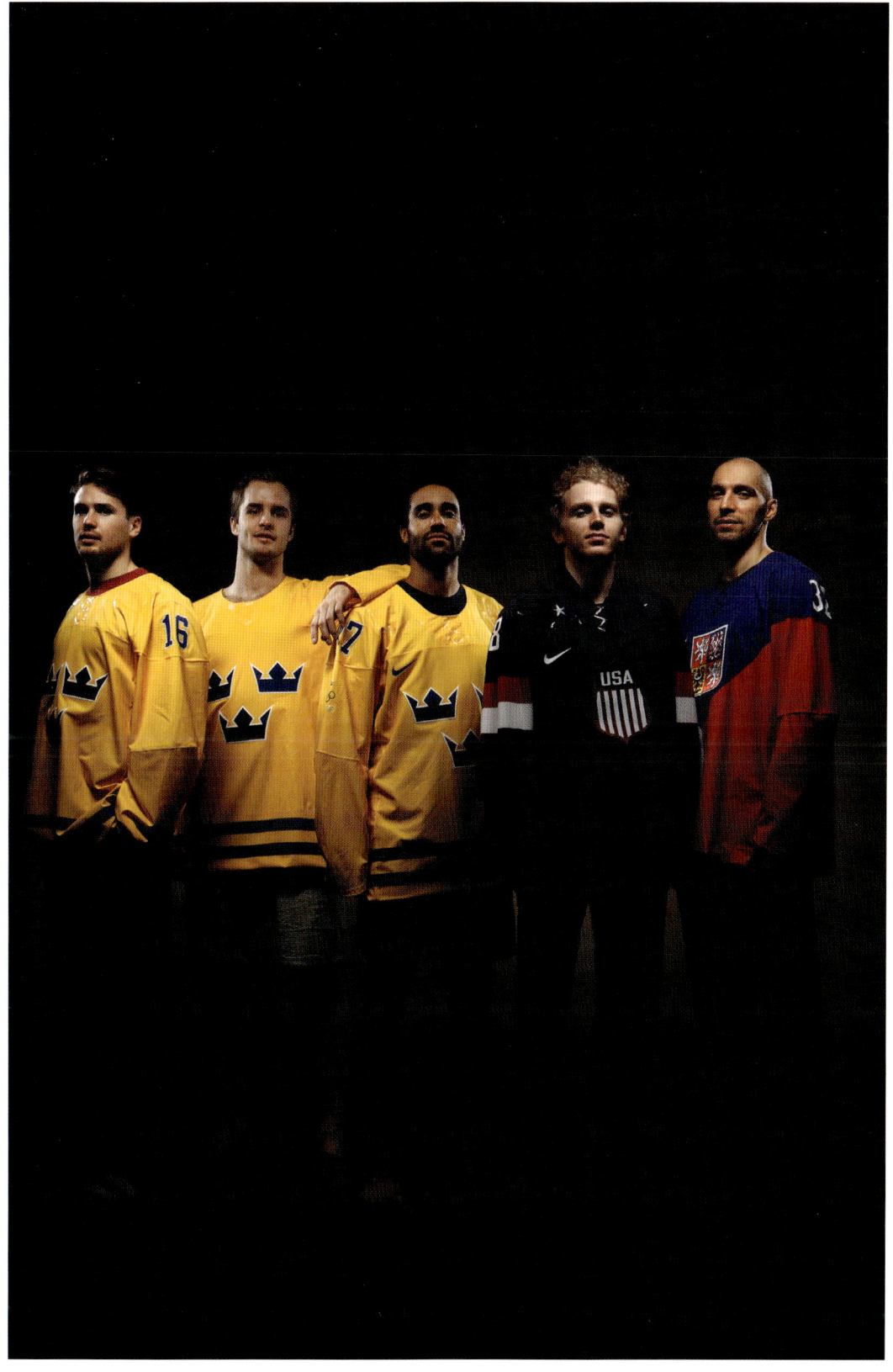

Chicago Blackhawks

Members of the Chicago Blackhawks prepare to represent their nations in the 2014 Sochi Winter Olympics.

OPPOSITE PAGE: From left, Team Canada: Patrick Sharp, Jonathan Toews, Duncan Keith; Team Slovakia: Marian Hossa, Michal Handzus.

THIS PAGE: From left, Team Sweden: Marcus Kruger, Niklas Hjalmarsson, Johnny Oduya; Team U.S.A.: Patrick Kane. Team Czech Republic: Michal Rozsival.

E. JASON WAMBSGANS, MICHAEL TERCHA 2014

Ron Santo

Chicago Cubs player Ron Santo cools down at spring training in Arizona in 1968. Santo finished his career with 342 home runs and a .277 batting average. A nine-time All-Star, Santo also won five Gold Gloves in 14 seasons with the Cubs. He played his final season with the White Sox.

CHICAGO TRIBUNE HISTORICAL PHOTO, 1968

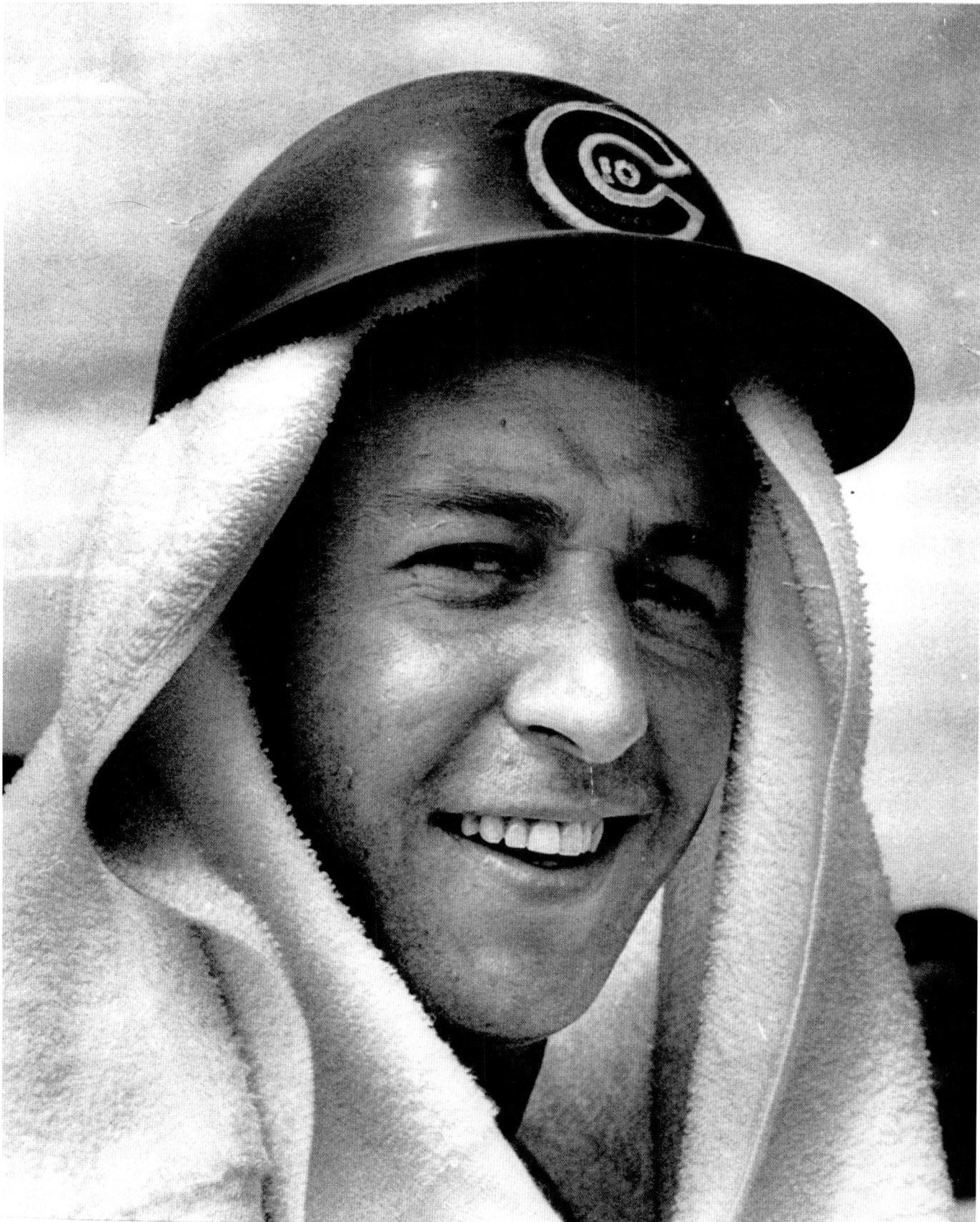

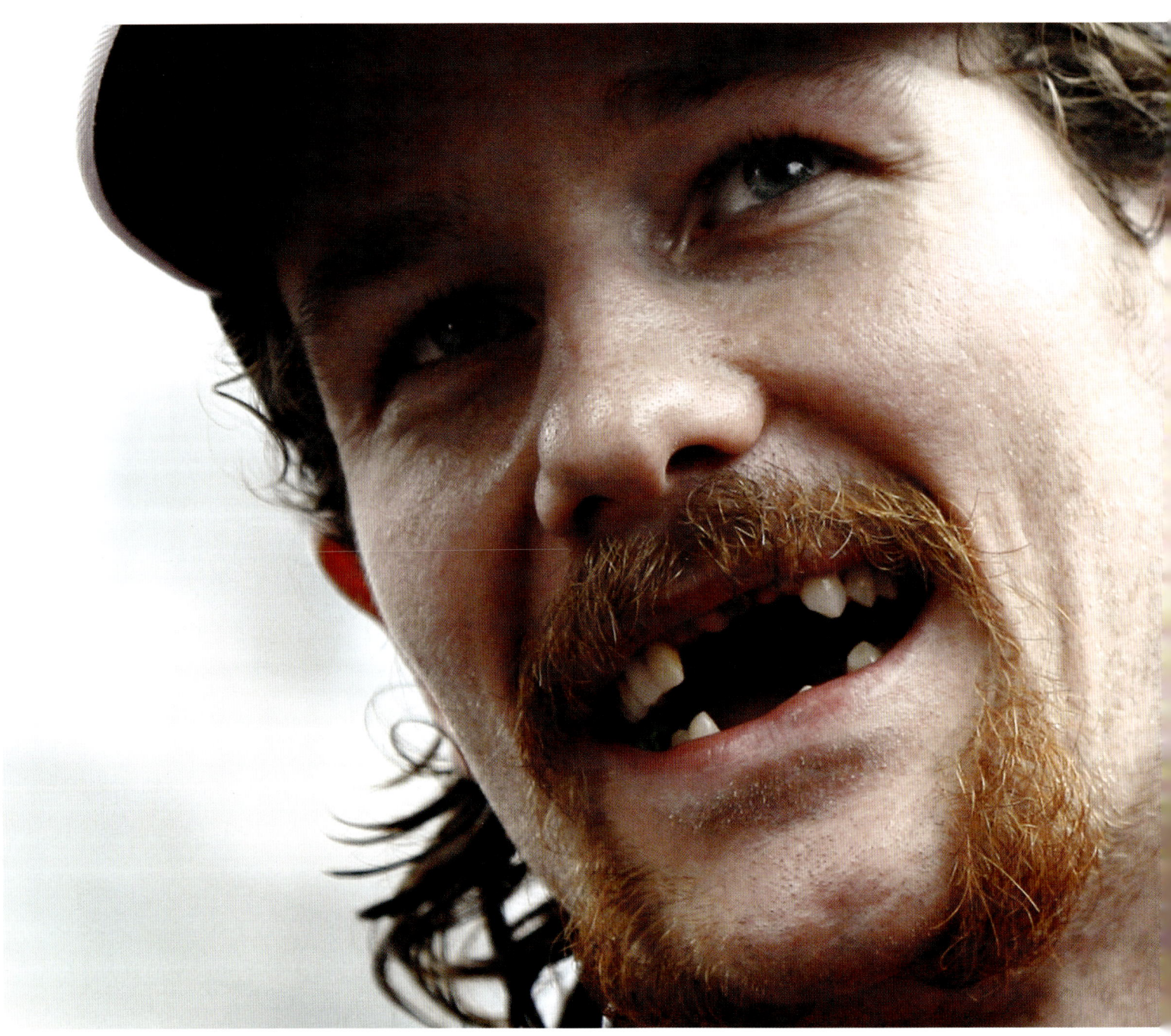

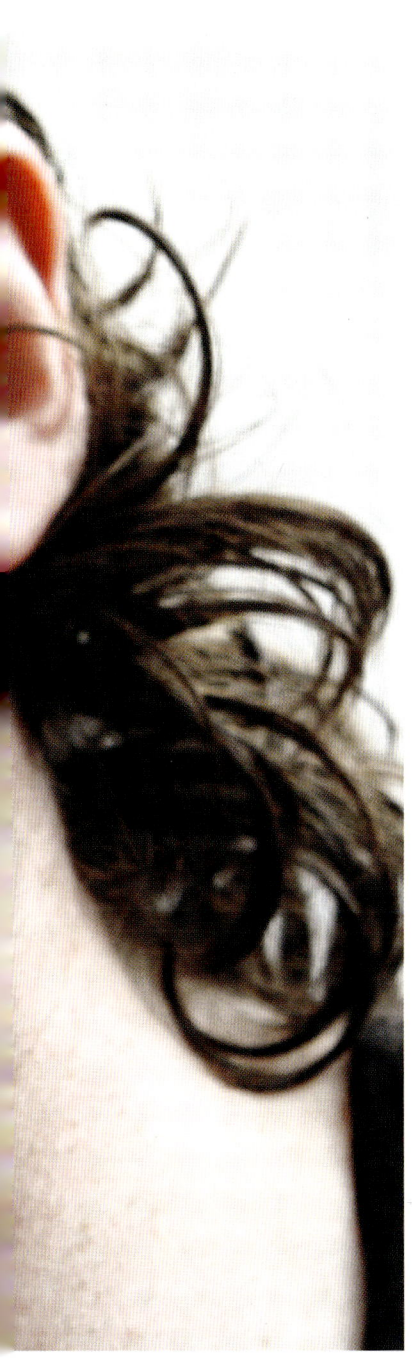

Duncan Keith

Player Duncan Keith smiles during the Chicago Blackhawks Stanley Cup victory rally in Chicago. The win gave the team its first NHL title since 1961.

BRIAN CASSELLA, 2010

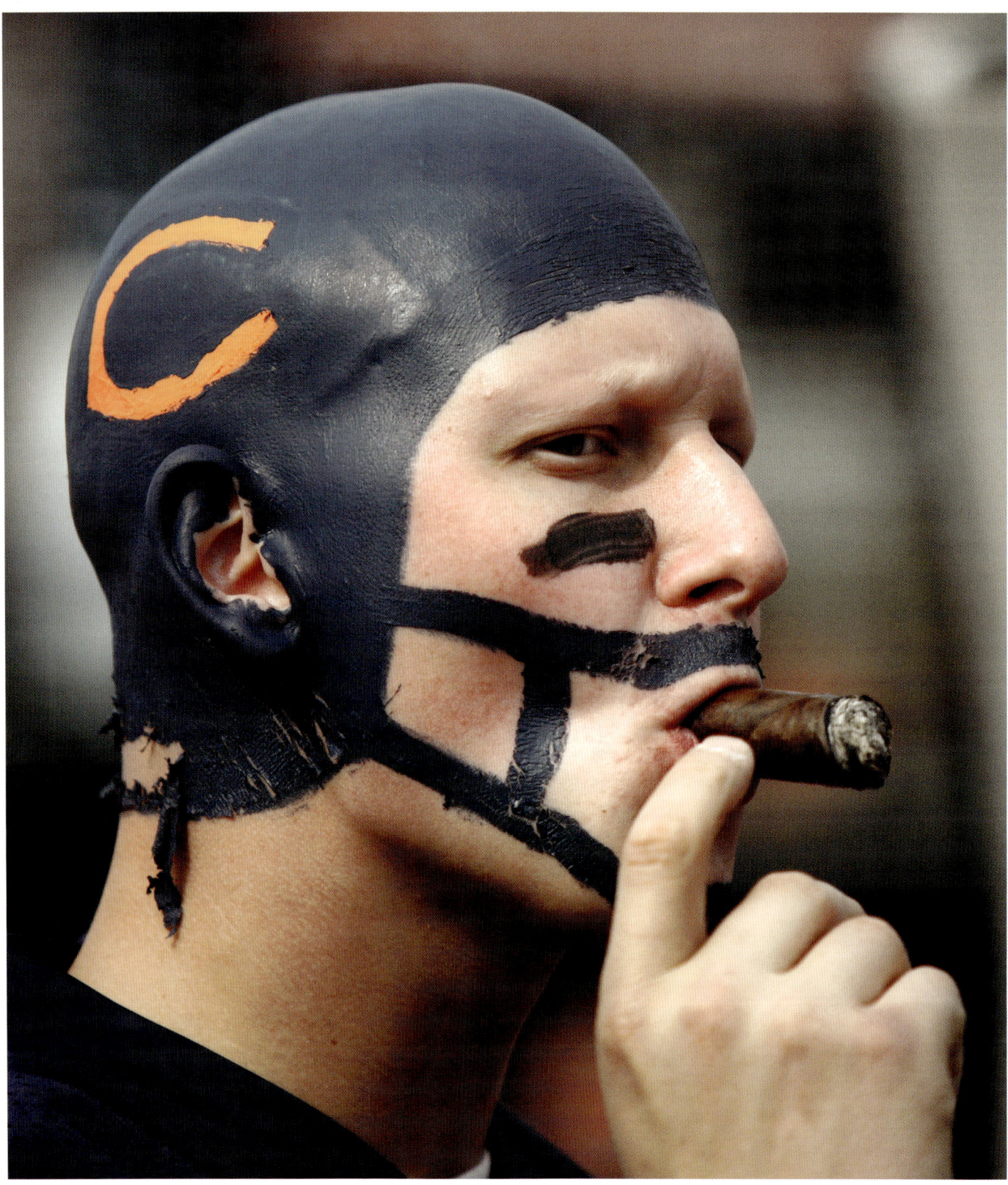

Kevin Bozelka

Kevin Bozelka sports a painted-on helmet before the Chicago Bears game against the Cincinnati Bengals at Paul Brown Stadium in Cincinnati.

BRIAN CASSELLA, 2009

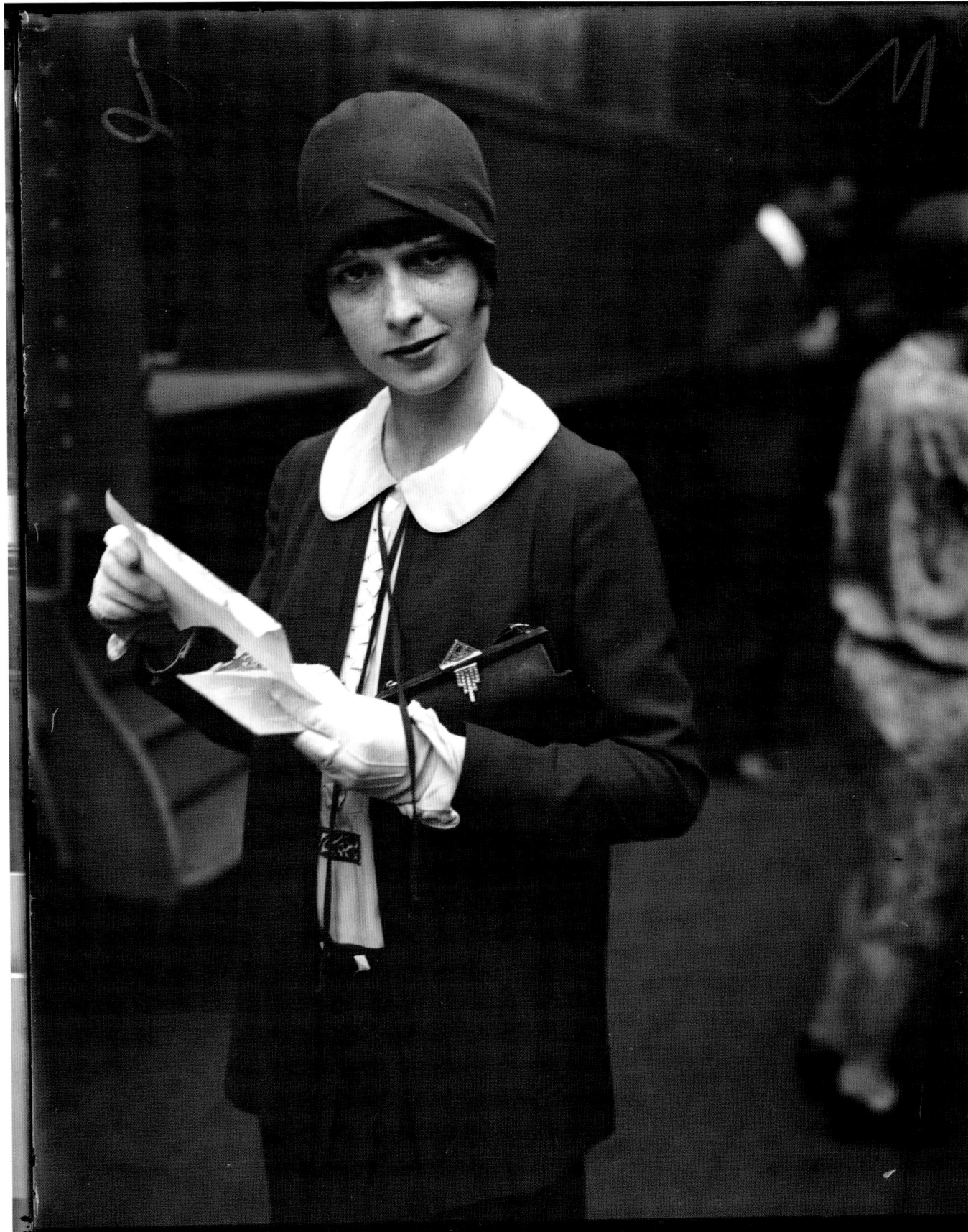

Louise Brooks

Film icon Louise Brooks was a trendsetter with her bobbed hairstyle. She commanded leading roles in films such as Howard Hawks' 1928 "A Girl in Every Port."

CHICAGO TRIBUNE HISTORICAL PHOTO, 1928

Jeremy Allen White

Jeremy Allen White, who stars in Showtime's "Shameless," stops for a burger in Chicago's Ukrainian Village neighborhood. He's particularly partial to burgers at Kuma's Corner on the Northwest Side when he's in town to shoot exterior scenes for the cable series.

ABEL URIBE, 2012

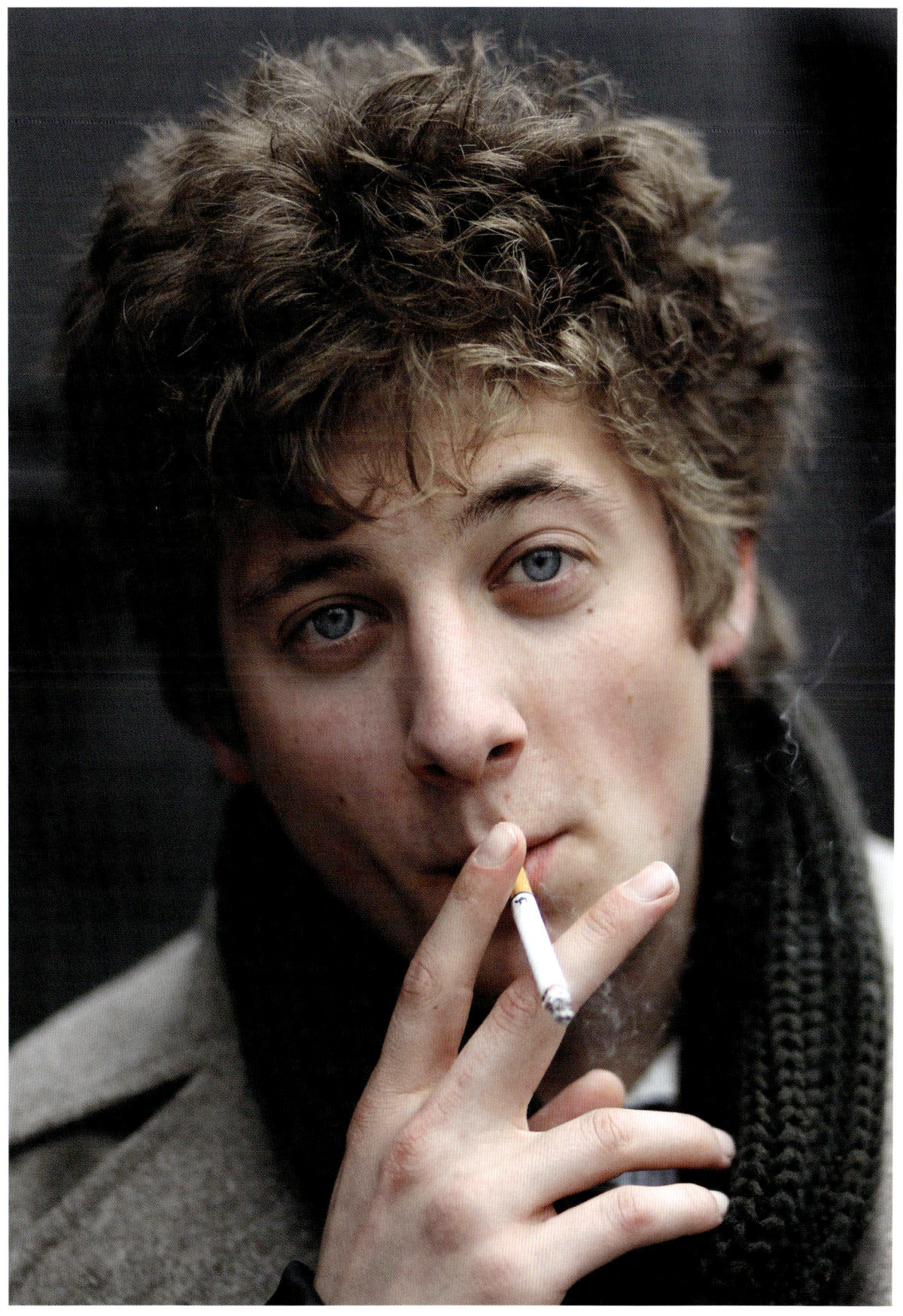

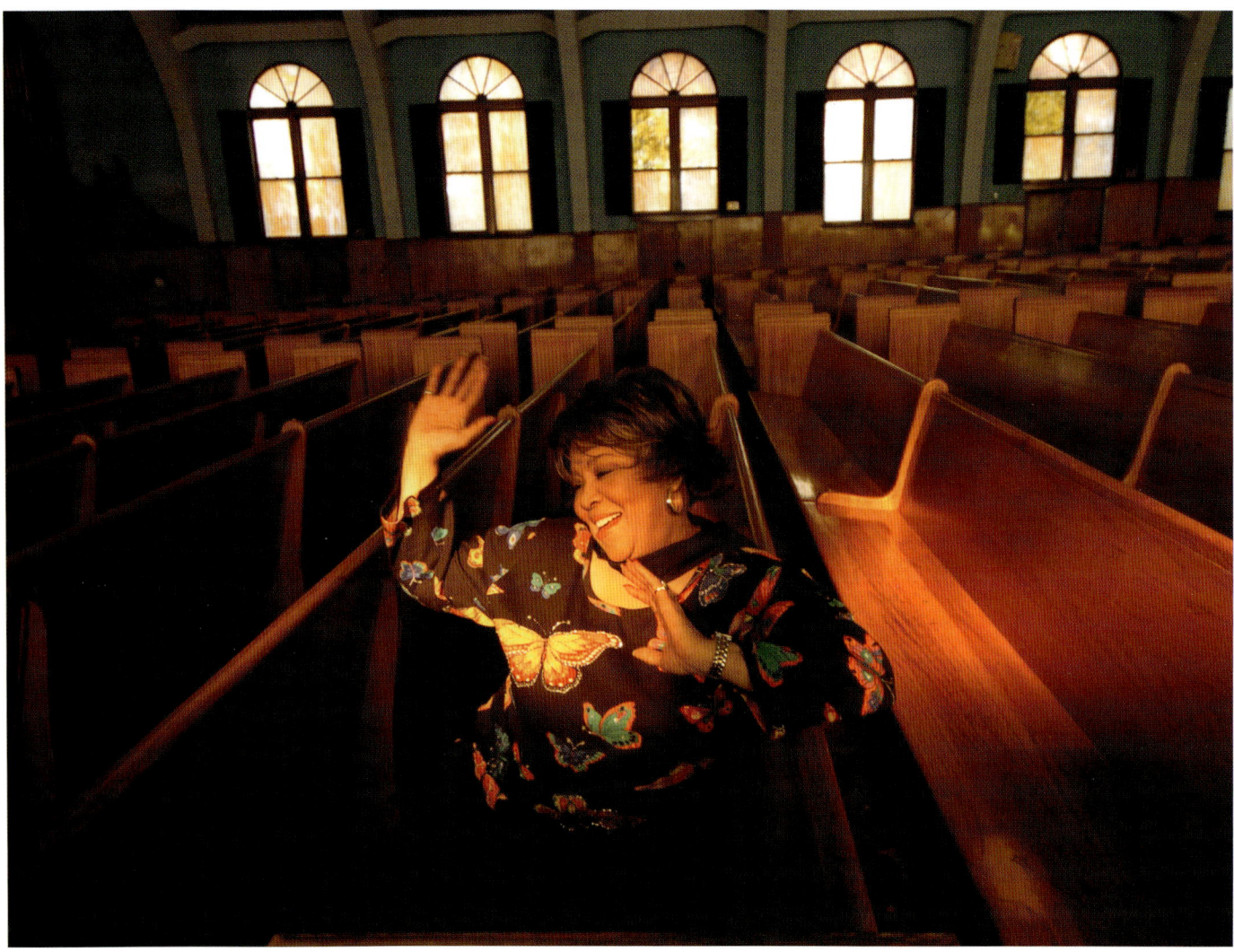

Mavis Staples

Tabernacle Baptist Church is a place of great significance to singer Mavis Staples. She once sang at the church with fellow gospel singer Mahalia Jackson. The Chicago native first came to fame as a member of The Staples Singers.

NANCY STONE, 2004

Dennis Farina

Dennis Farina, shown in Chicago's Lincoln Park neighborhood, was a Chicago police officer when he was hired in 1978 to help advise film director Michael Mann on the cops-and-robbers tale "Thief." Mann liked Farina so much that he wrote a small role for him, launching Farina's 30-plus-year career as an actor.

VAL MAZZENGA, 1988

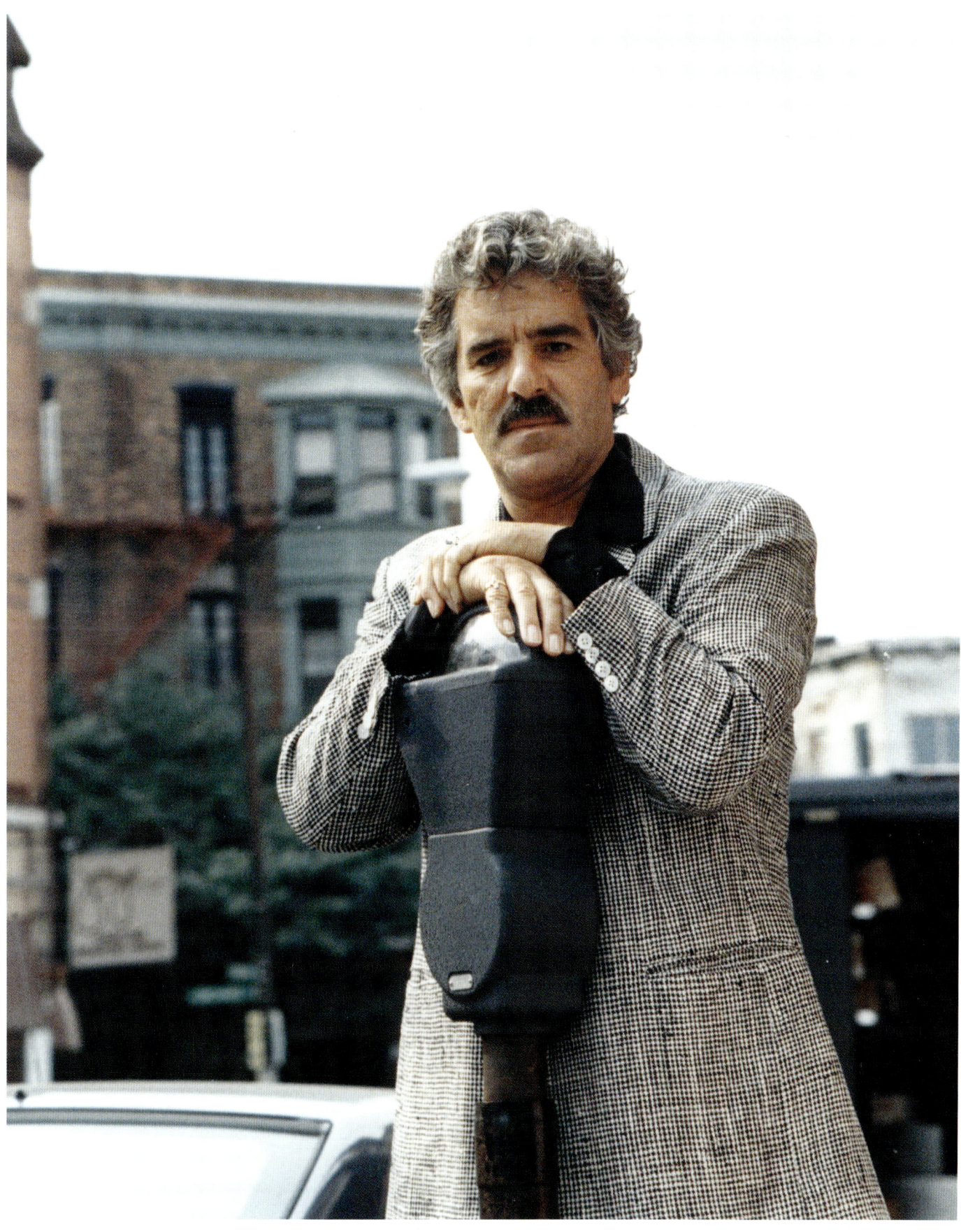

Bobby Rush

Before Bobby Rush became a congressman representing Illinois, he led the Black Panther party of Illinois.

CHICAGO TRIBUNE HISTORICAL PHOTO, 1970

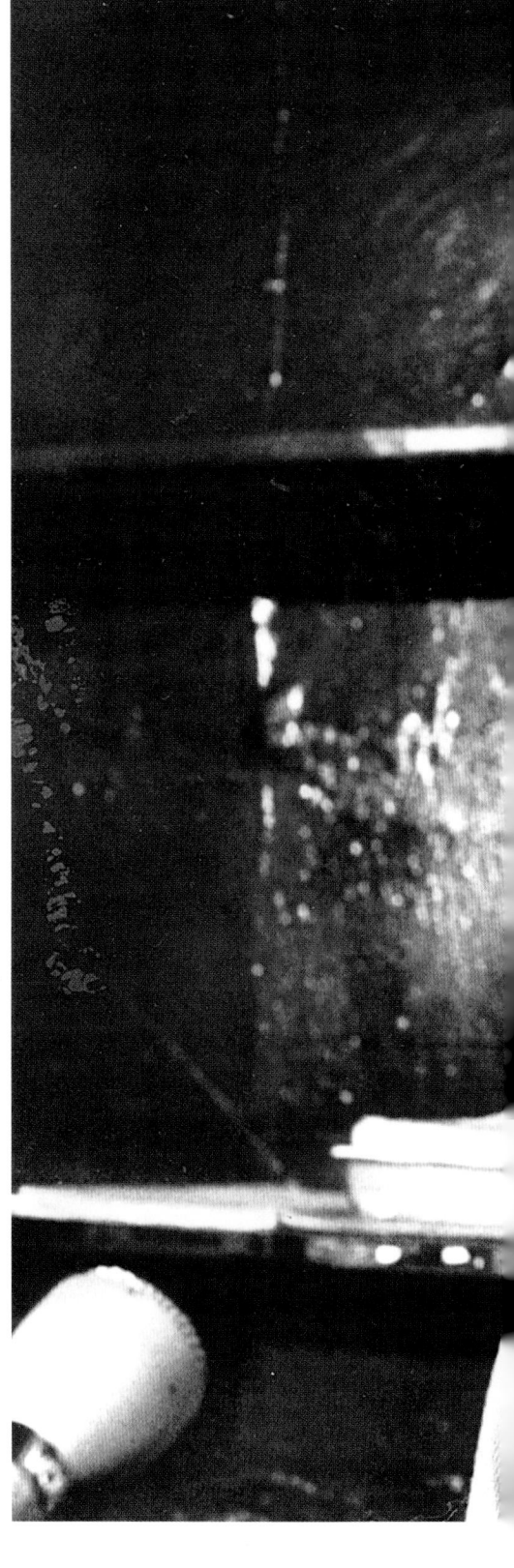

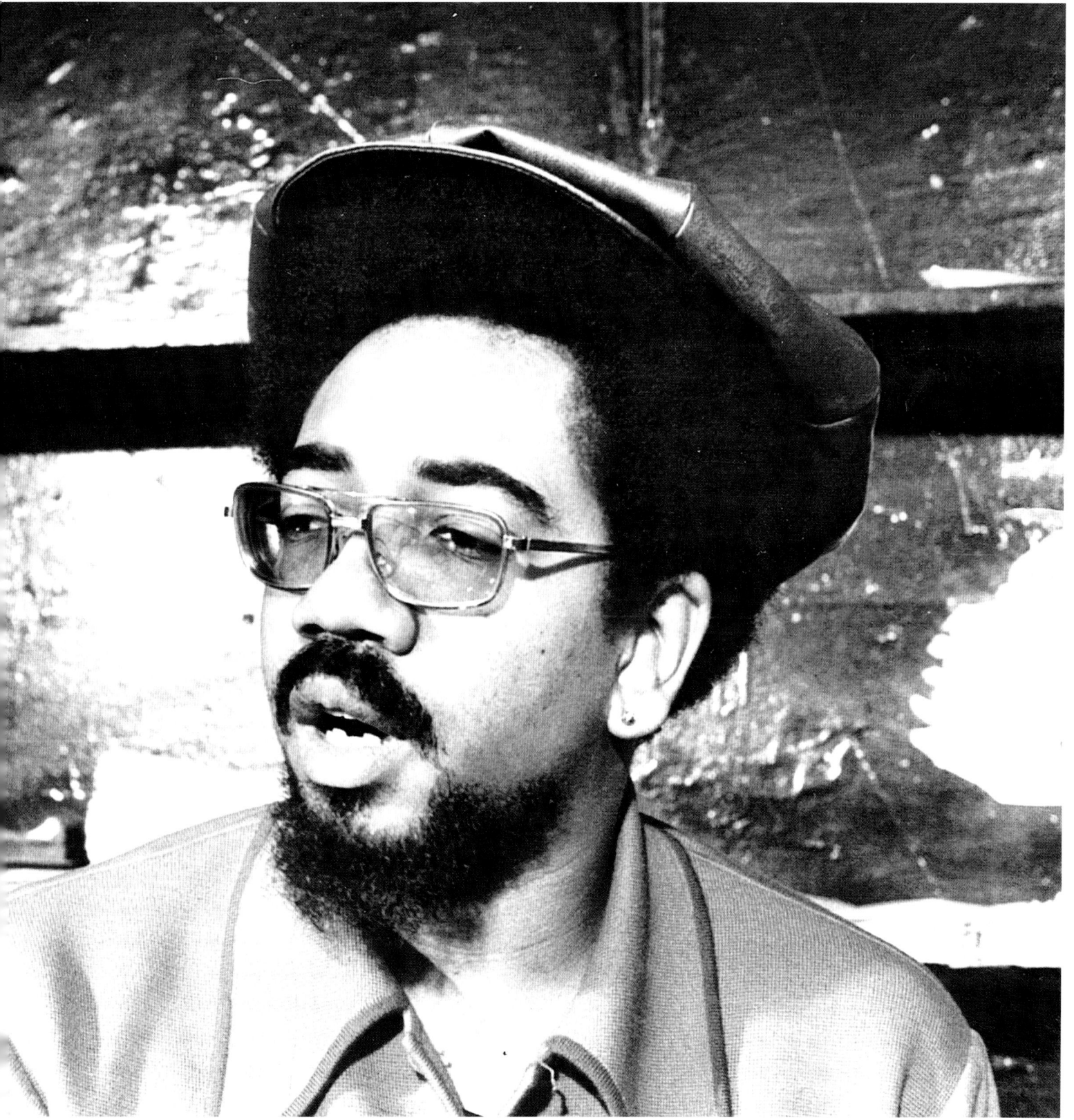

Barack Obama

Then-U.S. Sen. Barack Obama, D-Ill., a former Illinois state senator and Chicago community organizer, won the presidential election that year, becoming the nation's first black president.

CHRIS WALKER, 2008

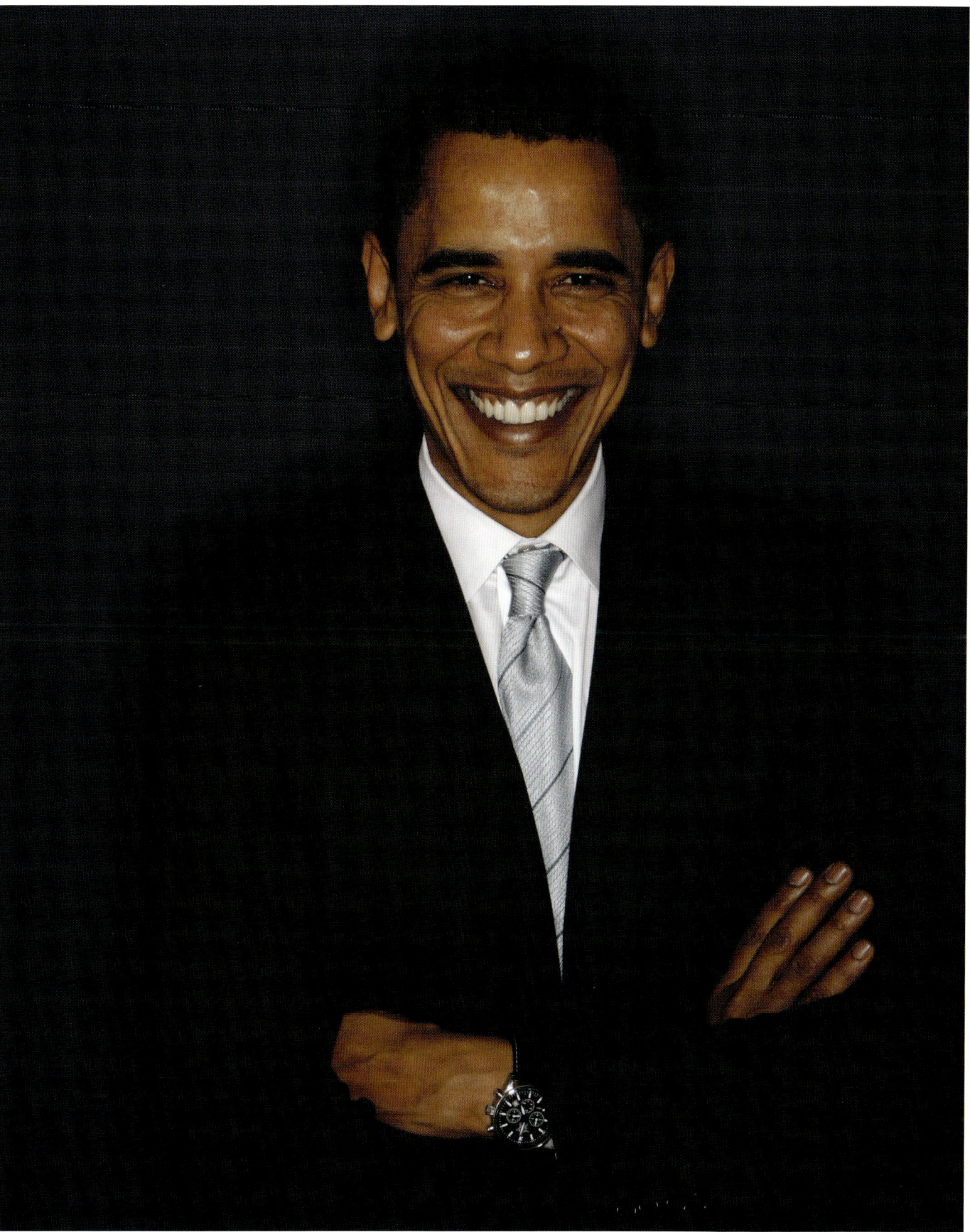

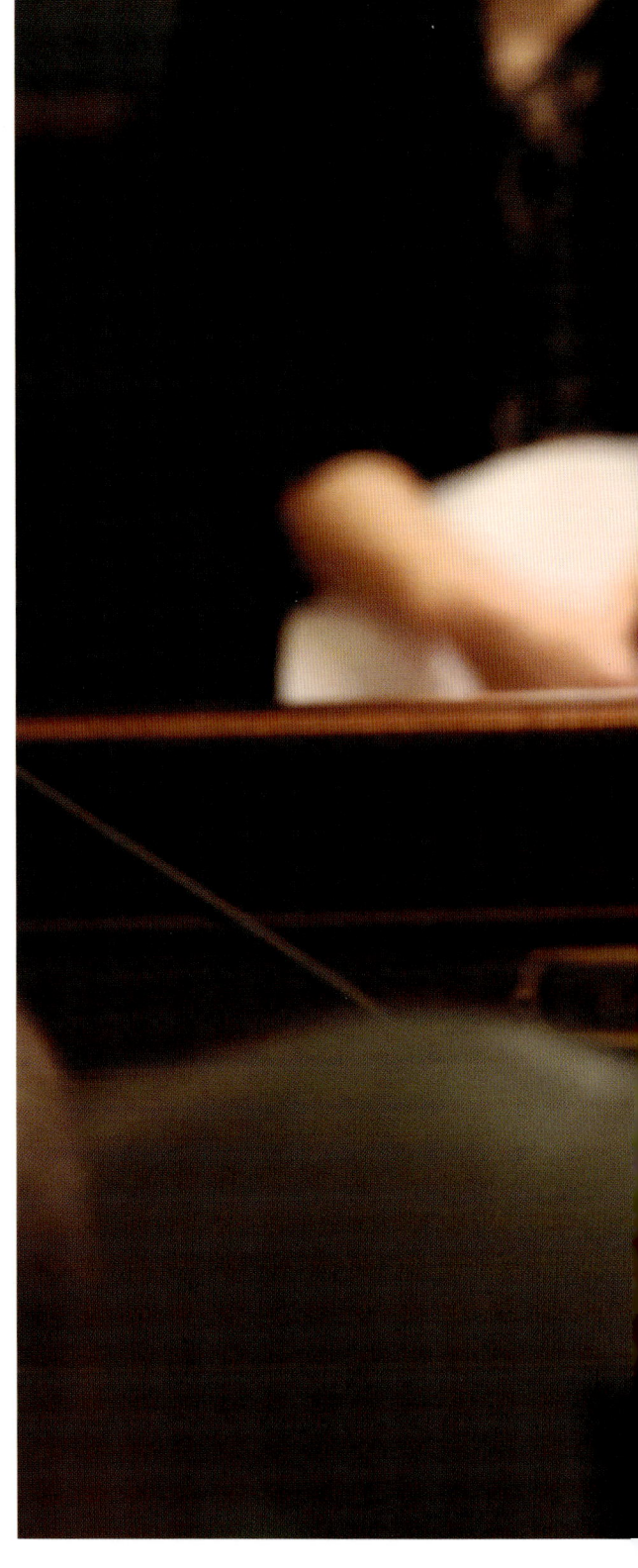

Michael Madigan

Longtime Illinois House Speaker Michael Madigan listens in the House chambers at the Capitol in Springfield. The Chicago Democrat is Illinois' most influential politician.

ZBIGNIEW BZDAK, 2013

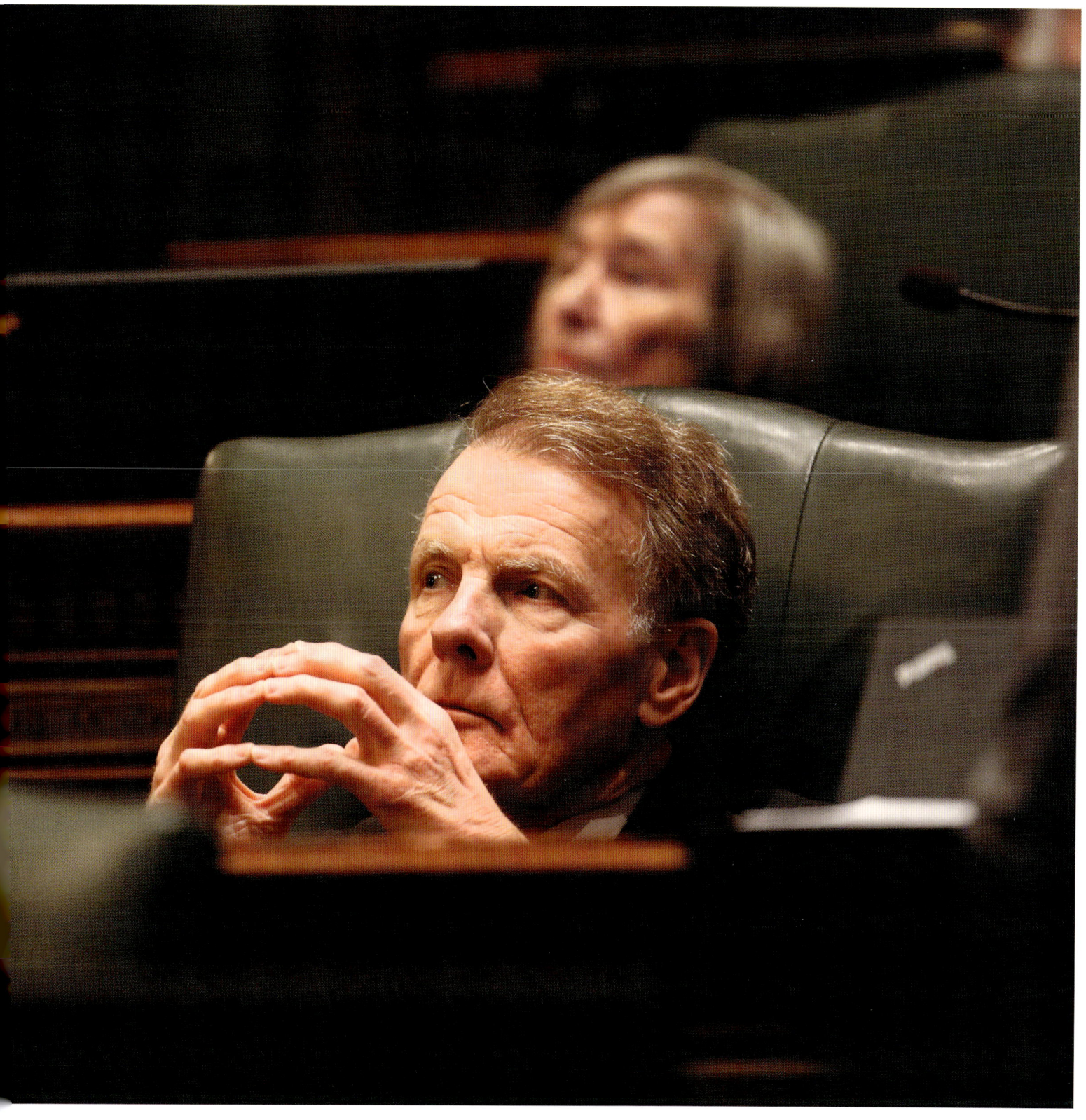

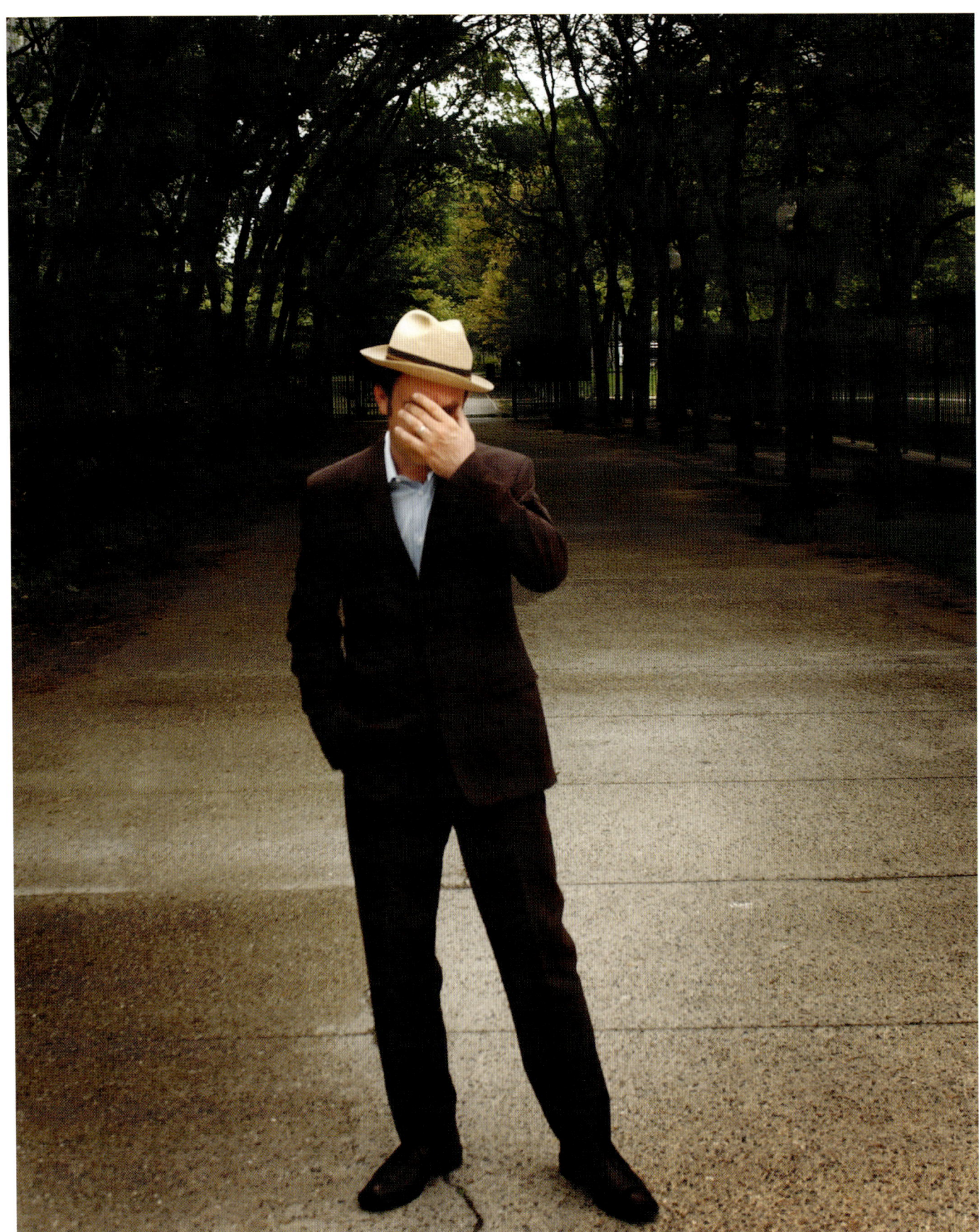

John C. Reilly

Actor John C. Reilly poses for a portrait while promoting his film "Criminal." Reilly was born and raised on Chicago's South Side.

E. JASON WAMBSGANS, 2004

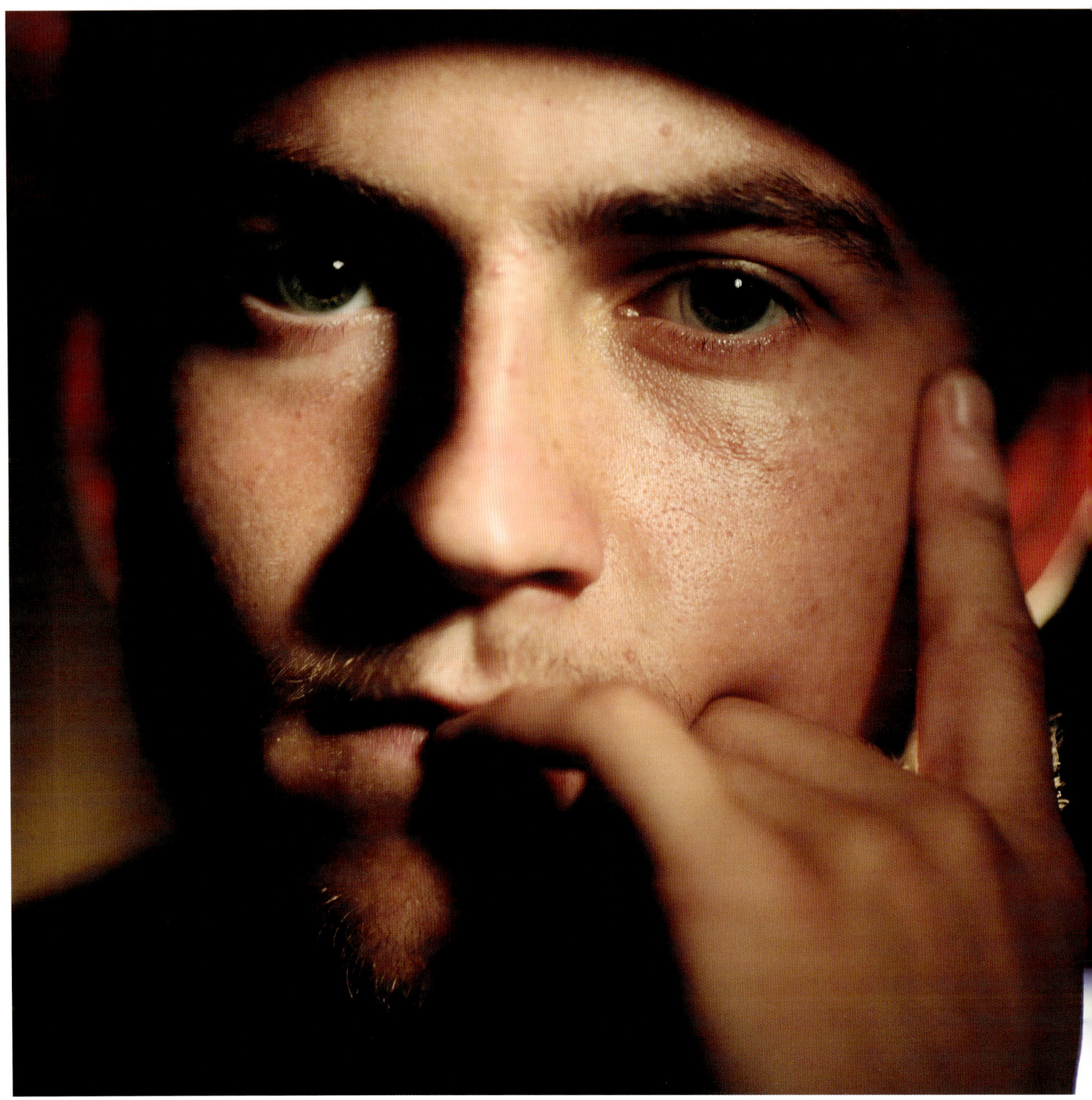

Clancy McCartney

Stage actor Clancy McCartney, shown at Chicago's Steep Theatre, left a lasting impression as a hyperaggressive bully in Steep's production of "The Knowledge." The Tribune declared him one of the hot new faces of Chicago theater in 2013.

ANTHONY SOUFFLE, 2013

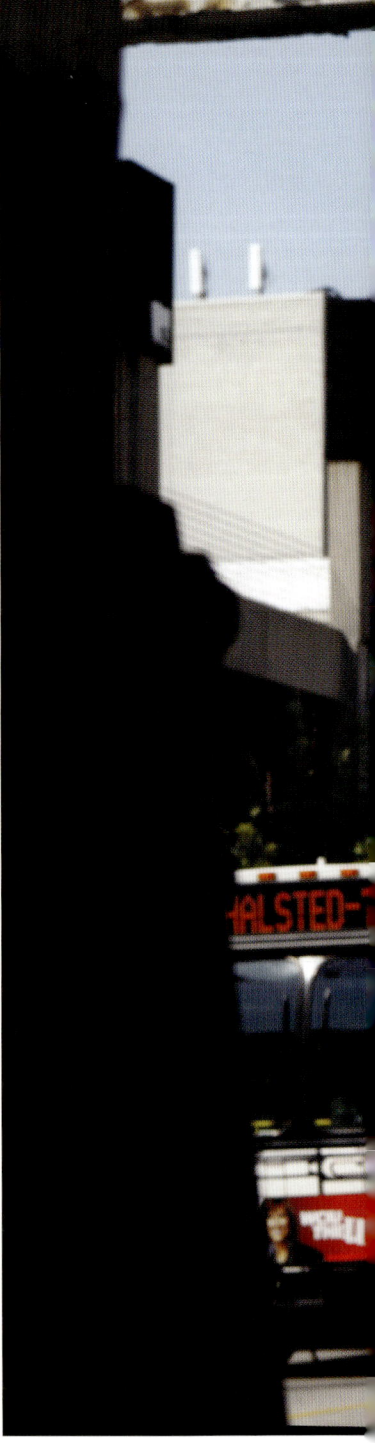

Tracy Letts

Playwright Tracy Letts stands outside Chicago's Steppenwolf Theatre, where his Pulitzer Prize- and Tony Award-winning play "August: Osage County" premiered in 2007. The searing multigenerational tale about a family was turned into a 2013 film that earned two acting Oscar nominations.

ALEX GARCIA, 2009

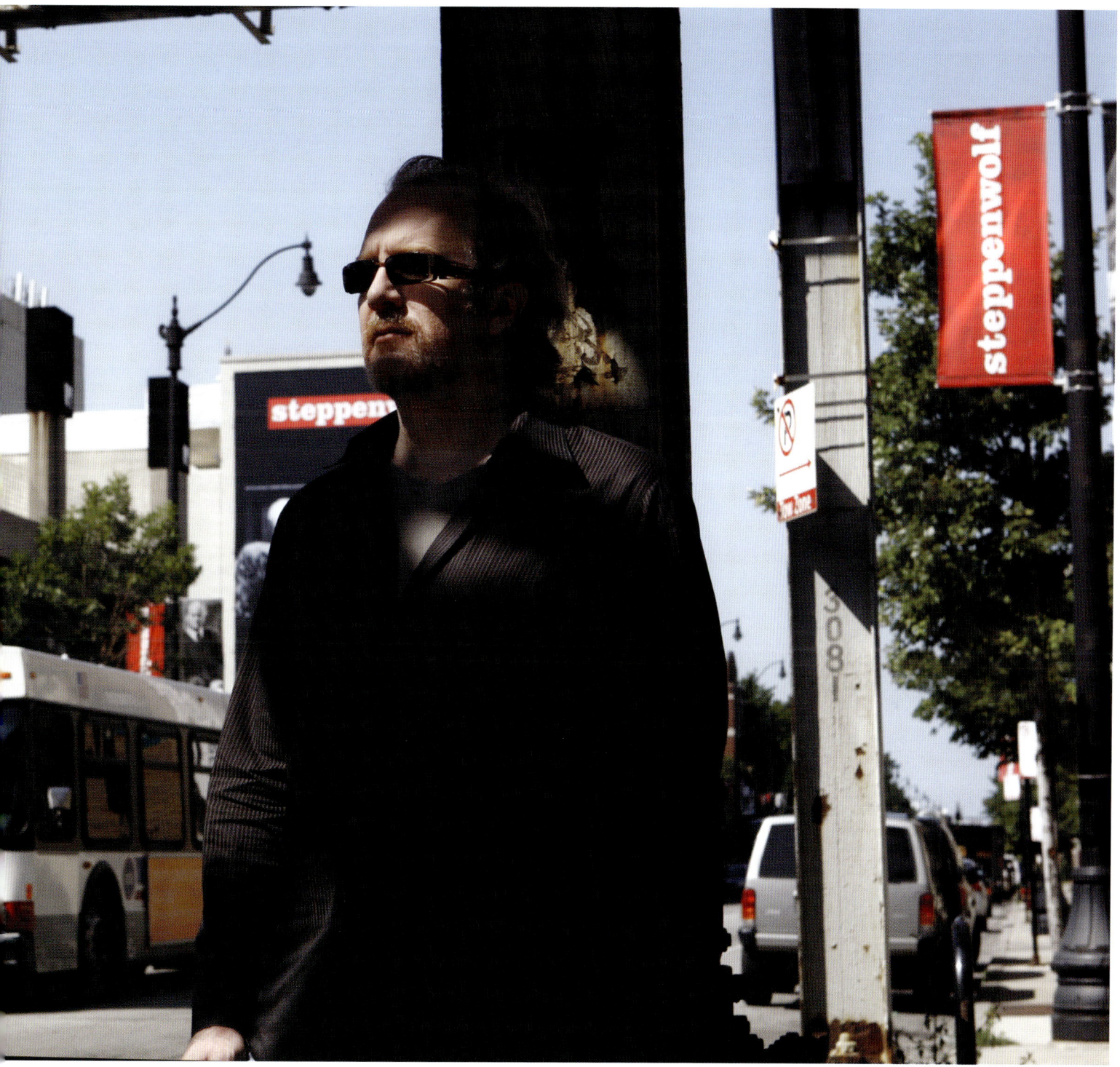

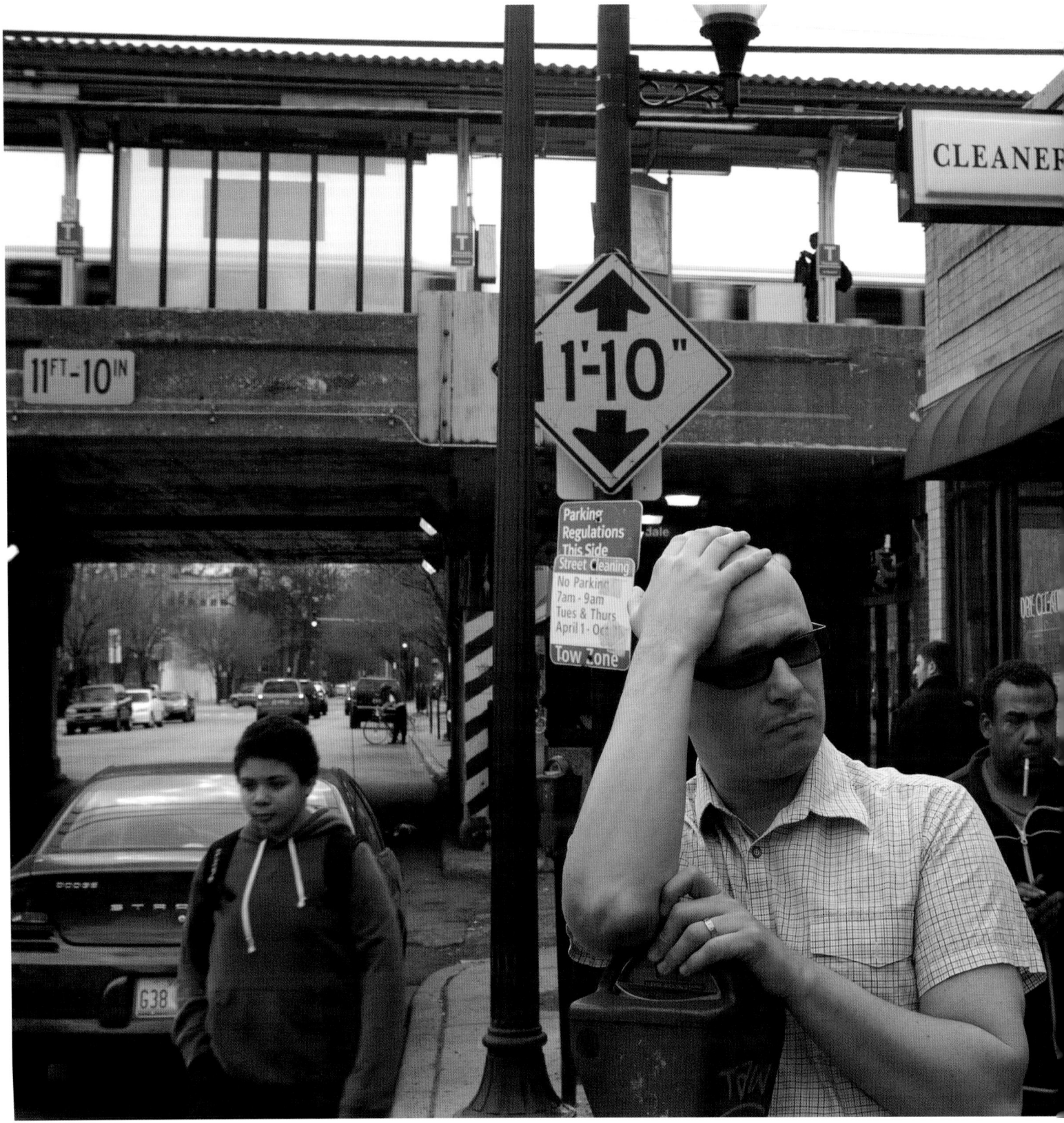

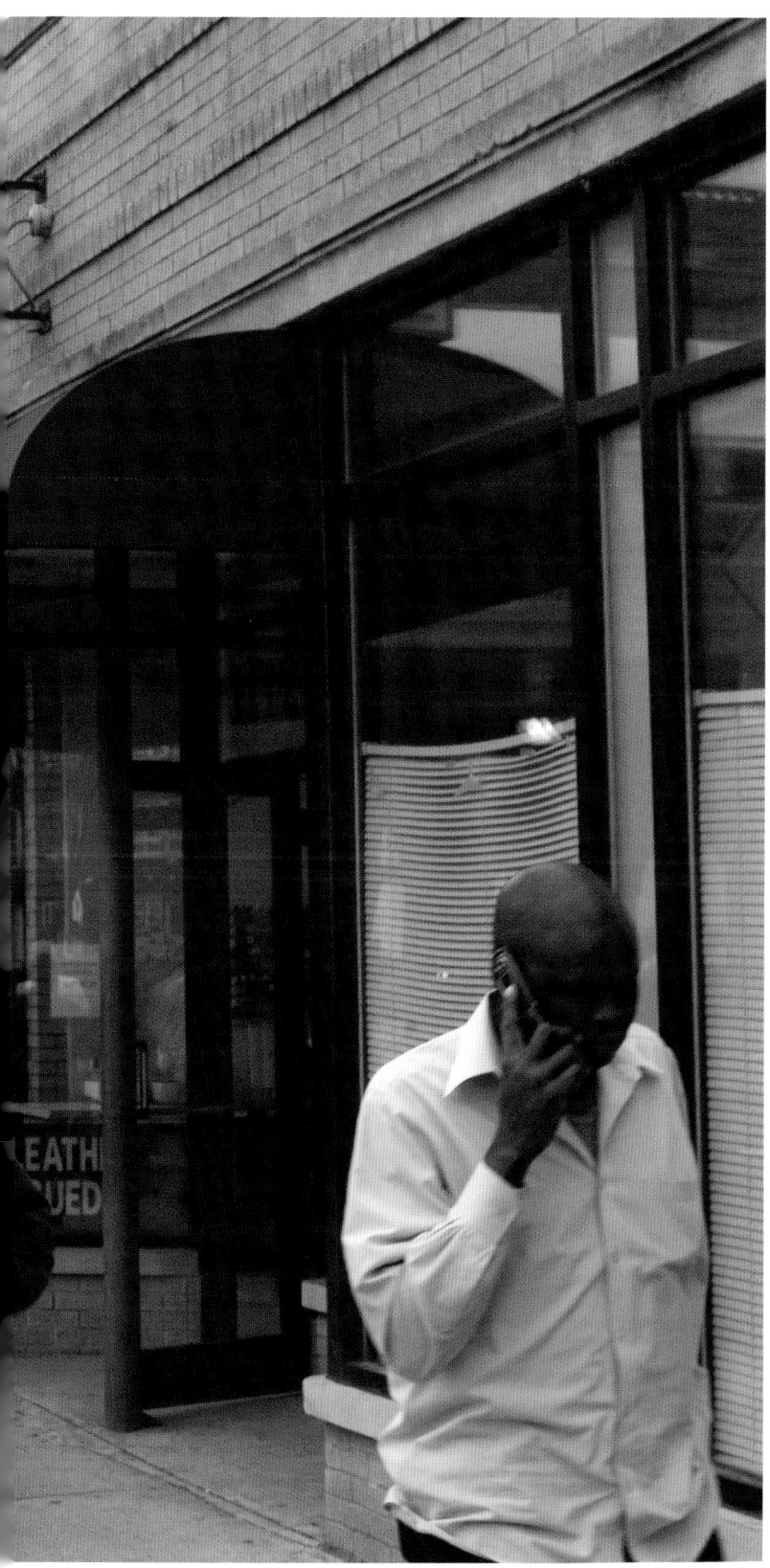

Aleksandar Hemon

Author Aleksandar Hemon stands on Chicago's Thorndale Avenue outside the deli author Saul Bellow, a fellow Chicago transplant, used to frequent.

ALEX GARCIA, 2008

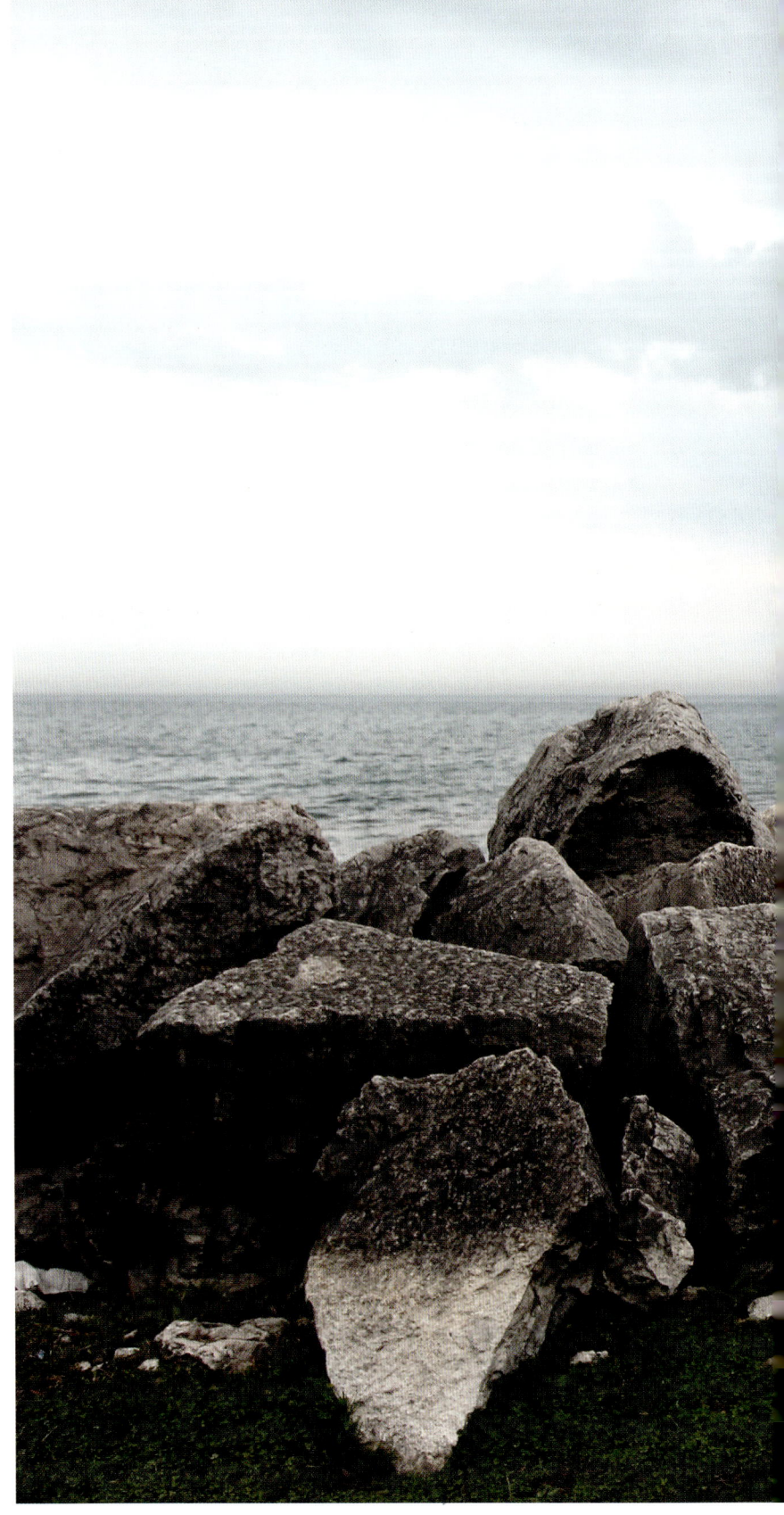

Rick Wunder

Rick Wunder plays his trombone near the Lake Michigan shoreline in Evanston, Ill. The retired systems analyst participated in a Northwestern University study that found playing musical instruments at least three times a week into adulthood has a positive impact on the brain.

CHRIS SWEDA, 2012

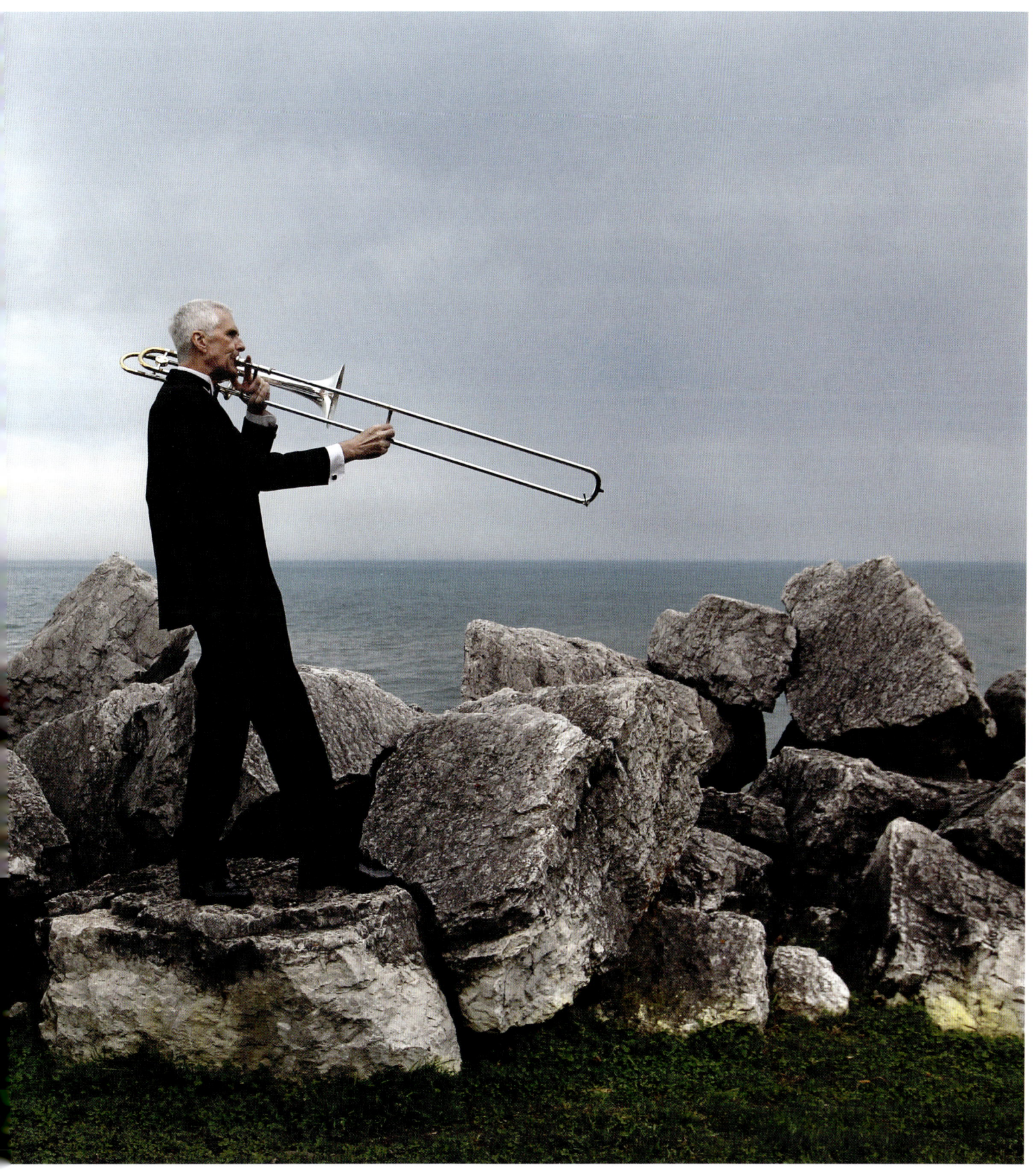

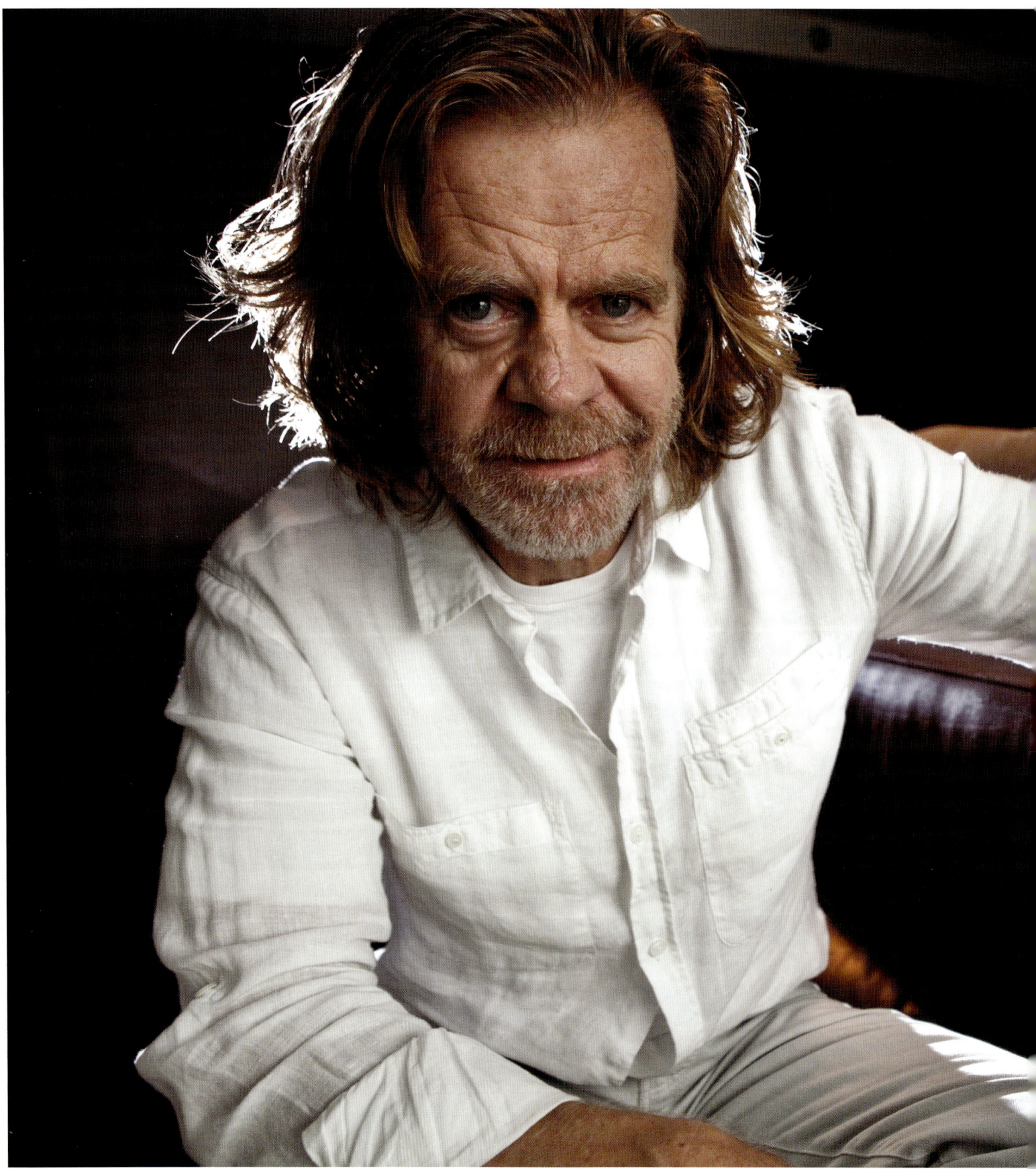

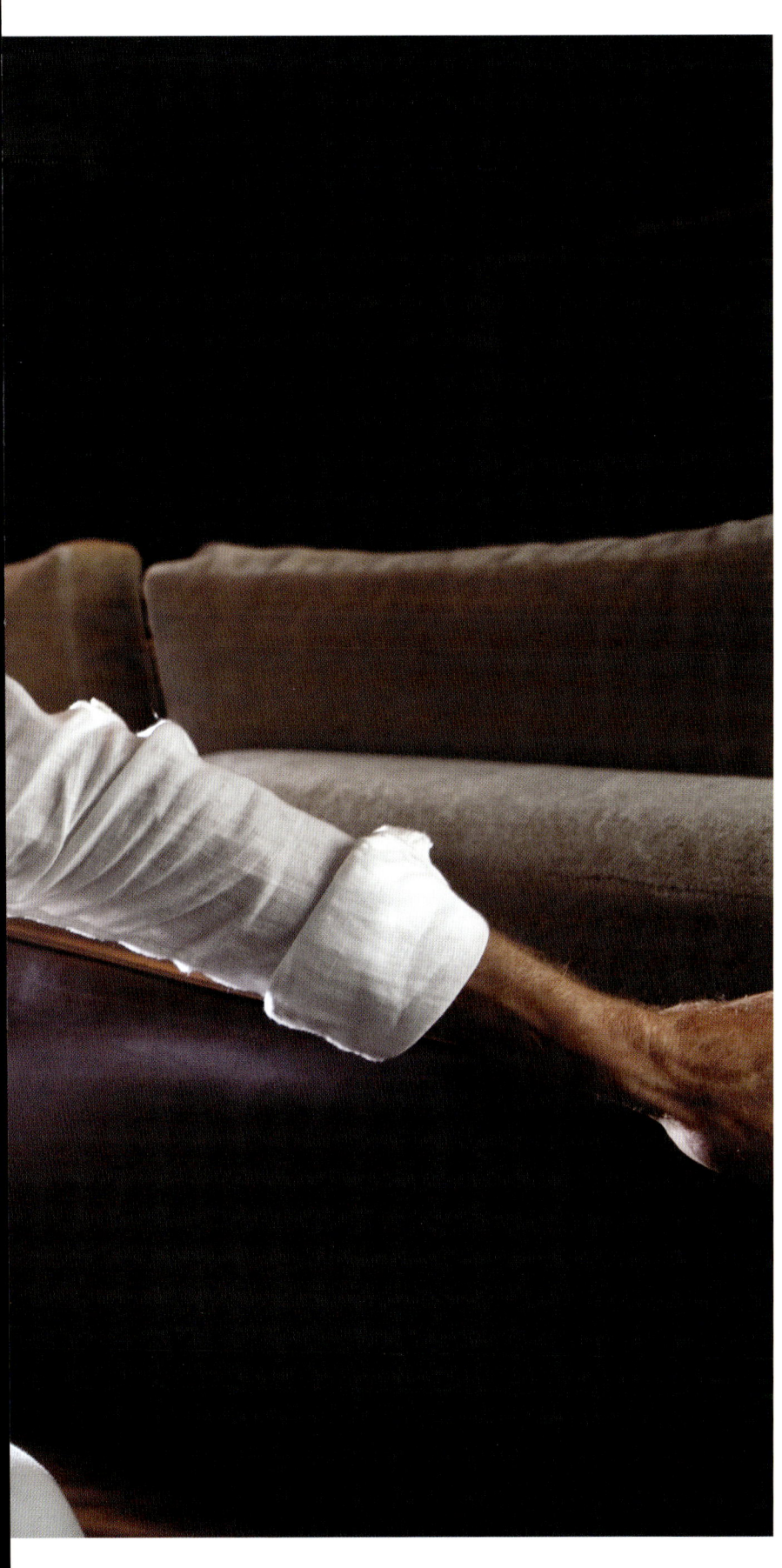

William H. Macy

Actor William H. Macy stars in Showtime's "Shameless," which films in Chicago.

ZBIGNIEW BZDAK, 2012

Maurice Chevalier

A Pabst Blue Ribbon beer is Maurice Chevalier's drink of choice at a Chicago tavern. The French-born actor came to the U.S. after World War I to make it in show business. His most famous role may have been "Gigi" (1958), in which he sang his signature songs, "Thank Heaven for Little Girls" and "I Remember it Well."

CHICAGO TRIBUNE HISTORICAL PHOTO, 1933

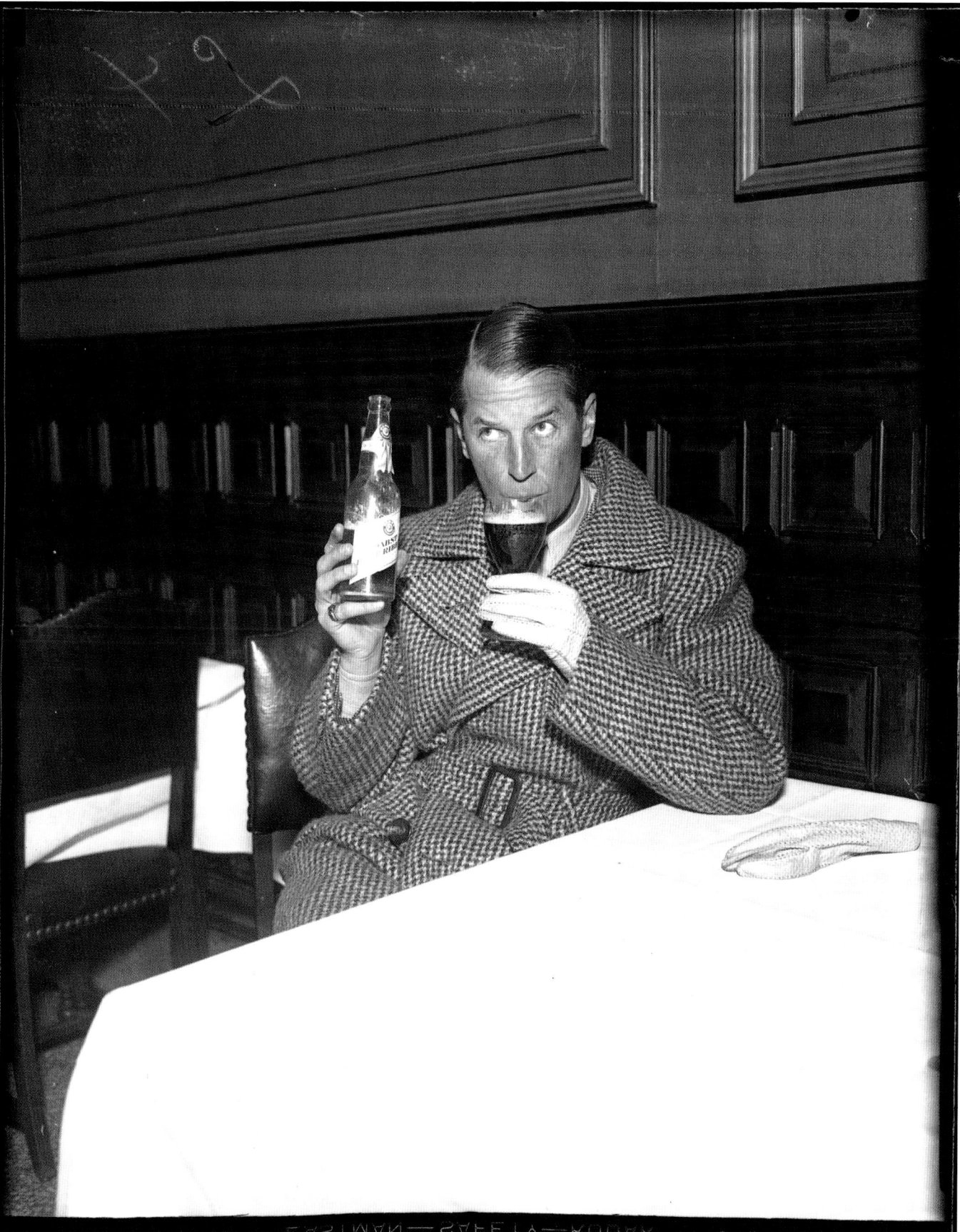

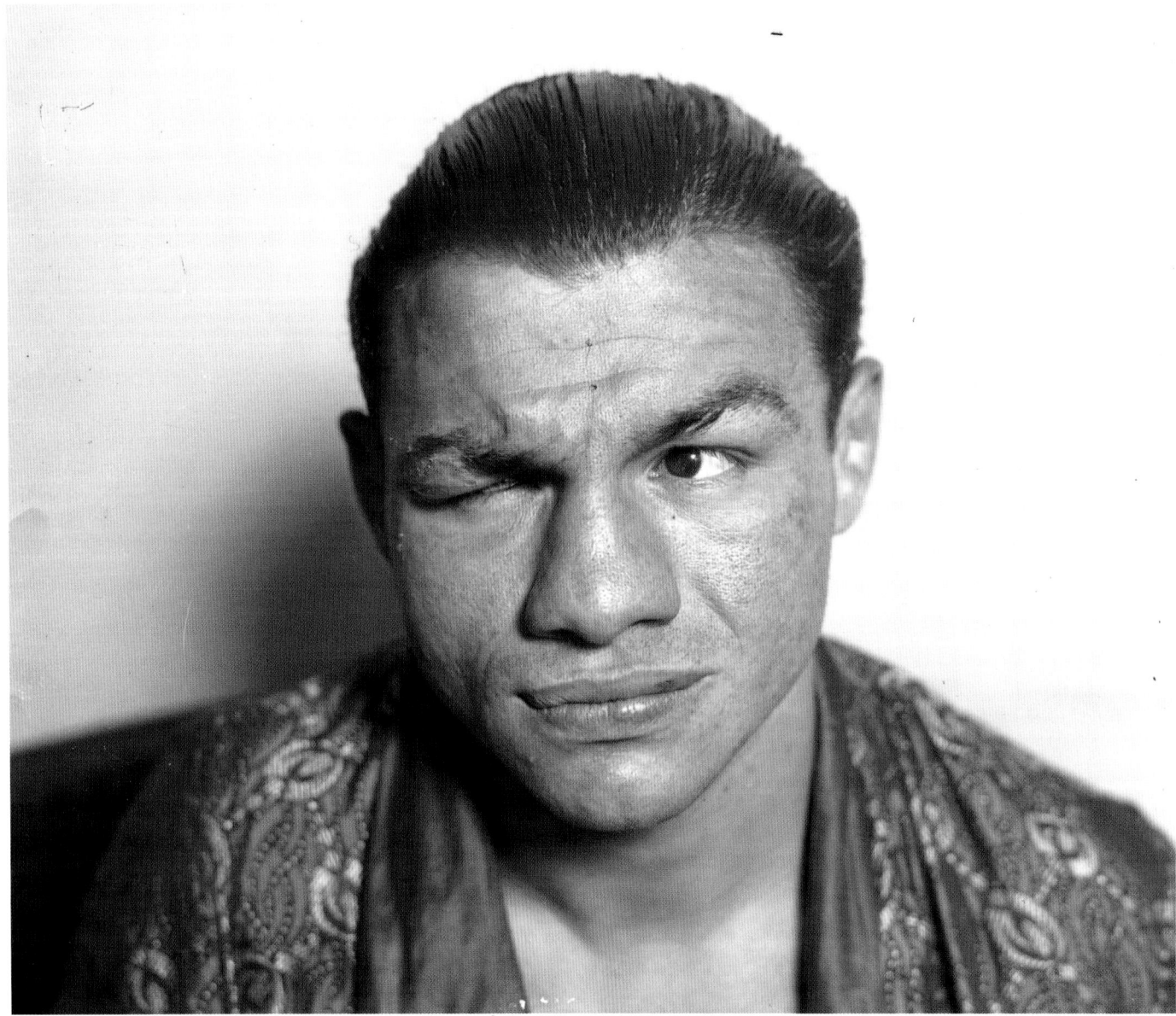

Tony Canzoneri

Boxer Tony Canzoneri, shown Sept. 20, 1932, was a three-time world champion and held five world titles, including world featherweight champion, world light welterweight champion and world lightweight champion.

CHICAGO TRIBUNE HISTORICAL PHOTO, 1932

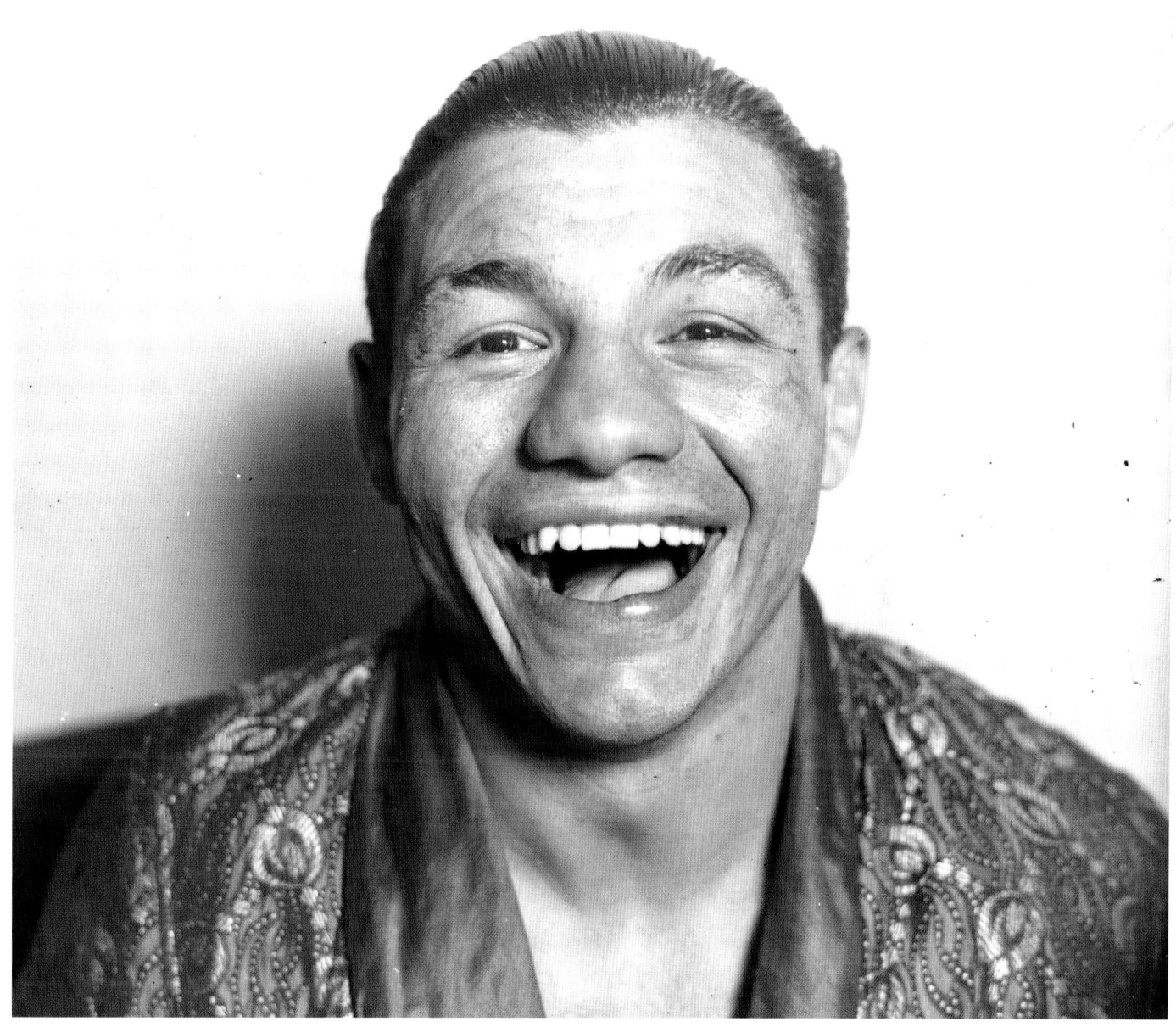

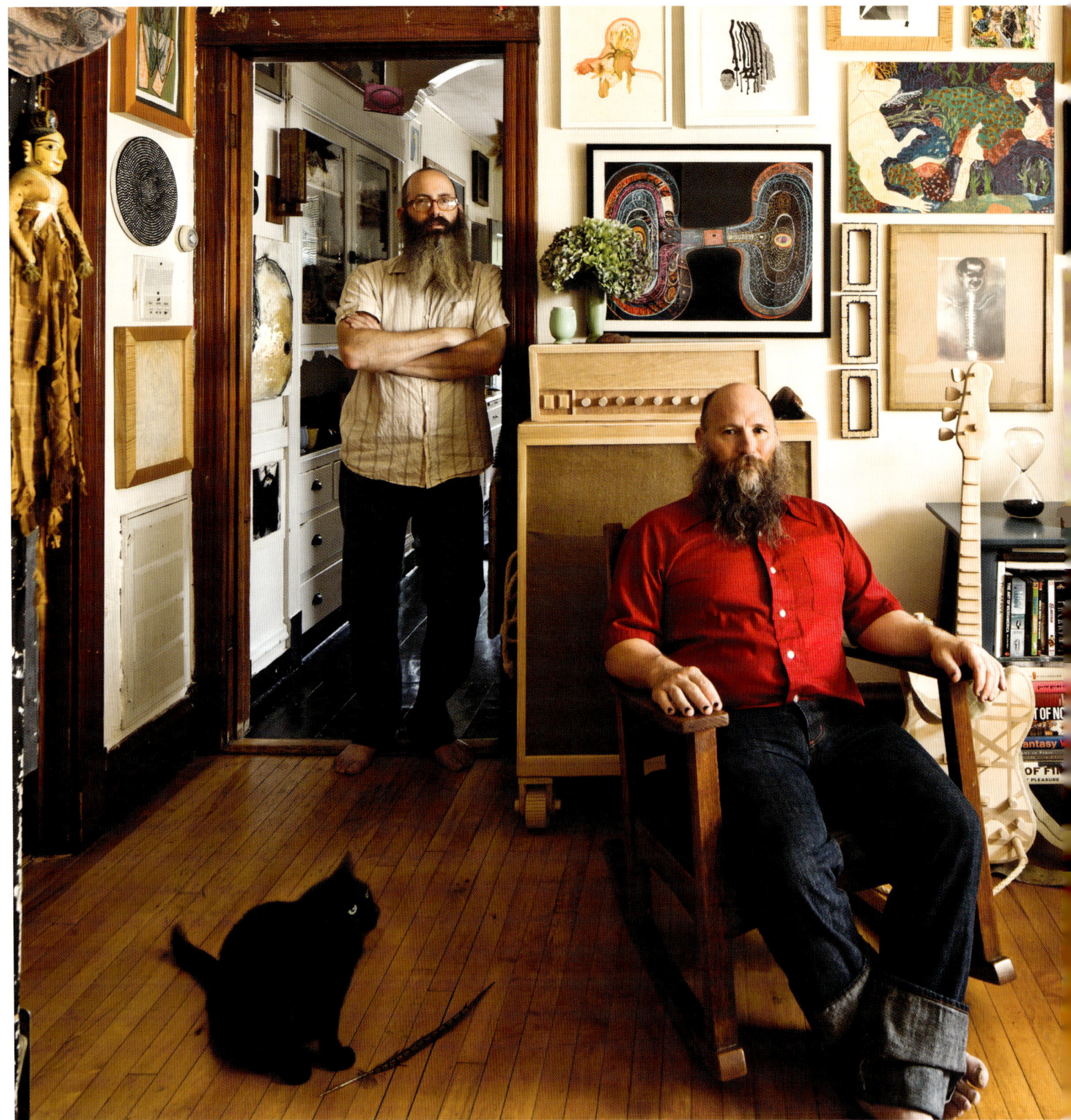

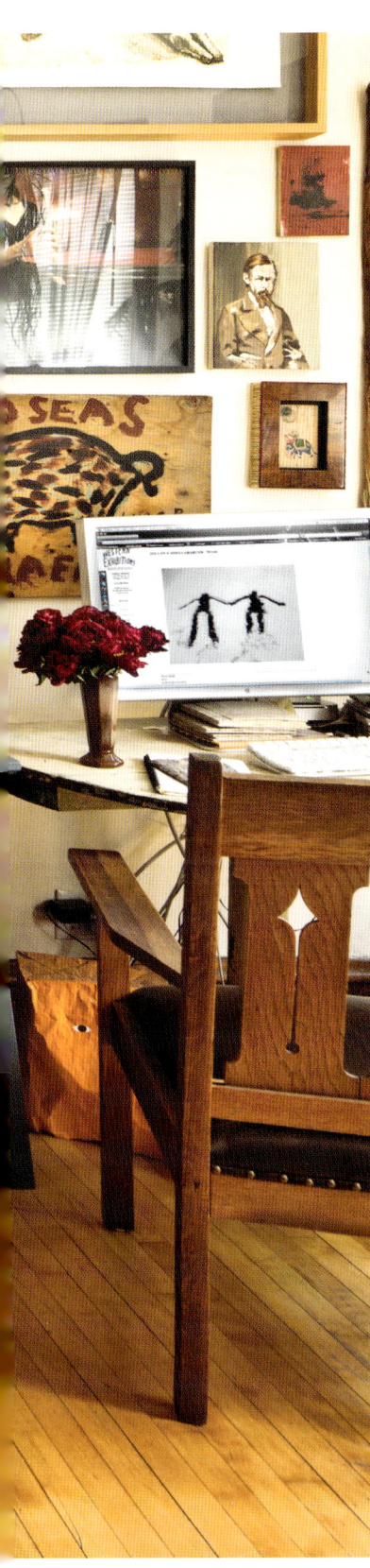

Stan Shellabarger AND Dutes Miller

Chicago-based artists and couple Stan Shellabarger, left, and Dutes Miller at home June 20, 2012, in Chicago's Avondale neighborhood. Their apartment functions like a life-size shadow box. The walls are lined with contemporary art, much of it made by artist friends and acquired through purchase, gift or swap.

BILL HOGAN, 2012

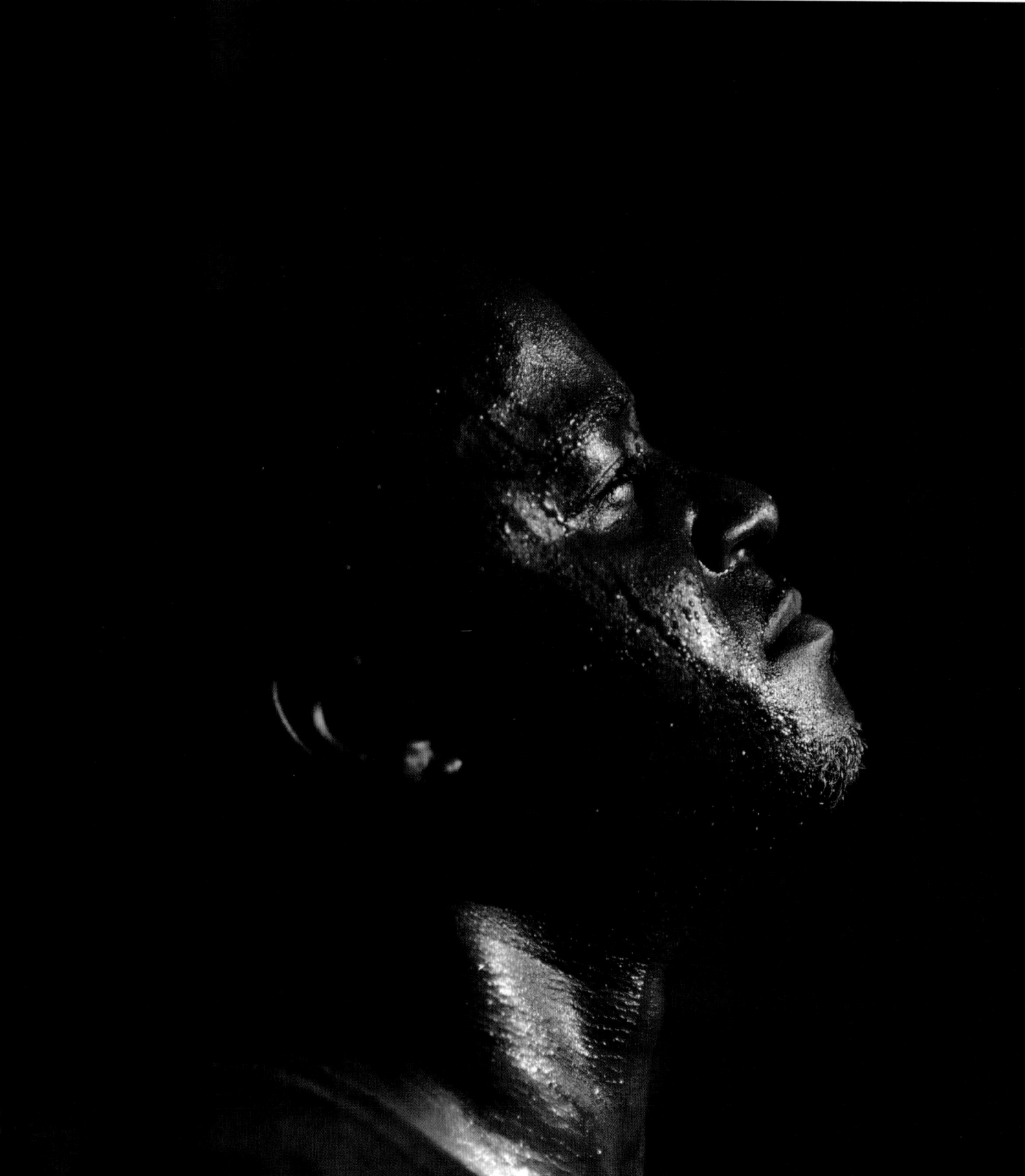

Daniel Taylor

Daniel Taylor takes a brief break before taking another load up to his new apartment in Evanston, Ill. Taylor served nearly 20 years after his wrongful conviction in a 1992 double murder before he was exonerated and freed in June 2013.

Most of his new belongings came from Margaret Rosetta, who had also been incarcerated and had died a week before Taylor's move.

CAROLYN VAN HOUTEN, 2013

Seminole Indians

Seminole Indian children at the closing of the World's Fair hosted by Chicago.

CHICAGO TRIBUNE HISTORICAL PHOTO, 1933

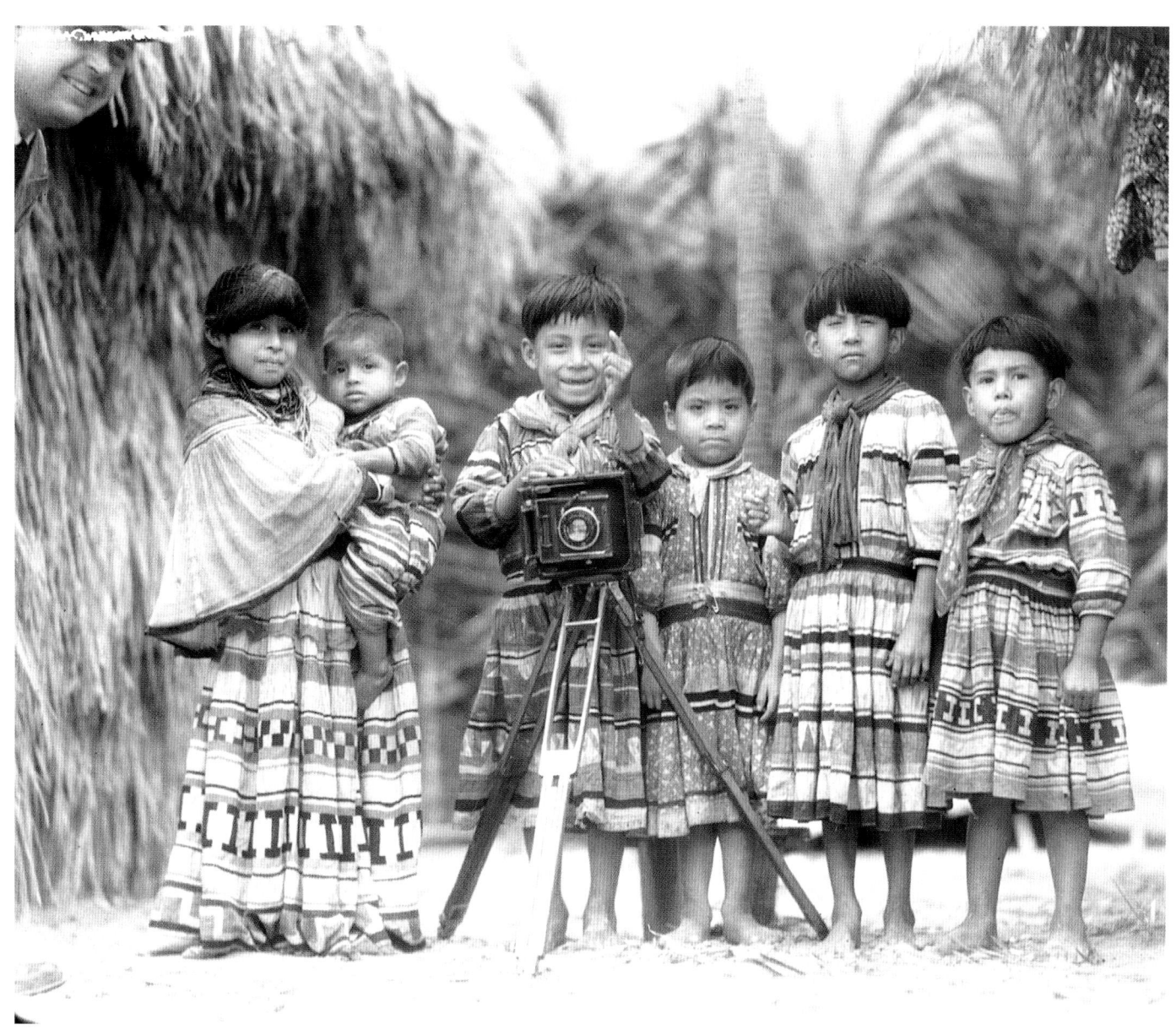

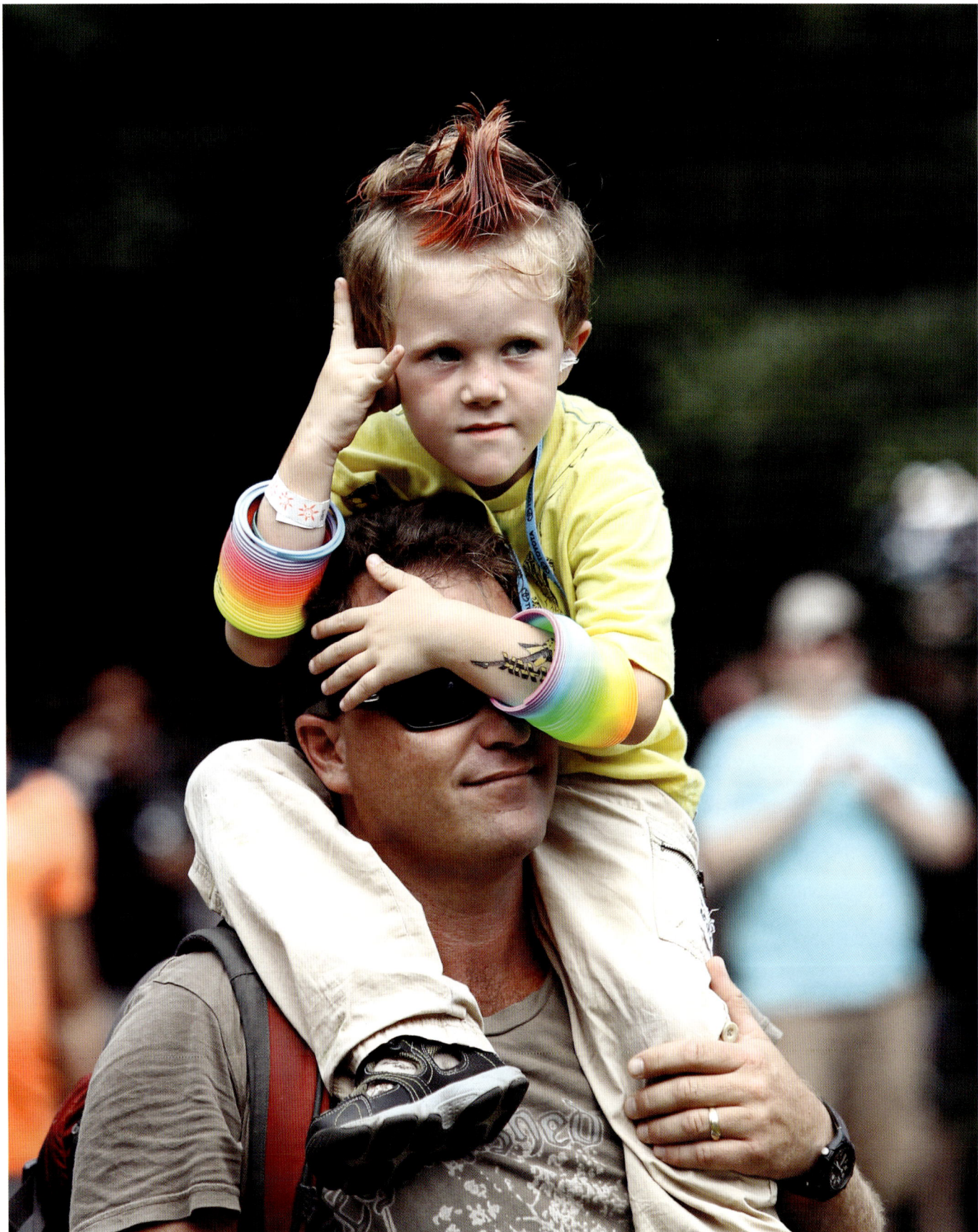

Pierce King AND **Brian King**

Pierce King, 4, and his father, Brian King, watch Le Butcherettes perform during opening day of the Lollapalooza music festival in Chicago's Grant Park.

BRIAN CASSELLA, 2011

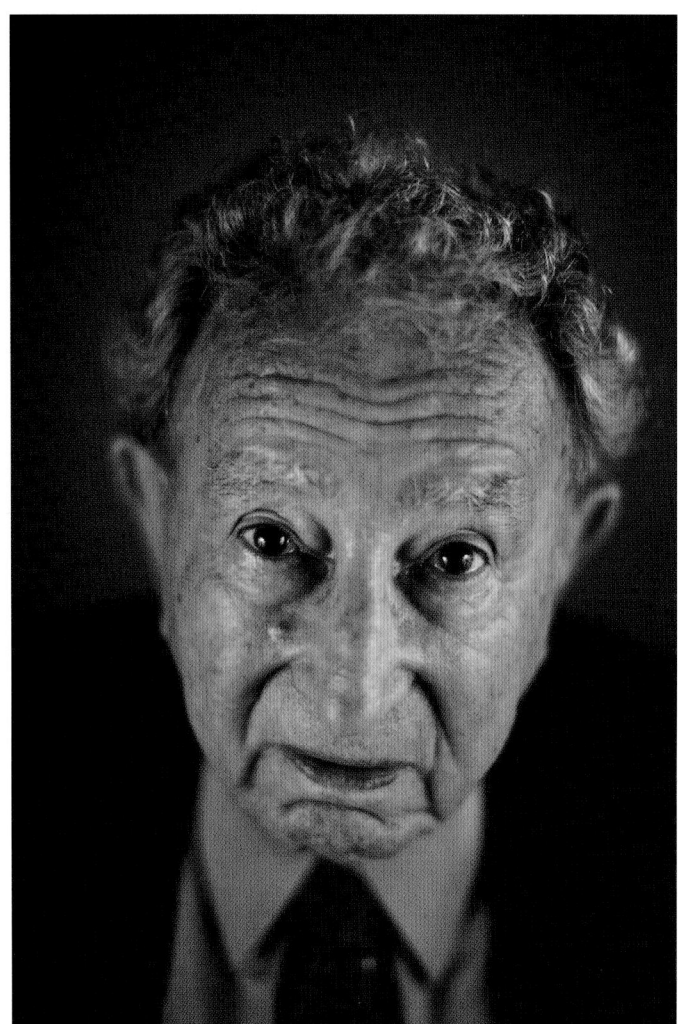 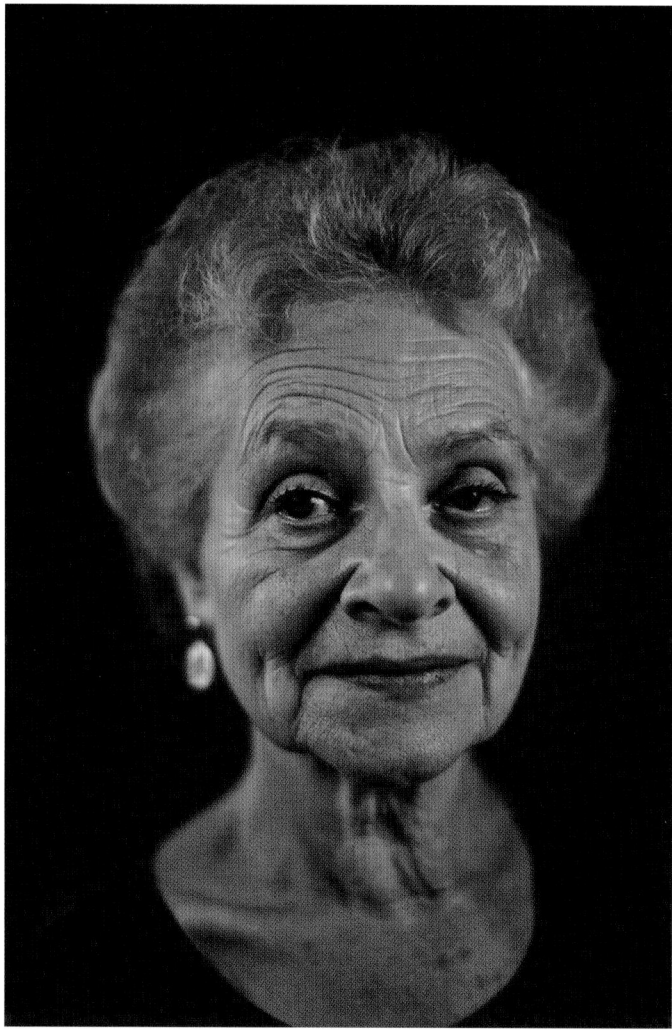

David Figman, Ursula Levy, Bill Pineless AND Regina Samelson

David Figman, from left, Ursula Levy, Bill Pineless and Regina Samelson, like many other Holocaust survivors, found refuge and community in the village of Skokie when they moved to the United States. About 7,000 to 8,000 survivors lived in Skokie a couple of generations ago, opening synagogues and Hebrew schools, kosher markets and butcher shops, Jewish delis and bagel bakeries — and remaking a town barely 10 miles square.

ZBIGNIEW BZDAK, 2008

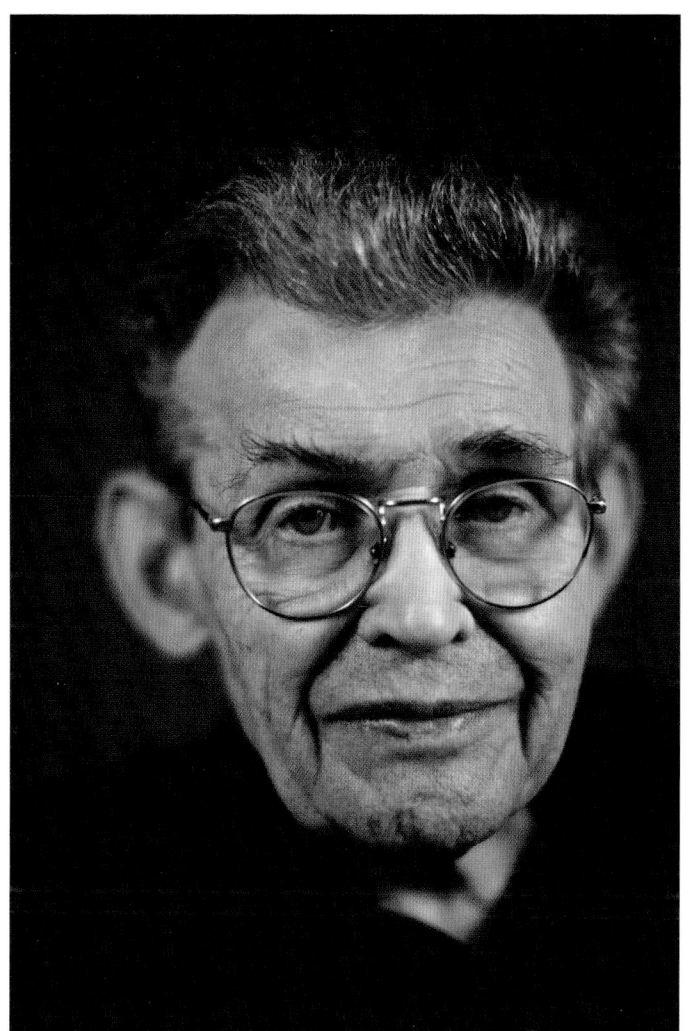
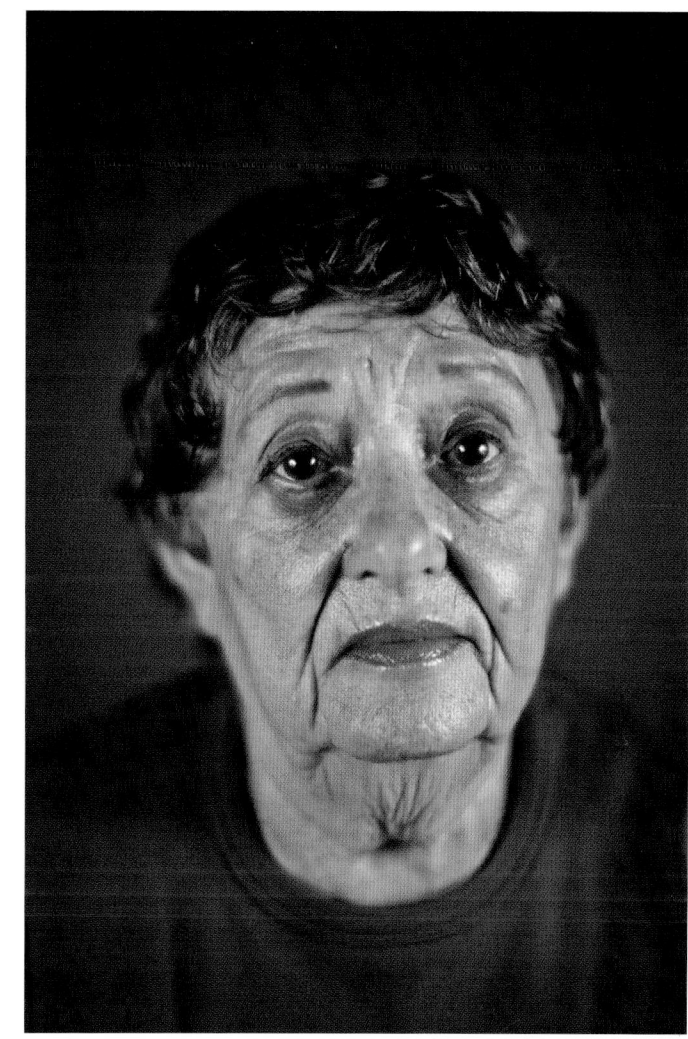

Richard Cozzi

Richard Cozzi, 11, rushes home to South Morgan Street, Chicago, with a turkey for Thanksgiving dinner.

CHICAGO TRIBUNE HISTORICAL PHOTO, 1955

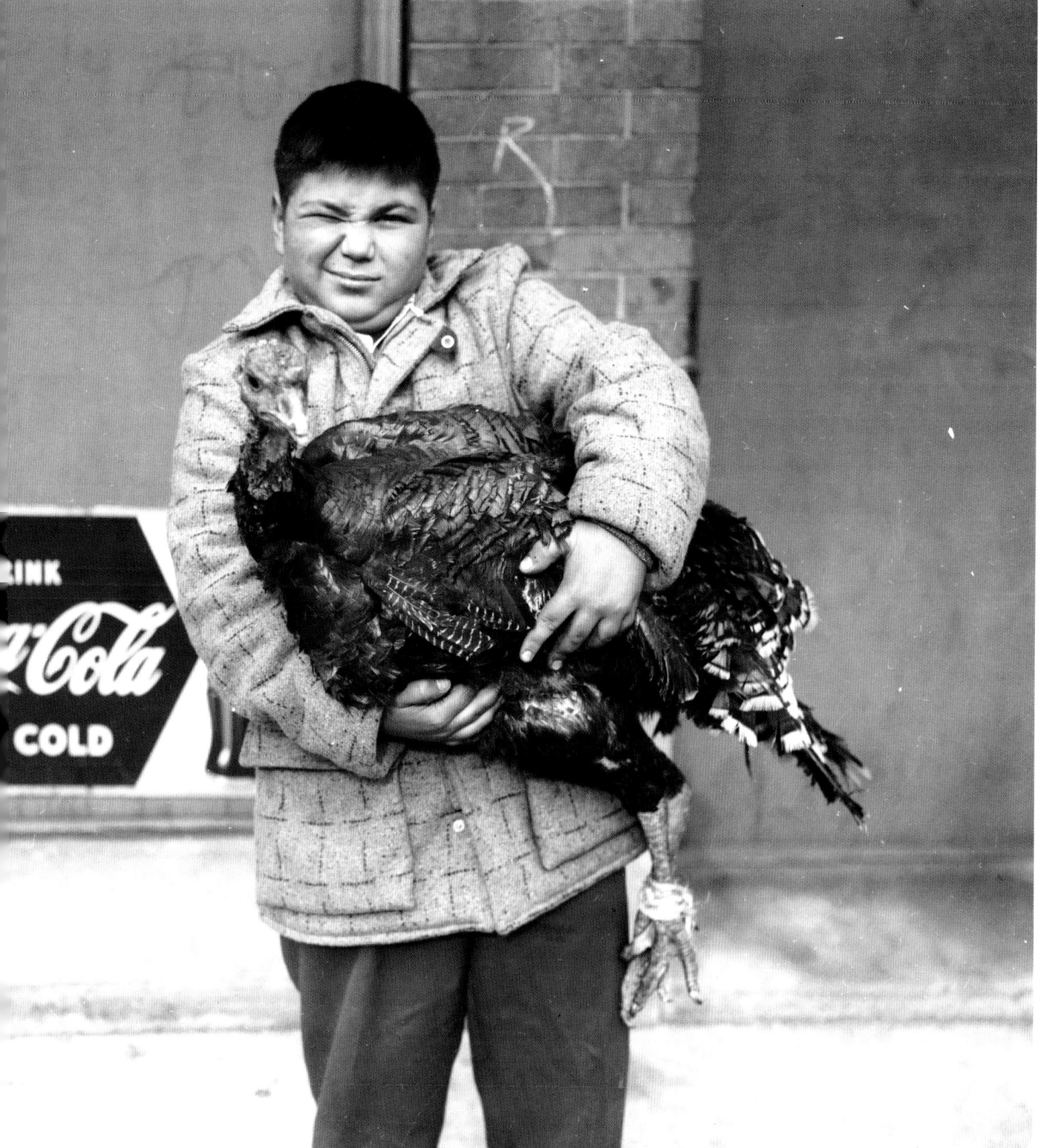

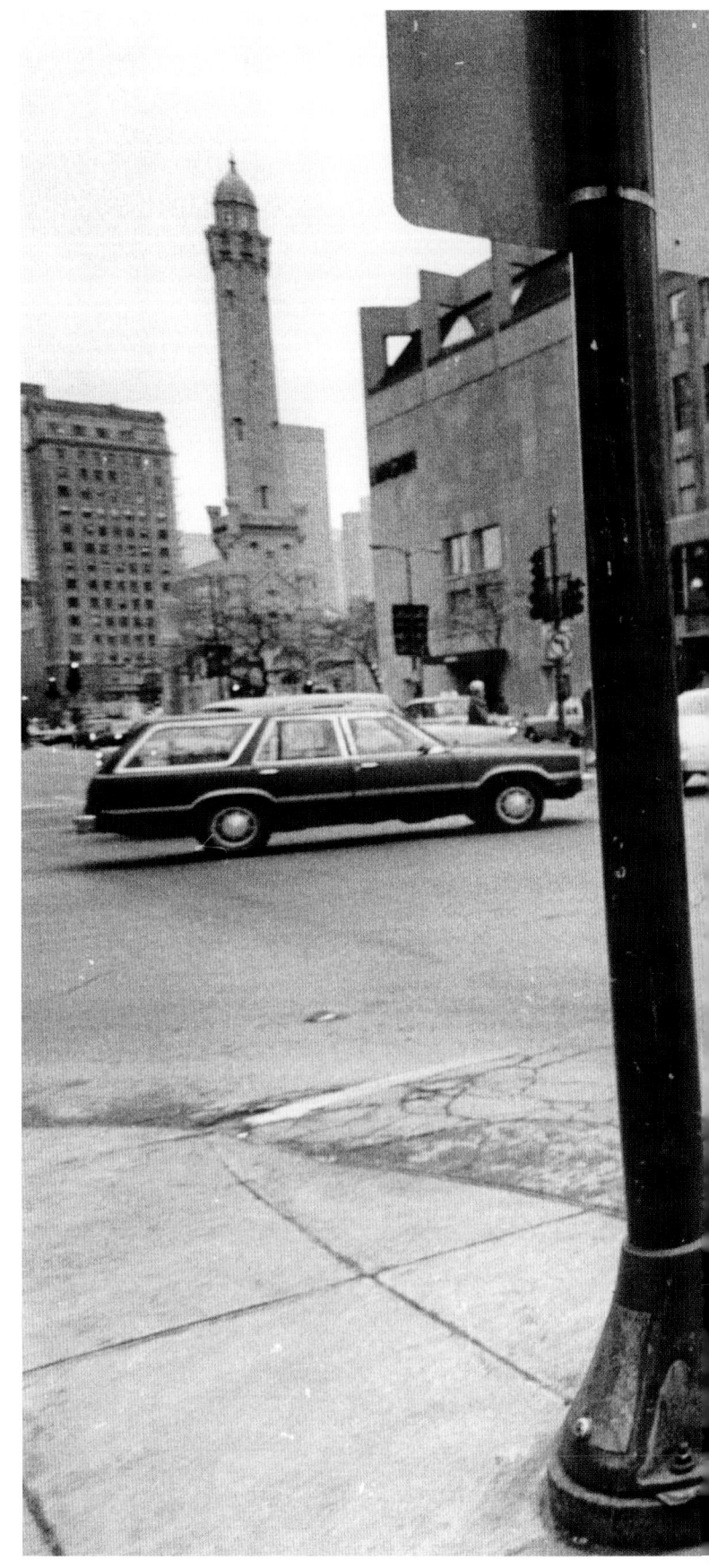

Jim Belushi

Sitcom and film actor Jim Belushi, shown on Michigan Avenue, grew up in west suburban Wheaton with his famous older brother, John.

SALLY GOOD 1982

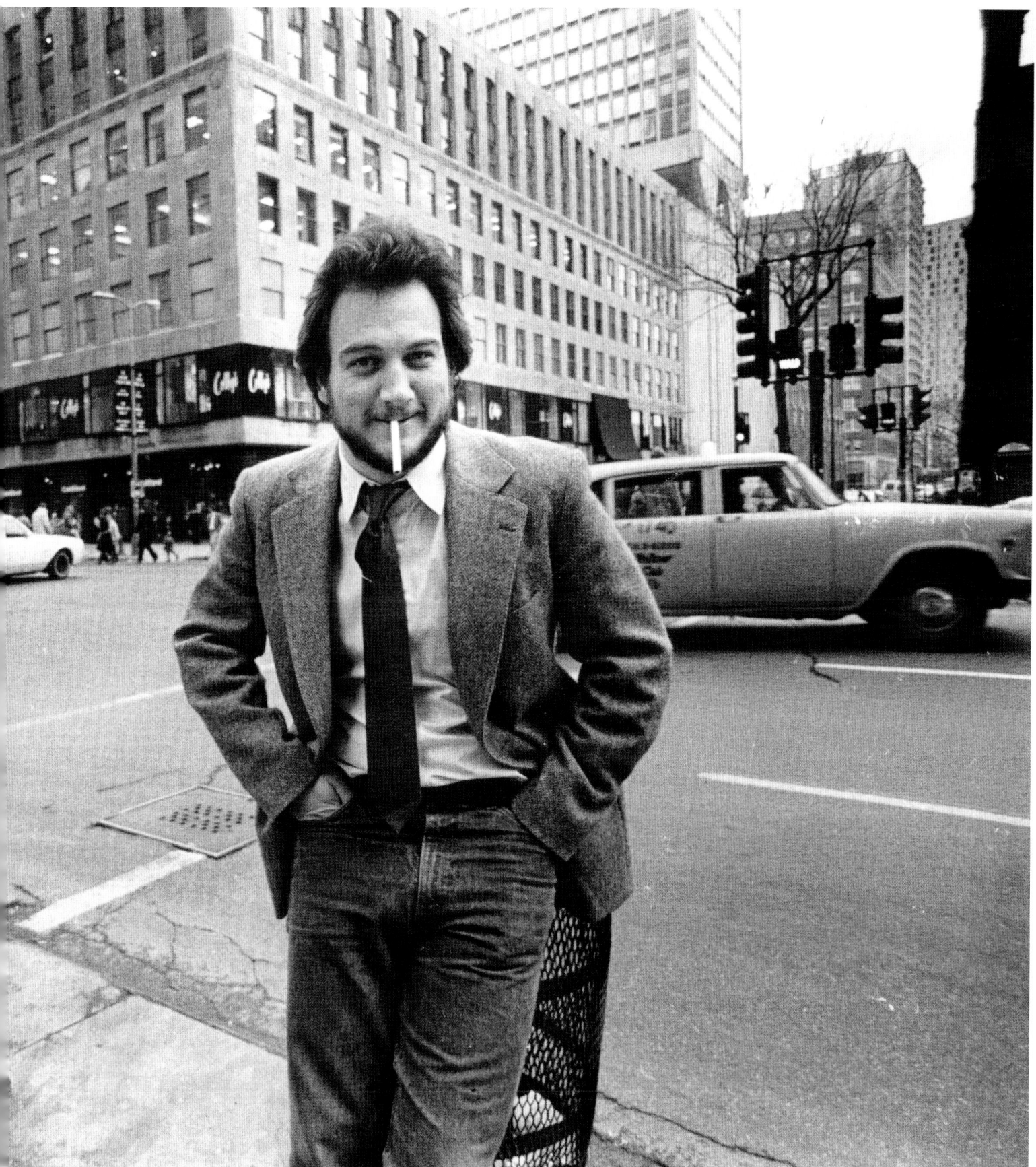

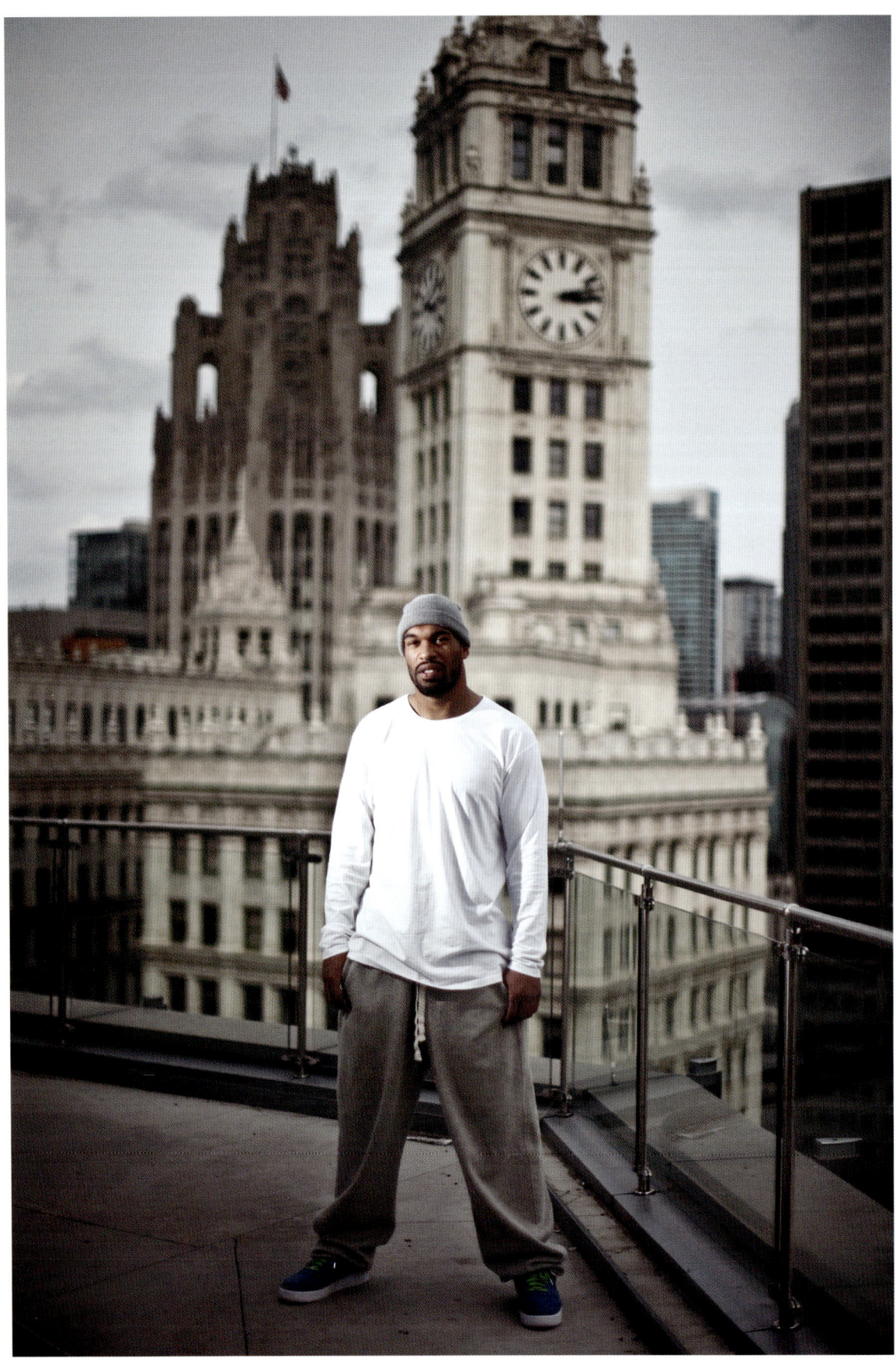

Julius Peppers

Julius Peppers, then a defensive end for the Chicago Bears, poses in downtown Chicago with the iconic Wrigley Building and Tribune Tower in the background.

ZBIGNIEW BZDAK, 2010

Oprah Winfrey

Oprah Winfrey, then the host of "AM Chicago," strikes a celebratory pose on State Street in Chicago. "AM Chicago" was the precursor to her monstrously successful daytime talk show, "The Oprah Winfrey Show." The latter ran for 25 seasons as a nationally syndicated program based in Chicago and turned Oprah into a household name — and a billionaire.

CHICAGO TRIBUNE HISTORICAL PHOTO, 1984

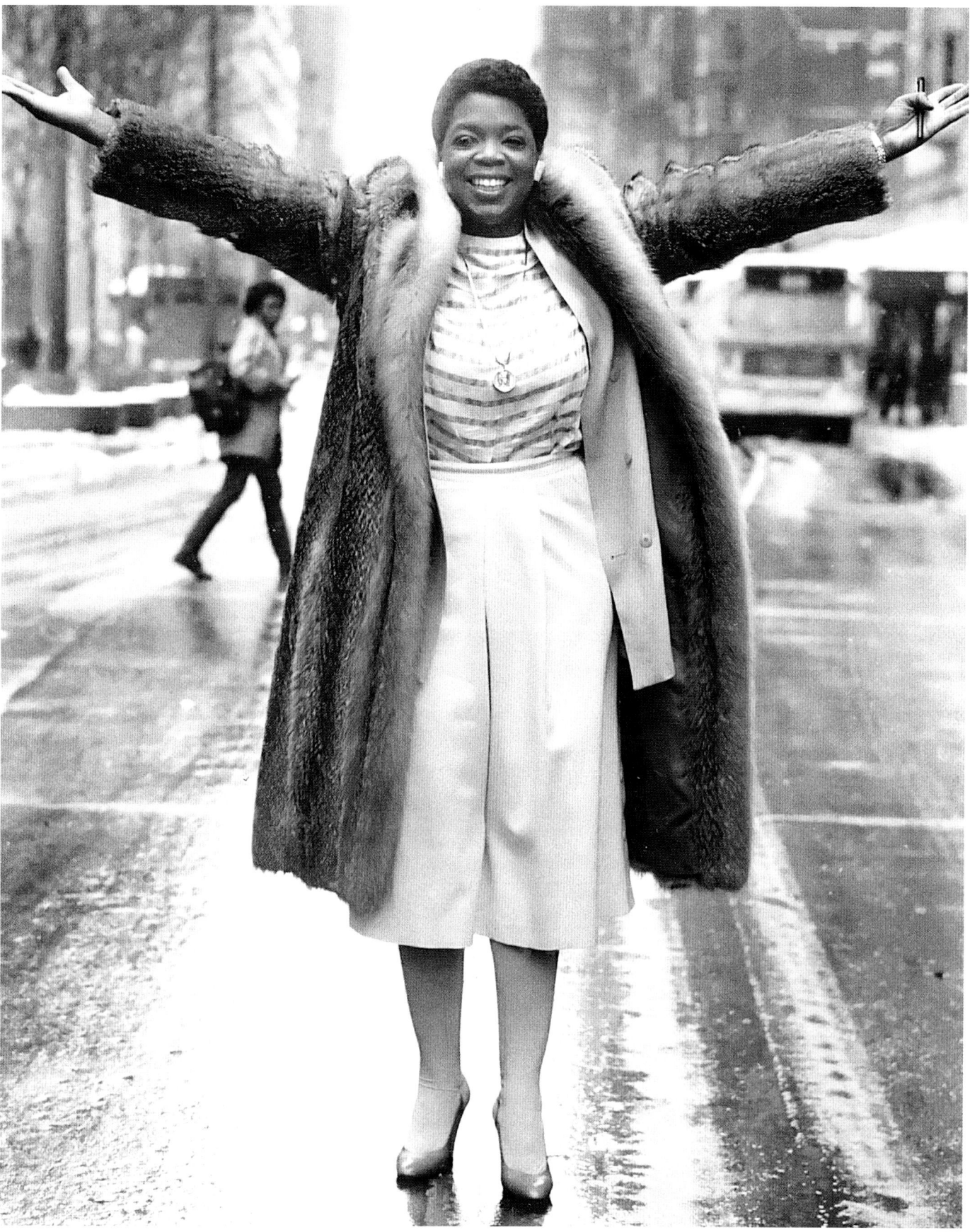

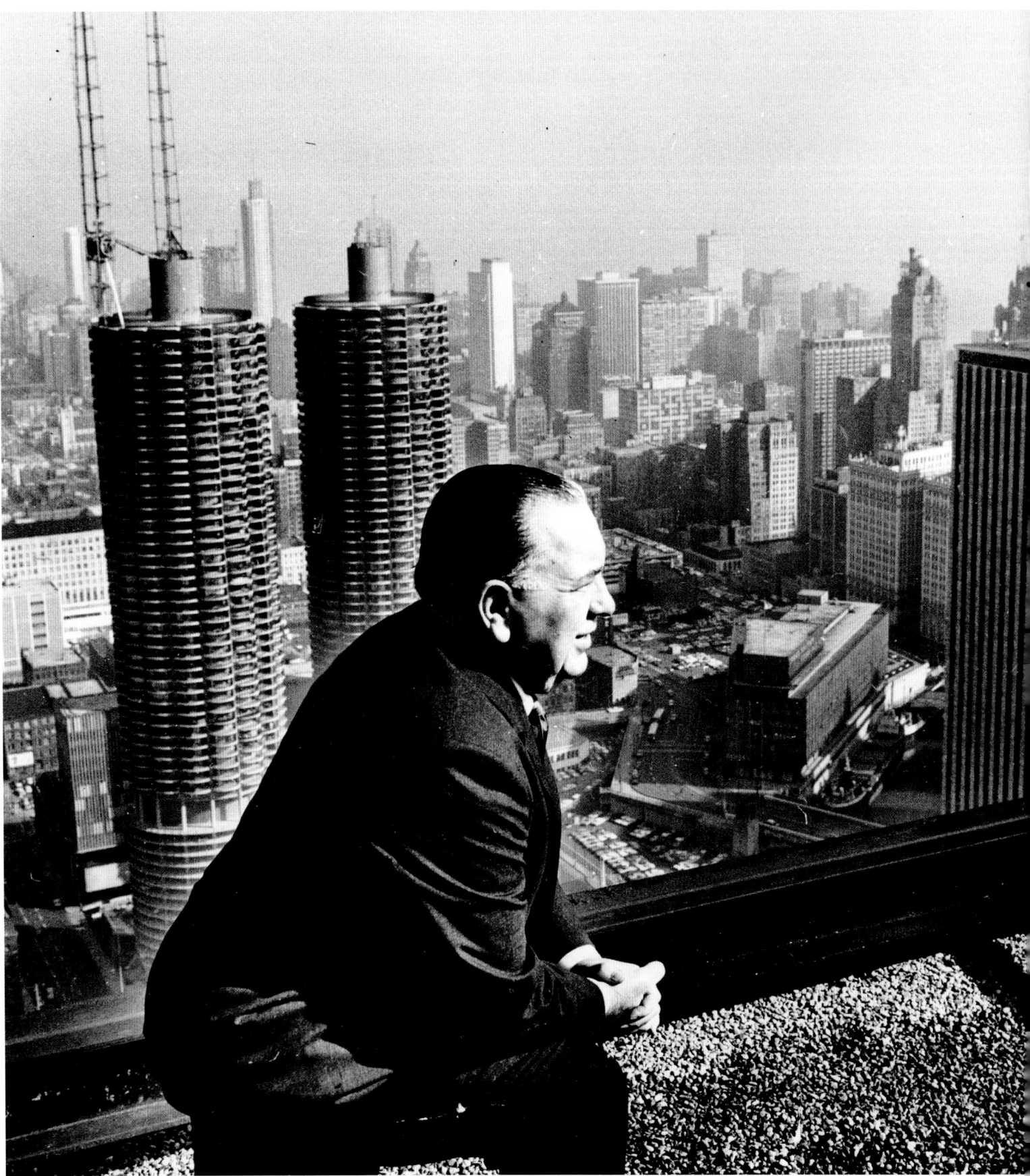

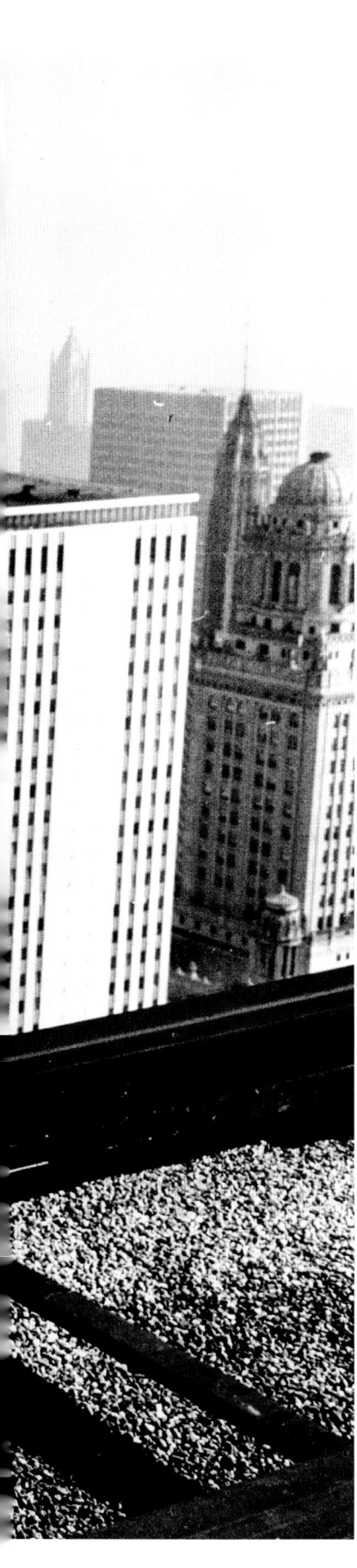

Richard J. Daley

Chicago Mayor Richard J. Daley looks out across his city in a photo that was one of his favorites. Daley left an indelible stamp on Chicago as one of America's most powerful big-city bosses. His son, Richard M. Daley, followed in his footsteps.

CHICAGO TRIBUNE HISTORICAL PHOTO, 1966

Richard J. Daley AND
Richard M. Daley

Mayor Richard J. Daley, right, and his son Richard M. Daley walk down a City Hall corridor on the way to the mayor's office.

JAMES F. QUINN, 1972

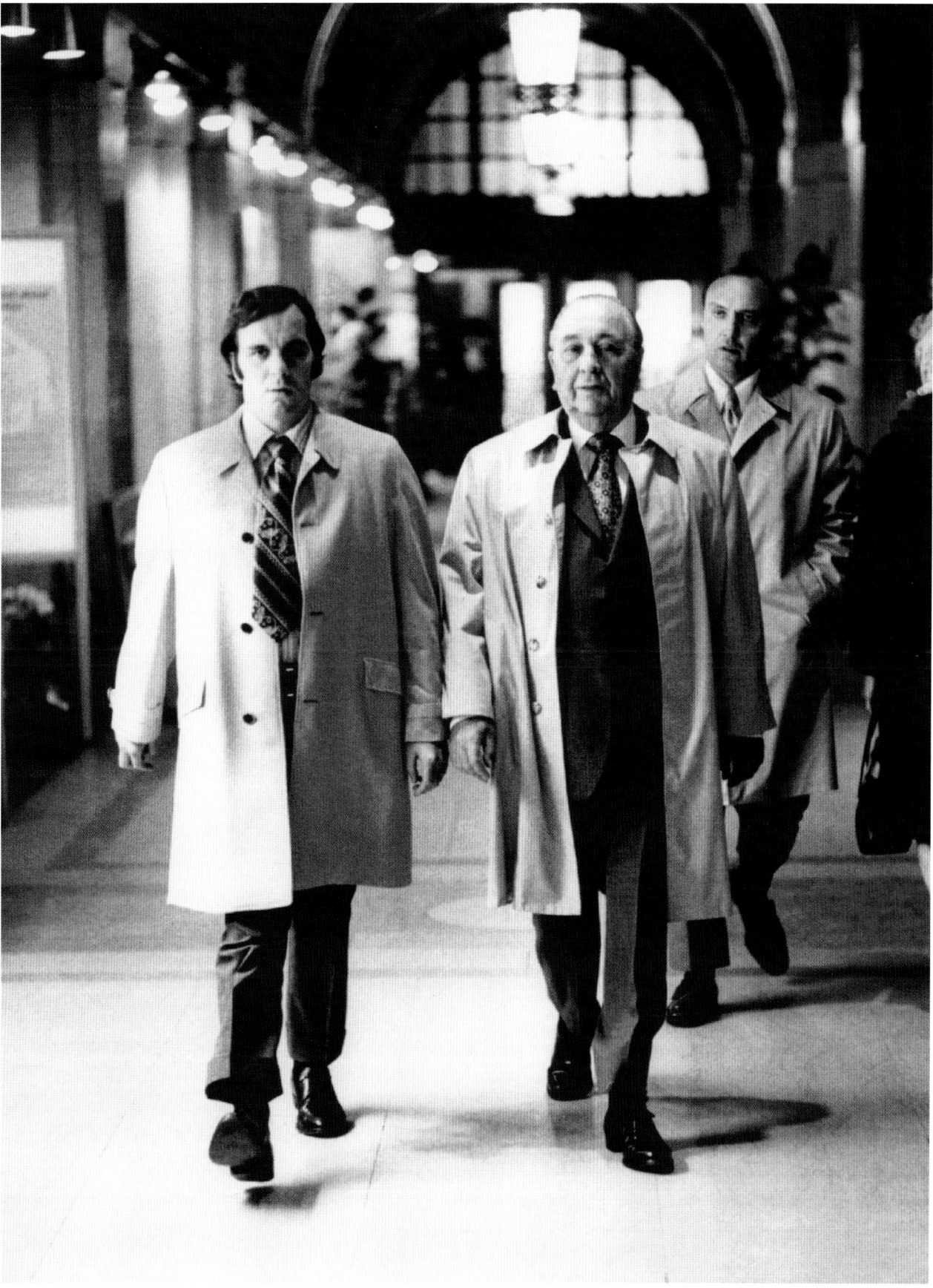

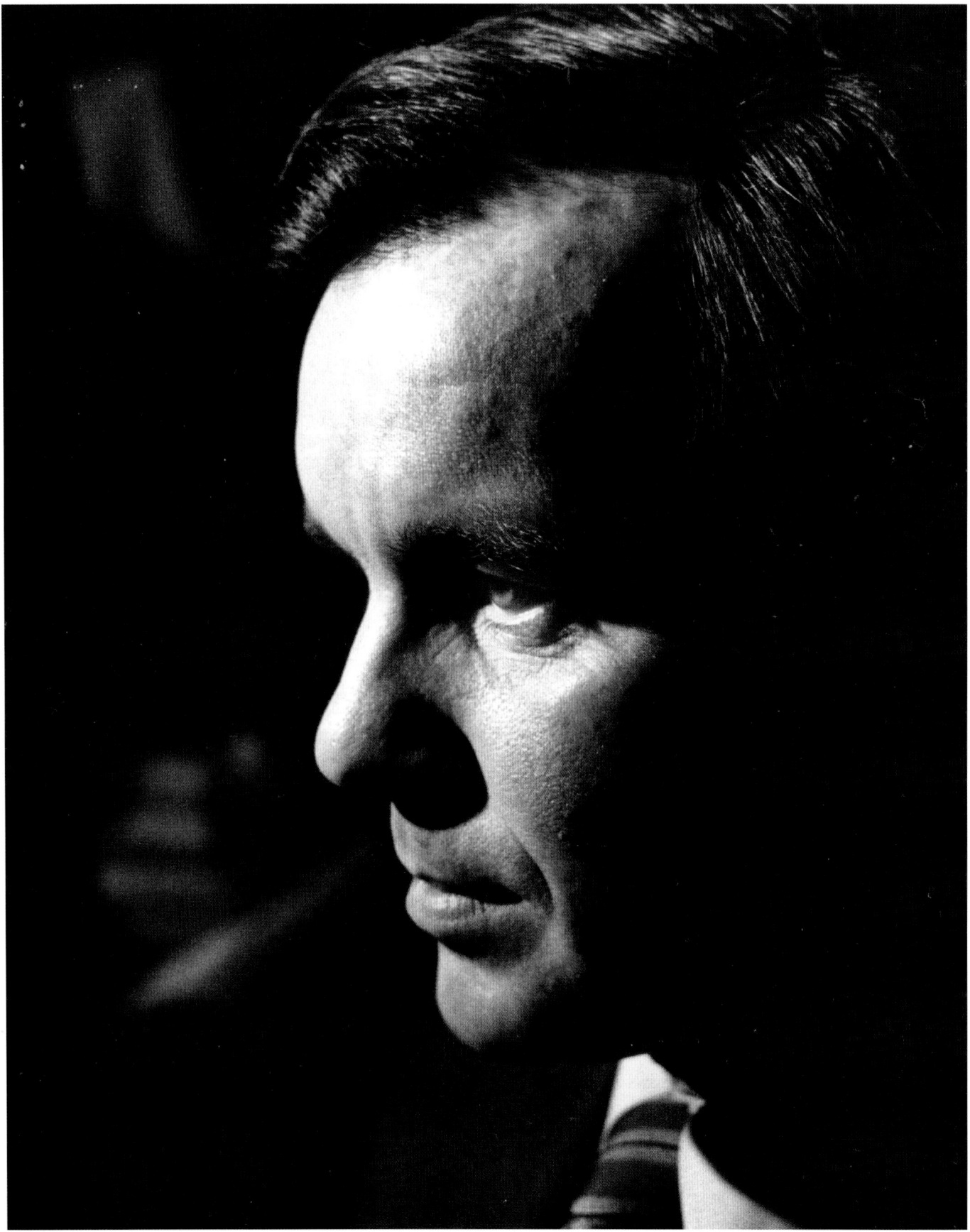

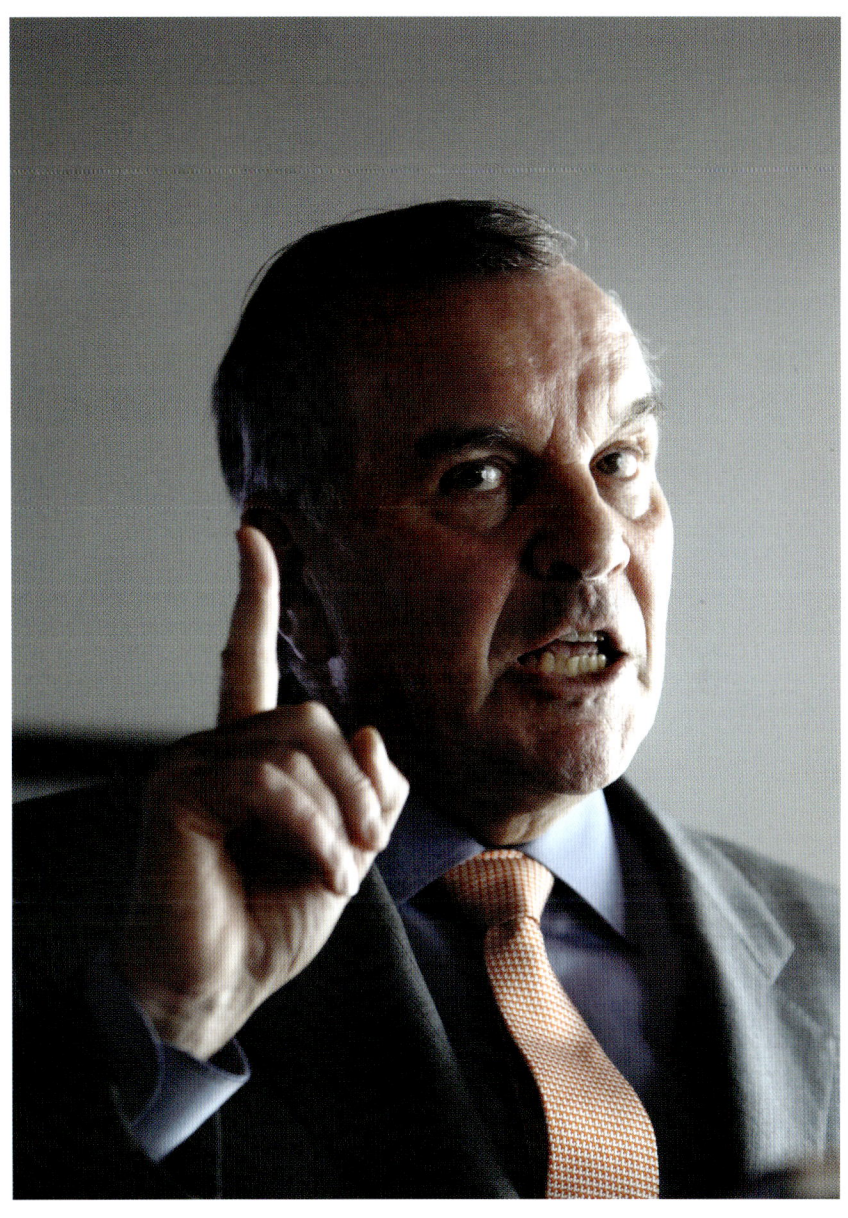

Richard M. Daley

LEFT: Mayoral candidate Richard M. Daley, then state's attorney, announced his 10-point plan to revitalize Chicago's ailing economy Jan. 25, 1983, in remarks at the Association of Industrial Real Estate Brokers luncheon at the Como Inn in Chicago. The third debate between Democratic candidates Mayor Jane Byrne, Harold Washington and Daley was held a few days later. Daley lost the Democratic nomination to Washington, though he successfully followed in his father's footsteps when he was elected mayor in 1989 in a special contest.

JAMES MAYO, 1983

RIGHT: Mayor Richard M. Daley meets with reporters in Chicago. Daley, a member of a family that held sway in the city for decades, left office in 2011 after more than 20 years in power.

DAVID PIERINI, 2009

The Rev. Jesse Jackson

The Rev. Jesse Jackson became a famous civil rights activist based in Chicago after working alongside the Rev. Martin Luther King Jr. and has continued to fight for equality in many arenas. Here, he speaks at the funeral for fellow activist and Black Panther party leader Fred Hampton.

ERNIE COX, 1969

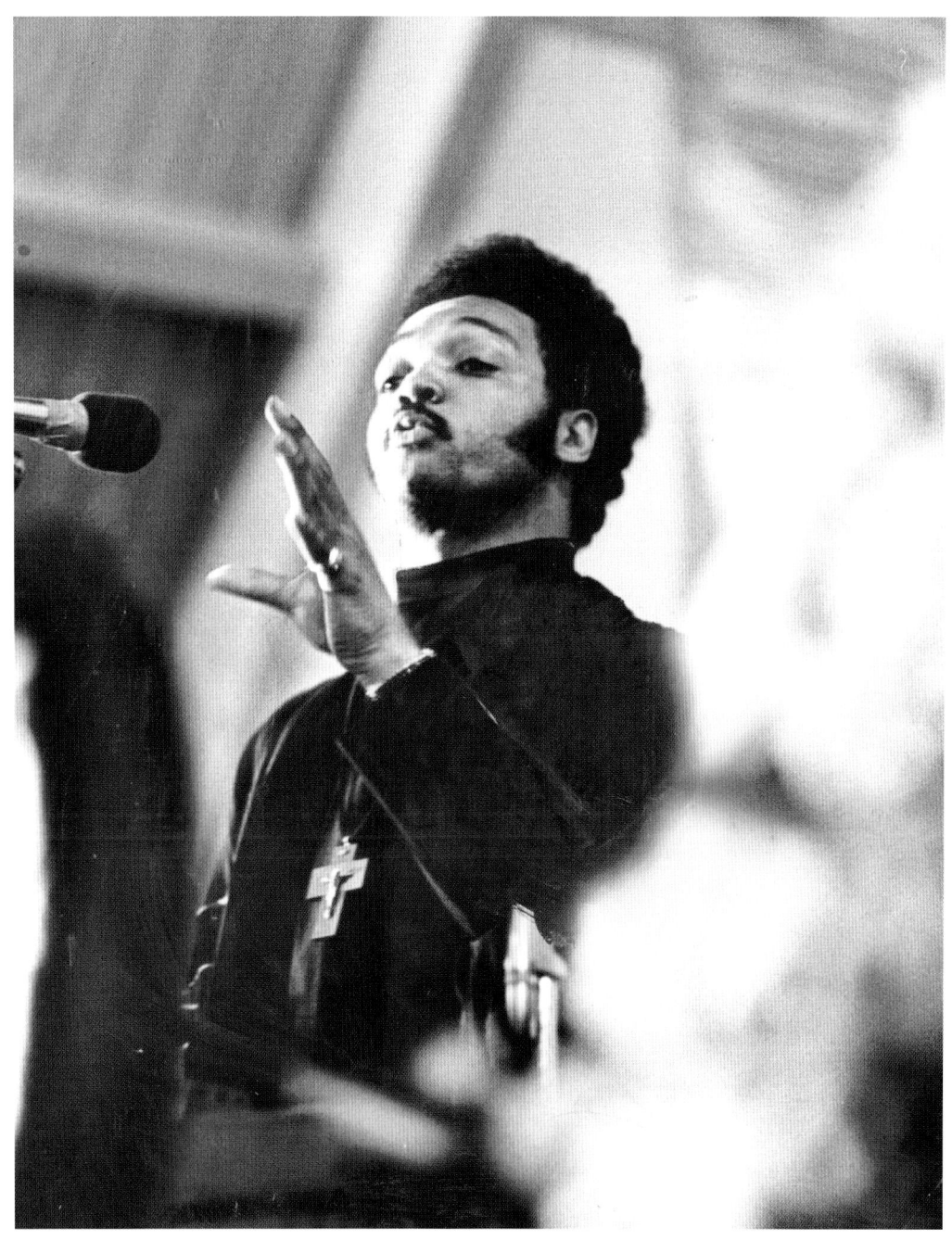

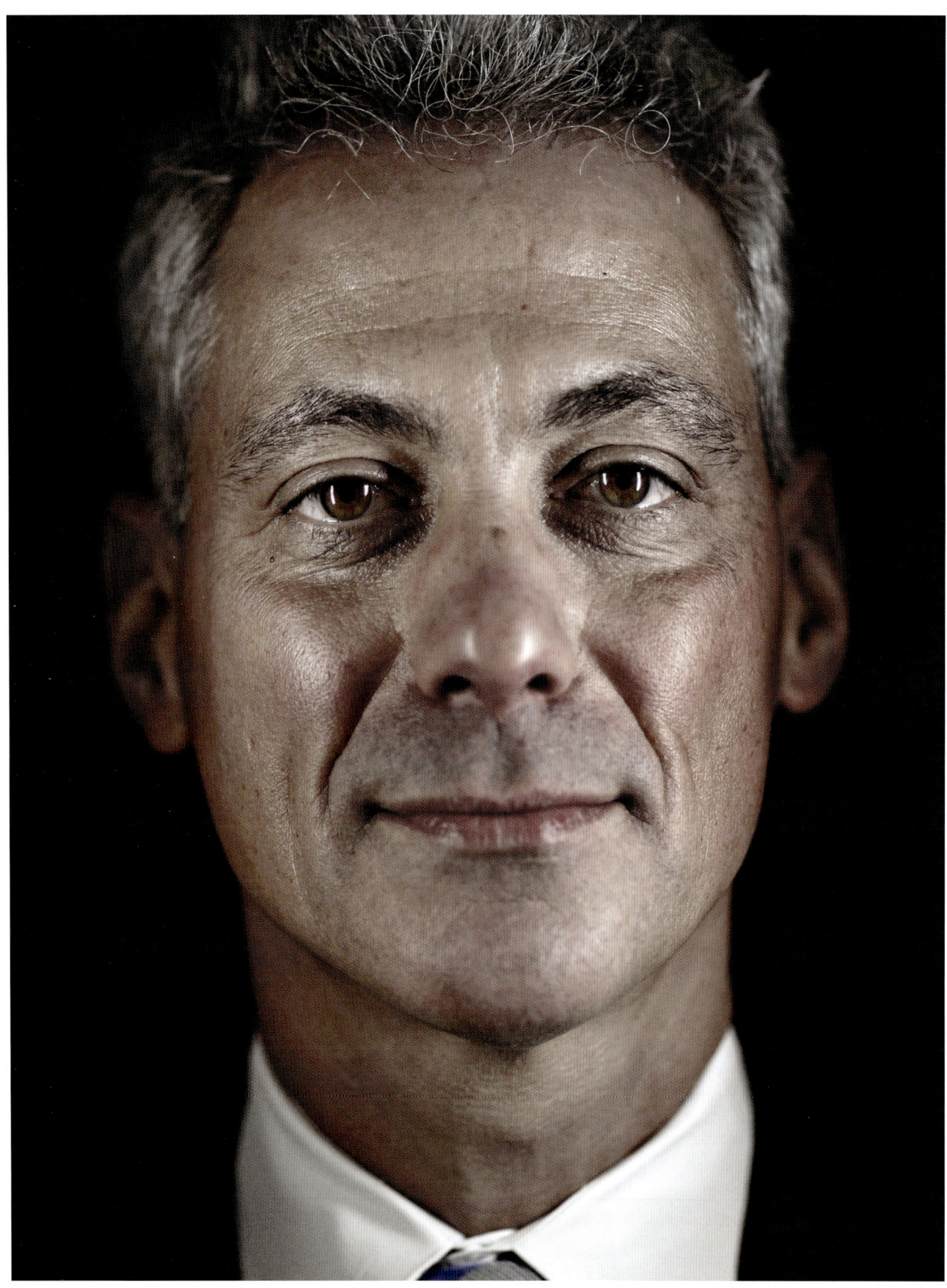

Rahm Emanuel

Rahm Emanuel was elected Chicago's mayor Feb. 22, 2011, in a special contest to fill the vacancy left by Richard M. Daley. "All I can say, you sure know how to make a guy feel at home," Emanuel, who faced a high-profile legal challenge to his residency, told a packed room at a plumbers' union hall on the Near West Side. "Because of the people of Chicago, this is the warmest place in America."

BRIAN CASSELLA, 2011

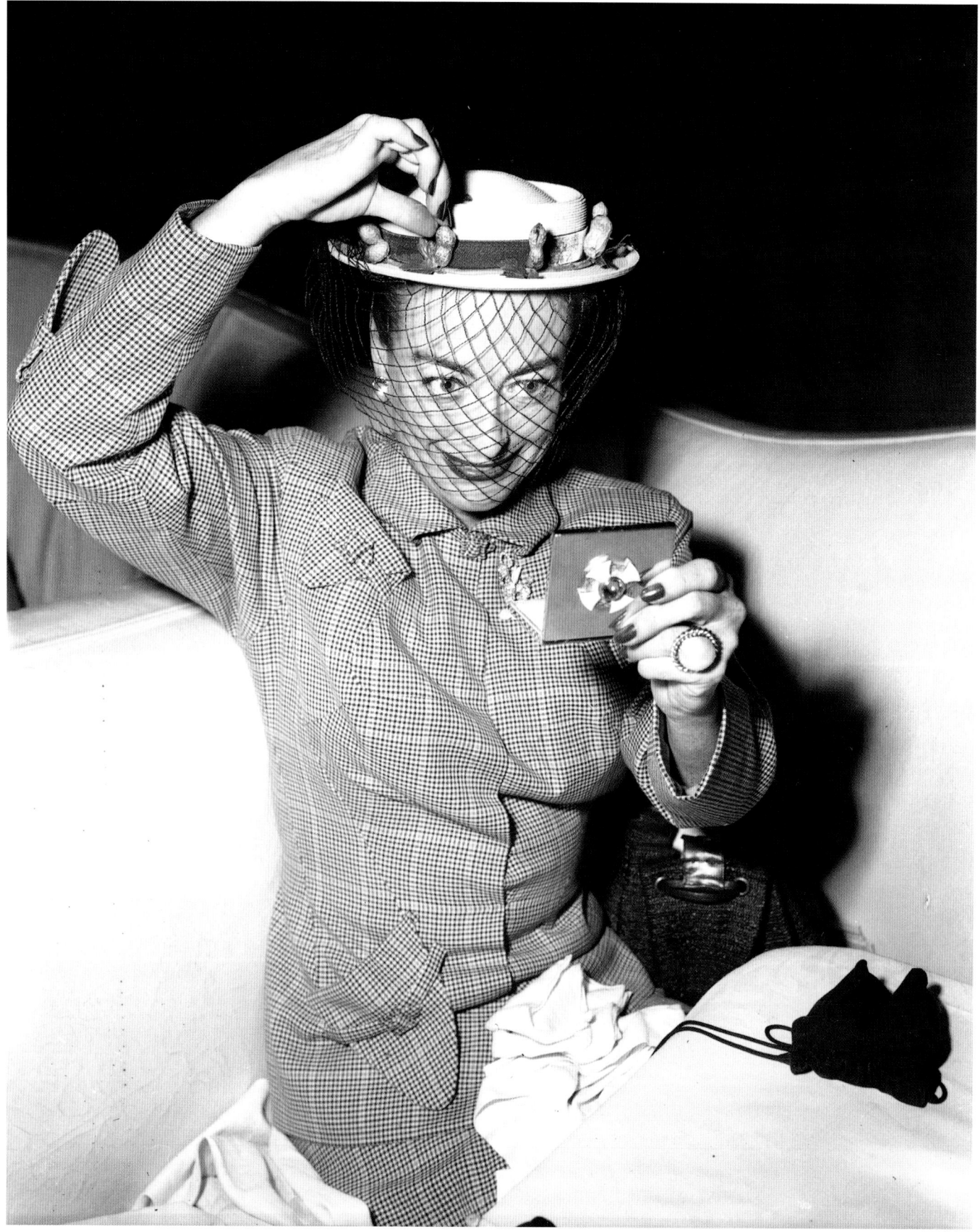

Joan Crawford

Film star Joan Crawford primps at the Pump Room in Chicago. Her role in 1945's "Mildred Pierce" proved to be a turning point in her career, earning her an Academy Award.

CHICAGO TRIBUNE HISTORICAL PHOTO, 1952

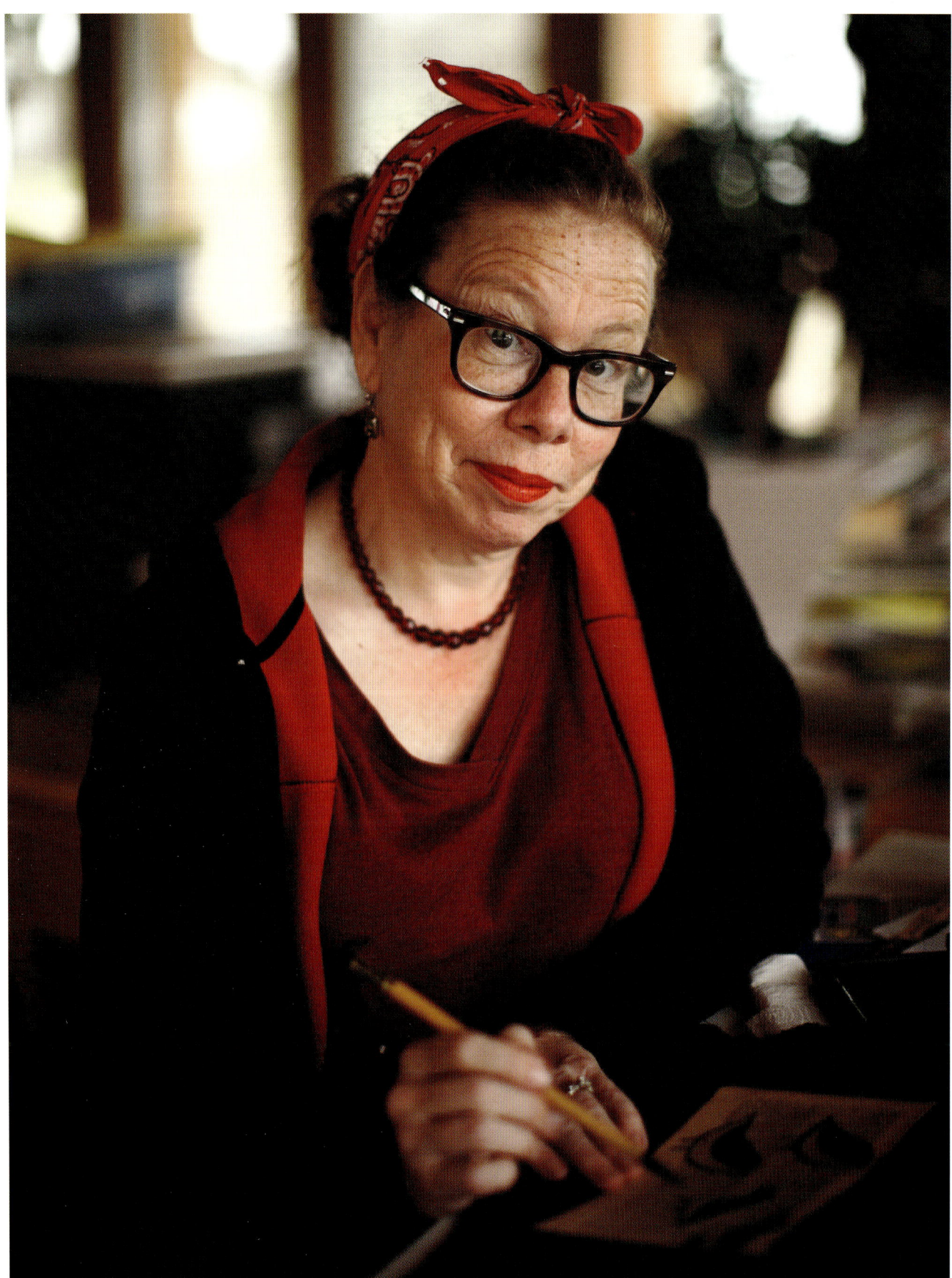

Lynda Barry

Cartooninst Lynda Barry at work in her Wisconsin studio. Barry moved to Chicago in 1989 after her comic strip "Ernie Pook's Comeek" started in the Chicago Reader. The comic became a standard of alterative weeklies across the country.

E. JASON WAMBSGANS, 2008

Rudolph Valentino

Back when traveling by rail was the only way to go, Chicago's train stations were a stopping point for the nation's celebrities, including Rudolph Valentino, a film star of the 1920s.

CHICAGO TRIBUNE HISTORICAL PHOTO, UNDATED

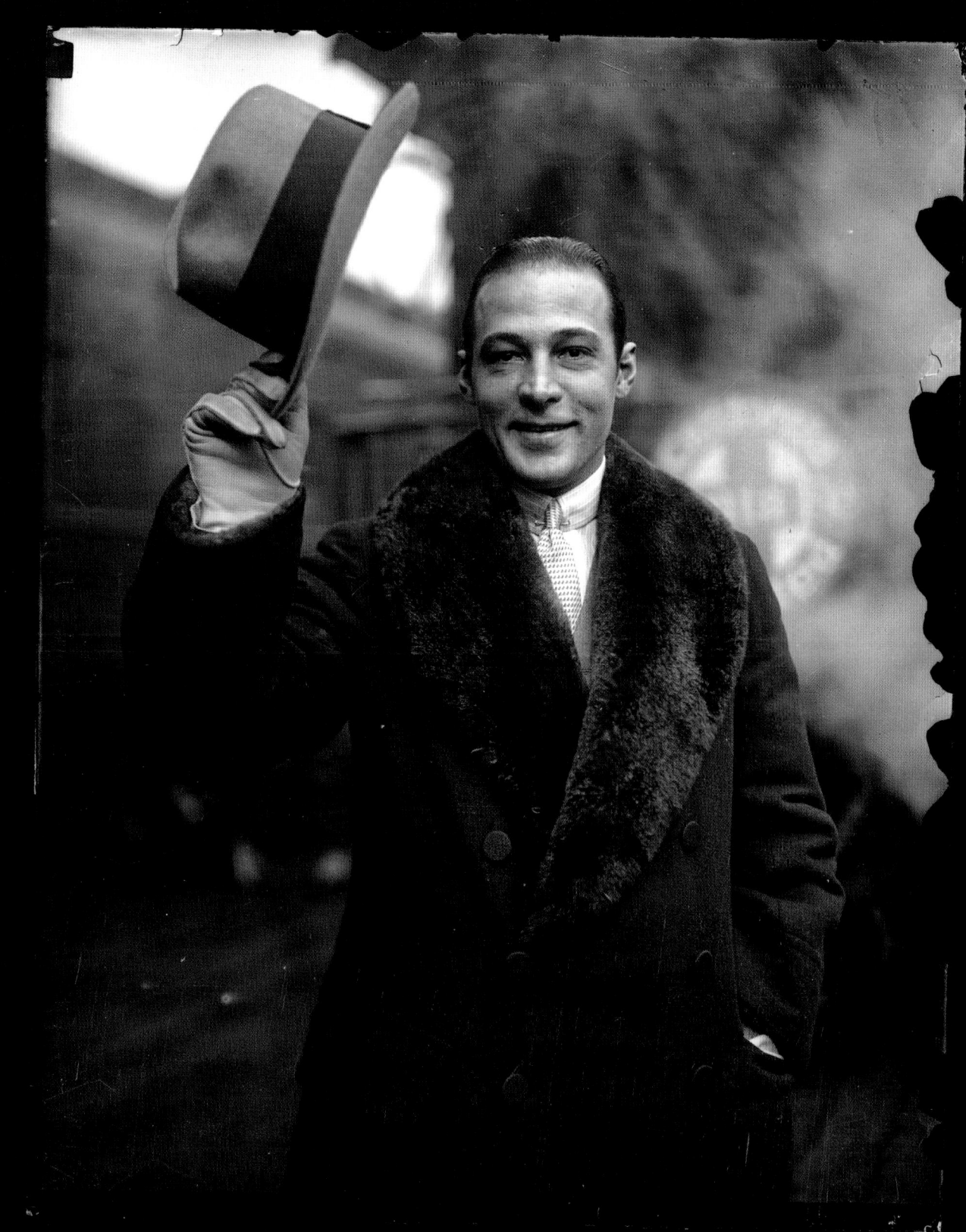

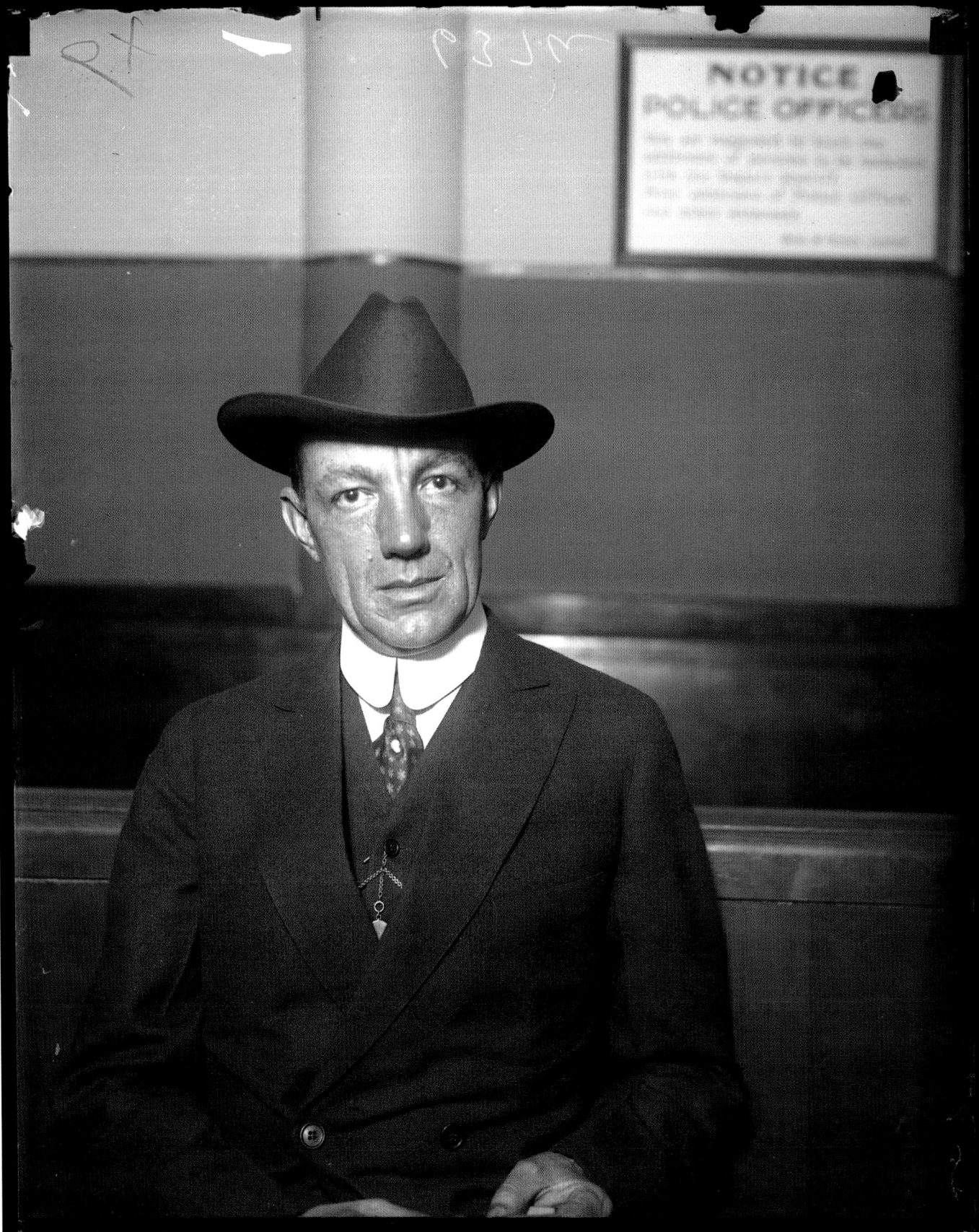

William Veeck Sr.

William Veeck Sr. was president of the Chicago Cubs from 1919 to 1933.

CHICAGO TRIBUNE HISTORICAL PHOTO, 1920s

D.J. Stone

Saddle bronc rider D.J. Stone, of Davis, Ill., listens as Ronald "Budda" Gatons, left, talks with Brett Mix before Gatons' bull ride at a rodeo competition in Gillette, Wyo. More than 30 students from Illinois made it that year to the national rodeo finals for high school students.

ZBIGNIEW BZDAK, 2005

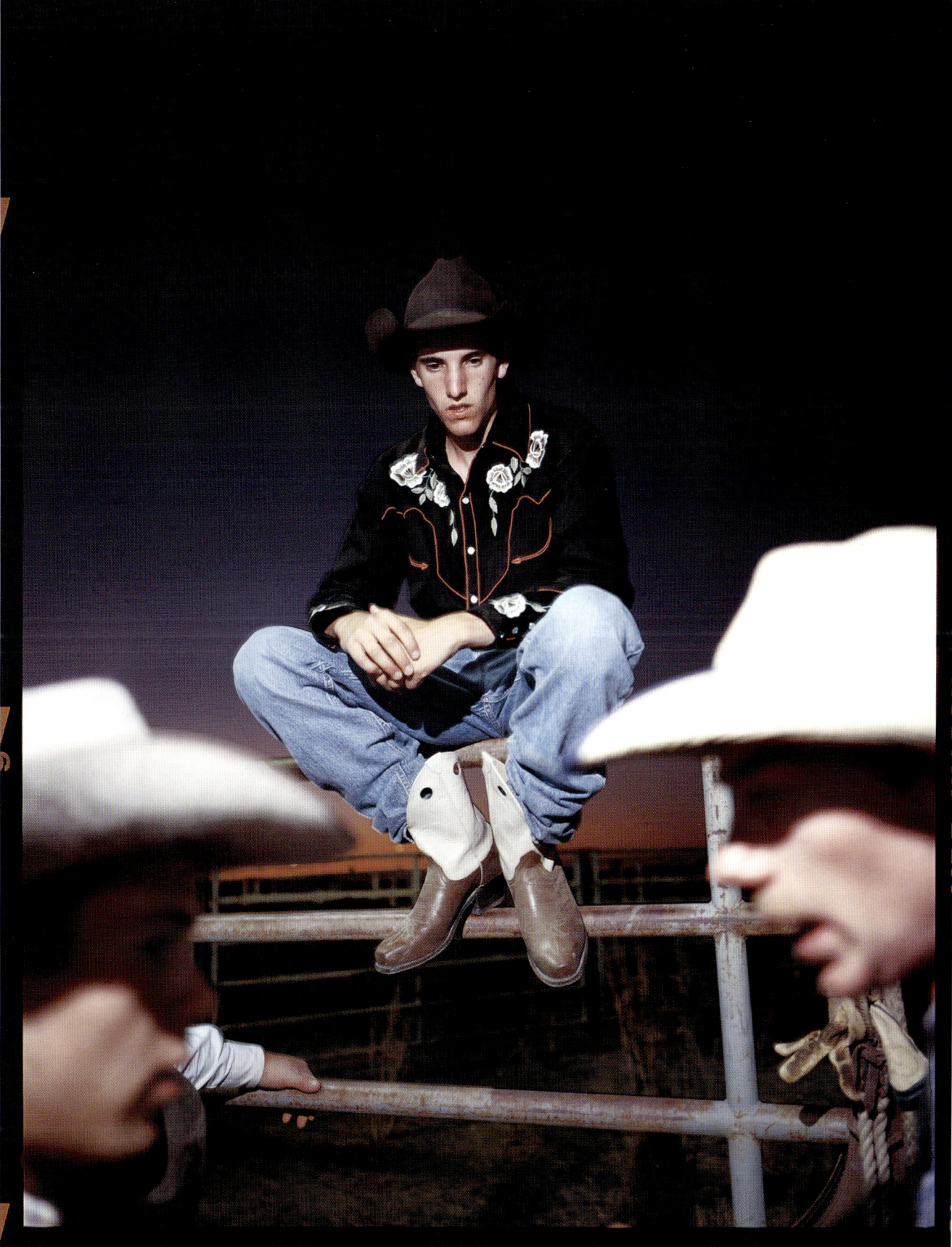

Jack Earle AND Major Mite

Circus performers Jack Earle and Major Mite, shown Sept. 15, 1926.

CHICAGO TRIBUNE HISTORICAL PHOTO, 1926

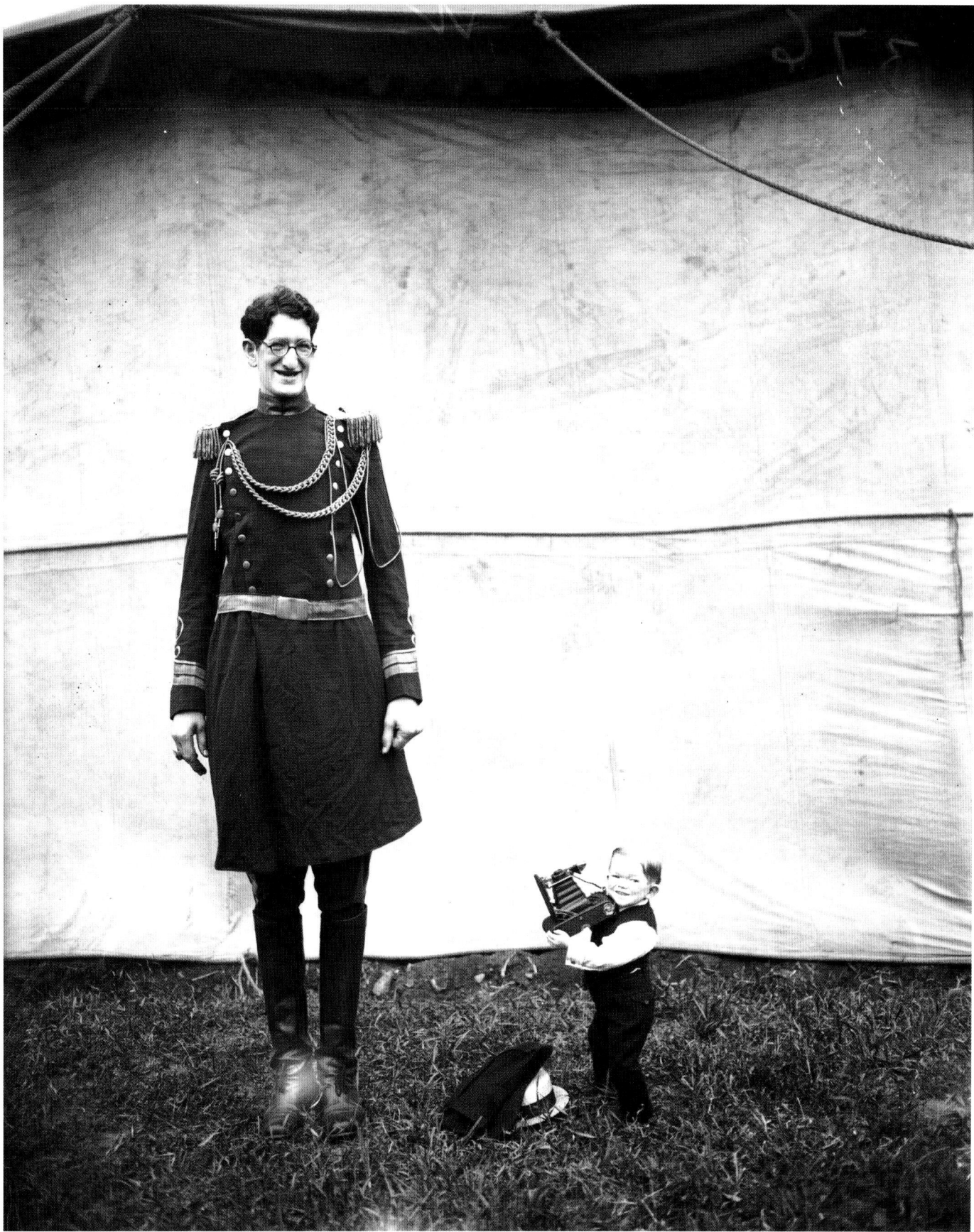

Jean Harlow

Jean Harlow lived in Highland Park, Ill., in her teens before she hit it big in Hollywood as an actress and a sex symbol.

CHICAGO TRIBUNE HISTORICAL PHOTO, 1930

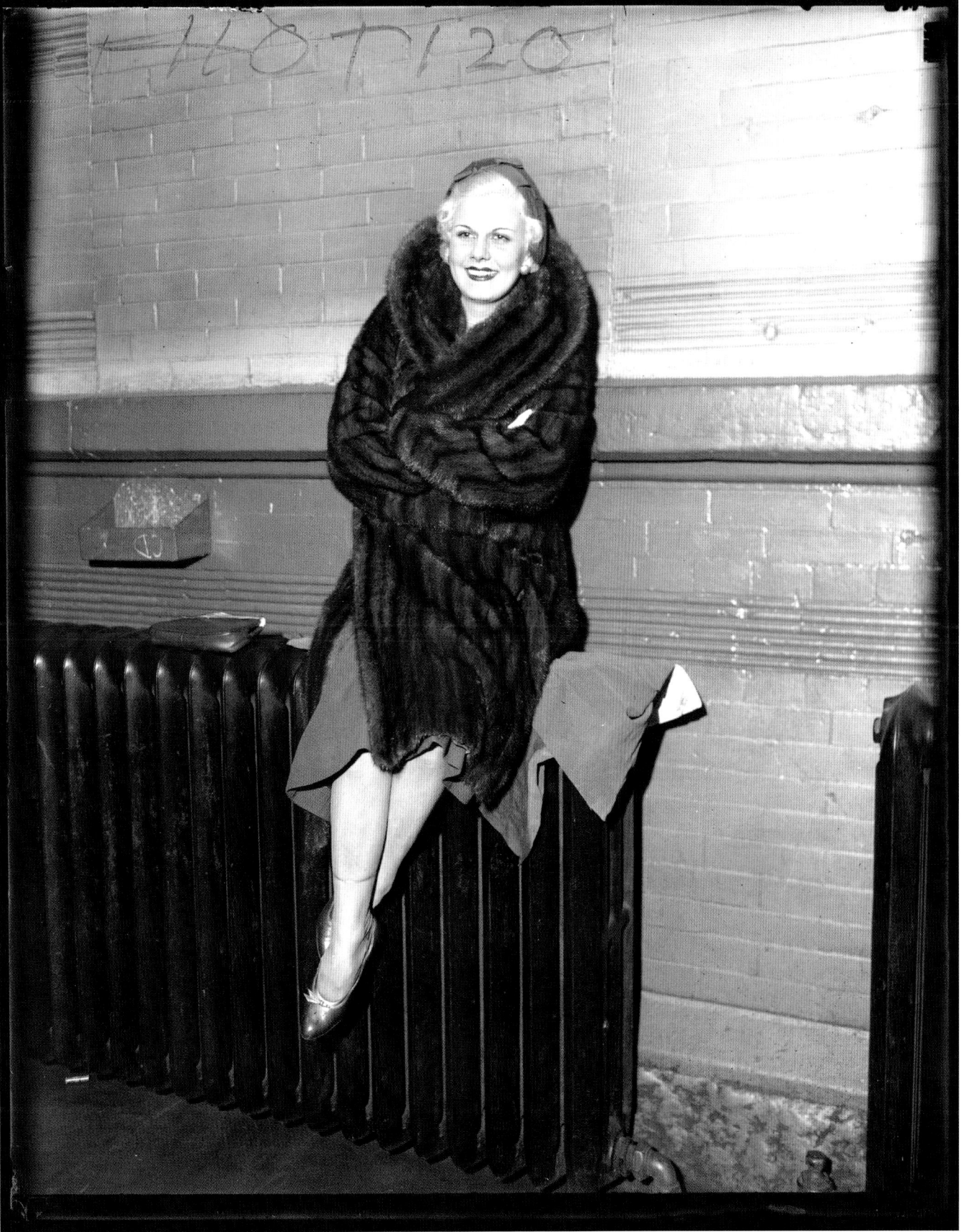

Andy Samberg

Actor Andy Samberg was in town at a taping of "Conan" at the Chicago Theatre, where he impersonated Chicago Mayor Rahm Emanuel. Samberg has shown a knack for impressions while part of the ensemble on "Saturday Night Live."

BRIAN CASSELLA, 2012

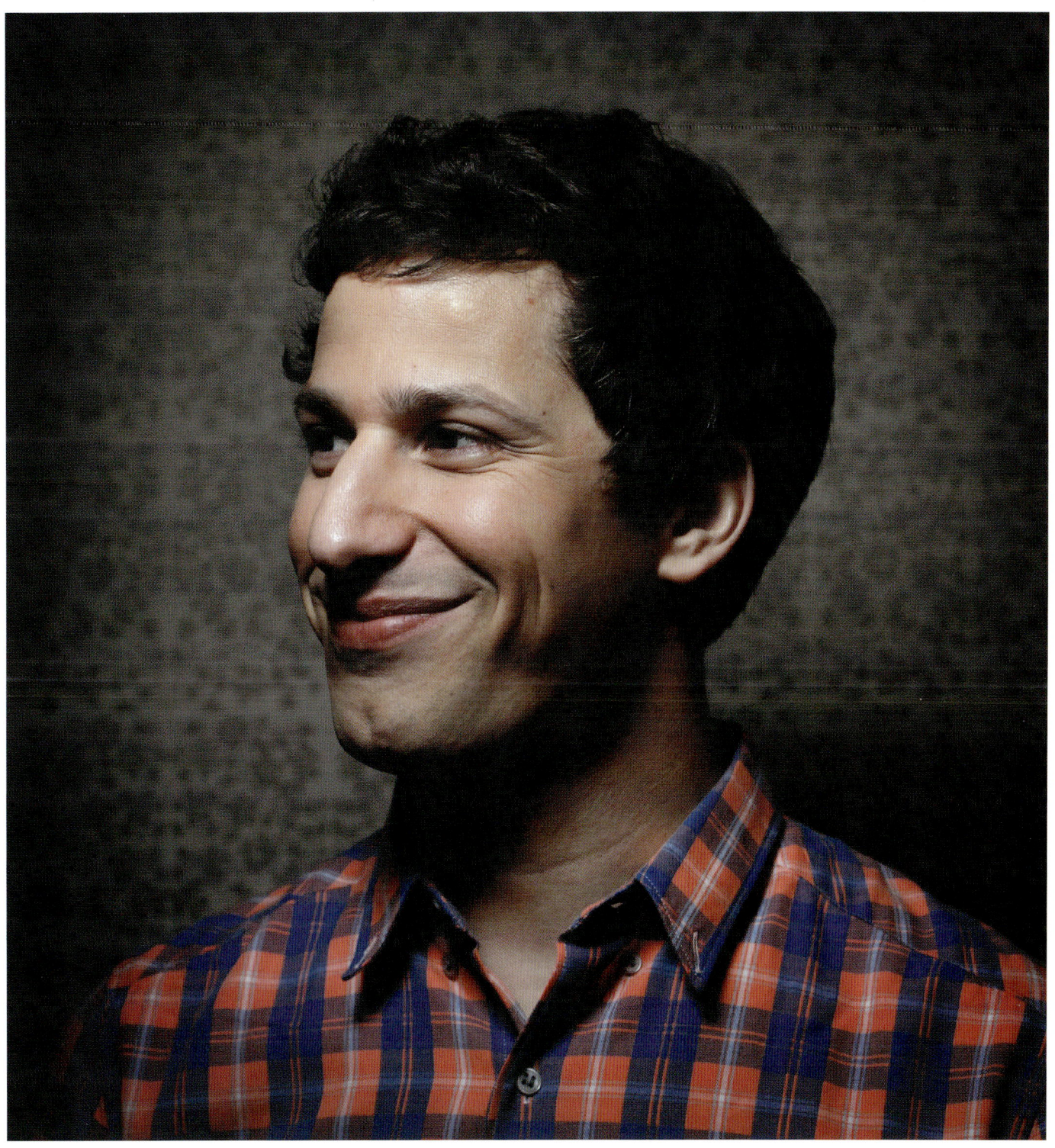

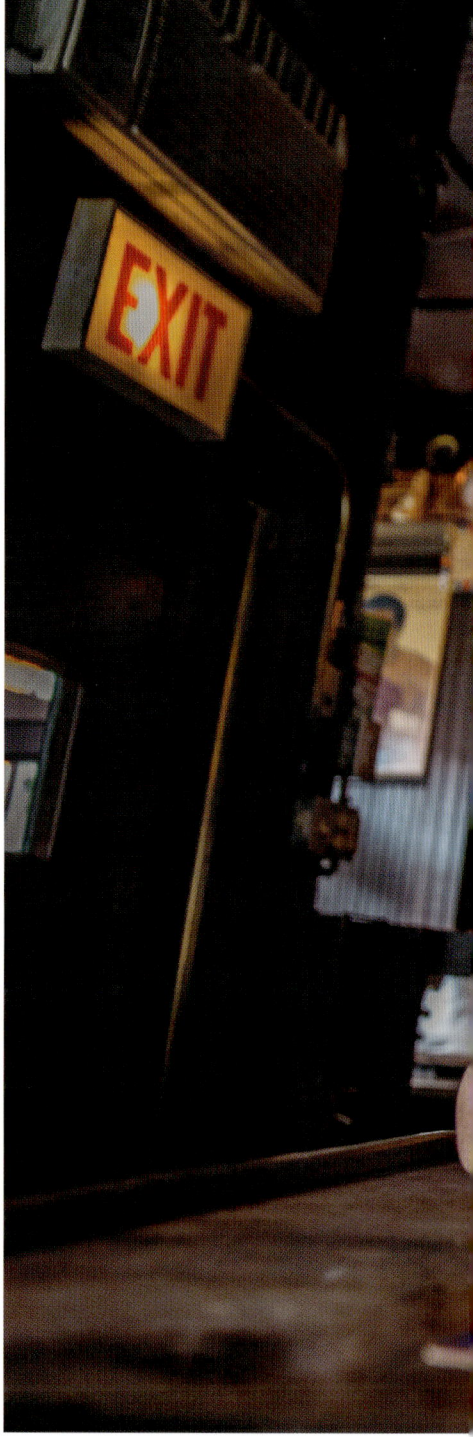

Michael Shannon

Chicago-trained actor Michael Shannon stops at Old Town Ale House in the city after rehearsing "Simpatico" at the Red Orchid Theatre, which he co-founded two decades ago.

ZBIGNIEW BZDAK, 2013

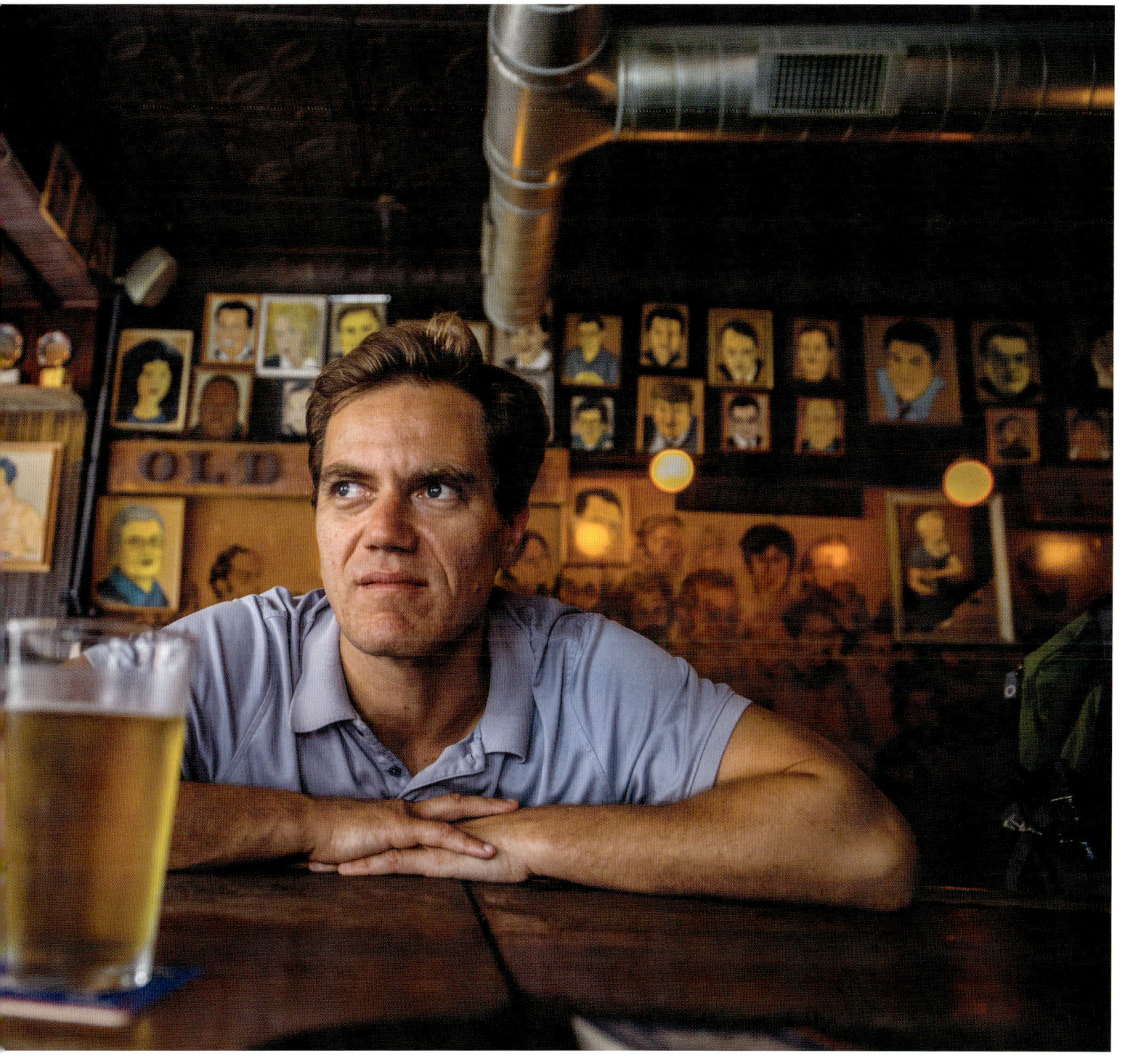

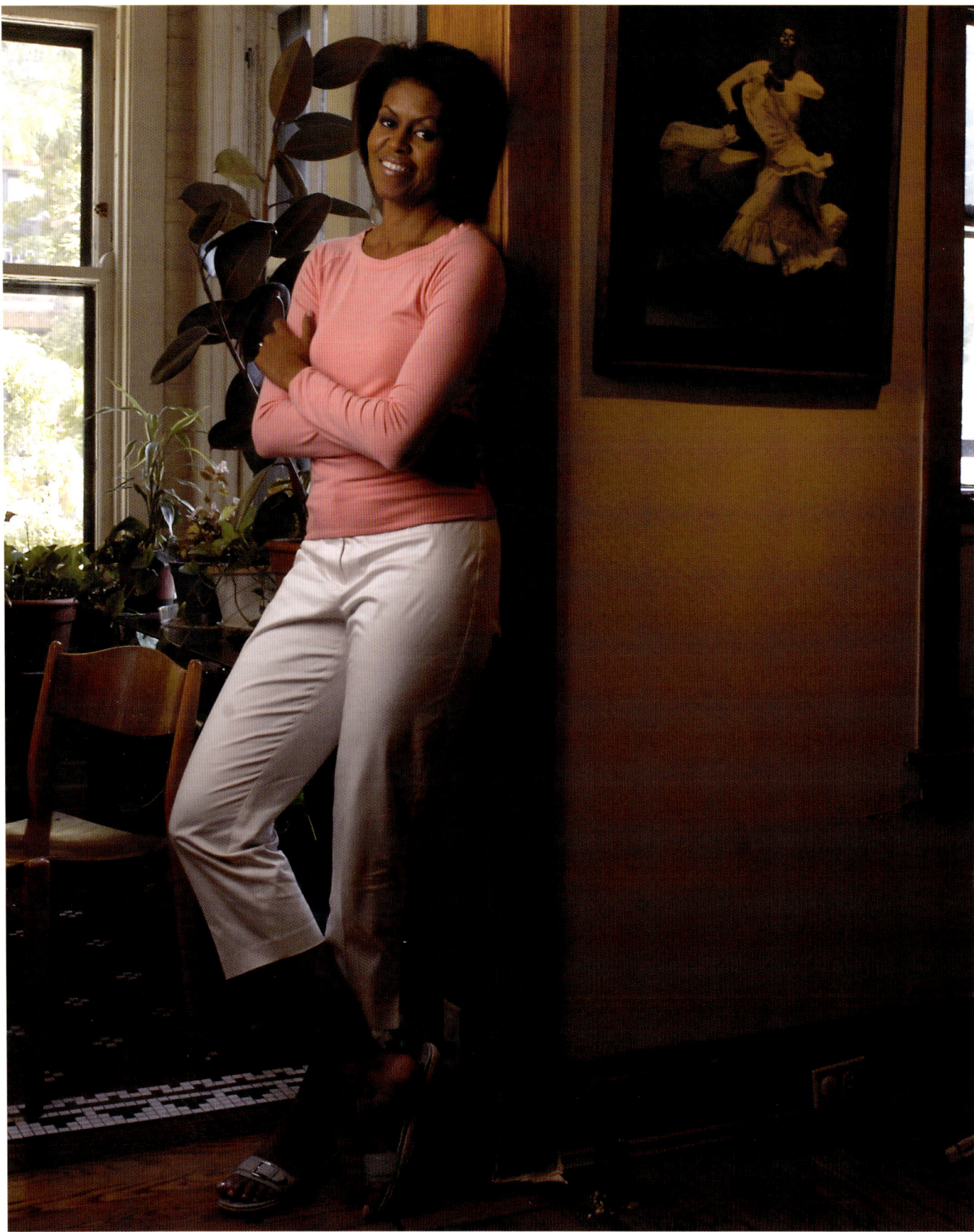

Michelle Obama

Michelle Obama at home in Chicago's Hyde Park neighborhood while her husband, Barack Obama, a candidate for the U.S. Senate, hit the campaign trail. She said in 2004 that politics is not her passion, but if it were, "I'd find out how to do it and make it work." Since becoming first lady, Obama has used her national spotlight to advocate for healthier lifestyles.

ZBIGNIEW BZDAK, 2004

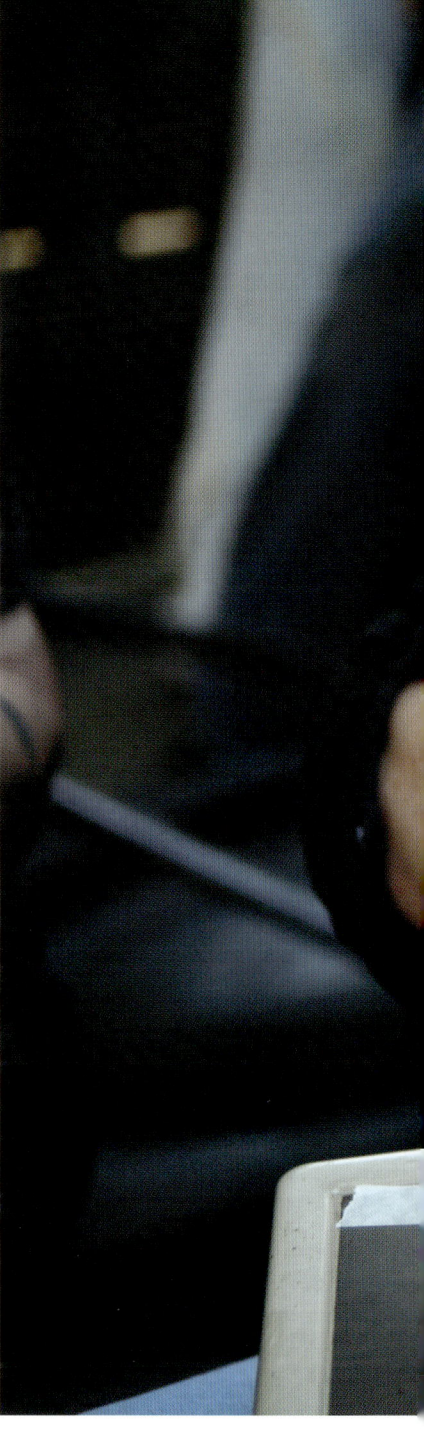

Betty Loren-Maltese

Former Cicero Town President Betty Loren-Maltese autographs a dollar bill during a garage sale of her belongings at a friend's house in Forest View, Ill. The former convict, who spent seven years in federal custody for bilking Cicero residents of more than $12 million in a mob-related insurance scam, said she was in need of money for living expenses.

E. JASON WAMBSGANS, 2011

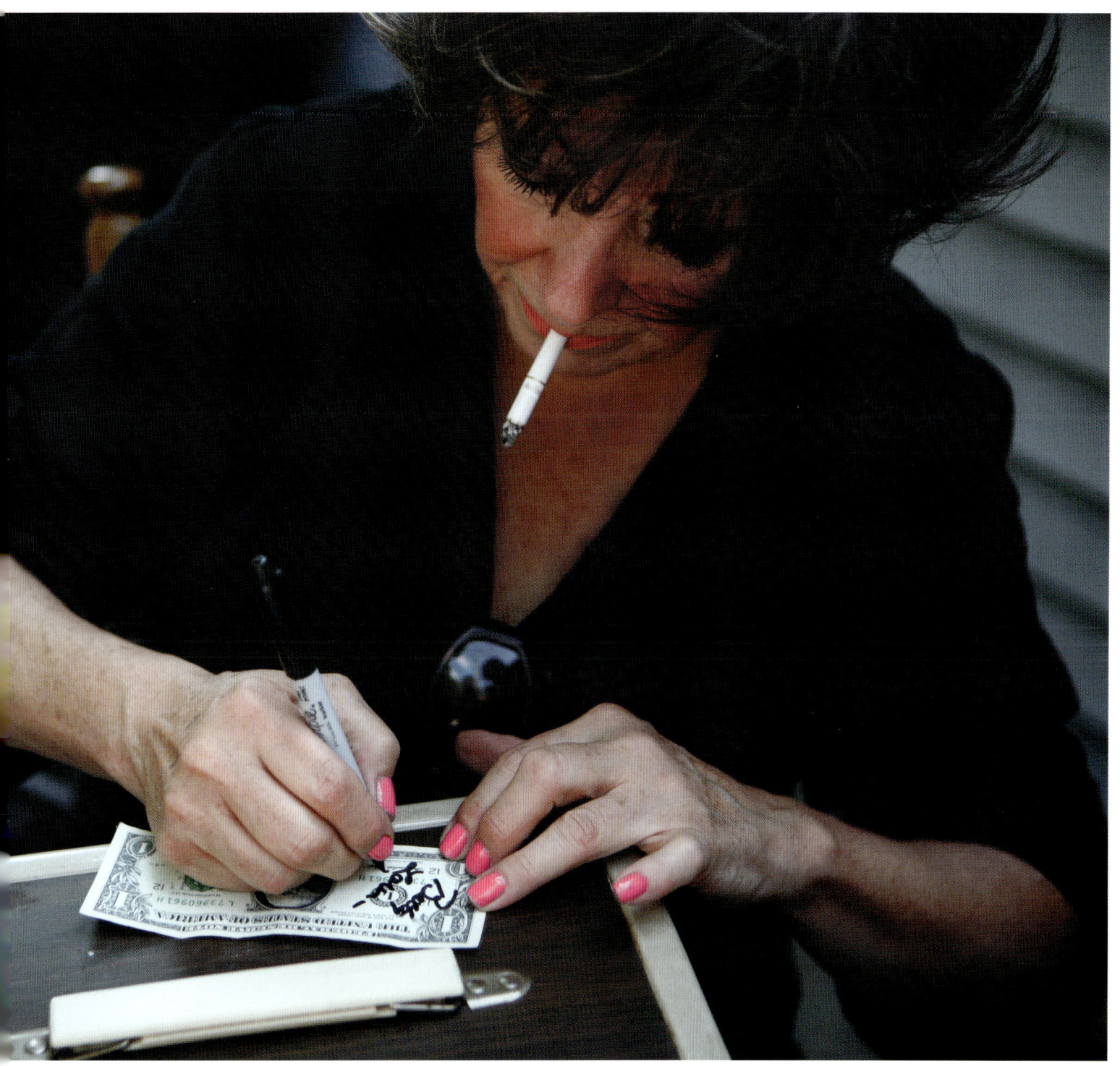

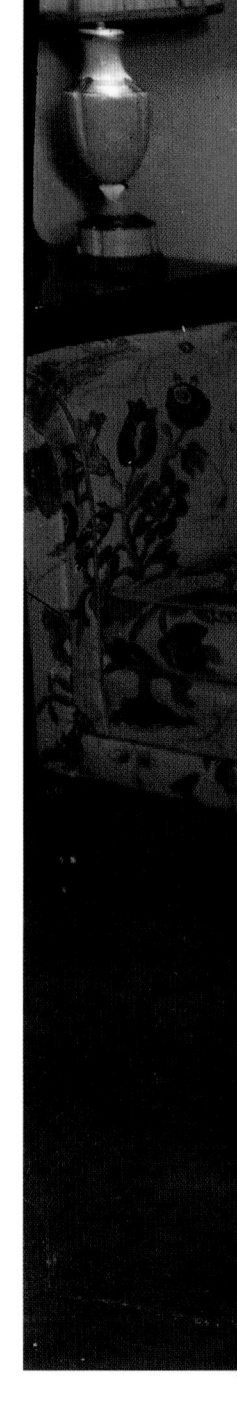

Pola Negri

Polish actress Pola Negri poses at Chicago's State-Lake Theater. She came to the U.S. in the mid-1920s after a successful European career. After a very public display at actor Rudolph Valentino's funeral, where she claimed they were engaged and placed a wreath containing her name on his coffin, as well as fainting whenever a photographer was near, she fell out of favor with the public.

TRIBUNE HISTORICAL PHOTO, 1933

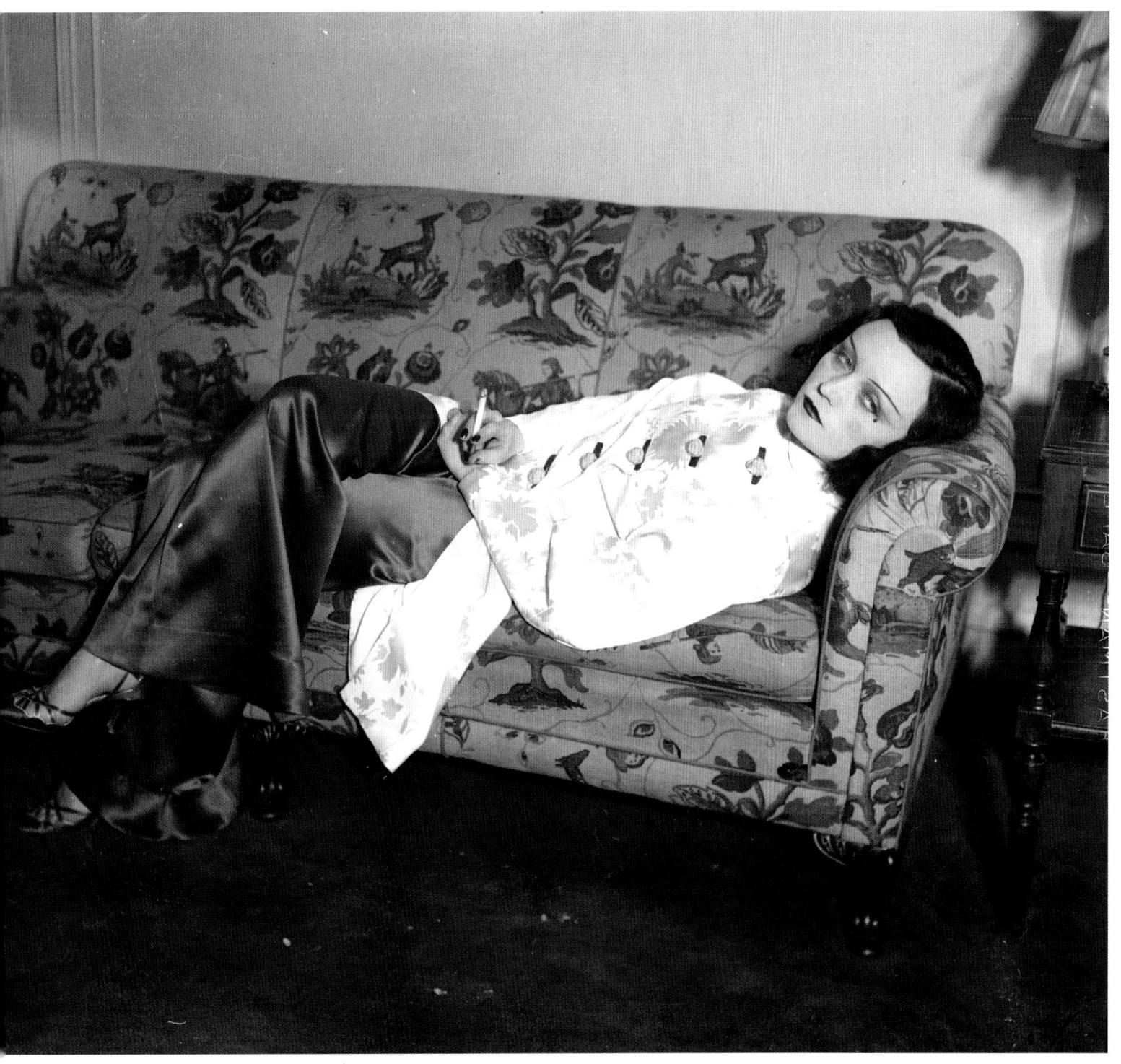

John Keating

Stage actor John Keating brought the house down as a singing mail carrier in the Black Ensemble Theater's production of "From Doo Wop to Hip Hop." His acting chops inspired the Tribune to declare him a hot new face in Chicago theater in the summer of 2013.

ANTHONY SOUFFLE, 2013

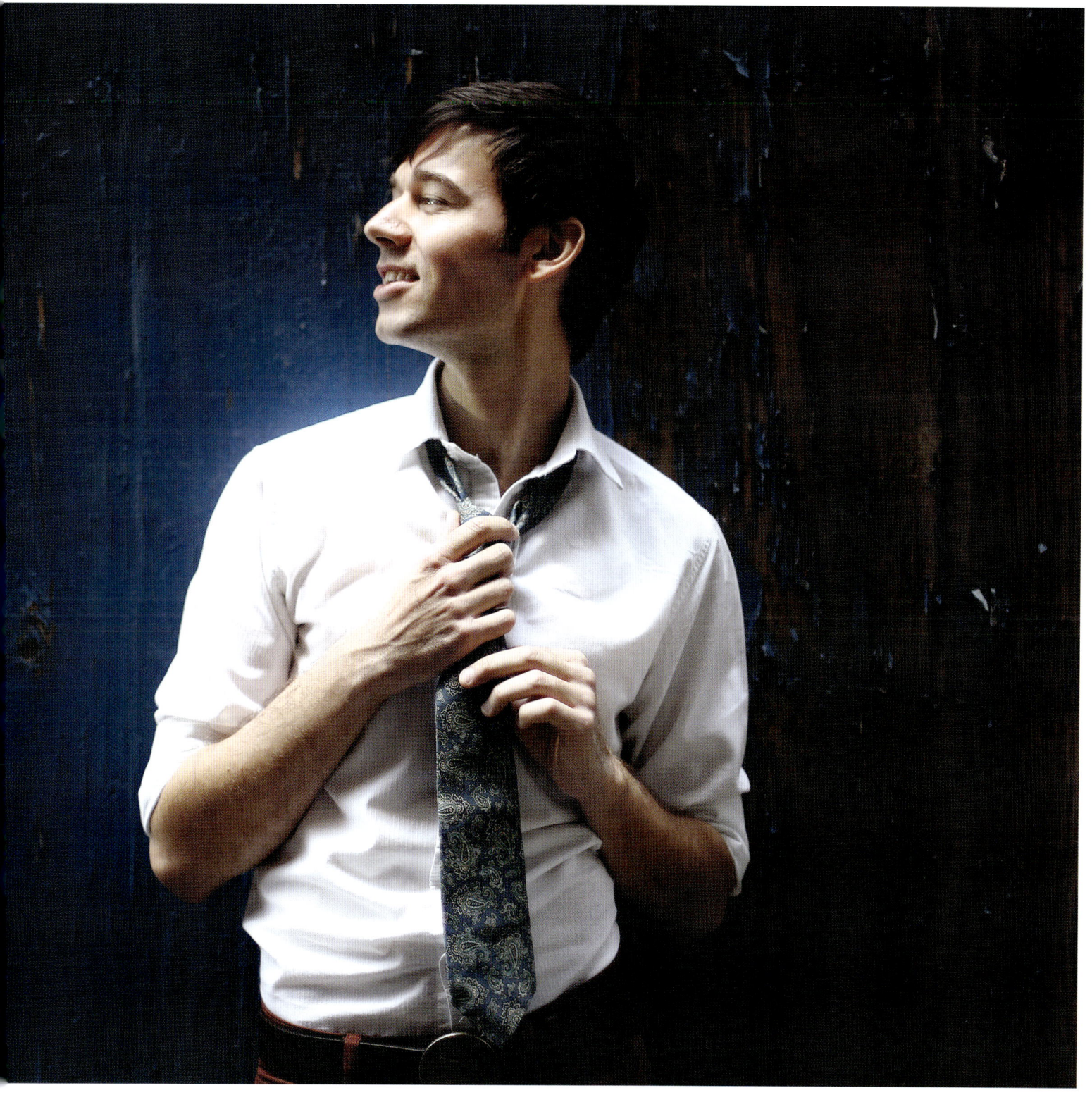

Rod Blagojevich AND
Frank Vincent

Illinois Gov. Rod Blagojevich leaves a bill-signing ceremony at a Chicago restaurant. The new law authorized a tax credit for filmmakers. Behind the governor is actor Frank Vincent who, among other roles, played mobster Phil Leotardo on the HBO series "The Sopranos."

CHRIS WALKER 2008

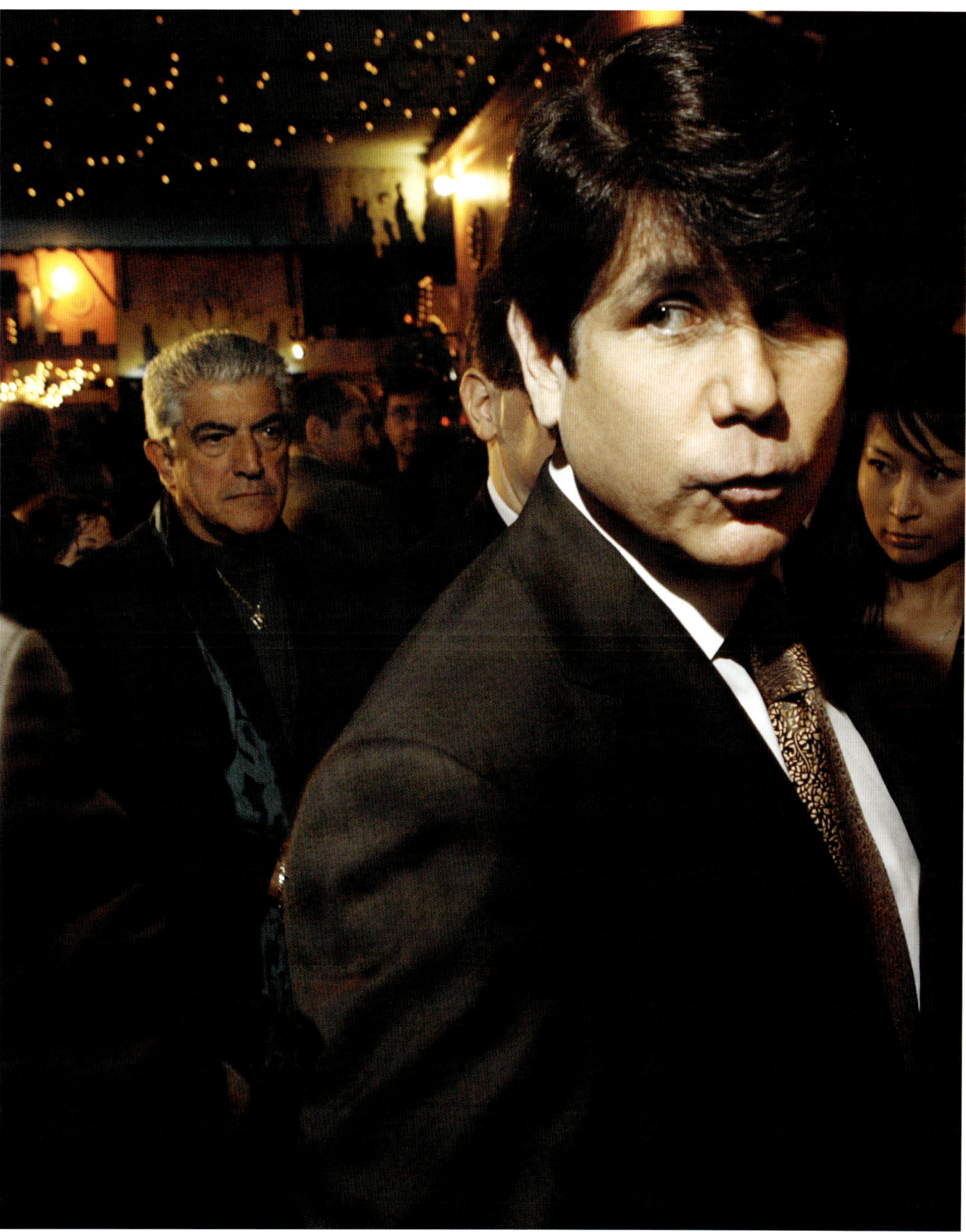

Rod Blagojevich

Former Illinois Gov. Rod Blagojevich talks briefly with reporters after returning home from a jog. Blagojevich became the first governor in state history to be impeached and ousted from office. His fall from grace came after he was charged with corruption that included allegations he tried to sell President Barack Obama's vacated U.S. Senate seat. He was convicted in June 2011 of numerous charges and is serving time in federal prison.

CHRIS SWEDA, 2010

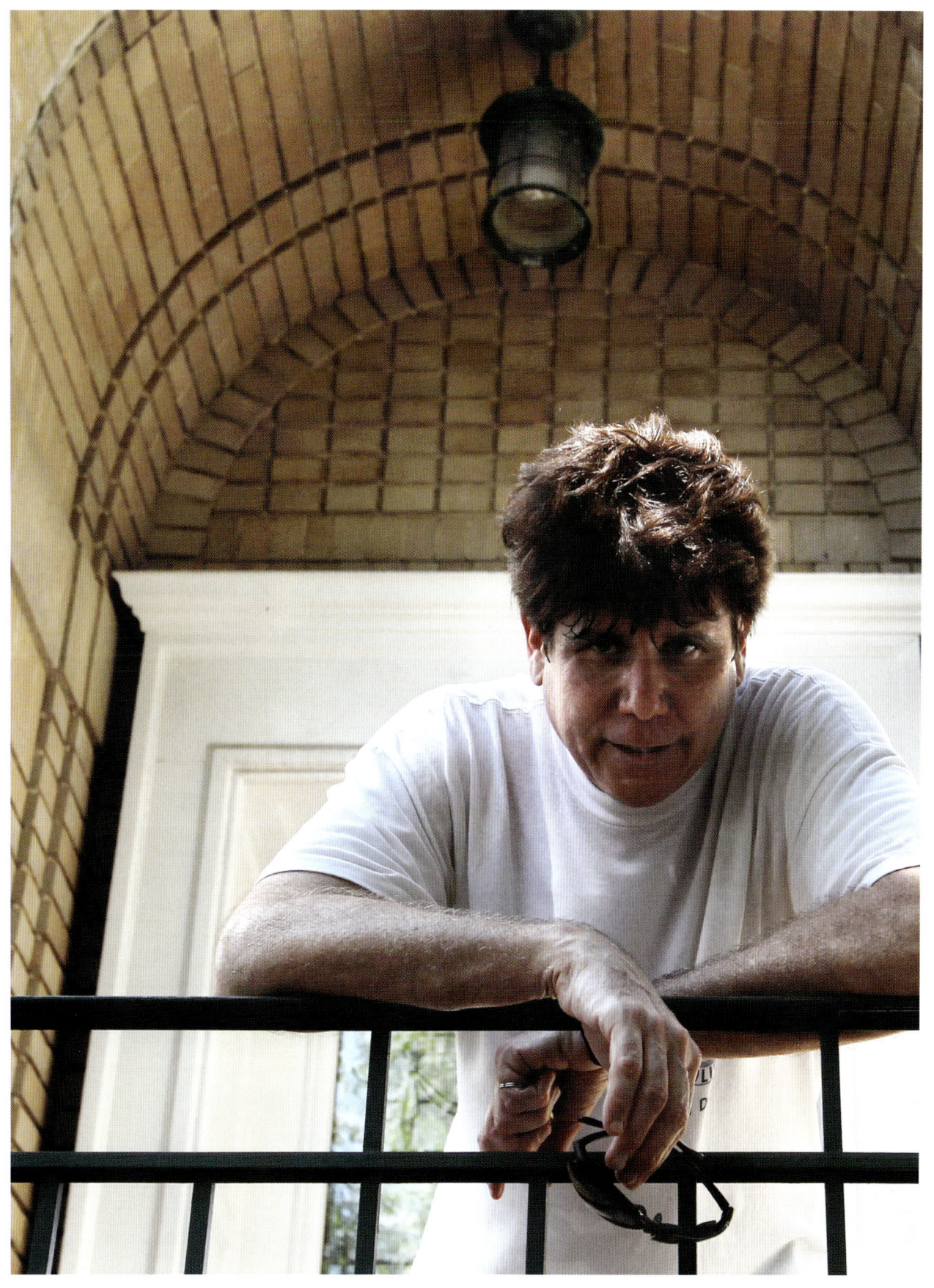

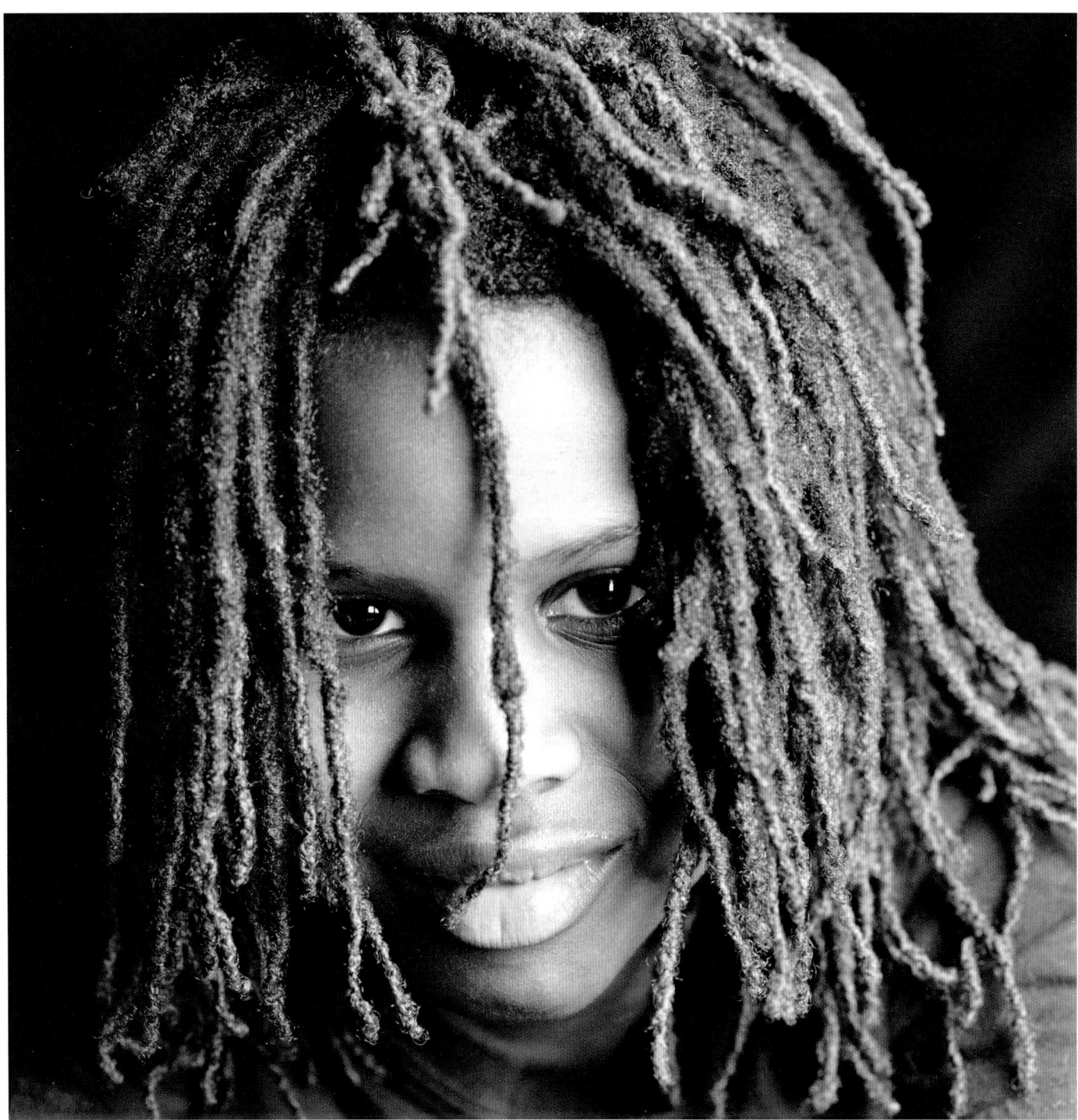

Jessica Hubert

Jessica Hubert, 9, a third-grader at the University of Chicago Laboratory School, spent her Sunday attending Mass with her dad, practicing karate and hanging out at home.

STACEY WESCOTT 2003

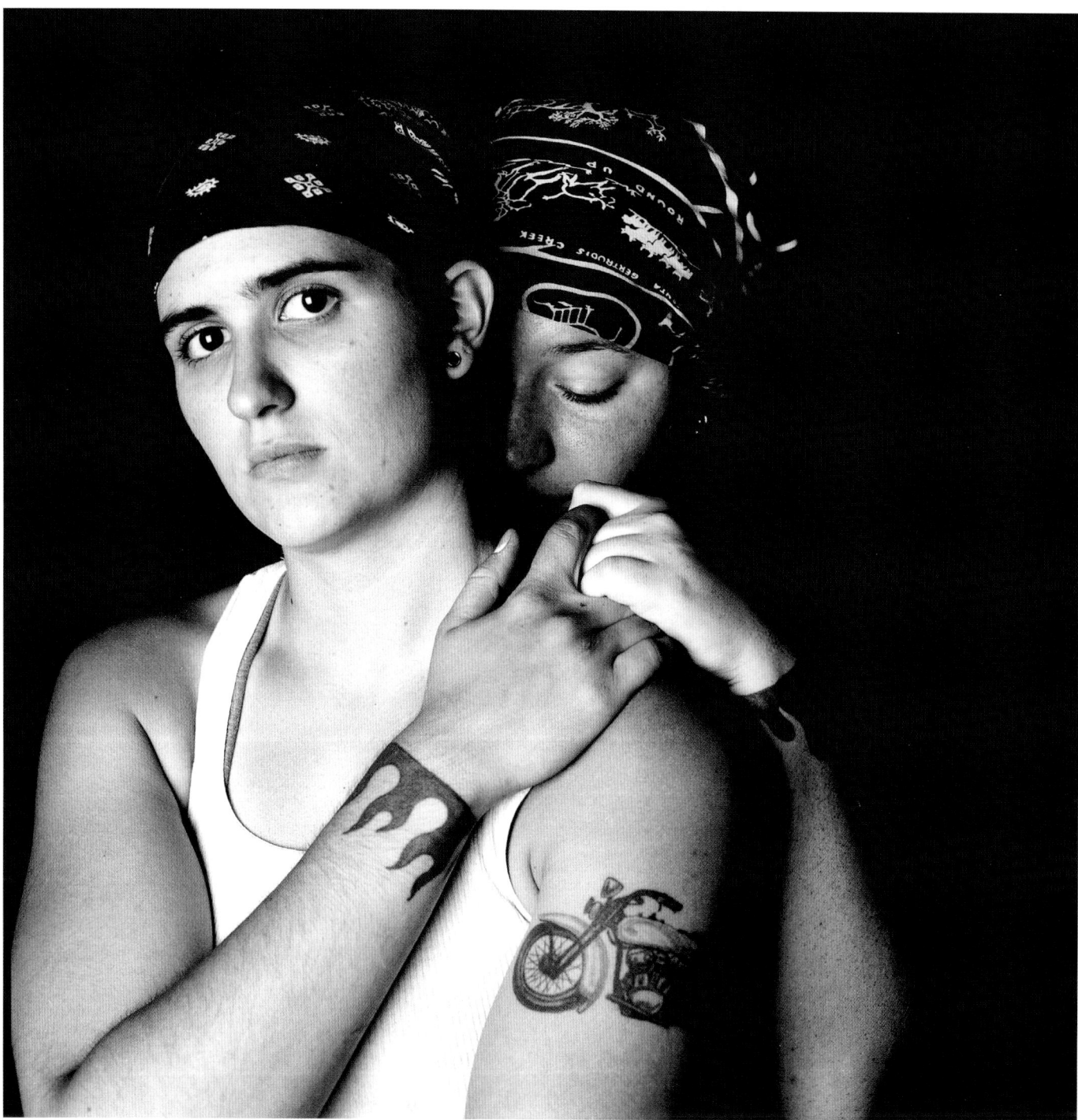

Sarah Stigler AND Missy Davellis

Sarah Stigler, 21, of Chicago, with her partner, Missy Davellis. Stigler, an avid labor rights advocate, was in her first week of a five-year apprenticeship with Local 130 of the plumbers union when this photo appeared in the Chicago Tribune. "It's important visibility," she said. "For me personally, (the attention) is embarrassing, but as a tradeswoman, it's important. We can't afford to be average."

STACEY WESCOTT, 2003

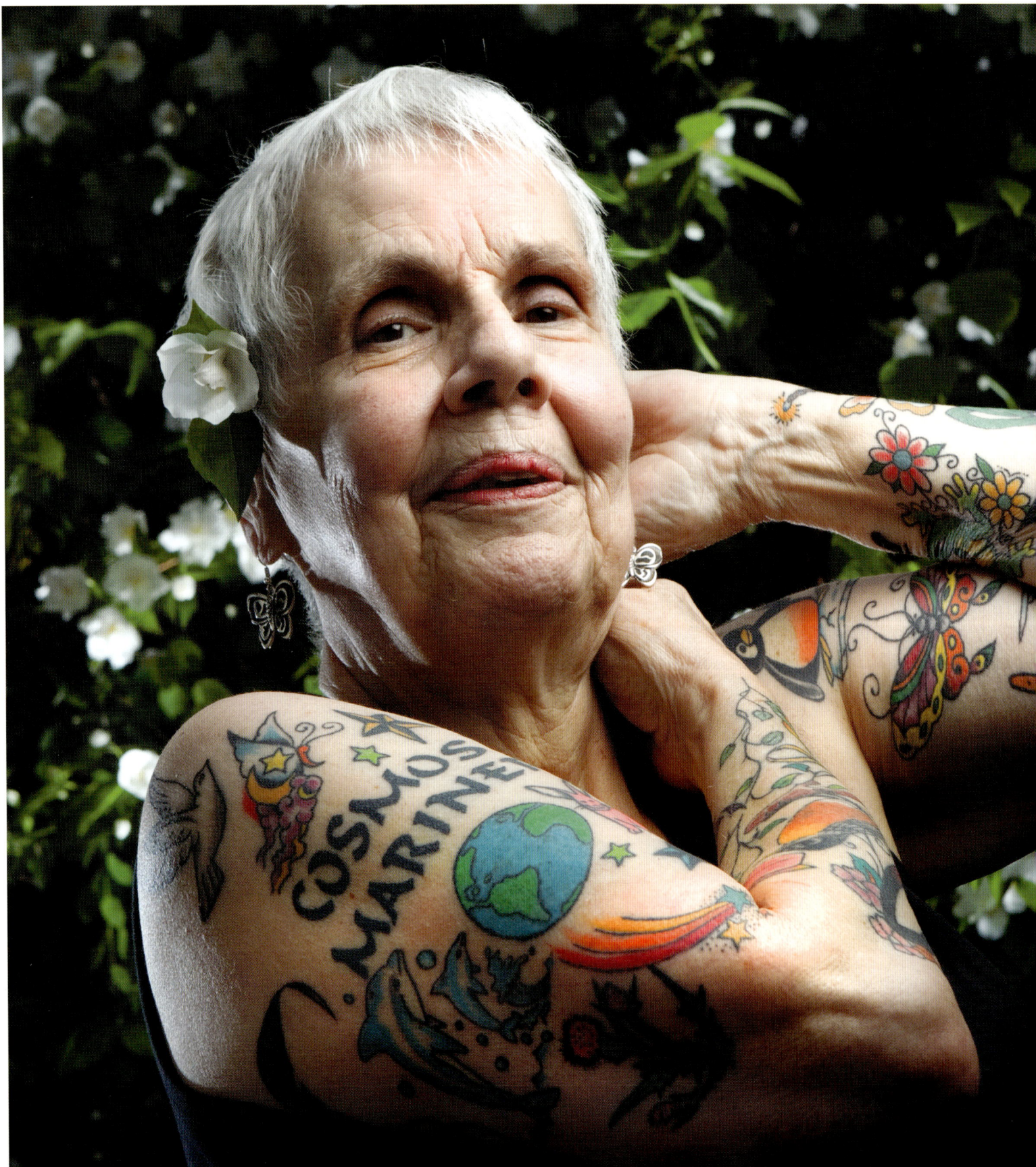

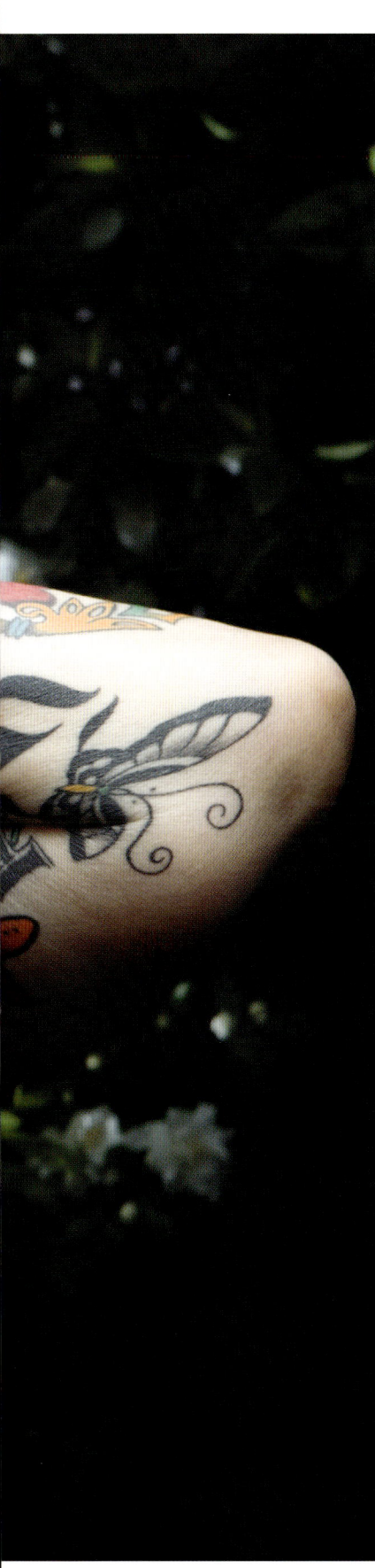

Helen Lambin

Helen Lambin shows off her tattoos while standing in the backyard of her Edgewater neighborhood home in Chicago. She feared growing old gracefully, so she got tattoos, which attract a lot of attention on the street during summer months.

ALEX GARCIA, 2010

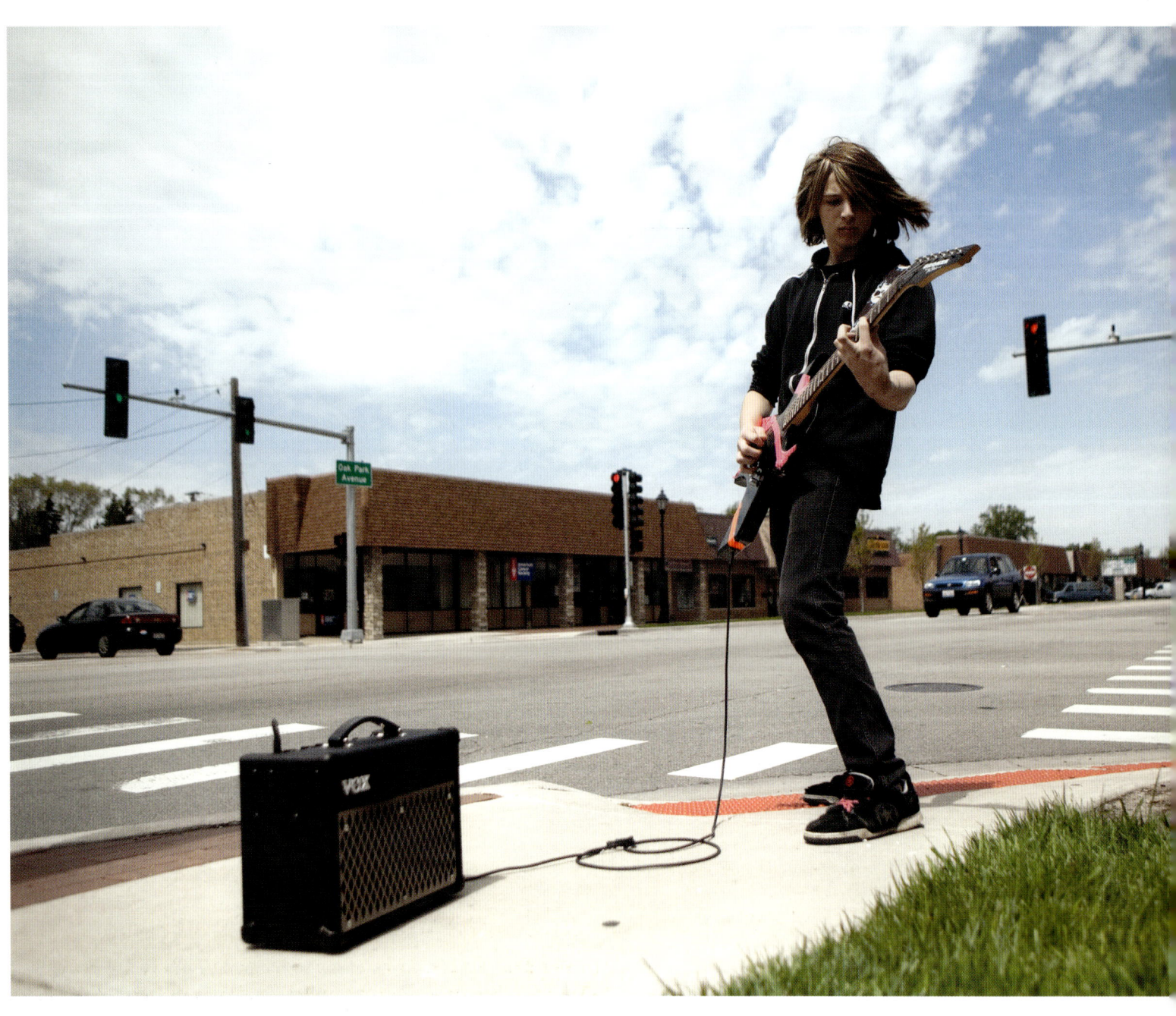

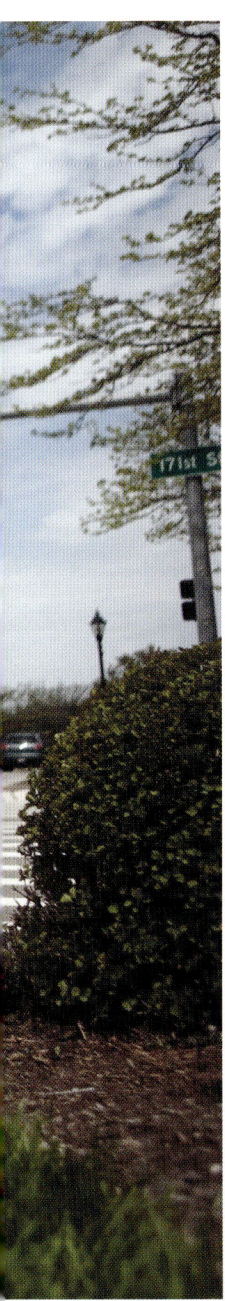

Jetta Tomlianovich

Jetta Tomlianovich, 15, was on his way to a Subway restaurant with friends in Tinley Park, Ill., when he stopped at the corner of Oak Park Avenue and 171st Street, plugged his guitar into his amplifier and played an impromptu concert for his friends and passing motorists. He performed a medley of rock classics plus edgy interpretations of "Somewhere Over the Rainbow" and the "Star Wars" theme song. "I've only been playing a year, but I practice all day, every day," said Jetta, taking advantage of a half-day of school. "I try to do this when it's nice out. I like showing off."

DAVID PIERINI, 2010

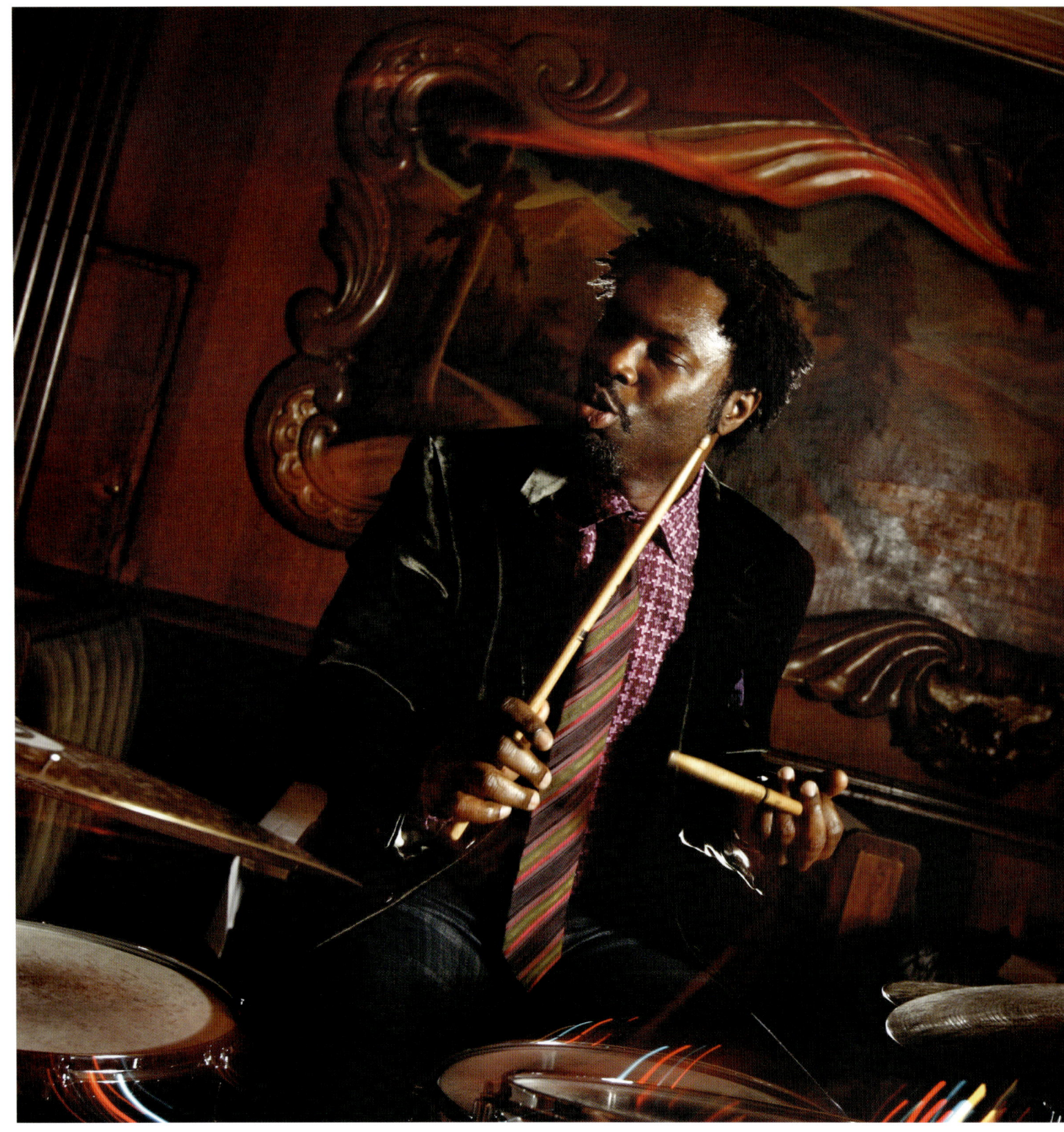

Dana Hall

Jazz drummer Dana Hall, shown at the Chicago jazz club the Green Mill, has won critical acclaim for his work in other bands and as the leader of his own quintet.

BRIAN CASSELLA, 2009

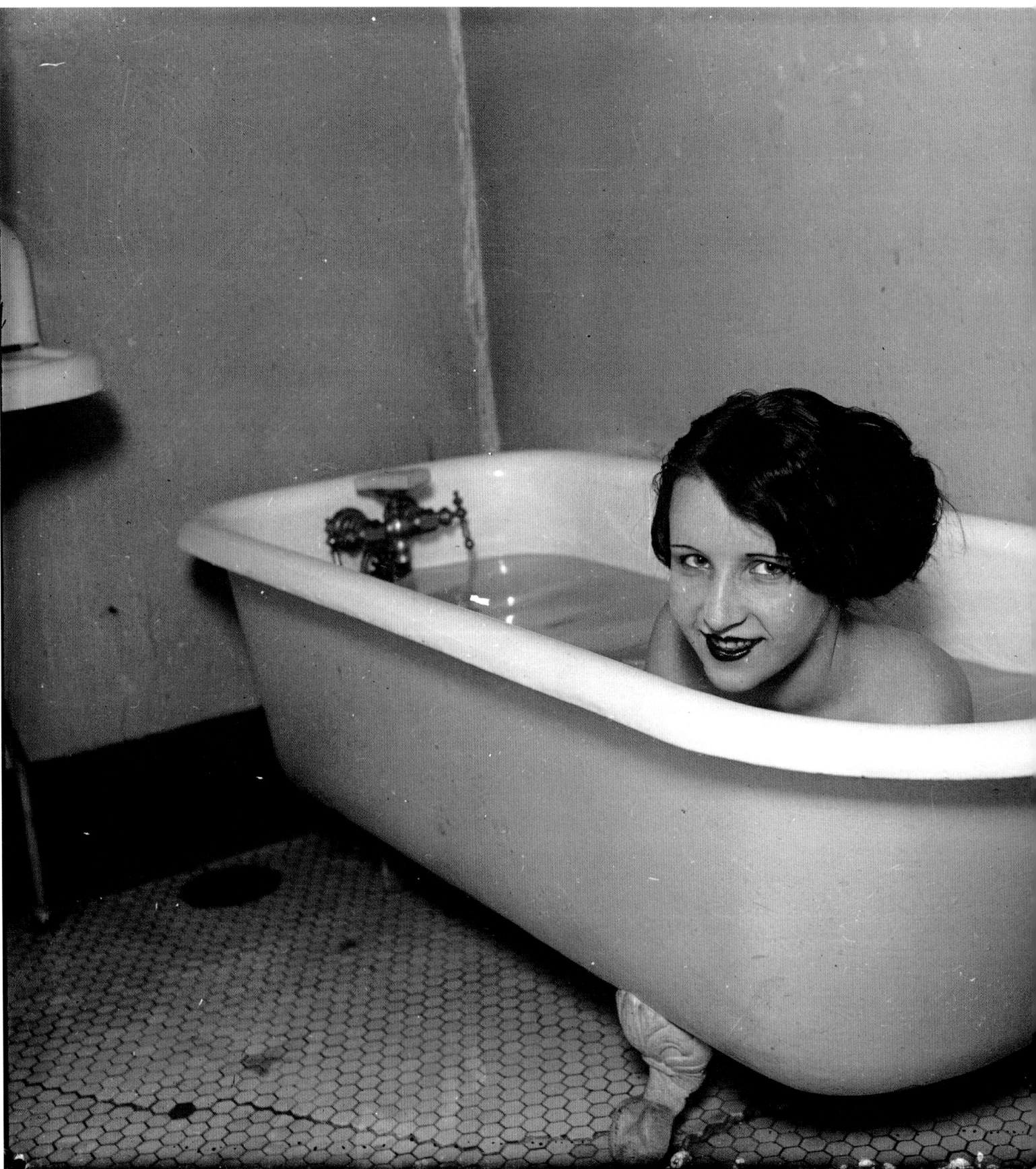

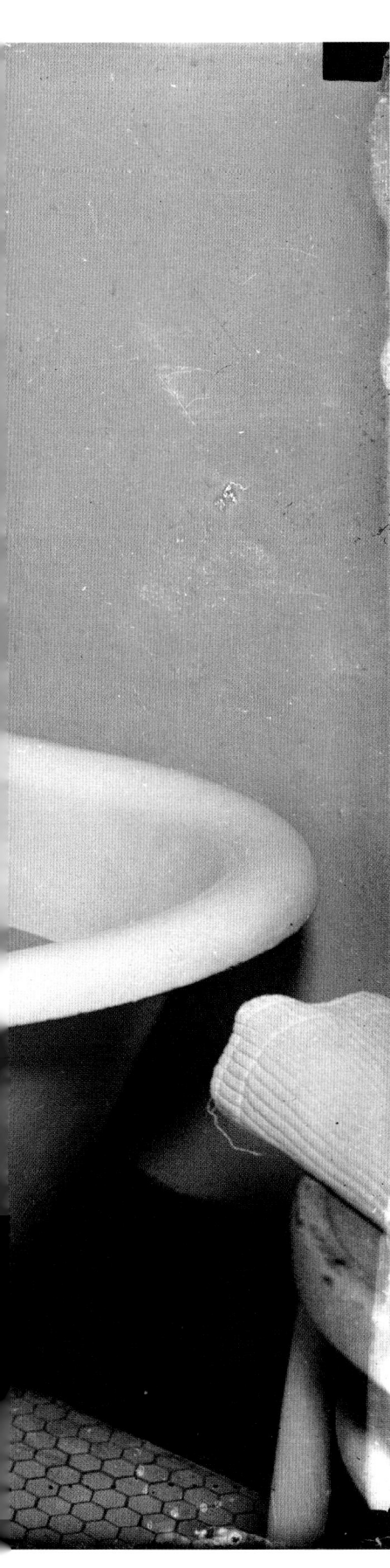

Marci Sanders

Marci Sanders, a flapper, displays the free-spirit reminiscent of the Roaring '20s, a time remembered for its postwar throw-caution-to-the-wind zeitgeist and the early stirrings of restlessness that presaged the women's liberation movement.

CHICAGO TRIBUNE HISTORICAL PHOTO, 1920s

Anna May Wong

Chinese-American actress and film star Anna May Wong was best known in the '20s for her smoky villainess part in Douglas Fairbanks' 1924 "Thief of Baghdad."

CHICAGO TRIBUNE HISTORICAL PHOTO, 1924

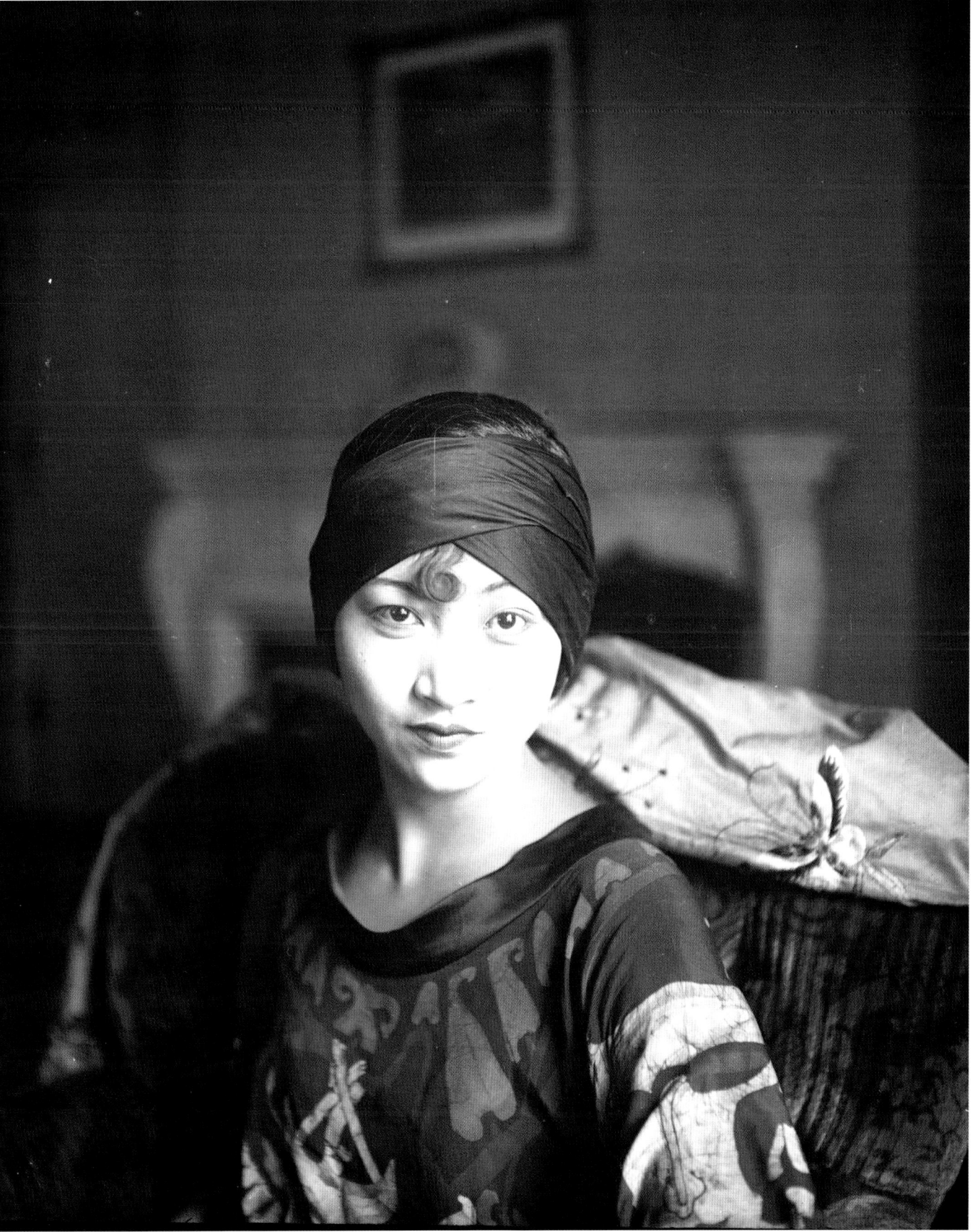

Bill Ayers

Author and retired professor Bill Ayers, shown at a California coastal park, earned notoriety in the 1970s as a member of the Weather Underground, a group that bombed government property in protest of the Vietnam War. His name came up in 2008 in connection with then-presidential candidate Barack Obama during a debate between Obama and Hillary Rodham Clinton. Ayers taught at the University of Illinois at Chicago.

CHRIS WALKER, 2001

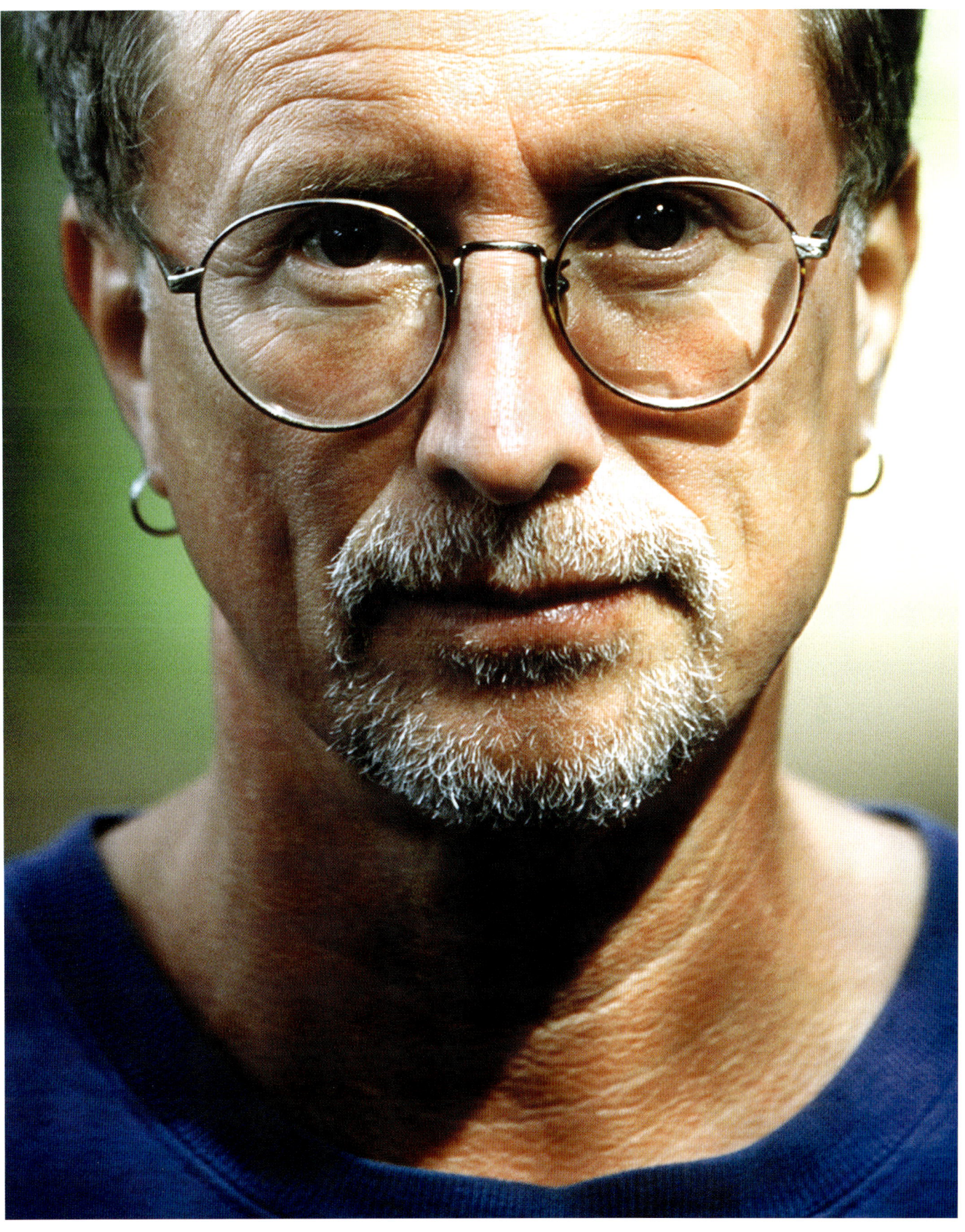

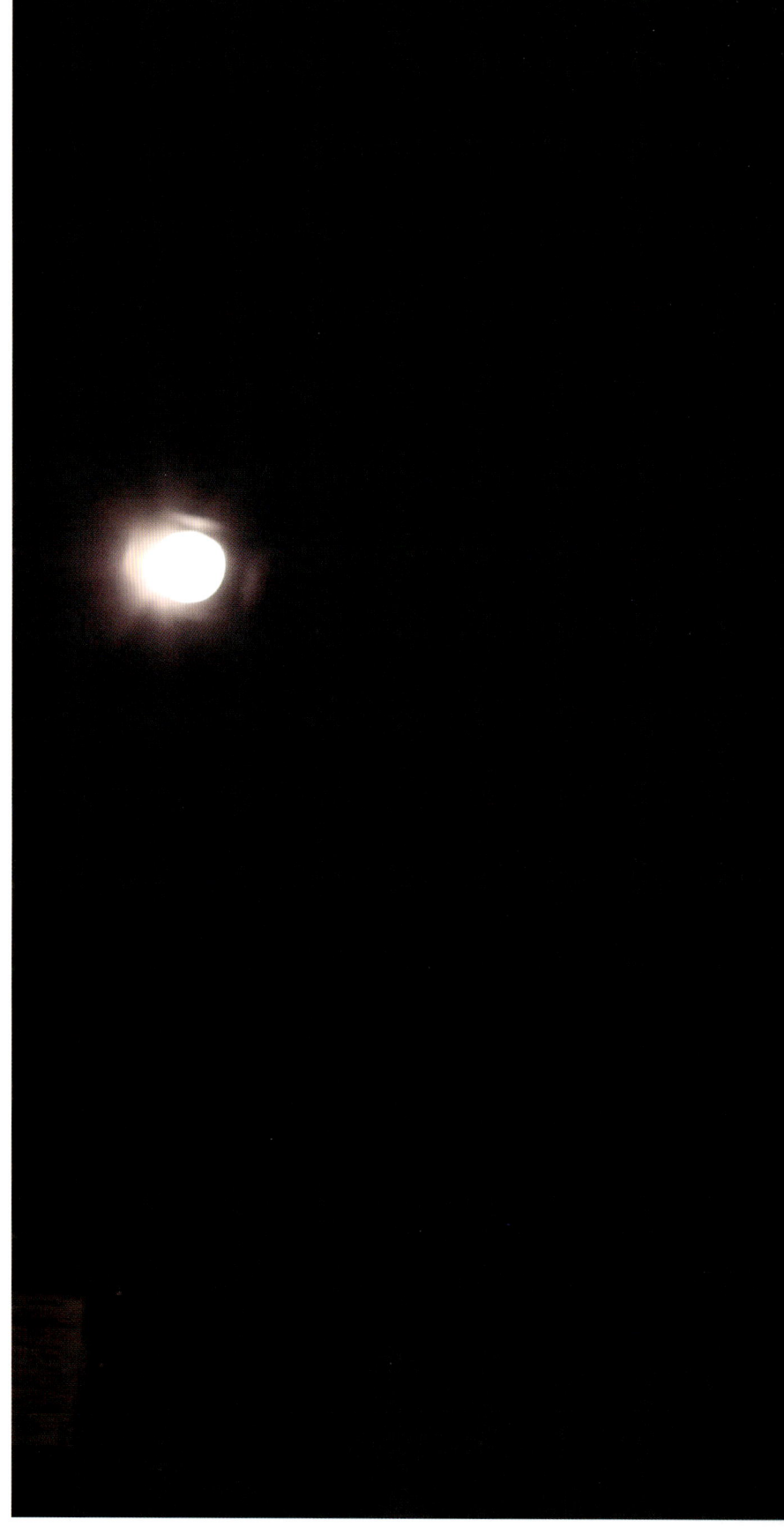

Richard Lewis

Comedian Richard Lewis catches his breath — "doing the rope-a-dope," he calls it — at Zanies Comedy Club in Vernon Hills, Ill.

NUCCIO DINUZZO, 2009

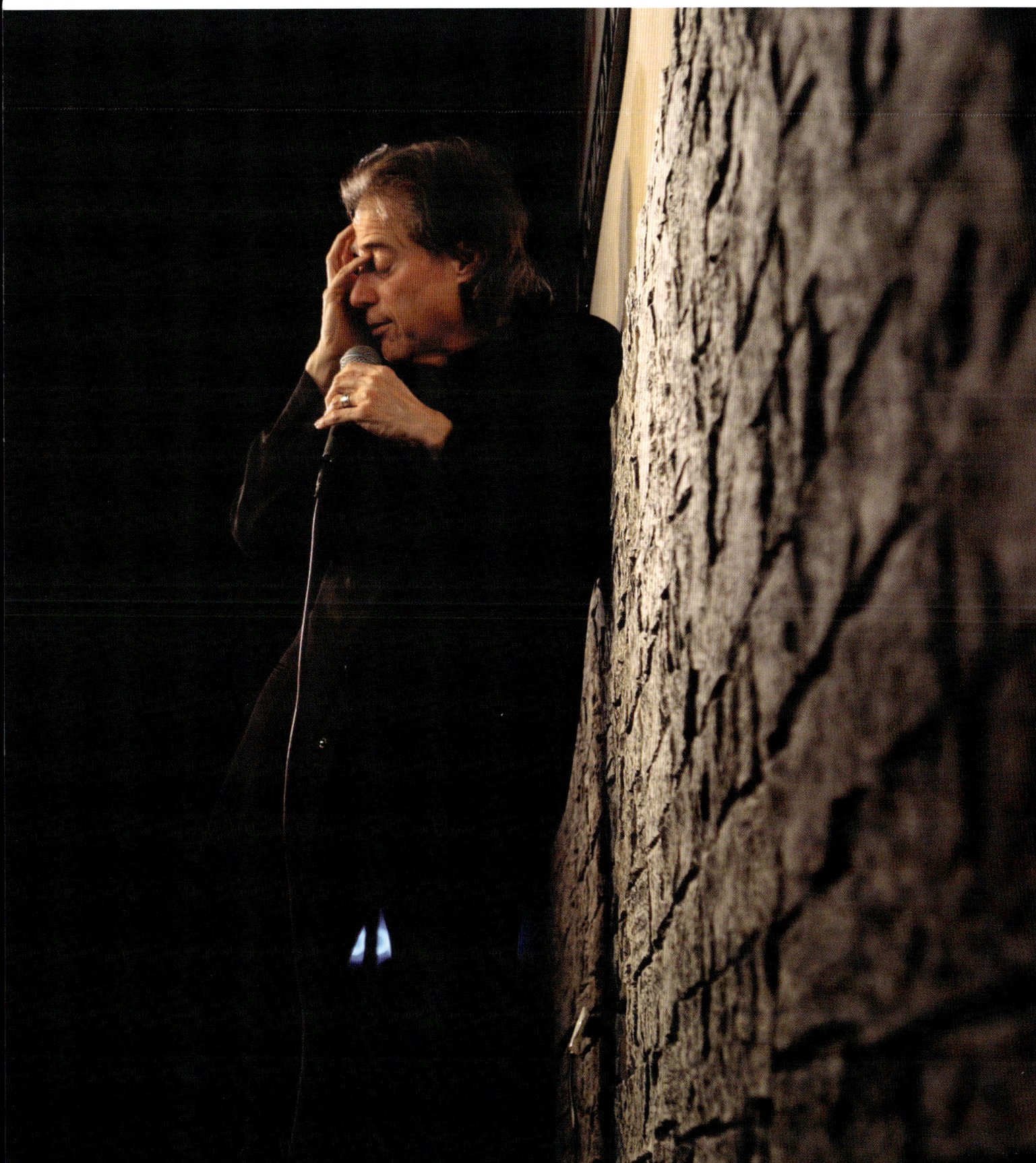

SUBJECT INDEX

Achatz, Grant 92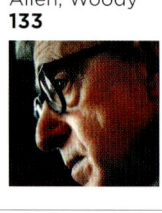

Allen, Woody 133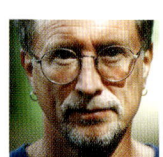

Arpino, Gerald 54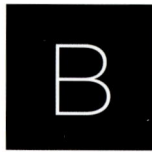

Ayers, Bill 280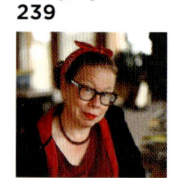

Bannon, Brian 10

Barry, Lynda 239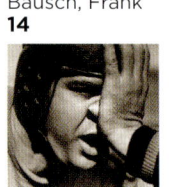

Bausch, Frank 14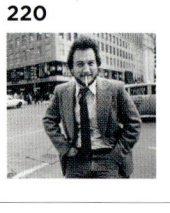

Belushi, Jim 220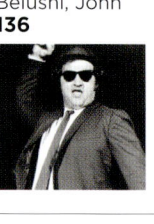

Belushi, John 136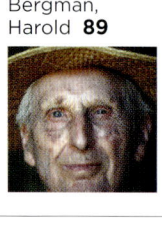

Bergman, Harold 89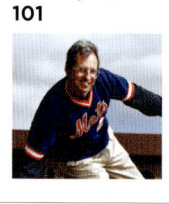

Berton, Joe 101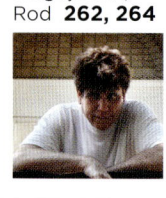

Blagojevich, Rod 262, 264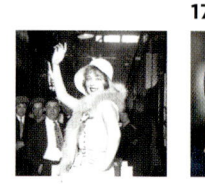

Bow, Clara 120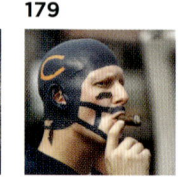

Bozelka, Kevin 179

Brooks, Gwendolyn 16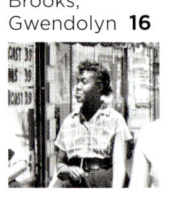

Brooks, Louise 181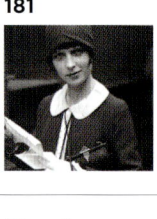

Butkus, Dick 166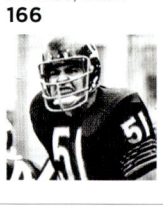

Byrne, Jane 136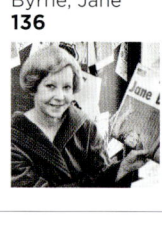

Canzoneri, Tony 206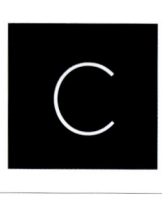

Capra, Frank 130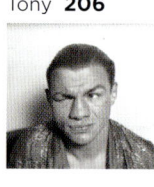

Cave, Nick 96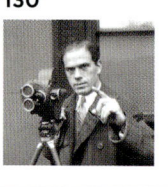

Chaplin, Charlie 119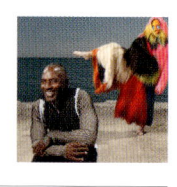

Chevalier, Maurice 204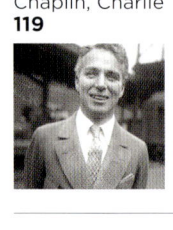

Chicago Blackhawks 173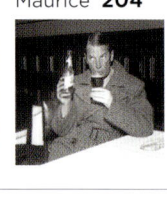

Cole-Kweli, Johari 86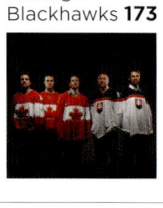

Contreras, Jose 28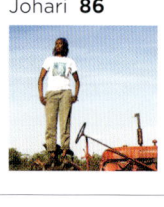

Corgan, Billy 111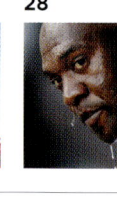

Cozzi, Richard 218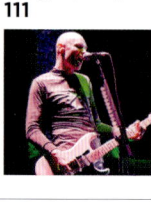

Crawford, Joan 237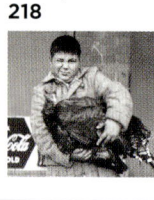

Cruz, Fernando 127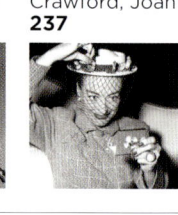

Daley, Richard J. 227, 228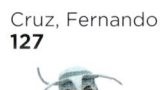

Daley, Richard M. 228, 231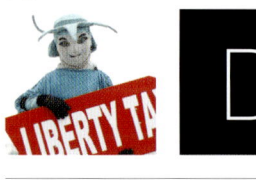

Davellis, Missy 269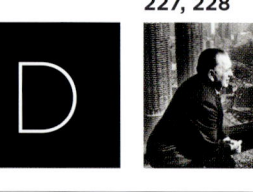

Dickinson, Janice 18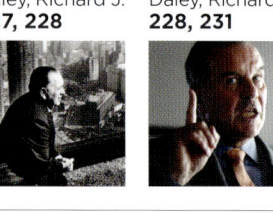

Earle, Jack 246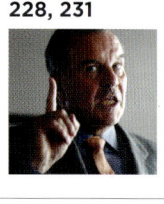

Eckman, Autumn 56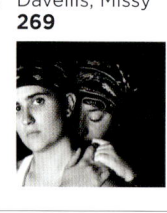

Efron, Zac 59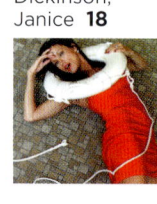

Emanuel, Rahm 235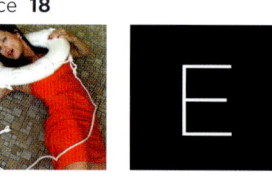

Fairbanks, Douglas 78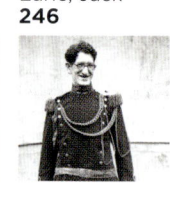

Farina, Dennis 184

Fayson, Jarred 141

Fedor, Ron 45

Figman, David 216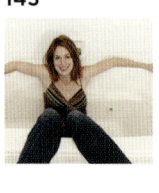

Flynn, Gillian 143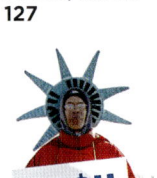

Fowler, Corina 127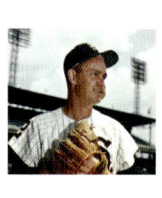

Fox, Nellie 152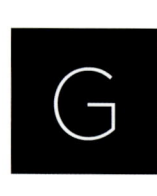

Gevinson, Tavi 149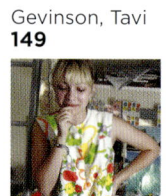

Halas, George 168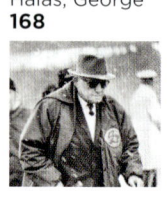

284

Hall, Dana **275**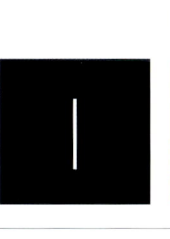
Hanson, Robert **34**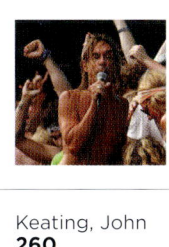
Harlow, Jean **248**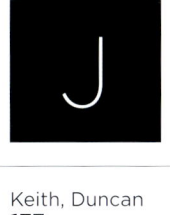
Hartnett, Charles Leo "Gabby" **161**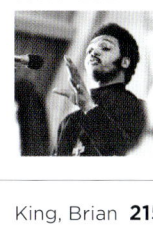
Hassan, Tahani **75**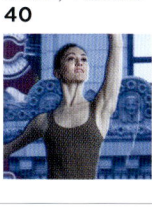
Hemon, Aleksandar **199**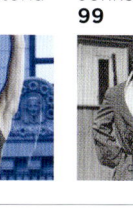
Hendricks, Christina **134**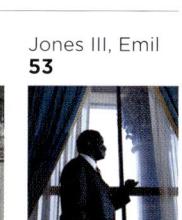
Hubert, Jessica **267**

Huh, Ben **102**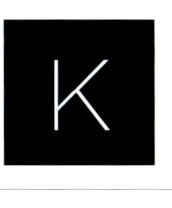
I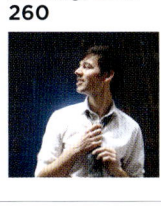
Iggy Pop **68**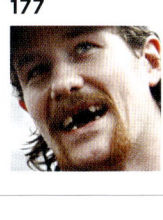
J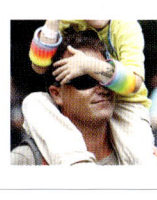
Jackson, Rev. Jesse **232**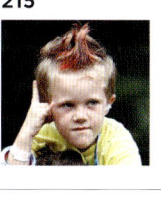
Jaiani, Victoria **40**
Johnson, Jack **99**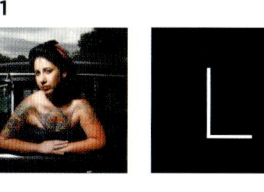
Jones III, Emil **53**

Judy, Atalee **84**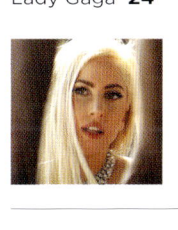
K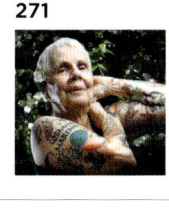
Keating, John **260**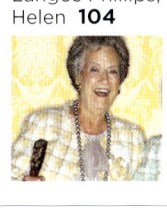
Keith, Duncan **177**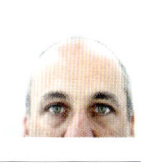
King, Brian **215**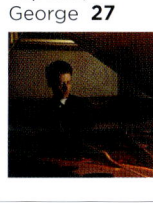
King, Pierce **215**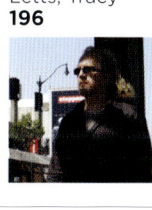
Kush, Patricia **151**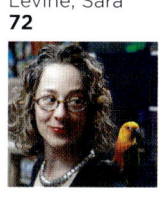
L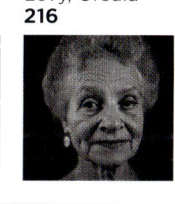

Lady Gaga **24**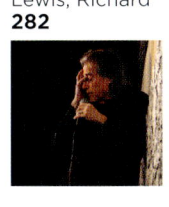
Lambin, Helen **271**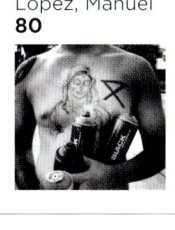
Langos Phillips, Helen **104**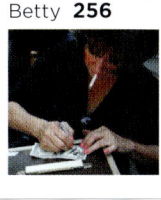
Lasko, Jim **117**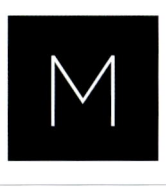
Lepauw, George **27**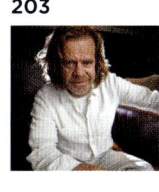
Letts, Tracy **196**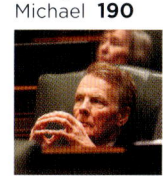
Levine, Sara **72**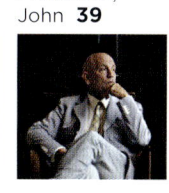
Levy, Ursula **216**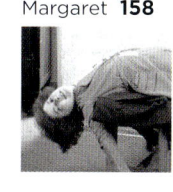

Lewis, Richard **282**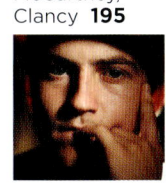
Lopez, Manuel **80**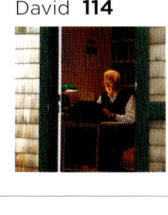
Loren-Maltese, Betty **256**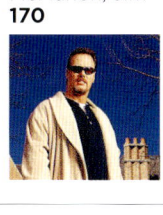
M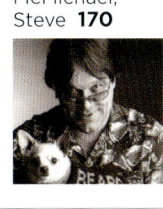
Macy, William H. **203**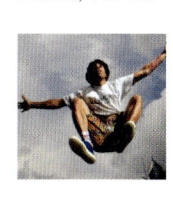
Madigan, Michael **190**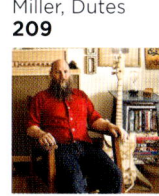
Malkovich, John **39**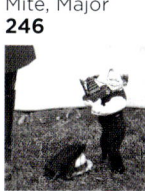
Marsh, Margaret **158**

McCartney, Clancy **195**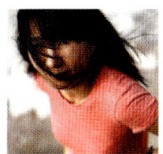
McCullough, David **114**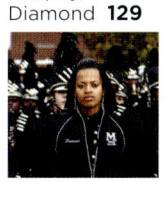
McMahon, Jim **170**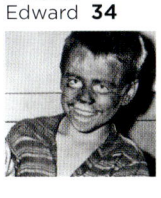
McMichael, Steve **170**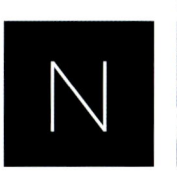
Mensa, Vic **83**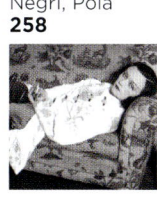
Miller, Dutes **209**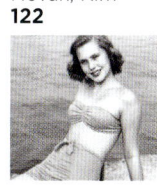
Mite, Major **246**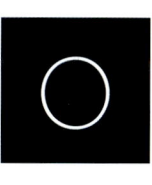
Monroe, Marilyn **124**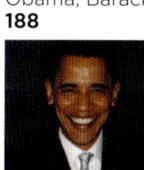

Mun, Nami **49**
Murphy, Diamond **129**
Murphy, Edward **34**
N
Negri, Pola **258**
Novak, Kim **122**
O
Obama, Barack **188**

Obama, Michelle **255**

O.J. **77**

O'Malley Graham, Irene **104**

P

Palmer, Pauline **22**

Payton, Walter **63**

Peppers, Julius **223**

Perry, Kurt **162**

Phair, Liz **112**

Pineless, Bill **216**

Q

R

Reilly, John C. **193**

Robinson, Reginald **109**

Rush, Bobby **186**

S

Sagal, Peter **17**

Samberg, Andy **250**

Samelson, Regina **216**

Sanders, Marci **277**

Santo, Ron **174**

Schroeder, Eddie **47**

Secrist, Carrie **32**

Seminole Indians **212**

Seyferlich, Arthur **31**

Shannon, Michael **252**

Shellabarger, Stan **209**

Simpson, Rosie **50**

Sinise, Gary **164**

Staples, Mavis **184**

Stevens, June **107**

Stigler, Sarah **269**

Stone, D.J. **244**

Sullivan, Jesse **156**

T

Taylor, Daniel **211**

Terkel, Studs **13**

Thomas, Eugene **91**

Thompson, William Hale **37**

Tomlianovich, Jetta **273**

Tree **60**

Turco, Andy **145**

U

V

Valentino, Rudolph **240**

Van Ek, Jeremy **146**

Van Lier, Norm **155**

Vaughn, Vince **138**

Veeck Sr., William **243**

Vincent, Frank **262**

W

Warlick, Derek **127**

Washington, Harold **42**

Washington, Isaiah **142**

Waters, Muddy **71**

Westenberger, Michael **21**

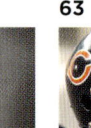
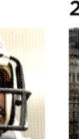
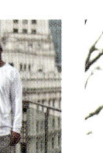

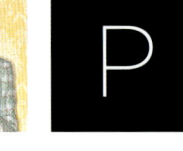
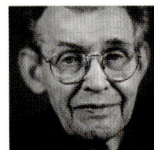
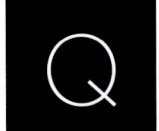
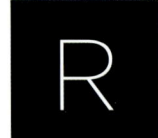
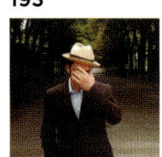
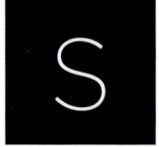
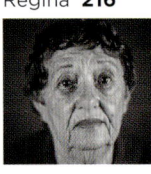
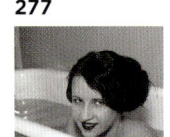
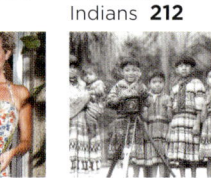
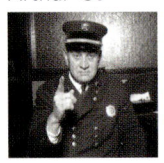
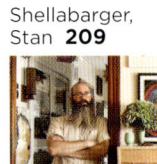
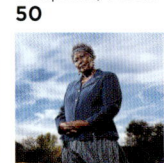
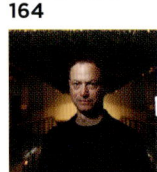
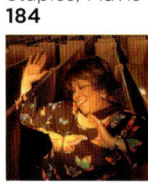
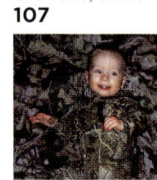
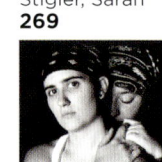
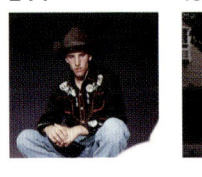
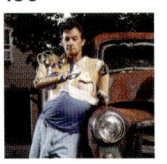
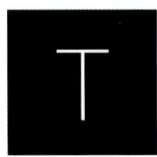
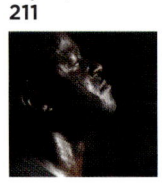
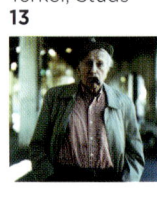
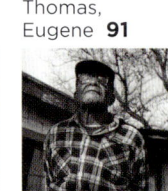
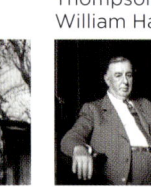
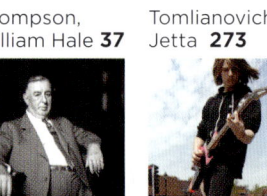
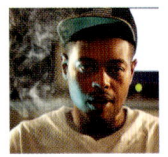
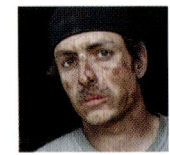
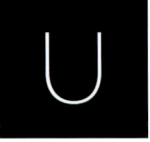
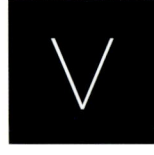
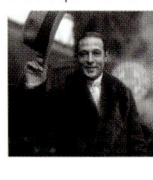
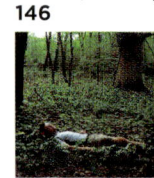
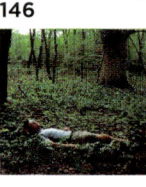
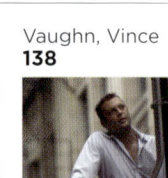
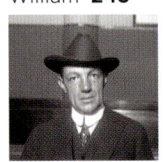
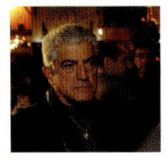
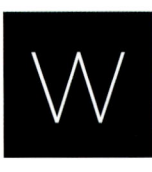
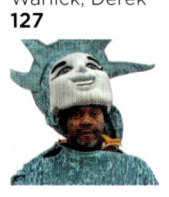
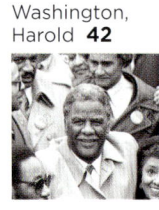
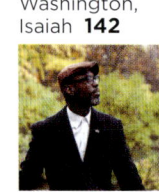
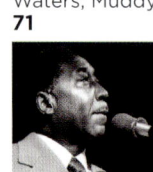
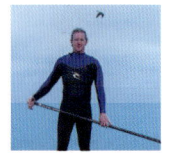

White, Jeremy Allen **182**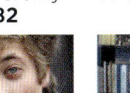
Wiesel, Elie **67**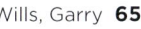
Wills, Garry **65**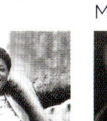
Winfrey, Oprah **224**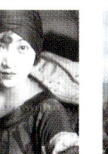
Wong, Anna May **278**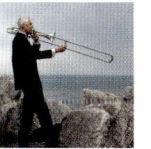
Wunder, Rick **200**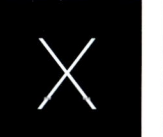

X

Y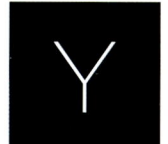

Yano, Sho **94**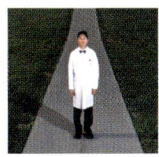

Z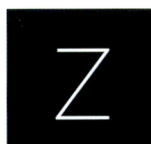

Photo editing and research by Robin Daughtridge, associate managing editor for photography and video; Katherine Manker, Marianne Mather, Erin Mystkowski and Michael Zajakowski

Captions by Colleen Kujawa

Copy editing by Valentina Djeljosevic and Kathleen O'Malley